Rev. Erwin E.
Admission year. 1929

JOHN WESLEY

"The noblest portrait of all."

# SELECTIONS

## FROM THE WRITINGS OF THE

# Rev. JOHN WESLEY, M.A.
SOMETIME FELLOW OF LINCOLN COLLEGE, OXFORD

COMPILED AND ARRANGED WITH A PREFACE

BY

HERBERT WELCH

Bishop of the Methodist Episcopal Church

THE METHODIST BOOK CONCERN
NEW YORK          CINCINNATI

COPYRIGHT, 1901, BY
EATON & MAINS

COPYRIGHT, 1918, BY
HERBERT WELCH

Printed in the United States of America

First Edition Printed January, 1901
Reprinted June, 1902; September, 1904; March, 1906; March, 1910;
May, 1918; March, 1922; October, 1923; October, 1925

# CONTENTS.

|  | PAGE |
|---|---|
| PREFACE | 5 |
| PREFACE TO REVISED EDITION | 12 |
| WESLEY'S OWN PREFACE TO HIS SERMONS | 13 |

SERMONS:

| Salvation by Faith | 17 |
|---|---|
| Free Grace | 30 |
| The New Birth | 46 |
| The Way to the Kingdom | 61 |
| The Danger of Riches | 74 |
| The More Excellent Way | 92 |
| Catholic Spirit | 106 |
| Charity | 122 |
| Scriptural Christianity | 137 |
| The General Spread of the Gospel | 157 |

TREATISES:

| A Plain Account of the People Called Methodists | 171 |
|---|---|
| A Short History of Methodism | 199 |
| Thoughts upon Methodism | 205 |
| An Earnest Appeal to Men of Reason and Religion | 209 |
| A Letter to the Rev. Mr. Downes | 236 |
| A Letter to a Clergyman | 249 |
| A Letter on Preaching Christ | 254 |
| Thoughts Concerning Gospel Ministers | 259 |
| An Address to the Clergy | 262 |
| Farther Thoughts on Separation from the Church | 287 |
| The Character of a Methodist | 291 |
| A Letter to a Roman Catholic | 303 |
| A Plain Account of Genuine Christianity | 312 |
| Thoughts Concerning the Origin of Power | 328 |
| Thoughts on the Power of Music | 337 |

LETTERS:

| To His Brother Samuel | 343 |
|---|---|
| To His Brother Charles | 349 |
| To Mr. Richard Tompson | 353 |
| To Mr. John Trembath | 354 |
| To Lady Maxwell | 356 |

# Contents.

LETTERS—*Continued*.                                     PAGE

| | |
|---|---|
| To the Rev. Mr. Venn | 360 |
| To Mr. Thomas Rankin | 364 |
| To Mrs. Emma Moon, of Yarm | 366 |
| To Mr. John Mason | 367 |
| To Mr. Joseph Benson | 368 |
| To Mrs. Crosby | 370 |
| To a Young Disciple | 371 |
| To the Rev. John Fletcher | 373 |
| To Mr. George Shadford | 375 |
| To Miss Bolton | 376 |
| To Samuel Sparrow, Esq. | 378 |
| To Mr. John King | 379 |
| To a Member of the Society | 379 |
| To Mr. ——— | 383 |
| To Bishop Lowth | 384 |
| To Mr. ——— | 386 |
| To the Commanding Officer in Lowestoft | 387 |
| To Dr. Coke, Mr. Asbury, and Our Brethren in North America | 388 |
| To the Rev. Freeborn Garrettson | 390 |
| To Dr. Adam Clarke | 392 |
| To the Rev. Peard Dickinson | 393 |
| To the Rev. Francis Asbury | 394 |
| To Mrs. Adam Clarke | 395 |
| To Robert C. Brackenbury, Esq., of Raithby, Lincolnshire | 397 |
| To the Rev. Ezekiel Cooper, of Philadelphia | 398 |
| To a Friend | 399 |
| INDEX | 400 |

# LIST OF ILLUSTRATIONS.

JOHN WESLEY.................................................*Frontispiece*

                                              FACING PAGE

| | |
|---|---|
| DR. JAMES HAMILTON, THE REV. JOHN WESLEY, THE REV. JOSEPH COLE | 35 |
| WESLEY'S HOUSE, CITY ROAD, LONDON | 199 |
| FACSIMILE OF A PAGE OF JOHN WESLEY'S JOURNAL IN GEORGIA | 303 |
| THE REV. SAMUEL WESLEY, JR. | 345 |
| AN EARLY PORTRAIT OF JOSEPH BENSON | 369 |

# PREFACE.

THE religious revival of the eighteenth century in England was more than an incident; it was an epoch. Its connection not simply with theology and church organization, but with literature, education, philanthropy, social reform, and national temper, gives it significance for all students of their own and the preceding generations.

In this revival the central personage is not far to seek. "We do not, of course, forget that Wesley was but one of a number of religious teachers and reformers whom we identify with the movement towards what we may call 'vital religion.' But when all is said and done, John Wesley remains the one supreme and towering figure, a characteristic product of England, and one of the noblest and most saintly of her sons."*

The people called Methodists are clearly not alone in their high appreciation of their founder's work. Passing over the better known words of Macaulay and Buckle and Lecky, of Southey and Stanley and Green and Huxley, we may note two recent tributes. "England, as a whole, is as truly interested in Wesley as in Shakespeare; and it may well be doubted whether in the long course of her history any one person has ever influenced her life in so direct, palpable, and powerful a way as John Wesley."† "You cannot cut him out of our national life. No single figure influenced so many minds, no single voice touched so many hearts. No other man did such a life's work for England."‡

This book is an attempt, not to characterize the man or his work, but to let him speak for himself. To a degree not common even among literary men, we may discover in Wesley's writings his opinions, his peculiarities, his methods of life, the sources of his power. He was not only an omnivorous reader,

---

*Wesley's Services to England* (editorial), in *The Spectator* (London), July 15, 1899.　　　　　　　　　　　　　　　　　　　　　†*Ibid.*

‡*John Wesley*, by Augustine Birrell, in *Scribner's Magazine*, December, 1899.

but a writer, the quantity and range of whose output were astounding. Burdened as he was with details of administration, taxed by immense ministerial labors in travel and preaching, he still maintained his studious and meditative habit, and found time for the exercise of his inherited taste for literary pursuits. Coke, Fletcher, Benson, and Clarke, all made contributions of value to the literature of the church; but it was Wesley who stood in the forefront. From *A Collection of Forms of Prayer*, in 1733, to *The Arminian Magazine* for 1791 his publications, original, edited, or abridged, were unceasing. In the latest and most accurate list,* 371 such publications are named, besides a score more of Charles Wesley's books which probably received his brother's editorial oversight. Of the total 391, 14 are musical, 62 poetical, and 315 prose. In 30 of these, John and Charles Wesley seem to have shared the labor, or at least their work cannot be distinguished; the other 341 are to be credited to John Wesley alone. Of these, 233 are original works. Only 15 publications, including à Kempis and some sermons and devotional books, appeared before 1740. Then began a freer use of the press. From 1740 to 1750, and beyond, came the defenses of Methodism; from 1740 to 1760, many controversial and theological works; beyond 1760, a larger number of letters. In 1768 the first of the political tracts was printed. After 1780, except the *Minutes* and *The Arminian Magazine*, there are only a few publications of importance. *Sermons, Hymns,* and *Journals* appeared at intervals all through this half century of literary activity.

The character of these publications varies widely, from *A Christian Library*, in fifty volumes (containing extracts, with notes, of theological writings from the apostolic fathers to the eighteenth century), and *The Arminian Magazine*, in fourteen volumes (a monthly devoted especially to the defense of "universal redemption"), to tracts addressed to smugglers, swearers, drunkards, and bribe-takers. They include prose and poetry, in English and Latin. Among them are sermons, letters, biographies, devotional manuals, polemical pamphlets; grammars of the English, French, Latin, Greek, and Hebrew languages;

---

*\*The Works of John and Charles Wesley; a Bibliography*, by the Rev. Richard Green. London; C. H. Kelly, 1896.

treatises on logic, medicine, literary criticism, theology, philosophy, and public affairs; histories of Rome, England, and the Christian church; a comprehensive, though concise, system of natural philosophy; commentaries on the entire Scriptures; and *The Complete English Dictionary.*

The ventures into so many fields of learning did not, in this case, imply the gross egotism that might be suspected. Popular literature was then unknown. It was highly desirable to teach and train the converts of the Methodist preachers, and to defend the Methodist doctrine and practice. Under the urgency of friends or the pressure of circumstances, Wesley undertook literary tasks to which he felt himself unequal in knowledge and in time, but for which no other man was available. His ambition was to meet a need of the hour, to produce a literature simple enough for plain men to understand, cheap enough for poor men to buy. Two thirds of his publications up to 1756 were for sale at less than a shilling each, and more than a quarter of them at one penny.*

This desire to produce cheap and plain publications naturally determined the style of their composition. Wesley tried to avoid dulness, verbosity, and obscurity.† He loved brevity, and regarded "a great book as a great evil," remarking once, "I believe if angels were to write books, we should have very few folios."‡ He cultivated a somewhat Puritan simplicity. In the preface to his *Sermons* (1746.—*Works,* i, xviii) he said: "Nothing here appears in an elaborate, elegant, or oratorical dress. . . . I design plain truth for plain people: therefore, of set purpose, I abstain from all nice and philosophical speculations; from all perplexed and intricate reasonings; and, as far as possible, from even the show of learning, unless in sometimes citing the original Scriptures." And in publishing the later *Sermons* (1788.—*Works,* ii, iv); "I dare no more write in a *fine style* than wear a fine coat. . . . Let who will admire the French frippery; I am still for plain, sound English." His language, especially in the earliest period, lacks flexibility and richness. Formed on classic models, his style seems sometimes stiff and

---

*Stevens, *History of Methodism,* ii, 494.
†*Letter to the Rev. Mr. G.,* 1761.—*Works,* vi, 756.
‡Preface to *The Arminian Magazine,* vol. iv, 1784.—*Works,* vii, 570.

stilted. Practice, however, made him more nearly perfect. From being like the fencer whose regard is for the handling of his weapon and the rules of the play rather than for the disarming of his opponent, he came into the ease and energy of the later days. He is not wanting in imagination and picturesqueness; but the distinctive traits of his best writing are still his careful and correct English, his apt use of words, his compactness of statement, his clear and logical method. Mr. Leslie Stephen remarks: "We admire his [Wesley's] sense and his sincerity. He remains on the plane of terse, vigorous sense. But it is also true that his eloquence never soars above the ground; if there is no bombast, there is little more rhetoric than may be found in a vigorous leading article; and if he wins our respect, he does not excite our admiration, or add to the stores of English rhetorical prose."* But Mr. Stephen justly recognizes that Wesley's writings are not to be judged as mere pieces of rhetorical composition, but as a means to a direct practical end.† He best appreciates them who regards them not simply as literature, but as the literary expression of a splendid personality, and one of the instruments for the achievement of a magnificent work.

Flaws may readily be found by the critic in Wesley's opinions as in his style. (This to him would seem no disrespect. Independent in his own thinking, taking "no author for better, for worse," calling no man master,‡ he would have bound no person, no church, to his own views as a final test of truth.) Strained interpretations of Scripture may be pointed out, and ingenious special pleading. His conservatism was extreme, in both religion and politics. He clung to the old and established. He had no sympathy with popular government. He was in early manhood inclined to ritualism, tending to be abstruse and precise. Later, when his doctrinal views had been modified, he was undoubtedly dogmatic and absolute. But he had what in his circumstances was a marvelous grace—a teachable spirit. He loved truth supremely, and welcomed it from every quarter. His was an alert and acquisitive mind, which retained its vivacity to the

---

*History of English Thought in the Eighteenth Century, ii, 423.
†Ibid., ii, 409.
‡Preface to *A Christian Library*, 1749.—*Works*, vii, 526.

very end. Always tolerant, serene, and wholesome, he became, despite a touch of the pessimism common to old age, more mellow, tender, playful, sympathetic, and discriminating. Yet, like the earlier St. John of gospel days, he never lost the sharpness of his distinctions, the clear views of the eternal difference between good and evil, and the eternal consequences of action and character.

In Wesley's works will be noticed the frequent repetition of a few thoughts that for him were central and dominant. His emphasis on the religious consciousness, his regard for experience as a source of theology, were most modern. But, pre-eminently, he thrust into the background names, rituals, creeds, and asserted the supremacy of character. The nature of true religion, consisting in love to God and man, as opposed to mere opinions, or forms, or good works, constitutes the message of Methodism. Wesley is at his best when proclaiming the reality and the attainability of this inward, vital religion; when emphasizing character as the meaning of salvation. Methodists have prided themselves more on their doctrinal liberty than on their doctrinal uniformity, and rightly; for the thing of greatest value which they have received from John Wesley is not a system of theology, nor even an admirable form of church organization for efficient work; but, above all, a spiritual inspiration, and a true view of the essence of Christianity. He did not build a theological monument; he did better: he planted a living seed that had in it the germ of all true theologies. He judged, and rightly, that what his age most needed was not a new philosophy, but a new life; that this life would shape its own creeds, would create its own forms, but that it could not be produced by the imposition of creeds, however correct, or the adoption of forms of worship and government, however perfect, but only by the power of God working in men yielded to His hand. He therefore sought not elaboration in theology more than in style, and those who look for a complete and scientific system of religious theory may be disappointed in him. He attained the simplicity at which he aimed; and because his thought was simple, it has by some been judged insignificant. Such judgment would rate the Matterhorn below the hudding hills!

As a sermonizer Wesley was doctrinal and argumentative,

but direct, convincing, arousing. He had the "plain and familiar manner" which Dr. Samuel Johnson thought the secret of the success of Methodist preaching, and he had much more. As a controversialist, he was an expert. In answer to the abuse abundantly heaped upon him and upon his people, he was frank and fearless, sometimes severe, sarcastic, indignant, but prevailingly Christian, "loving his brother only less than the truth."*
As a correspondent, he was not leisurely and elegant. His were the terse letters of an orderly mind and a crowded life—letters with hurry written over them, stirring with zeal, concerned with a hundred matters, spiritual, financial, disciplinary, political—letters showing the astonishing knowledge of the details of church work, the shrewd understanding of human nature, the grasp of fundamental principles, the bold judgment, the vital common sense, that made him eminent as an administrator.

Of all Wesley's writings, he himself esteemed most highly the *Sermons*, the *Appeals*, *The Christian's Pattern* (his edition of the *Imitation of Christ*), and the *Primitive Physic*, saying of the two latter, "It is a great pity that any Methodist should be without them."†

But his judgment of his own works has hardly been confirmed by the men of later days. Readers of different schools of thought unite in declaring that his *"Journal* is the most interesting product of his pen."‡ Mr. Augustine Birrell, the English lawyer and literary critic already quoted, speaks of it as "the most amazing record of human exertion ever penned or endured . . . a book full of plots, and plays, and novels, which quivers with life, and is crammed full of character. If you want to get into the last century, to feel its pulses throb beneath your finger, be content sometimes to leave the letters of Horace Walpole unturned . . . nay, even deny yourself your annual reading of Boswell or your biennial retreat with Sterne, and ride up

---

*\*The Principles of a Methodist*, 1740.—*Works*, v. 254-5.
†*Letter to Mr. Merryweather, of Yarm*, 1760.—*Works*, vi, 760.
‡The limits of space forbid the inclusion of any parts of this remarkable record here. Such extracts have already been made, giving, in eight volumes, an admirable notion of Wesley's labors: *Journal of the Rev. John Wesley, Edited by Nehemiah Curnock*. Published by the Methodist Book Concern. Price of series, $21.00. The volumes are not sold separately.

## Preface.

and down the country with the greatest force of the eighteenth century in England."*

Other selections from the writings of John Wesley have been gathered and published. But it is believed that in purpose, method, and range this volume differs from those to such a degree as to justify its production. It has been prepared at the request of the Committee of the Board of Bishops on the Conference Course of Study. Its contents have been largely determined by the special purpose for which it is intended. But while the book is planned primarily for the preachers, possibly it may come with interest to a wider circle of those who are concerned with the great men and the great movements of Christian history, and especially to those who count themselves the spiritual descendants of John Wesley. In its preparation, helpful suggestions have been received from various friends, in particular from the Rev. Bishop Cyrus D. Foss and the Rev. Dr. James M. Buckley, to whom special acknowledgments are due.

Most of the articles are printed in complete form. In the few cases where omissions have seemed wise, the omissions are indicated by dots . . . . . Footnotes without any distinguishing mark are Wesley's own. Notes to which is affixed EDIT. were added by the English editor, the Rev. Thomas Jackson. Brackets [ ] are used to inclose footnotes and also translations in the text which are to be credited to the American editor, the Rev. Dr. (late Bishop) John Emory. The only additions to the pages made by the present editor are the references to the date of writing or publication and to the location of articles in Wesley's *Works* (inserted in brackets when at the head of articles), and footnotes consisting almost exclusively of quotations from other writings of Wesley, and inclosed in quotation marks. These quotations have been added to suggest the variety and extent of Wesley's literary work, and to explain, modify, or enforce the statements of the text. References in all cases are to the standard American edition of Wesley's *Works,* published by the Book Concern in 1831; Vols. I and II including

---

*\*John Wesley*, by Augustine Birrell, in *Scribner's Magazine*, December, 1899.

the *Sermons,* Vols. III and IV the *Journals,* Vols. V. VI, and VII the miscellaneous writings.

The selections here published were not chosen because the present editor agrees with all that they contain—because he thinks the interpretations of Scripture always right, the arguments always sound, or the conclusions always just. But this volume has been compiled with the hope that it may bring to its readers some fuller appreciation of the breadth and beauty of Wesley's teaching, some clearer apprehension of the prophetic quality of Methodism's founder, and may show from the original documents the providential mission, the message, and the spirit of the Methodism which has proved so mighty a factor in the Anglo-Saxon world of to-day.

HERBERT WELCH.

*Middletown, Conn., November 24, 1900.*

# PREFACE TO REVISED EDITION.

AFTER various printings of this little book since its original publication, a new and somewhat revised edition has been asked for by the Commission on the Conference Course of Study appointed by the last General Conference.

The changes in the contents are not numerous. Three sermons and one treatise have been omitted. As the fifty-eight standard sermons formerly designated for reading in the Conference Course are no longer included, it has been thought best to transfer here a few of these foundation discourses, and seven of them touching upon some of the characteristic doctrines of Methodism have been chosen, together with Wesley's own preface to his sermons.

The editor sends forth this volume again with the prayer that it may be the bearer of light and help to those to whom it may come in these heavy crisis days of new need, and of new longing for the great truths and the splendid duties.

HERBERT WELCH.

Seoul, Korea,
February 19, 1918.

# PREFACE.

The following Sermons contain the substance of what I have been preaching for between eight and nine years last past.* During that time I have frequently spoken in public, on every subject in the ensuing collection: and I am not conscious, that there is any one point of doctrine, on which I am accustomed to speak in public, which is not here, incidentally, if not professedly, laid before every Christian reader. Every serious man, who peruses these, will therefore see in the clearest manner, what these doctrines are, which I embrace and teach, as the essentials of true religion.

2. But I am throughly sensible, these are not proposed in such a manner as some may expect. Nothing here appears in an elaborate, elegant, or oratorical dress. If it had been my desire or design to write thus, my leisure would not permit. But, in truth, I, at present, designed nothing less; for I now write, as I generally speak, *ad populum:* to the bulk of mankind, to those who neither relish nor understand the art of speaking; but who, notwithstanding, are competent judges of those truths, which are necessary to present and future happiness. I mention this, that curious readers may spare themselves the labour of seeking for what they will not find.

3. I design plain truth for plain people: therefore, of set purpose, I abstain from all nice and philosophical speculations; from all perplexed and intricate reasonings; and, as far as possible, from even the show of learning, unless in sometimes citing the original Scripture. I labour to avoid all words which are not easy to be understood, all which are not used in common life; and, in particular, those kinds of technical terms that so frequently occur in bodies of divinity,—those modes of speaking, which men of reading are intimately acquainted with, but which, to common people, are an unknown tongue. Yet I am not assured, that I do not sometimes slide into them unawares:

---

*In the year 1747.

it is so extremely natural to imagine, that a word which is familiar to ourselves is so to all the world.

4. Nay, my design is, in some sense, to forget all that ever I have read in my life. I mean to speak, in the general, as if I had never read one author, ancient or modern: (always excepting the inspired.) I am persuaded, that on the one hand, this may be a means of enabling me more clearly to express the sentiments of my heart, while I simply follow the chain of my own thoughts, without entangling myself with those of other men; and that, on the other, I shall come with fewer weights upon my mind, with less of prejudice and prepossession either to search for myself, or to deliver to others the naked truths of the Gospel.

5. To candid, reasonable men, I am not afraid to lay open what have been the inmost thoughts of my heart. I have thought, I am a creature of a day, passing through life, as an arrow through the air. I am a spirit come from God, and returning to God: just hovering over the great gulf; till a few moments hence, I am no more seen! I drop into an unchangeable eternity! I want to know one thing, the way to heaven: how to land safe on that happy shore. God himself has condescended to teach the way; for this very end he came from heaven. He hath written it down in a book! Oh give me that book! At any price, give me the book of God! I have it: here is knowledge enough for me. Let me be *homo unius libri.*\* Here then I am, far from the busy ways of men. I sit down alone: only God is here. In his presence I open, I read this book; for this end, to find the way to heaven. Is there a doubt concerning the meaning of what I read? Does any thing appear dark or intricate? I lift up my heart to the Father of lights.—Lord, is it not thy word, "If any man lack wisdom, let him ask of God?" Thou "givest liberally and upbraidest not." Thou hast said, "If any be willing to do thy will, he shall know." I am willing to do: let me know thy will. I then search after, and consider parallel passages of Scripture, "comparing spiritual things with spiritual." I meditate thereon, with all the attention and earnestness of which my mind is capable. If any doubt still remains, I consult those who are experienced in the things

---

\*A man of one book.

## Wesley's Own Preface to His Sermons. 15

of God; and then, the writings whereby, being dead, they yet speak. And what I thus learn, that I teach.

6. I have accordingly set down in the following sermons, what I find in the Bible concerning the way to heaven; with a view to distinguish this way of God, from all those which are the inventions of men. I have endeavoured to describe the true, the scriptural, experimental religion, so as to omit nothing which is a real part thereof, and to add nothing thereto which is not. And herein it is more especially my desire, first, to guard those who are just setting their faces towards heaven, (and who, having little acquaintance with the things of God, are the more liable to be turned out of the way,) from formality, from mere outside religion, which has almost driven heart religion out of the world; and, secondly, to warn those who know the religion of the heart, the faith which worketh by love, lest at any time they make void the law through faith, and so fall back into the snare of the devil.

7. By the advice, and at the request of some of my friends, I have prefixed to the other sermons contained in this volume, three sermons of my own,* and one of my brother's,† preached before the university of Oxford. My design required some discourses on those heads. And I preferred these before any others, as being a stronger answer than any which can be drawn up now, to those who have frequently asserted, that we have changed our doctrine of late, and do not preach now, what we did some years ago. Any man of understanding may now judge for himself, when he has compared the latter with the former sermons.

8. But some may say, I have mistaken the way myself, although I take upon me to teach it to others. It is probable many will think this, and it is very possible that I have. But I trust, whereinsoever I have mistaken, my mind is open to conviction. I sincerely desire to be better informed. I say to God and man, "What I know not, teach thou me!"

9. Are you persuaded you see more clearly than me? It is not unlikely that you may. Then treat me as you would desire to be treated yourself upon a change of circumstances. Point

---

*Salvation by Faith, The Almost Christian, and Scriptural Christianity.
†Awake, Thou that Sleepest.

me out a better way than I have yet known. Show me it is so, by plain proof of Scripture. And if I linger in the path I have been accustomed to tread, and am therefore unwilling to leave it, labour with me a little; take me by the hand, and lead me as I am able to bear. But be not displeased if I entreat you not to beat me down in order to quicken my pace: I can go but feebly and slowly at best; then, I should not be able to go at all. May I not request of you, farther, not to give me hard names in order to bring me into the right way. Suppose I were ever so much in the wrong, I doubt this would not set me right. Rather, it would make me run so much the farther from you, and so get more and more out of the way.

10. Nay, perhaps, if you are angry, so shall I be too; and then there will be small hopes of finding the truth. If once anger arise, ηυτε καπνος, (as Homer somewhere expresses it,) this smoke will so dim the eyes of my soul, that I shall be able to see nothing clearly. For God's sake, if it be possible to avoid it, let us not provoke one another to wrath. Let us not kindle in each other this fire of hell; much less blow it up into a flame. If we could discern truth by that dreadful light, would it not be loss, rather than gain? For, how far is love, even with many wrong opinions, to be preferred before truth itself without love! We may die without the knowledge of many truths, and yet be carried into Abraham's bosom. But if we die without love, what will knowledge avail? Just as much as it avails the devil and his angels!

The God of love forbid we should ever make the trial! May he prepare us for the knowledge of all truth, by filling our hearts with all his love, and with all joy and peace in believing!

# SERMONS.

## SALVATION BY FAITH.

[*Preached at St. Mary's, Oxford, before the University, June 18, 1738.*]

"By grace are ye saved, through faith."—Eph. ii, 8.

ALL the blessings which God hath bestowed upon man, are of his mere grace, bounty, or favour; his free, undeserved favour; favour altogether undeserved; man having no claim to the least of his mercies. It was free grace that "formed man of the dust of the ground, and breathed into him a living soul," and stamped on that soul the image of God, and "put all things under his feet." The same free grace continues to us, at this day, life and breath, and all things. For there is nothing we are, or have, or do, which can deserve the least thing at God's hand. "All our works, thou, oh God! hast wrought in us." These, therefore, are so many more instances of free mercy: and, whatever righteousness may be found in man, this is also the gift of God.

Wherewithal then shall a sinful man atone for any, the least of his sins? With his own works? No. Were they ever so many or holy, they are not his own, but God's. But indeed they are all unholy and sinful themselves, so that every one of them needs a fresh atonement. Only corrupt fruit grows on a corrupt tree. And his heart is altogether corrupt and abominable; being "come short of the glory of God," the glorious righteousness at first impressed on his soul, after the image of his great Creator. Therefore having nothing, neither righteousness nor works to plead, his mouth is utterly stopped before God.

If then sinful men find favour with God, it is "grace upon grace!" If God vouchsafe still to pour fresh blessings upon us, yea, the greatest of all blessings, salvation; what can we say to these things, but, "Thanks be unto God for his unspeakable gift!" And thus it is. Herein "God commendeth his love towards us, in that while we were yet sinners, Christ died" to save us. "By grace, then, are ye saved, through faith." Grace is the source, faith the condition, of salvation.

Now, that we fall not short of the grace of God, it concerns us carefully to inquire,

I. What Faith it is through which we are saved?
II. What is the Salvation which is through Faith?
III. How we may answer some Objections.

I. What faith it is through which we are saved?

And first. It is not barely the faith of a heathen.

Now God requireth of a heathen to believe, "That God is; that he is a rewarder of them that diligently seek him;" and that he is to be sought by glorifying him as God, by giving him thanks for all things, and by a careful practice of moral virtue, of justice, mercy and truth towards their fellow creatures. A Greek or Roman therefore, yea, a Scythian or Indian, was without excuse if he did not believe thus much: The being and attributes of God, a future state of reward and punishment, and the obligatory nature of moral virtue. For this is barely the faith of a heathen.

Nor, secondly. Is it the faith of a devil, though he goes much farther than that of a heathen. For the devil believes, not only that there is a wise and powerful God, gracious to reward, and just to punish; but also that Jesus is the Son of God, the Christ, the Saviour of the world. So we find him declaring in express terms, Luke iv, 34,

## Salvation by Faith.

"I know thee, who thou art; the Holy One of God." Nor can we doubt but that unhappy spirit believes all those words which came out of the mouth of the Holy One; yea, and whatsoever else was written by those holy men of old, of two of whom he was compelled to give that glorious testimony, "These men are the servants of the Most High God, who show unto you the way of salvation." Thus much, then, the great enemy of God and man believes, and trembles in believing, that God was made manifest in the flesh; that he will "tread all enemies under his feet;" and that "all Scripture was given by inspiration of God." Thus far goeth the faith of a devil.

Thirdly. The faith through which we are saved, in that sense of the word which will hereafter be explained, is not barely that which the apostles themselves had while Christ was yet upon earth; though they so believed on him as to "leave all and follow him;" although they had then power to work miracles, to "heal all manner of sickness, and all manner of disease;" yea, they had then "power and authority over all devils;" and, which is beyond all this, were sent by their Master to "preach the kingdom of God."

What faith is it then through which we are saved? It may be answered, first, in general, it is a faith in Christ; Christ, and God through Christ, are the proper objects of it. Herein, therefore, it is sufficiently, absolutely distinguished from the faith, either of ancient or modern heathens. And from the faith of a devil, it is fully distinguished by this, it is not barely a speculative, rational thing, a cold, lifeless assent, a train of ideas in the head; but also a disposition of the heart. For thus saith the Scripture, "With the heart man believeth unto righteousness." And, "If thou shalt confess with thy mouth the Lord Jesus, and shalt believe with thy heart, that God hath raised him from the dead, thou shalt be saved."

And herein does it differ from that faith which the

apostles themselves had while our Lord was on earth, that it acknowledges the necessity and merit of his death, and the power of his resurrection. It acknowledges his death as the only sufficient means of redeeming man from death eternal, and his resurrection as the restoration of us all to life and immortality; inasmuch as he "was delivered for our sins, and rose again for our justification." Christian faith is then, not only an assent to the whole Gospel of Christ, but also a full reliance on the blood of Christ; a trust in the merits of his life, death, and resurrection; a recumbency upon him as our atonement and our life, *as given for us,* and *living in us.* It is a sure confidence which a man hath in God, that through the merits of Christ, *his* sins are forgiven, and *he* reconciled to the favour of God; and, in consequence hereof, a closing with him, and cleaving to him, as our "wisdom, righteousness, sanctification, and redemption," or, in one word, our salvation.

II. What salvation it is, which is through this faith, is the second thing to be considered.

And first, whatsoever else it imply, it is a present salvation. It is something attainable, yea, actually attained on earth, by those who are partakers of this faith. For thus saith the apostle to the believers at Ephesus, and in them to the believers of all ages, not *ye shall be,* (though that also is true,) but *"ye are saved* through faith."

Ye are saved (to comprise all in one word) from sin. This is the salvation which is through faith. This is that great salvation foretold by the angel, before God brought his First-begotten into the world: "Thou shalt call his name JESUS, for he shall save his people from their sins." And neither here, nor in other parts of the Holy Writ, is there any limitation or restriction. All his people, or as it is elsewhere expressed, "all that believe in him," he will save from all their sins; from original and actual, past and present sin, "of the flesh and of the spirit." Through

## Salvation by Faith.

faith that is in him, they are saved both from the guilt and from the power of it.

First from the guilt of all past sin: for, whereas all the world is guilty before God, insomuch, that should he "be extreme to mark what is done amiss, there is none that could abide it;" and whereas, "by the law is" only "the knowledge of sin," but no deliverance from it, so that, "by fulfilling the deeds of the law, no flesh can be justified in his sight;" now, "the righteousness of God, which is by faith of Jesus Christ, is manifested unto all that believe." Now, "they are justified freely by his grace, through the redemption that is in Jesus Christ." "Him God hath set forth to be a propitiation, through faith in his blood; to declare his righteousness for (or by) the remission of the sins that are past." Now hath Christ taken away "the curse of the law, being made a curse for us." He hath "blotted out the hand writing that was against us, taking it out of the way, nailing it to his cross." "There is, therefore, no condemnation now, to them which" believe in Christ Jesus.

And being saved from guilt, they are saved from fear. Not indeed from the filial fear of offending; but, from all servile fear; from that fear which hath torment; from fear of punishment; from fear of the wrath of God, whom they no longer regard as a severe Master, but as an indulgent Father. "They have not received again the spirit of bondage, but the spirit of adoption, whereby they cry Abba, Father; the Spirit itself also bearing witness with their spirits, that they are the children of God." They are also saved from the fear, though not from the possibility, of falling away from the grace of God, and coming short of the great and precious promises: they are "sealed with the Holy Spirit of promise, which is the earnest of their inheritance," Eph. i, 13. Thus have they "peace with God through our Lord Jesus Christ. They rejoice in hope of the glory of God. And the love of God is shed abroad in their hearts, through the Holy Ghost, which is given unto them." And hereby they are persuaded, (though perhaps not at all times, nor with the same fulness of persuasion,) that "neither death, nor life, nor things present, nor things to come, nor height, nor depth, nor any other creature, shall be able to separate them from the love of God which is in Christ Jesus our Lord."

Again, through this faith they are saved from the power of sin, as well as from the guilt of it. So the apostle declares, "Ye know that he was manifested to take away our sins, and in him is no sin. Whosoever abideth in him, sinneth not," 1 John iii, 5, &c. Again, "Little children, let no man deceive you. He that committeth sin is of the devil. Whosoever believeth is born of God. And whosoever is born of God doth not commit sin, for his seed remaineth in him: and he cannot sin, because he is born of God." Once more, "We know, that whosoever is born of God sinneth not: but he that is begotten of God, keepeth himself, and that wicked one toucheth him not," chap. v, 18.

He that is, by faith, born of God, sinneth not, 1, by any habitual sin; for all habitual sin, is sin reigning: but sin cannot reign in any that believeth. Nor, 2, by any wilful sin, for his will, while he abideth in the faith, is utterly set against all sin, and abhorreth it as deadly poison. Nor, 3, by any sinful desire; for he continually desireth the holy and perfect will of God; and any tendency to an unholy desire, he, by the grace of God, stifleth in the birth. Nor, 4, doth he sin by infirmities, whether in act, word or thought: for his infirmities have no concurrence of his will; and without this they are not properly sins. Thus, "He that is born of God doth not commit sin." And though he cannot say, he hath not sinned, yet, now "he sinneth not."

This then is the salvation which is through faith, even

in the present world: a salvation from sin, and the consequences of sin, both often expressed in the word justification; which, taken in the largest sense, implies, a deliverance from guilt and punishment, by the atonement of Christ actually applied to the soul of the sinner now believing on him, and a deliverance from the whole body of sin, through Christ, formed in his heart. So that he who is thus justified, or saved by faith, is indeed born again. He is born again of the Spirit unto a new life, "which is hid with Christ in God." "He is a new creature: old things are passed away: all things in him are become new." And as a newborn babe he gladly receives the αδολον, "sincere milk of the word, and grows thereby;" going on in the might of the Lord his God, from faith to faith, from grace to grace, until at length he comes unto "a perfect man, unto the measure of the stature of the fulness of Christ."

III. The first usual objection to this is,

That to preach salvation, or justification, by faith only, is to preach against holiness and good works. To which a short answer might be given: It would be so, if we spake, as some do, of a faith which was separate from these: but we speak of a faith which is not so but necessarily productive of all good works and all holiness.

But it may be of use to consider it more at large; especially since it is no new objection, but as old as St. Paul's time: for even then it was asked, "Do we not make void the law through faith?" We answer, first, All who preach not faith, do manifestly make void the law; either directly and grossly by limitations and comments, that eat out all the spirit of the text; or, indirectly, by not pointing out the only means whereby it is possible to perform it. Whereas, secondly, "we establish the law," both by showing its full extent and spiritual meaning; and by calling all to that living way, whereby "the righteousness of the law may be fulfilled in them." These, while they trust in the blood of Christ alone, use all the ordinances which he hath appointed, do all the "good works which he had before prepared that they should walk therein," and enjoy and manifest all holy and heavenly tempers, even the same mind that was in Christ Jesus.

But does not preaching this faith lead men into pride? We answer, Accidentally it may: therefore ought every believer to be earnestly cautioned, in the words of the great apostle, "Because of unbelief, the first branches were broken off; and thou standest by faith. Be not high minded, but fear. If God spared not the natural branches, take heed lest he spare not thee. Behold, therefore, the goodness and severity of God! On them which fell, severity; but towards thee, goodness, if thou continue in his goodness; otherwise thou also shalt be cut off." And while he continues therein, he will remember those words of St. Paul, foreseeing and answering this very objection, Rom. iii, 27, "Where is boasting then? It is excluded. By what law? Of works? Nay, but by the law of faith. If a man were justified by his works, he would have whereof to glory." But there is no glorying for him "that worketh not, but believeth on him that justifieth the ungodly," Rom. iv, 5. To the same effect are the words both preceding and following the text: Eph. ii, 4, &c, "God, who is rich in mercy, even when we were dead in sins, hath quickened us together with Christ, (by grace ye are saved,) that he might show the exceeding riches of his grace, in his kindness toward us through Christ Jesus. For, by grace are ye saved, through faith; and that not of yourselves." Of yourselves cometh neither your faith nor your salvation: "It is the gift of God;" the free, undeserved gift; the faith through which ye are saved, as well as the salvation, which he of his own good pleasure, his mere favour, annexes thereto. That ye believe, is one instance of his grace; that believing ye are saved, another. "Not of works, lest any man should

## Salvation by Faith.

boast." For all our works, all our righteousness, which were before our believing, merited nothing of God but condemnation. So far were they from deserving faith, which, therefore, whenever given, is not *of works.* Neither is salvation of the works we do when we believe: for *it is then God that worketh in us:* and, therefore, that he giveth us a reward for what he himself worketh, only commendeth the riches of his mercy, but leaveth us nothing whereof to glory.

However, may not the speaking thus of the mercy of God, as saving or justifying freely by faith only, encourage men in sin? Indeed it may and will: many will "continue in sin that grace may abound:" But their blood is upon their own head. The goodness of God ought to lead them to repentance; and so it will those who are sincere of heart. When they know there is yet forgiveness with him, they will cry aloud that he would blot out their sins also, through faith which is in Jesus. And if they earnestly cry and faint not; if they seek him in all the means he hath appointed; if they refuse to be comforted till he come; "he will come and will not tarry." And he can do much work in a short time. Many are the examples, in the Acts of the Apostles, of God's shedding abroad this faith in men's hearts, even like lightning falling from heaven. So in the same hour that Paul and Silas began to preach, the jailer "repented, believed, and was baptized:" as were three thousand, by St. Peter, on the day of Pentecost, who all repented and believed at his first preaching. And blessed be God, there are now many living proofs that he is still "mighty to save."

Yet to the same truth, placed in another view, a quite contrary objection is made: "If a man cannot be saved by all that he can do, this will drive men to despair." True, to despair of being saved by their own works, their own merits, or righteousness. And so it ought; for none can trust in the merits of Christ, till he has utterly renounced his own. He that "goeth about to establish his own righteousness," cannot receive the righteousness of God. The righteousness which is of faith cannot be given him while he trusteth in that which is of the law.

But this, it is said, is an uncomfortable doctrine. The devil spoke like himself, that is, without either truth or shame, when he dared to suggest to men that it is such. It is the only comfortable one, it is "very full of comfort," to all self-destroyed, self-condemned sinners. That "whosoever believeth on him shall not be ashamed: that the same Lord over all, is rich unto all that call upon him:" Here is comfort, high as heaven, stronger than death! What! Mercy for all? For Zaccheus, a public robber? For Mary Magdalene, a common harlot? Methinks I hear one say, Then I, even I, may hope for mercy! And so thou mayest, thou afflicted one, whom none hath comforted! God will not cast out thy prayer. Nay, perhaps he may say the next hour, "Be of good cheer, thy sins are forgiven thee;" so forgiven, that they shall reign over thee no more; yea, and that "the Holy Spirit shall bear witness with thy spirit that thou art a child of God." O glad tidings! Tidings of great joy, which are sent unto all people! "Ho, every one that thirsteth, come ye to the waters: Come ye, and buy, without money and without price." Whatsoever your sins be, "though red, like crimson," though more than the hairs of your head, "return ye unto the Lord, and he will have mercy upon you; and to our God, for he will abundantly pardon."

When no more objections occur, then we are simply told, that salvation by faith only ought not to be preached as the first doctrine, or, at least, not to be preached to all. But what saith the Holy Ghost? "Other foundation can no man lay, than that which is laid, even Jesus Christ." So then, that "whosoever believeth on him, shall be saved," is, and must be, the foundation of all our preaching; that is, must be preached first. "Well, but not to all." To whom then are we not to preach it? Whom shall we except? The poor? Nay; they have a peculiar right to have the gospel preached unto them. The unlearned? No. God hath revealed these things unto unlearned and ignorant men from the beginning. The young? By no means. Suffer these, in any wise, to come unto Christ, and forbid them not. The sinners? Least of all. "He came not to call the righteous, but sinners to repentance." Why then, if any, we are to except the rich, the learned, the reputable, the moral men. And, it is true, they too often except themselves from hearing; yet we must speak the words of our Lord. For thus the tenor of our commission runs, "Go and preach the gospel to every creature." If any man wrest it, or any part of it, to his destruction, he must bear his own burden. But still, "as the Lord liveth, whatsoever the Lord saith unto us, that we will speak."

At this time, more especially, will we speak, that, "by grace ye are saved, through faith:" because, never was the maintaining this doctrine more seasonable than it is at this day. Nothing but this can effectually prevent the increase of the Romish delusion among us. It is endless to attack, one by one, all the errors of that church. But salvation by faith strikes at the root, and all fall at once where this is established. It was this doctrine, which our church justly calls *the strong rock and foundation of the Christian religion,* that first drove popery out of these kingdoms, and it is this alone can keep it out. Nothing but this can give a check to that immorality which hath "overspread the land as a flood." Can you empty the great deep, drop by drop? Then you may reform us by dissuasives from particular vices. But let the "righteousness which is of God by faith" be brought in, and so shall its proud waves be stayed. Nothing but this can stop the mouths of those who "glory in their shame, and openly deny the Lord that bought them." They can talk as sublimely of the law, as he that hath it written, by God, in his heart. To hear them speak on this head, might incline one to think they were not far from the kingdom of God: but take them out of the law into the gospel; begin with the righteousness of faith; with Christ, "the end of the law, to every one that believeth;" and those who but now appeared almost, if not altogether Christians, stand confessed the sons of perdition; as far from life and salvation (God be merciful unto them!) as the depth of hell from the height of heaven.

For this reason the adversary so rages, whenever "salvation by faith" is declared to the world: for this reason did he stir up earth and hell, to destroy those who first preached it. And for the same reason, knowing that faith alone could overturn the foundations of his kingdom, did he call forth all his forces, and employ all his arts of lies and calumny to affright that champion of the Lord of Hosts, Martin Luther, from reviving it. Nor can we wonder thereat; for as that man of God observes, "How would it enrage a proud strong man armed, to be stopped and set at nought by a little child coming against him with a reed in his hand?" Especially, when he knew that little child would surely overthrow him, and tread him under foot. Even so, Lord Jesus! Thus hath thy strength been ever "made perfect in weakness!" Go forth then, thou little child that believest in him, and "his right hand shall teach thee terrible things!" Though thou art helpless and weak as an infant of days, the strong man shall not be able to stand before thee. Thou shalt prevail over him, and subdue him, and overthrow him, and trample him under thy feet. Thou shalt march on, under the great Captain of thy salvation, "conquering, and to conquer," until all thine enemies are destroyed, and "death is swallowed up in victory."

"Now, thanks be to God, which giveth us the victory through our Lord Jesus Christ," to whom with the Father and the Holy Ghost, be blessing, and glory, and wisdom, and thanksgiving, and honour, and power, and might, for ever. Amen.

## FREE GRACE.

*[Preached at Bristol]*

"He that spared not his own Son, but delivered him up for us all, how shall he not with him also freely give us all things?"—Rom. viii, 32.

How freely does God love the world! While we were yet sinners, "Christ died for the ungodly." While we were "dead in sin," God "spared not his own Son, but delivered him up for us all." And how freely with him does he "give us all things!" Verily, FREE GRACE is all in all!

The grace or love of God, whence cometh our salvation, is FREE IN ALL, and FREE FOR ALL.

First: It is free IN ALL to whom it is given. It does not depend on any power or merit in man; no, not in any degree, neither in whole, nor in part. It does not in any wise depend either on the good works or righteousness of the receiver; not on any thing he has done, or any thing he is. It does not depend on his endeavours. It does not depend on his good tempers, or good desires, or good purposes and intentions; for all these flow from the free grace of God; they are the streams only, not the fountain. They are the fruits of free grace, and not the root. They are not the cause, but the effects of it. Whatsoever good is in man, or is done by man, God is the author and doer of it. Thus is his grace free in all; that is, no way depending on any power or merit in man, but on God alone, who freely gave us his own Son, and "with him freely giveth us all things."

But is it free FOR ALL, as well as IN ALL? To this some have answered, "No: it is free only for those whom God hath ordained to life; and they are but a little flock. The greater part of mankind God hath ordained to death; and it is not free for them. Them God hateth; and therefore, before they were born, decreed they should die eternally. And this he absolutely decreed; because so was his good pleasure; because it was his sovereign will. Accordingly they are born for this, to be destroyed body and soul in hell. And they grow up under the irrevocable curse of God, without any possibility of redemption; for what grace God gives, he gives only for this, to increase, not prevent, their damnation."

This is that decree of predestination. But methinks I hear one say, "This is not the predestination which I hold: I hold only, the election of grace. What I believe is no more than this: that God, before the foundation of the world, did elect a certain number of men to be justified, sanctified, and glorified. Now all these will be saved, and none else: for the rest of mankind God leaves to themselves; so they follow the imaginations of their own hearts, which are only evil continually, and, waxing worse and worse, are at length justly punished with everlasting destruction."

Is this all the predestination which you hold? Consider: perhaps this is not all. Do not you believe, God ordained them to this very thing? If so, you believe the whole decree; you hold predestination in the full sense, which has been above described. But it may be, you think you do not. Do not you then believe, God hardens the hearts of them that perish? Do not you believe, he (literally) hardened Pharaoh's heart, and that for this end he raised him up, or created him? Why this amounts to just the same thing. If you believe Pharaoh, or any one man upon earth, was created for this end, to be damned, you hold all that has been said of predestination. And there is no need you should add, that God seconds his decree, which is supposed unchangeable and irresistible, by hardening the hearts of those vessels of wrath, whom that decree had before fitted for destruction.

Well; but it may be you do not believe even this: you do not hold any decree of reprobation: you do not think God decrees any man to be damned, nor hardens, irresistibly fits him for damnation: you only say, "God eternally decreed, that all being dead in sin, he would say to some of the dry bones, Live, and to others he would not; that, consequently, these should be made alive, and those abide in death,—these should glorify God by their salvation, and those by their destruction."

Is not this what you mean by the election of grace? If it be, I would ask one or two questions: Are any who are not thus elected, saved? Or, were any, from the foundation of the world? Is it possible any man should be saved, unless he be thus elected? If you say, No; you are but where you were: you are not got one hair's breadth farther: you still believe, that in consequence of an unchangeable, irresistible decree of God, the greater part of mankind abide in death, without any possibility of redemption; inasmuch as none can save them but God, and he will not save them. You believe he hath absolutely decreed not to save them; and what is this, but decreeing to damn them? It is, in effect, neither more nor less: it comes to the same thing: for if you are dead, and altogether unable to make yourself alive; then, if God has absolutely decreed he will make only others alive, and not you, he hath absolutely decreed your everlasting death; you are absolutely consigned to damnation. So then, though you use softer words than some, you mean the self same thing; and God's decree concerning the election of grace, according to your own account of it, amounts to neither more nor less than what others call, "God's decree of reprobation."

Call it therefore by whatever name you please, election, preterition, predestination, or reprobation, it comes in the end to the same thing. The sense of all is plainly this: by virtue of an eternal, unchangeable, irresistible decree

## Free Grace. 33

of God, one part of mankind are infallibly saved, and the rest infallibly damned; it being impossible that any of the former should be damned, or that any of the latter should be saved.

But if this be so, then is all preaching vain. It is needless to them that are elected; for they, whether with preaching or without, will infallibly be saved. Therefore the end of preaching, to save souls, is void with regard to them. And it is useless to them that are not elected, for they cannot possibly be saved. They, whether with preaching or without, will infallibly be damned. The end of preaching is therefore void with regard to them likewise; so that in either case, our preaching is vain, as your hearing is also vain.

This, then, is a plain proof that the doctrine of predestination is not a doctrine of God, because it makes void the ordinance of God: and God is not divided against himself. A second is, that it directly tends to destroy that holiness, which is the end of all the ordinances of God. I do not say, none who hold it are holy; (for God is of tender mercy to those who are unavoidably entangled in errors of any kind;) but that the doctrine itself,—That every man is either elected or not elected from eternity, and that the one must inevitably be saved, and the other inevitably damned,—has a manifest tendency to destroy holiness in general. For it wholly takes away those first motives to follow after it, so frequently proposed in Scripture, the hope of future reward and fear of punishment, the hope of heaven and fear of hell. That these shall go away into everlasting punishment, and those into life eternal, is no motive to him to struggle for life, who believes his lot is cast already: it is not reasonable for him so to do, if he thinks he is unalterably adjudged either to life or death. You will say, "But he knows not whether it is life or death." What then?—this helps not the matter: for if a sick man knows that he must unavoidably die, or unavoidably recover, though he knows not which, it is unreasonable for him to take any physic at all. He might justly say, (and so I have heard some speak, both in bodily sickness and in spiritual,) "If I am ordained to life, I shall live; if to death, I shall die: so I need not trouble myself about it." So directly does this doctrine tend to shut the very gate of holiness in general, to hinder unholy men from ever approaching thereto, or striving to enter in thereat.

As directly does this doctrine tend to destroy several particular branches of holiness. Such as meekness and love: love, I mean, of our enemies; of the evil and unthankful. I say not, but none who hold it have meekness and love; (for as is the power of God, so is his mercy;) but that it naturally tends to inspire, or increase, a sharpness or eagerness of temper, which is quite contrary to the meekness of Christ; as then especially appears, when they are opposed on this head. And it as naturally inspires contempt or coldness towards those whom we suppose outcasts from God. "Oh but," you say, "I suppose no particular man a reprobate." You mean, you would not if you could help it. But you cannot help sometimes applying your general doctrine to particular persons: the enemy of souls will apply it for you. You know how often he has done so. But you rejected the thought with abhorrence. True: as soon as you could: but how did it sour and sharpen your spirit in the mean time? You well know it was not the spirit of love which you then felt towards that poor sinner, whom you supposed or suspected, whether you would or no, to have been hated of God from eternity.

Thirdly, This doctrine tends to destroy the comfort of religion, the happiness of Christianity. This is evident as to all those who believe themselves to be reprobated; or who only suspect or fear it. All the great and precious promises are lost to them; they afford them no ray of

1. DR. JAMES HAMILTON.  2. REV. JOHN WESLEY.
3. REV. JOSEPH COLE

As seen walking in Edinburgh, 1790.

comfort: for they are not the elect of God; therefore they have neither lot nor portion in them. This is an effectual bar to their finding any comfort or happiness, even in that religion whose ways are designed to be "ways of pleasantness, and all her paths peace."

And as to you who believe yourselves the elect of God, what is your happiness? I hope not a notion; a speculative belief; a bare opinion of any kind; but a feeling possession of God in your heart, wrought in you by the Holy Ghost, or the witness of God's Spirit with your spirit that you are a child of God. This, otherwise termed "the full assurance of faith," is the true ground of a Christian's happiness. And it does indeed imply a full assurance that all your past sins are forgiven, and that you are *now* a child of God. But it does not necessarily imply a full assurance of our future perseverance. I do not say this is never joined to it, but that it is not necessarily implied therein; for many have the one who have not the other.

Now this witness of the Spirit, experience shows to be much obstructed by this doctrine; and not only in those who, believing themselves reprobated, by this belief thrust it far from them, but even in them that have tasted of that good gift, who yet have soon lost it again, and fallen back into doubts, and fears, and darkness,—horrible darkness, that might be felt! And I appeal to any of you who hold this doctrine, to say, between God and your own hearts, whether you have not often a return of doubts and fears concerning your election or perseverance? If you ask, who has not? I answer, very few of those that hold this doctrine,—but many, very many of those that hold it not, in all parts of the earth, many of those who know and feel they are in Christ to day, and "take no thought for the morrow," who "abide in him" by faith from hour to hour, or rather from moment to moment,—many of these have enjoyed the uninterrupted witness of his Spirit, the continual light of his countenance, from the moment wherein they first believed, for many months or years, to this day.

That assurance of faith, which these enjoy, excludes all doubt and fear. It excludes all kinds of doubt and fear concerning their future perseverance; though it is not properly, as was said before, an assurance of what is future, but only of what *now* is. And this needs not for its support a speculative belief that whoever is once ordained to life must live; for it is wrought, from hour to hour, by the mighty power of God, "by the Holy Ghost which is given unto them." And therefore that doctrine is not of God, because it tends to obstruct, if not destroy, this great work of the Holy Ghost, whence flows the chief comfort of religion, the happiness of Christianity.

Again: how uncomfortable a thought is this, that thousands and millions of men, without any preceding offence or fault of theirs, were unchangeably doomed to everlasting burnings! How peculiarly uncomfortable must it be to those who have put on Christ! To those who, being filled with bowels of mercy, tenderness, and compassion, could even "wish themselves accursed for their brethren's sake!"

Fourthly: This uncomfortable doctrine directly tends to destroy our zeal for good works. And this it does, first, as it naturally tends (according to what was observed before) to destroy our love to the greater part of mankind, namely, the evil and unthankful. For whatever lessens our love, must so far lessen our desire to do them good. This it does, secondly, as it cuts off one of the strongest motives to all acts of bodily mercy, such as feeding the hungry, clothing the naked, and the like; viz. the hope of saving their souls from death. For what avails it to relieve their temporal wants, who are just dropping into eternal fire? "Well: but run and snatch them as brands out of the fire."—Nay, this you suppose impossible. They were appointed thereunto, you say, from eternity, before they had done either good or evil. You believe it is the will of God they should die. And "who hath resisted his will?" But you say, you do not know whether these are elected or not. What then? If you know they are the one or the other, that they are either elected, or not elected, all your labour is void and vain. In either case, your advice, reproof, or exhortation, is as needless and useless as our preaching. It is needless to them that are elected; for they will infallibly be saved without it. It is useless to them that are not elected; for with or without it they will infallibly be damned: therefore you cannot, consistently with your principles, take any pains about their salvation. Consequently those principles directly tend to destroy your zeal for good works; for all good works; but particularly for the greatest of all, the saving of souls from death.

But, fifthly, This doctrine not only tends to destroy Christian holiness, happiness, and good works, but hath also a direct and manifest tendency to overthrow the whole Christian revelation. The point which the wisest of the modern unbelievers most industriously labour to prove, is that the Christian revelation is not necessary. They well know, could they once show this, the conclusion would be too plain to be denied, "If it be not necessary, it is not true." Now this fundamental point you give up. For supposing that eternal, unchangeable decree, one part of mankind must be saved though the Christian revelation were not in being, and the other part of mankind must be damned, notwithstanding that revelation. And what would an infidel desire more? You allow him all he asks. In making the gospel thus unnecessary to all sorts of men, you give up the whole Christian cause. "Oh tell it not in Gath! Publish it not in the streets of Askelon! lest the daughters of the uncircumcised rejoice;" lest the sons of unbelief triumph!

And as this doctrine manifestly and directly tends to overthrow the whole Christian revelation, so it does the same thing, by plain consequence, in making that revelation contradict itself. For it is grounded on such an interpretation of some texts (more or fewer it matters not) as flatly contradicts all the other texts, and indeed the whole scope and tenor of Scripture. For instance: the assertors of this doctrine interpret that text of Scripture, "Jacob have I loved, but Esau have I hated," as implying, that God in a literal sense hated Esau, and all the reprobated, from eternity. Now what can possibly be a more flat contradiction than this, not only to the whole scope and tenor of Scripture, but also to all those particular texts which expressly declare, "God is love?" Again: they infer from that text, "I will have mercy on whom I will have mercy," Rom. ix, 15, that God is love only to some men, viz. the elect, and that he hath mercy for those only; flatly contrary to which is the whole tenor of Scripture, as is that express declaration in particular, "The Lord is loving unto every man, and his mercy is over all his works," Psalm cxlv, 9. Again: they infer from that and the like texts, "It is not of him that willeth, nor of him that runneth, but of God that showeth mercy," that he showeth mercy only to those to whom he had respect from all eternity. Nay, but who replieth against God now? You now contradict the whole oracles of God, which declare throughout, "God is no respecter of persons," Acts x, 34; "There is no respect of persons with him," Rom. ii, 11. Again: from that text,—"The children being not yet born, neither having done any good or evil, that the purpose of God according to election might stand, not of works, but of him that calleth; it was said unto her, [unto Rebecca,] the elder shall serve the younger;"—you infer, that our being predestinated, or elect, no way depends on the foreknowledge of God; flatly contrary to this are all the Scriptures; and those in

## Free Grace. 39

particular, "Elect according to the foreknowledge of God," 1 Pet. i, 2: "Whom he did foreknow, he also did predestinate," Rom. viii, 29.

And, "the same Lord over all is rich in mercy to all that call upon him," Rom. x, 12: But you say, no; he is such only to those for whom Christ died. And those are not all, but only a few, whom God hath chosen out of the world; for he died not for all, but only for those who were "chosen in him before the foundation of the world," Eph. i, 4. Flatly contrary to your interpretation of these Scriptures, also, is the whole tenor of the New Testament; as are in particular those texts;—"Destroy not him with thy meat, for whom Christ died," Rom. xiv, 15; [a clear proof that Christ died, not only for those that are saved, but also for them that perish;] he is "The Saviour of the world," John iv, 42; he is "The Lamb of God that taketh away the sins of the world," John i, 29; "He is the propitiation, not for our sins only, but also for the sins of the whole world," 1 John ii, 2; "He [the living God] is the Saviour of all men," 1 Tim. iv, 10; "He gave himself a ransom for all," 1 Tim. ii, 6; "He tasted death for every man," Heb. ii, 9.

If you ask, why then are not all men saved? The whole law and the testimony answer, first, not because of any decree of God; not because it is his pleasure they should die; for, "as I live, saith the Lord God," "I have no pleasure in the death of him that dieth," Ezek. xviii, 32. Whatever be the cause of their perishing, it cannot be his will if the oracles of God are true; for they declare, "He is not willing that any should perish, but that all should come to repentance," 2 Pet. iii, 9; "He willeth that all men should be saved." And they, secondly, declare what is the cause why all men are not saved, namely, that they will not be saved: so our Lord expressly; "Ye will not come unto me that ye may have life," John v, 40. "The power of the Lord is present to heal" them, but they will not be healed. "They reject the counsel," the merciful counsel of God "against themselves," as did their stiff necked forefathers. And therefore are they without excuse; because God would save them, but they will not be saved: this is the condemnation, "How often would I have gathered you together, and ye would not," Matt. xxiii, 37.

Thus manifestly does this doctrine tend to overthrow the whole Christian revelation, by making it contradict itself; by giving such an interpretation of some texts, as flatly contradicts all the other texts, and indeed the whole scope and tenor of Scripture;—an ambundant proof that it is not of God. But neither is this all: for, seventhly, it is a doctrine full of blasphemy; of such blasphemy as I should dread to mention, but that the honour of our gracious God, and the cause of his truth, will not suffer me to be silent. In the cause of God, then, and from a sincere concern for the glory of his great name, I will mention a few of the horrible blasphemies, contained in this horrible doctrine. But first, I must warn every one of you that hears, as ye will answer it at the great day, not to charge me (as some have done) with blaspheming, because I mention the blasphemy of others. And the more you are grieved with them that do thus blaspheme, see that ye "confirm your love towards them" the more, and that your hearts' desire, and continual prayer to God, be, "Father, forgive them, for they know not what they do."

This premised, let it be observed, that this doctrine represents our blessed Lord, "Jesus Christ, the righteous," "the only begotten Son of the Father, full of grace and truth," as a hypocrite, a deceiver of the people, a man void of common sincerity. For it cannot be denied, that he every where speaks as if he was willing that all men should be saved. Therefore, to say he was not willing that all men should be saved, is to represent him as a mere hypocrite and dissembler. It cannot be denied that the gracious words which came out of his mouth, are full of invitations to all sinners. To say then, he did not intend to save all sinners, is to represent him as a gross deceiver of the people. You cannot deny that he says, "Come unto me, all ye that are weary and heavy laden." If, then, you say he calls those that cannot come; those whom he knows to be unable to come; those whom he can make able to come, but will not; how is it possible to describe greater insincerity? You represent him as mocking his helpless creatures, by offering what he never intends to give. You describe him as saying one thing, and meaning another; as pretending the love which he had not. Him, in "whose mouth was no guile," you make full of deceit, void of common sincerity;—then especially, when, drawing nigh the city, he wept over it, and said, "Oh Jerusalem, Jerusalem, thou that killest the prophets, and stonest them that are sent unto thee, how often *would I* have gathered thy children together,—and *ye would not;*" ηθελησα—και ουκ ηθελησατε. Now if you say, *they would,* but *he would not,* you represent him (which who could hear?) as weeping crocodile's tears; weeping over the prey which himself had doomed to destruction!

Such blasphemy this, as one would think might make the ears of a Christian to tingle! But there is yet more behind; for just as it honours the Son, so doth this doctrine honour the Father. It destroys all his attributes at once: it overturns both his justice, mercy, and truth: yea, it represents the most holy God as worse than the devil, as both more false, more cruel, and more unjust. More *false;* because the devil, liar as he is, hath never said, "He willeth all men to be saved:" more *unjust;* because the devil cannot, if he would, be guilty of such injustice as you ascribe to God, when you say, that God condemned millions of souls to everlasting fire, prepared for the devil and his angels, for continuing in sin, which, for want of that grace *he will not* give them, they cannot avoid: and more *cruel;* because that unhappy spirit "seeketh rest and findeth none;" so that his own restless misery is a kind of temptation to him to tempt others. But God resteth in his high and holy place; so that to suppose him, of his own mere motion, of his pure will and pleasure, happy as he is, to doom his creatures, whether they will or no, to endless misery, is to impute such cruelty to him, as we cannot impute even to the great enemy of God and man. It is to represent the Most High God (he that hath ears to hear, let him hear!) as more cruel, false, and unjust than the devil!

This is the blasphemy clearly contained in *the horrible decree* of predestination! And here I fix my foot. On this I join issue with every assertor of it. You represent God as worse than the devil; more false, more cruel, more unjust. But you say, you will prove it by Scripture. Hold! What will you prove by Scripture? That God is worse than the devil? It cannot be. Whatever that Scripture proves, it never can prove this; whatever its true meaning be, this cannot be its true meaning. Do you ask, What is its true meaning then? If I say, I know not, you have gained nothing; for there are many scriptures, the true sense whereof neither you nor I shall know, till death is swallowed up in victory. But this I know, better it were to say it had no sense at all, than to say it had such a sense as this. It cannot mean, whatever it mean besides, that the God of truth is a liar. Let it mean what it will, it cannot mean that the Judge of all the world is unjust. No scripture can mean that God is not love, or that his mercy is not over all his works: that is, whatever it prove besides, no scripture can prove predestination.

This is the blasphemy for which (however I love the persons who assert it) I abhor the doctrine of predestina-

## Free Grace.  43

tion; a doctrine, upon the supposition of which, if one could possibly suppose it for a moment, (call it election, reprobation, or what you please, for all comes to the same thing,) one might say to our adversary the devil, "Thou fool, why dost thou roar about any longer? Thy lying in wait for souls is as needless and useless as our preaching. Hearest thou not, that God hath taken thy work out of thy hands; and that he doeth it much more effectually? Thou, with all thy principalities and powers, canst only so assault that we may resist thee; but he can irresistibly destroy both body and soul in hell! Thou canst only entice; but his unchangeable decree, to leave thousands of souls in death, compels them to continue in sin, till they drop into everlasting burnings. Thou temptest; he forceth us to be damned: for we cannot resist his will. Thou fool, why goest thou about any longer, seeking whom thou mayest devour? Hearest thou not that God is the devouring lion, the destroyer of souls, the murderer of men? Moloch caused only children to pass through the fire; and that fire was soon quenched; or, the corruptible body being consumed, its torment was at an end: but God, thou art told, by his eternal decree, fixed before they had done good or evil, causes not only children of a span long, but the parents also, to pass through the fire of hell, the 'fire which never shall be quenched:' and the body which is cast thereinto, being now incorruptible and immortal, will be ever consuming and never consumed, but 'the smoke of their torment,' because it is God's good pleasure, 'ascendeth up for ever and ever.' "

Oh how would the enemy of God and man rejoice to hear these things were so! How would he cry aloud and spare not! How would he lift up his voice and say, "To your tents, oh Israel! Flee from the the face of this God, or ye shall utterly perish! But whither will ye flee? Into heaven? He is there. Down to hell? He is there also. Ye cannot flee from an omnipresent, almighty tyrant. And whether ye flee or stay, I call heaven his throne, and earth his footstool, to witness against you, ye shall perish, ye shall die eternally. Sing, oh hell, and rejoice, ye that are under the earth! for God, even the mighty God, hath spoken, and devoted to death thousands of souls, from the rising of the sun, unto the going down thereof! Here, oh death, is thy sting! They shall not, cannot escape, for the mouth of the Lord hath spoken it. Here, oh grave, is thy victory! Nations yet unborn, or ever they have done good or evil, are doomed never to see the light of life, but thou shalt gnaw upon them for ever and ever: Let all those morning stars sing together, who fell with Lucifer, son of the morning! Let all the sons of hell shout for joy! For the decree is past, and who can disannul it?"

Yea, the decree is past: and so it was before the foundation of the world. But what decree? Even this: "I will set before the sons of men, 'life and death, blessing and cursing.' And the soul that chooseth life shall live, as the soul that chooseth death shall die." This decree, whereby "whom God did foreknow, he did predestinate," was indeed from everlasting: this, whereby all who suffer Christ to make them alive are "elect, according to the foreknowledge of God," now standeth fast, even as the moon, and as the faithful witnesses in heaven; and when heaven and earth shall pass away, yet this shall not pass away, for it is as unchangeable and eternal, as is the being of God that gave it. This decree yields the strongest encouragement to abound in all good works, and in all holiness; and it is a well spring of joy, of happiness also, to our great and endless comfort. This is worthy of God: it is every way consistent with all the perfections of his nature. It gives us the noblest view both of his justice, mercy, and truth. To this agrees the whole scope of the Christian revelation, as well as all the parts thereof. To this Moses and all the prophets bear witness, and our blessed Lord and all his apostles. Thus Moses, in the name of his Lord, "I call heaven and earth to record against you this day, that I have set before you life and death, blessing and cursing; therefore choose life, that thou and thy seed may live." Thus Ezekiel: (to cite one prophet for all:) "The soul that sinneth, it shall die: the son shall not bear [eternally] the iniquity of the father. The righteousness of the righteous shall be upon him, and the wickedness of the wicked shall be upon him," chap. xviii, 20. Thus our blessed Lord: "If any man thirst, let him come unto me and drink," John vii, 37. Thus his great apostle, St. Paul, Acts xvii, 30, "God commandeth all men every where to repent;"—"all men, every where;" every man in every place, without any exception, either of place or person. Thus St. James: "If any of you lack wisdom, let him ask of God, who giveth to all men liberally, and upbraideth not, and it shall be given him," James i, 5. Thus St. Peter: 2 Pet. iii, 9, "The Lord is not willing that any should perish, but that all should come to repentance." And thus St. John: "If any man sin, we have an advocate with the Father: and he is the propitiation for our sins: and not for ours only, but for the sins of the whole world," 1 John ii, 1, 2.

Oh hear ye this, ye that forget God! Ye cannot charge your death upon him! "Have I any pleasure at all, that the wicked should die, saith the Lord God? Ezek. xviii, 23, &c. Repent, and turn from all your transgressions: so iniquity shall not be your ruin. Cast away from you all your transgressions whereby ye have transgressed,— for why will ye die, oh house of Israel? For I have no pleasure in the death of him that dieth, saith the Lord God. Wherefore turn yourselves and live ye." "As I live, saith the Lord God, I have no pleasure in the death of the wicked.—Turn ye, turn ye, from your evil ways: for why will ye die, oh house of Israel?" Ezek. xxxiii, 11.

## THE NEW BIRTH.

"Ye must be born again."—John iii, 7.

If any doctrines within the whole compass of Christianity may be properly termed fundamental, they are doubtless these two; the doctrine of justification, and that of the new birth: the former relating to that great work which God does *for us,* in forgiving our sins; the latter, to the great work which God does *in us,* in renewing our fallen nature. In order of *time,* neither of these is before the other; in the moment we are justified by the grace of God, through the redemption that is in Jesus, we are also "born of the Spirit;" but in order of *thinking* as it is termed, justification precedes the new birth. We first conceive his wrath to be turned away, and then his Spirit to work in our hearts.

How great importance then must it be of, to every child of man, thoroughly to understand these fundamental doctrines? From a full conviction of this, many excellent men have written very largely concerning justification, explaining every point relating thereto, and opening the scriptures which treat upon it. Many likewise have written on the new birth: and some of them largely enough: but yet not so clearly as might have been desired; nor so deeply and accurately, having either given a dark, abstruse account of it, or a slight and superficial one. Therefore a full, and at the same time a clear account of the new birth, seems to be wanting still; such as may enable us to give a satisfactory answer to these three questions: first, Why must we be born again? What is the foundation of this doctrine of the new birth? Secondly, How must we be born again? What is the nature of the new birth? And, thirdly, Wherefore must we be born again? To what end is it necessary? These questions, by the assistance of God, I shall briefly and plainly an-

## The New Birth.

swer, and then subjoin a few inferences which will naturally follow.

I. And first, Why must we be born again? What is the foundation of this doctrine? The foundation of it lies near as deep as the creation of the world; in the scriptural account whereof we read, "And God," the three-one God, "said, Let us make man in our image, after our likeness. So God created man in his own image, in the image of God created he him," Gen. i, 26, 27:—not barely in his *natural image,* a picture of his own immortality; a spiritual being, endued with understanding, freedom of will, and various affections;—nor merely in his *political image,* the governor of this lower world, having "dominion over the fishes of the sea, and over all the earth;"—but chiefly in his *moral image;* which, according to the apostle, is "righteousness and true holiness," Eph. iv, 24. In this image of God was man made. "God is love;" accordingly man at his creation was full of love; which was the sole principle of all his tempers, thoughts, words, and actions. God is full of justice, mercy, and truth; so was man as he came from the hands of his Creator. God is spotless purity; and so man was in the beginning pure from every sinful blot; otherwise God could not have pronounced him, as well as all the other works of his hands, "very good," Gen. i, 31. This he could not have been, had he not been pure from sin, and filled with righteousness and true holiness. For there is no medium: if we suppose an intelligent creature not to love God, not to be righteous and holy, we necessarily suppose him not to be good at all; much less to be "very good."

But, although man was made in the image of God, yet he was not made immutable. This would have been inconsistent with that state of trial in which God was pleased to place him. He was therefore created able to stand, and yet liable to fall. And this God himself apprized him of, and gave him a solemn warning against it. Nevertheless, man did not abide in honour: he fell from his high estate. He "ate of the tree whereof the Lord had commanded him, Thou shalt not eat thereof." By this wilful act of disobedience to his Creator, this flat rebellion against his Sovereign, he openly declared that he would no longer have God to rule over him; that he would be governed by his own will, and not the will of him that created him; and that he would not seek his happiness in God, but in the world, in the works of his hands. Now God had told him before, "In the day that thou eatest [of that fruit] thou shalt surely die." And the word of the Lord cannot be broken. Accordingly, in that day he did die, he died to God, the most dreadful of all deaths. He lost the life of God: he was separated from him, in union with whom his spiritual life consisted. The body dies when it is separated from the soul; the soul, when it is separated from God. But this separation from God, Adam sustained in the day, the hour, he ate of the forbidden fruit. And of this he gave immediate proof; presently showing by his behaviour, that the love of God was extinguished in his soul, which was now "alienated from the life of God." Instead of this he was now under the power of servile fear, so that he fled from the presence of the Lord. Yea, so little did he retain even of the knowledge of him who filleth heaven and earth, that he endeavoured to "hide himself from the Lord God, among the trees of the garden," Gen. iii, 8: so had he lost both the knowledge and the love of God, without which the image of God could not subsist. Of this therefore he was deprived at the same time, and became unholy as well as unhappy. In the room of this he had sunk into pride and self will, the very image of the devil; and into sensual appetites and desires, the image of the beasts that perish.

If it be said, "Nay, but that threatening, 'In the day

## The New Birth. 49

that thou eatest thereof, thou shalt surely die,' refers to temporal death and that alone, to the death of the body only;" the answer is plain: To affirm this is flatly and palpably to make God a liar; to aver that the God of truth positively affirmed a thing contrary to truth. For it is evident, Adam did not *die* in this sense, "in the day that he ate thereof." He lived in the sense opposite to this death, above nine hundred years after, so that this cannot possibly be understood of the death of the body, without impeaching the veracity of God. It must therefore be understood of spiritual death, the loss of the life and image of God.

And in Adam all died, all human kind, all the children of men who were then in Adam's loins. The natural consequence of this is, that every one descended from him comes into the world spiritually dead, dead to God, wholly dead in sin; entirely void of the life of God; void of the image of God, of all that righteousness and holiness wherein Adam was created. Instead of this, every man born into the world now bears the image of the devil, in pride and self will; the image of the beast, in sensual appetites and desires. This then is the foundation of the new birth,—the entire corruption of our nature. Hence it is, that being born in sin, we must be "born again." Hence every one that is born of a woman, must be born of the Spirit of God.

II. But how must a man be born again? What is the nature of the new birth? This is the second question. And a question it is of the highest moment that can be conceived. We ought not therefore, in so weighty a concern, to be content with a slight inquiry; but to examine it with all possible care; and to ponder it in our hearts, till we fully understand this important point, and clearly see how we are to be born again.

Not that we are to expect any minute, philosophical account of the manner how this is done. Our Lord sufficiently guards us against any such expectation, by the words immediately following the text; wherein he reminds Nicodemus of as indisputable a fact as any in the whole compass of nature, which notwithstanding the wisest man under the sun is not able fully to explain. "The wind bloweth where it listeth,"—not by thy power or wisdom; "and thou hearest the sound thereof;"—thou art absolutely assured, beyond all doubt, that it doth blow; "but thou canst not tell whence it cometh, nor whither it goeth;"—the precise manner how it begins and ends, rises and falls, no man can tell. "So is every one that is born of the Spirit:"—thou mayest be as absolutely assured of the fact, as of the blowing of the wind; but the precise manner how it is done, how the Holy Spirit works this in the soul, neither thou nor the wisest of the children of men is able to explain.

However, it suffices for every rational and Christian purpose that without descending into curious, critical inquiries, we can give a plain scriptural account of the nature of the new birth. This will satisfy every reasonable man, who desires only the salvation of his soul. The expression, being born again, was not first used by our Lord in his conversation with Nicodemus: it was well known before that time, and was in common use among the Jews when our Saviour appeared among them. When an adult heathen was convinced that the Jewish religion was of God, and desired to join therein, it was the custom to baptize him first, before he was admitted to circumcision. And when he was baptized, he was said to be born again; by which they meant, that he who was before a child of the devil, was now adopted into the family of God, and accounted one of his children. This expression, therefore, which Nicodemus, being "a teacher in Israel," ought to have understood well, our Lord uses in conversing with him; only in a stronger sense than he was accustomed to. And this might be the reason of his asking,

"how can these things be?" They cannot be literally:—
a man cannot "enter a second time into his mother's
womb, and be born:"—but they may, spiritually: a man
may be born from above, born of God, born of the Spirit,
in a manner which bears a very near analogy to the natural birth.

Before a child is born into the world, he has eyes, but
sees not; he has ears, but does not hear. He has a very
imperfect use of every other sense. He has no knowledge of any of the things of the world, or any natural
understanding. To that manner of existence which he
then has, we do not even give the name of life. It is then
only when a man is born, that we say, he begins to live.
For as soon as he is born, he begins to see the light, and
the various objects with which he is encompassed. His
ears are then opened, and he hears the sounds which successively strike upon them. At the same time, all the
other organs of sense begin to be exercised upon their
proper objects. He likewise breathes, and lives in a
manner wholly different from what he did before. How
exactly doth the parallel hold in all these instances?
While a man is in a mere natural state, before he is born
of God, he has, in a spiritual sense, eyes and sees not; a
thick impenetrable veil lies upon them: he has ears, but
hears not; he is utterly deaf to what he is most of all concerned to hear. His other spiritual senses are all locked
up: he is in the same condition as if he had them not.
Hence he has no knowledge of God; no intercourse with
him; he is not at all acquainted with him. He has no
true knowledge of the things of God, either of spiritual or eternal things; therefore, though he is a living
man, he is a dead Christian. But as soon as he is born
of God, there is a total change in all these particulars. The "eyes of his understanding are opened;"
(such is the language of the great apostle;) and, he who
of old "commanded light to shine out of darkness shin-

ing on his heart, he sees the light of the glory of God," his glorious love "in the face of Jesus Christ." His ears being opened, he is now capable of hearing the inward voice of God, saying, "Be of good cheer; thy sins are forgiven thee;" "go and sin no more." This is the purport of what God speaks to his heart; although perhaps not in these very words. He is now ready to hear whatsoever "He that teacheth man knowledge" is pleased from time to time to reveal to him. He "feels in his heart (to use the language of our church) the mighty working of the Spirit of God;" not in a gross, carnal sense, as the men of the world stupidly and wilfully misunderstand the expression; though they have been told again and again, we mean thereby neither more nor less than this: he feels, is inwardly sensible of, the graces which the Spirit of God works in his heart. He feels, he is conscious of, a "peace which passeth all understanding." He many times feels such a joy in God, as is "unspeakable, and full of glory." He feels "the love of God shed abroad in his heart by the Holy Ghost which is given unto him;" and all his spiritual senses are then exercised to discern spiritual good and evil. By the use of these, he is daily increasing in the knowledge of God, of Jesus Christ whom he hath sent, and of all the things pertaining to his inward kingdom. And now he may be properly said to live: God having quickened him by his Spirit, he is alive to God through Jesus Christ. He lives a life which the world knoweth not of, a "life which is hid with Christ in God." God is continually breathing, as it were, upon the soul; and his soul is breathing unto God. Grace is descending into his heart; and prayer and praise ascending to heaven: and by this intercourse between God and man, this fellowship with the Father and the Son, as by a kind of spiritual respiration, the life of God in the soul is sustained; and the child of God grows up, till he comes to the "full measure of the stature of Christ."

## The New Birth.

From hence it manifestly appears, what is the nature of the new birth. It is that great change which God works in the soul, when he brings it into life; when he raises it from the death of sin to the life of righteousness. It is the change wrought in the whole soul by the almighty Spirit of God, when it is "created anew in Christ Jesus," when it is "renewed after the image of God, in righteousness and true holiness;" when the love of the world is changed into the love of God; pride into humility; passion into meekness; hatred, envy, malice, into a sincere, tender, disinterested love for all mankind. In a word, it is that change whereby the earthly, sensual, devilish mind is turned into the "mind which was in Christ Jesus." This is the nature of the new birth: "So is every one that is born of the Spirit."

III. It is not difficult for any who has considered these things, to see the necessity of the new birth, and to answer the third question, Wherefore, to what end, is it necessary that we should be born again? It is very easily discerned, that this is necessary, first, in order to holiness. For what is holiness according to the oracles of God? Not a bare external religion, a round of outward duties, how many soever they be, and how exactly soever performed. No: gospel holiness is no less than the image of God stamped upon the heart; it is no other than the whole mind which was in Christ Jesus; it consists of all heavenly affections and tempers mingled together in one. It implies such a continual, thankful love to him who hath not withheld from us his Son, his only Son, as makes it natural, and in a manner necessary to us, to love every child of man; as fills us "with bowels of mercies, kindness, gentleness, long suffering:" it is such a love of God as teaches us to be blameless in all manner of conversation; as enables us to present our souls and bodies, all we are, and all we have, all our thoughts, words, and actions, a continual sacrifice to God, acceptable through Christ

Jesus. Now this holiness can have no existence, till we are renewed in the image of our mind. It cannot commence in the soul, till that change be wrought; till by the power of the highest overshadowing us, we are "brought from darkness to light, from the power of Satan unto God;" that is, till we are born again; which therefore is absolutely necessary in order to holiness.

But "without holiness no man shall see the Lord," shall see the face of God in glory. Of consequence, the new birth is absolutely necessary in order to eternal salvation. Men may indeed flatter themselves, (so desperately wicked, and so deceitful is the heart of man!) that they may live in their sins till they come to the last gasp, and yet afterwards live with God; and thousands do really believe, that they have found a broad way which leadeth not to destruction. "What danger," say they, "can a woman be in that is so *harmless* and so *virtuous?* What fear is there that so *honest* a man, one of so strict *morality*, should miss of heaven? Especially, if over and above all this, they constantly attend on church and sacrament." One of these will ask with all assurance, "What, shall not I do as well as my neighbours?" Yes, as well as your unholy neighbours; as well as your neighbours that die in their sins! For you will all drop into the pit together, into the nethermost hell! You will all lie together in the lake of fire; "the lake of fire burning with brimstone." Then, at length, you will see, (but God grant you may see it before!) the necessity of holiness in order to glory; and consequently of the new birth, since none can be holy, except he be born again.

For the same reason, except he be born again, none can be happy even in this world. For it is not possible, in the nature of things, that a man should be happy who is not holy. Even the poor ungodly poet could tell us, *Nemo malus felix:* no wicked man is happy. The reason is plain: all unholy tempers are uneasy tempers: not only

## The New Birth.

malice, hatred, envy, jealousy, revenge, create a present hell in the breast, but even the softer passions, if not kept within due bounds, give a thousand times more pain than pleasure. Even "hope," when "deferred," (and how often must this be the case?) "maketh the heart sick;" and every desire which is not according to the will of God, is liable to "pierce [us] through with many sorrows:" and all those general sources of sin, pride, self will, and idolatry, are, in the same proportion as they prevail, general sources of misery. Therefore, as long as these reign in any soul, happiness has no place there. But they must reign till the bent of our nature is changed, that is, till we are born again; consequently, the new birth is absolutely necessary in order to happiness in this world, as well as in the world to come.

IV. I proposed in the last place to subjoin a few inferences, which naturally follow from the preceding observations.

And, first, it follows, that baptism is not the new birth; they are not one and the same thing. Many indeed seem to imagine that they are just the same; at least, they speak as if they thought so; but I do not know that this opinion is publicly avowed by any denomination of Christians whatever. Certainly it is not by any within these kingdoms, whether of the established church, or dissenting from it. The judgment of the latter is clearly declared, in their large catechism:[*] Q. "What are the parts of a sacrament? A. The parts of a sacrament are two: the one, an outward and sensible sign; the other, an inward and spiritual grace, thereby signified. Q. What is baptism? A. Baptism is a sacrament, wherein Christ hath ordained the washing with water, to be a sign and seal of regeneration by his Spirit." Here it is manifest, baptism, the sign, is spoken of as distinct from regeneration, the thing signified.

---

[*] Q. 163, 165.

In the church catechism likewise, the judgment of our church is declared with the utmost clearness: "What meanest thou by this word, sacrament? A. I mean an outward and visible sign of an inward and spiritual grace. Q. What is the outward part, or form, in baptism? A. Water, wherein the person is baptized, in the name of the Father, Son, and Holy Ghost. Q. What is the inward part, or thing signified? A. A death unto sin, and a new birth unto righteousness." Nothing therefore is plainer, than that according to the church of England, baptism is not the new birth.

But indeed the reason of the thing is so clear and evident, as not to need any other authority. For what can be more plain, than that the one is an external, the other an internal work; that the one is a visible, the other an invisible thing, and therefore wholly different from each other?—the one being an act of man, purifying the body; the other a change wrought by God in the soul: so that the former is just as distinguishable from the latter, as the soul from the body, or water from the Holy Ghost.

From the preceding reflections we may, secondly, observe, that as the new birth is not the same thing with baptism, so it does not always accompany baptism: they do not constantly go together. A man may possibly be "born of water," and yet not be "born of the Spirit." There may sometimes be the outward sign, where there is not the inward grace. I do not now speak with regard to infants: it is certain our church supposes, that all who are baptized in their infancy, are at the same time born again; and it is allowed that the whole office for the baptism of infants proceeds upon this supposition. Nor is it an objection of any weight against this, that we cannot comprehend how this work can be wrought in infants. For neither can we comprehend how it is wrought in a person of riper years. But whatever be the case with infants, it is sure all of riper years, who are

## The New Birth.

baptized, are not at the same time born again. "The tree is known by its fruits:" and hereby it appears too plain to be denied that divers of those, who were children of the devil before they were baptized, continue the same after baptism; "for the works of their father they do:" they continue servants of sin, without any pretence either to inward or outward holiness.

A third inference which we may draw from what has been observed, is, that the new birth is not the same with sanctification. This is indeed taken for granted by many; particularly by an eminent writer, in his late treatise on "The Nature and Grounds of Christian Regeneration." To waive several other weighty objections which might be made to that tract, this is a palpable one: it all along speaks of regeneration as a progressive work, carried on in the soul by slow degrees from the time of our first turning to God. This is undeniably true of sanctification; but of regeneration, the new birth, it is not true. This is a part of sanctification, not the whole; it is the gate to it, the entrance into it. When we are born again, then our sanctification, our inward and outward holiness, begins; and thenceforward we are gradually to "grow up in him who is our Head." This expression of the apostle admirably illustrates the difference between one and the other, and farther points out the exact analogy there is between natural and spiritual things. A child is born of a woman in a moment, or at least in a very short time: afterwards he gradually and slowly grows, till he attains to the stature of a man. In like manner, a child is born of God in a short time, if not in a moment. But it is by slow degrees that he afterwards grows up to the measure of the full stature of Christ. The same relation, therefore, which there is between our natural birth and our growth, there is also between our new birth and our sanctification.

One point more we may learn from the preceding observations. But it is a point of so great importance, as may excuse the considering it the more carefully, and prosecuting it at some length. What must one who loves the souls of men, and is grieved that any of them should perish, say to one whom he sees living in sabbath breaking, drunkenness, or any other wilful sin? What can he say, if the foregoing observations are true, but, "You must be born again?" "No," says a zealous man, "that cannot be. How can you talk so uncharitably to the man? Has he not been baptized already? He cannot be born again now." Can he not be born again? Do you affirm this? Then he cannot be saved. Though he be as old as Nicodemus was, yet "except he be born again, he cannot see the kingdom of God." Therefore in saying, "he cannot be born again," you in effect deliver him over to damnation. And where lies the uncharitableness now? On my side, or on yours? I say, he may be born again, and so become an heir of salvation. You say, "he cannot be born again:" and if so, he must inevitably perish! So you utterly block up his way to salvation, and send him to hell, out of mere charity!

But perhaps the sinner himself, to whom in real charity we say, "You must be born again," has been taught to say, "I defy your new doctrine; I need not be born again: I was born again when I was baptized. What! Would you have me deny my baptism?" I answer, first, there is nothing under heaven which can excuse a lie; otherwise I should say to an open sinner, If you have been baptized, do not own it. For how highly does this aggravate your guilt! How will it increase your damnation! Was you devoted to God at eight days old, and have you been all these years devoting yourself to the devil? Was you, even before you had the use of reason, consecrated to God the Father, the Son, and the Holy Ghost? And have you, ever since you had the use of it, been flying in the face of God, and consecrating yourself to Satan?

## The New Birth.

Does the abomination of desolation,—the love of the world, pride, anger, lust, foolish desire, and a whole train of vile affections,—stand where it ought not? Have you set up all these accursed things in that soul, which was once a temple of the Holy Ghost; set apart for a "habitation of God through the Spirit;" yea, solemnly given up to him? And do you glory in this, that you once belonged to God? Oh be ashamed! Blush! Hide yourself in the earth! Never boast more of what ought to fill you with confusion, to make you ashamed before God and man! I answer, secondly, you have already denied your baptism; and that in the most effectual manner. You have denied it a thousand and a thousand times; and you do so still, day by day. For in your baptism you renounced the devil and all his works. Whenever, therefore, you give place to him again, whenever you do any of the works of the devil, then you deny your baptism. Therefore you deny it by every wilful sin; by every act of uncleanness, drunkenness, or revenge; by every obscene or profane word; by every oath that comes out of your mouth. Every time you profane the day of the Lord, you thereby deny your baptism; yea, every time you do any thing to another, which you would not he should do to you I answer, thirdly, be you baptized, or unbaptized, "you must be born again;" otherwise it is not possible you should be inwardly holy; and without inward as well as outward holiness, you cannot be happy, even in this world, much less in the world to come. Do you say, "Nay, but I do no harm to any man; I am honest and just in all my dealings; I do not curse, or take the Lord's name in vain; I do not profane the Lord's day; I am no drunkard; I do not slander my neighbour, nor live in any wilful sin." If this be so, it were much to be wished that all men went as far as you do. But you must go farther yet, or you cannot be saved: still, "you must be born again." Do you add, "I do go farther yet; for I not only do no harm; but do all the good I can." I doubt that fact; I fear you have had a thousand opportunities of doing good, which you have suffered to pass by unimproved, and for which therefore you are accountable to God. But if you had improved them all, if you really had done all the good you possibly could to all men, yet this does not at all alter the case; still "you must be born again." Without this, nothing will do any good to your poor, sinful, polluted soul. "Nay, but I constantly attend all the ordinances of God: I keep to my church and sacrament." It is well you do: but all this will not keep you from hell, except you be born again. Go to church twice a day; go to the Lord's table every week; say ever so many prayers in private; hear ever so many good sermons; read ever so many good books; still, "you must be born again." None of these things will stand in the place of the new birth; nor any thing under heaven. Let this, therefore, if you have not already experienced this inward work of God, be your continual prayer: "Lord, add this to all thy blessings,—let me be born again! Deny whatever thou pleasest, but deny not this; let me be 'born from above!' Take away whatsoever seemeth thee good; reputation, fortune, friends, health; only give me this, to be born of the Spirit, to be received among the children of God! Let me be born, not of corruptible seed, but incorruptible, by the word of God, which liveth and abideth for ever;' and then let me daily 'grow in grace, and in the knowledge of our Lord and Saviour Jesus Christ!'"

## THE WAY TO THE KINGDOM.

"The kingdom of God is at hand: repent ye, and believe the gospel."—Mark i, 15.

THESE words naturally lead us to consider, first, The nature of true religion, here termed by our Lord, "the kingdom of God;" which, saith he, "is at hand:" and, secondly, the way thereto, which he points out in those words, "Repent ye, and believe the gospel."

I. We are, first, to consider the nature of true religion, here termed by our Lord, "the kingdom of God." The same expression the great apostle uses in his epistle to the Romans, where he likewise explains his Lord's words, saying, "The kingdom of God is not meat and drink; but righteousness, and peace, and joy in the Holy Ghost," Rom. xiv, 17.

"The kingdom of God," or true religion, "is not meat and drink." It is well known, that not only the unconverted Jews, but great numbers of those who had received the faith of Christ, were, notwithstanding, "zealous of the law," Acts xxi, 20, even the ceremonial law of Moses. Whatsoever therefore they found written therein, either concerning meat and drink offerings, or the distinction between clean and unclean meats, they not only observed themselves, but vehemently pressed the same, even on those "among the Gentiles (or heathens) who were turned to God;" yea, to such a degree, that some of them taught, wheresoever they came among them, "Except ye be circumcised, and keep the law, (the whole ritual law,) ye cannot be saved," Acts xv, 1, 24.

In opposition to these, the apostle declares, both here and in many other places, that true religion does not consist in *meat* and *drink,* or in any ritual observances; nor, indeed, in any outward thing whatever; in any thing exterior to the heart; the whole substance thereof lying in "righteousness, peace, and joy in the Holy Ghost."

Not in any *outward thing;* such as forms or ceremonies, even of the most excellent kind. Supposing these to be ever so decent and significant, ever so expressive of inward things: supposing them ever so helpful, not only to the vulgar, whose thought reaches little farther than their sight; but even to men of understanding, men of stronger capacities, as doubtless they may sometimes be: yea, supposing them, as in the case of the Jews, to be appointed by God himself; yet even during the period of time wherein that appointment remains in force, true religion does not principally consist therein; nay, strictly speaking, not all. How much more must this hold concerning such rites and forms as are only of human appointment! The religion of Christ rises infinitely higher, and lies immensely deeper, than all these. These are good in their place; just so far as they are in fact subservient to true religion. And it were superstition to object against them, while they are applied only as occasional helps to human weakness. But let no man carry them farther. Let no man dream that they have any intrinsic worth; or that religion cannot subsist without them. This were to make them an abomination to the Lord.

The nature of religion is so far from consisting in these, in *forms* of worship, or *rites* and *ceremonies,* that it does not properly consist in any *outward actions,* of what kind soever. It is true, a man cannot have any religion who is guilty of vicious, immoral actions; or who does to others, what he would not they should do unto him, if he were in the same circumstances. And it is also true, that he can have no real religion, who "knows to do good, and doeth it not." Yet may a man both abstain from outward evil, and do good, and still have no religion. Yea, two persons may do the same outward work; suppose, feeding the hungry, or clothing the naked; and, in

## The Way to the Kingdom.

the mean time, one of these may be truly religious, and the other have no religion at all; for the one may act from the love of God, and the other from the love of praise. So manifest it is, that although true religion naturally leads to every good word and work, yet the real nature thereof lies deeper still, even in "the hidden man of the heart."

I say of *the heart*. For neither does religion consist in *orthodoxy,* or *right opinions;* which, although they are not properly outward things, are not in the heart, but the understanding. A man may be orthodox in every point; he may not only espouse right opinions, but zealously defend them against all opposers; he may think justly concerning the incarnation of our Lord, concerning the ever blessed Trinity, and every other doctrine, contained in the oracles of God; he may assent to all the three creeds,—that called the *Apostles',* the *Nicene,* and the *Athanasian;* and yet it is possible he may have no religion at all, no more than a Jew, Turk, or Pagan. He may be almost as orthodox,—as the devil; (though indeed, not altogether; for every man errs in something; whereas we cannot well conceive him to hold any erroneous opinion;) and may, all the while, be as great a stranger as he to the religion of the heart.

This alone is religion, truly so called: this alone is in the sight of God of great price. The apostle sums it all up in three particulars, "righteousness, and peace, and joy in the Holy Ghost." And, first, *righteousness.* We cannot be at a loss concerning this, if we remember the words of our Lord, describing the two grand branches thereof, on which "hang all the law and the prophets:" "Thou shalt love the Lord thy God with all thy heart, and with all thy mind, and with all thy soul, and with all thy strength. This is the first and great commandment," Mark xii, 30, the first and great branch of Christian righteousness. Thou shalt delight thyself in the Lord thy

God; thou shalt seek and find all happiness in him. He shall be "thy shield, and thy exceeding great reward," in time, and in eternity. All thy bones shall say, "Whom have I in heaven but thee? And there is none upon earth that I desire beside thee!" Thou shalt hear, and fulfil his word, who saith, "My son, give me thy heart." And, having given him thy heart, thy inmost soul, to reign there without a rival, thou mayest well cry out, in the fulness of thy heart, "I will love thee, O Lord, my strength. The Lord is my strong rock, and my defence; my Saviour, my God, and my might, in whom I will trust; my buckler, the horn also of my salvation, and my refuge."

And the second commandment is like unto this; the second great branch of Christian righteousness is closely and inseparably connected therewith; even "Thou shalt love thy neighbour as thyself." *Thou shalt love,*—Thou shalt embrace with the most tender good will, the most earnest and cordial affection, the most inflamed desires of preventing or removing all evil, and of procuring for him every possible good,—*Thy neighbour;*—that is, not only thy friend, thy kinsman, or thy acquaintance: not only the virtuous, the friendly, him that loves thee, that prevents or returns thy kindness; but every child of man, every human creature, every soul which God hath made; not excepting him whom thou never hast seen in the flesh, whom thou knowest not, either by face or name; not excepting him whom thou knowest to be evil and unthankful, him that still despitefully uses and persecutes thee: him thou shalt love *as thyself;* with the same invariable thirst after his happiness in every kind; the same unwearied care to screen him from whatever might grieve or hurt, either his soul or body.

Now is not this love "the fulfilling of the law?" The sum of all Christian righteousness?—Of all inward righteousness; for it necessarily implies "bowels of mercy, humbleness of mind," (seeing love "is not puffed up,") "gentleness, meekness, long suffering:" (for love "is not provoked;" but "believeth, hopeth, endureth all things:") and of all outward righteousness; for "love worketh no evil to his neighbour," either by word or deed. It cannot willingly either hurt or grieve any one. And it is zealous of good works. Every lover of mankind, as he hath opportunity, "doeth good unto all men," being (without partiality, and without hypocrisy) "full of mercy, and good fruits."

But true religion, or a heart right towards God and man, implies happiness, as well as holiness. For it is not only righteousness, but also "peace and joy in the Holy Ghost." What peace? *The peace of God,* which God only can give, and the world cannot take away; the peace which "passeth all understanding," all (barely) rational conception; being a supernatural sensation, a divine taste of "the powers of the world to come;" such as the natural man knoweth not, how wise soever in the things of this world, nor, indeed, can he know it, in his present state, "because it is spiritually discerned." It is a peace that banishes all doubt, all painful uncertainty; the Spirit of God bearing witness with the spirit of a Christian, that he is *a child of God.* And it banishes fear, all such fear as hath torment; the fear of the wrath of God; the fear of hell; the fear of the devil; and, in particular, the fear of death: he that hath the peace of God, desiring, if it were the will of God, "to depart, and to be with Christ."

With this peace of God, wherever it is fixed in the soul, there is also *"joy in the Holy Ghost;"* joy wrought in the heart by the Holy Ghost, by the ever blessed Spirit of God. He it is that worketh in us that calm, humble rejoicing in God, through Christ Jesus, "by whom we have now received the atonement," καταλλαγην, the reconciliation with God; and that enables us boldly to confirm the truth of the royal psalmist's declaration, "blessed is the man," (or rather *happy,*) אשרי היש, "whose unrighteous ness is forgiven, and whose sin is covered." He it is that inspires the Christian soul with that even, solid joy, which arises from the testimony of the Spirit that he is a child of God; and that gives him to "rejoice with joy unspeakable, in hope of the glory of God;" hope both of the glorious image of God, which is in part, and shall be full "revealed in him;" and of that crown of glory which fadeth not away, reserved in heaven for him.

This holiness and happiness, joined in one, are sometimes styled, in the inspired writings, "the kingdom of God," (as by our Lord in the text,) and sometimes, "the kingdom of heaven." It is termed "the kingdom of God," because it is the immediate fruit of God's reigning in the soul. So soon as ever he takes unto himself his mighty power, and sets up his throne in our hearts, they are instantly filled with this "righteousness, and peace, and joy in the Holy Ghost." It is called "the kingdom of heaven," because it is (in a degree) heaven opened in the soul. For whosoever they are that experience this, they can aver before angels and men,

> "Everlasting life is won,
> Glory is on earth begun:"

According to the constant tenor of Scripture, which everywhere bears record, God "hath given unto us eternal life, and this life is in his Son. He that hath the Son" (reigning in his heart) "hath life," (even life everlasting,) 1 John v, 11, 12. For "this is life eternal, to know thee the only true God, and Jesus Christ whom thou hast sent," John xvii, 3. And they, to whom this is given, may confidently address God, though they were in the midst of a fiery furnace,

> "Thee,—Lord, safe shielded by thy power,
> Thee, Son of God, JEHOVAH, we adore;
> In form of man, descending to appear
> To thee be ceaseless hallelujahs given.
> Praise, as in heaven thy throne, we offer here,
> For where thy presence is display'd, is heaven."

And this kingdom of God, or of heaven, *is at hand*. As these words were originally spoken, they implied, that *the time* was then fulfilled, God being "made manifest in the flesh," when he would set up his kingdom among men, and reign in the hearts of his people. And is not the time now fulfilled? For, "Lo! (saith he) I am with you always," you who preach remission of sins in my name, "even unto the end of the world," Matt. xxviii, 20. Wheresoever, therefore, the gospel of Christ is preached, this his "kingdom is nigh at hand." It is not far from every one of you. Ye may this hour enter thereinto, if so be ye hearken to this voice, "Repent ye, and believe the gospel."

II. This is the way: walk ye in it. And, first, *"Repent;"* that is, know yourselves. This is the first repentance previous to faith; even conviction, or self-knowledge. Awake then, thou that sleepest. Know thyself to be a sinner, and what manner of sinner thou art. Know that corruption of thy inmost nature, whereby thou art very far gone from original righteousness, whereby "the flesh lusteth" always "contrary to the Spirit," through that "carnal mind" which "is enmity against God," which "is not subject to the law of God, neither indeed can be." Know that thou art corrupted in every power, in every faculty of thy soul; that thou art totally corrupted in every one of these, all the foundations being out of course. The eyes of thine understanding are darkened, so that they cannot discern God, or the things of God. The clouds of ignorance and error rest upon thee, and cover thee with the shadow of death. Thou knowest nothing yet as thou oughtest to know, neither God, nor the world, nor thyself. Thy will is no longer the will of God, but is utterly perverse and distorted, averse from all good, from all which God loves, and prone to all evil, to every abomination which God hateth. Thy affections are alienated from God, and scattered abroad over all the earth. All thy passions, both thy desires and aversions, thy joys and sorrows, thy hopes and fears, are out of frame, are either undue in their degree, or placed on undue objects. So that there is no soundness in thy soul; but "from the crown of the head to the sole of the foot," (to use the strong expression of the prophet,) there are only "wounds, and bruises, and putrefying sores."

Such is the inbred corruption of thy heart, of thy very inmost nature. And what manner of branches canst thou expect to grow from such an evil root? Hence springs unbelief; ever departing from the living God; saying, "Who is the Lord, that I should serve him? Tush! Thou, God, carest not for it:" hence independence; affecting to be like the Most High: hence pride, in all its forms; teaching thee to say, "I am rich, and increased in goods, and have need of nothing." From this evil fountain flow forth the bitter streams of vanity, thirst of praise, ambition, covetousness, the lust of the flesh, the lust of the eye, and the pride of life. From this arise anger, hatred, malice, revenge, envy, jealousy, evil surmisings: from this, all the foolish and hurtful lusts that now "pierce thee through with many sorrows," and, if not timely prevented, will at length drown thy soul in everlasting perdition.

And what fruits can grow on such branches as these? Only such as are bitter and evil continually. Of pride cometh contention, vain boasting, seeking and receiving praise of men, and so robbing God of that glory which he cannot give unto another: of the lust of the flesh, come gluttony or drunkenness, luxury or sensuality, fornication, uncleanness; variously defiling that body which was designed for a temple of the Holy Ghost: of unbelief, every evil word and work. But the time would fail, shouldest thou reckon up all; all the idle words thou hast spoken, provoking the Most High, grieving the Holy One of Israel; all the evil works thou hast done, either wholly

## The Way to the Kingdom.

evil in themselves, or at least not done to the glory of God. For thy actual sins are more than thou art able to express, more than the hairs of thy head. Who can number the sands of the sea, or the drops of rain, or thy iniquities?

And knowest thou not that "the wages of sin is death?" —Death not only temporal, but eternal. "The soul that sinneth, it shall die:" for the mouth of the Lord hath spoken it. It shall die the second death. This is the sentence, to "be punished" with never ending death, "with everlasting destruction from the presence of the Lord, and from the glory of his power." Knowest thou not that every sinner, ενοχος ες τη γεεννη τ8 πυρος, not properly *is in danger of hell fire;* that expression is far too weak; but rather, *is under the sentence of hell fire;* doomed already, just dragging to execution. Thou art guilty of everlasting death. It is the just reward of thy inward and outward wickedness. It is just that the sentence should now take place. Dost thou see, dost thou feel this? Art thou thoroughly convinced that thou deservest God's wrath and everlasting damnation? Would God do thee no wrong, if he now commanded the earth to open, and swallow thee up? If thou wert now to go down quick into the pit, into the fire that never shall be quenched? If God hath given thee truly to repent, thou hast a deep sense that these things are so; and that it is of his mere mercy thou art not consumed, swept away from the face of the earth.

And what wilt thou do to appease the wrath of God, to atone for all thy sins, and to escape the punishment thou hast so justly deserved? Alas, thou canst do nothing: nothing that will in any wise make amends to God for one evil work, or word, or thought. If thou couldest now do all things well, if from this very hour, till thy soul should return to God, thou couldest perform perfect, uninterrupted obedience, even this would not atone for what is past. The not increasing thy debt would not discharge it. It would still remain as great as ever. Yea, the present and future obedience of all the men upon earth, and all the angels in heaven, would never make satisfaction to the justice of God for one single sin. How vain, then, was the thought of atoning for thy own sins by any thing thou couldest do! It costeth far more to redeem one soul, than all mankind is able to pay. So that were there no other help for a guilty sinner, without doubt he must have perished everlastingly.

But suppose perfect obedience, for the time to come, could atone for the sins that are past, this would profit thee nothing; for thou art not able to perform it; no, not in any one point. Begin now: make the trial. Shake off that outward sin that so easily besetteth thee. Thou canst not. How then wilt thou change thy life from all evil to all good? Indeed, it is impossible to be done, unless first thy heart be changed. For so long as the tree remains evil, it cannot bring forth good fruit. But art thou able to change thy own heart, from all sin to all holiness? To quicken a soul that is dead in sin, dead to God, and alive only to the world? No more than thou art able to quicken a dead body, to raise to life him that lieth in the grave. Yea, thou art not able to quicken thy soul in any degree, no more than to give any degree of life to the dead body. Thou canst do nothing, more or less, in this matter; thou art utterly without strength. To be deeply sensible of this, how helpless thou art, as well as how guilty and how sinful, this is that "repentance not to be repented of," which is the forerunner of the kingdom of God.

If to this lively conviction of thy inward and outward sins, of thy utter guiltiness and helplessness, there be added suitable affections,—sorrow of heart, for having despised thy own mercies,—remorse, and self condemnation, having thy mouth stopped,—shame to lift up thine

## The Way to the Kingdom.

eyes to heaven,—fear of the wrath of God abiding on thee, of his curse hanging over thy head, and of the fiery indignation ready to devour those who forget God, and obey not our Lord Jesus Christ,—earnest desire to escape from that indignation, to cease from evil, and learn to do well;—then I say unto thee, in the name of the Lord, "Thou art not far from the kingdom of God." One step more, and thou shalt enter in. Thou dost *repent*. Now, *"believe the gospel."*

*The gospel,* (that is, good tidings, good news for guilty, helpless sinners,) in the largest sense of the word, means, the whole revelation made to men by Jesus Christ; and sometimes the whole account of what our Lord did and suffered, while he tabernacled among men. The substance of all is, "Jesus Christ came into the world to save sinners:" or, "God so loved the world, that he gave his only begotten Son, to the end we might not perish, but have everlasting life:" or, "He was bruised for our transgressions; he was wounded for our iniquities; the chastisement of our peace was upon him; and with his stripes we are healed."

*"Believe"* this, and the kingdom of God is thine. By faith thou attainest the promise. "He pardoneth and absolveth all that truly repent, and unfeignedly believe his holy gospel." As soon as ever God hath spoken to thy heart, "Be of good cheer, thy sins are forgiven thee," his kingdom comes: thou hast "righteousness, and peace, and joy in the Holy Ghost."

Only beware thou do not deceive thy own soul, with regard to the nature of this faith. It is not, as some have fondly conceived, a bare assent to the truth of the Bible, of the articles of our creed, or of all that is contained in the Old and New Testament. The devils believe this, as well as I or thou! And yet they are devils still. But it is, over and above this, a sure trust in the mercy of God, through Christ Jesus. It is a confidence in a pardoning

God. It is a divine evidence or conviction, that "God was in Christ reconciling the world to himself, not imputing to them their former trespasses;" and, in particular, that the Son of God hath loved *me,* and given himself for *me,* and that I, even I, am now reconciled to God by the blood of the cross.

Dost thou thus believe? Then the peace of God is in thy heart, and sorrowing and sighing flee away. Thou art no longer in doubt of the love of God; it is clear as the noonday sun. Thou criest out, "My song shall be always of the loving kindness of the Lord: with my mouth will I ever be telling of thy truth, from one generation to another." Thou art no longer afraid of hell, or death, or him that had once the power of death, the devil; no, nor painfully afraid of God himself; only thou hast a tender, filial fear of offending him. Dost thou believe? Then thy "soul doth magnify the Lord," and thy "spirit rejoiceth in God thy Saviour." Thou rejoicest in that thou hast "redemption through his blood, even the forgiveness of sins." Thou rejoicest in that "spirit of adoption," which crieth in thy heart, "Abba, Father!" Thou rejoicest in a "hope full of immortality;" in reaching forth unto the "mark of the prize of thy high calling;" in an earnest expectation of all the good things which God hath prepared for them that love him.

Dost thou now believe? Then the love of God is now shed abroad in thy heart. Thou lovest him, because he first loved us. And, because thou lovest God, thou lovest thy brother also. And, being filled with "love, peace, joy," thou art also filled with "long suffering, gentleness, fidelity, goodness, meekness, temperance," and all the other fruits of the same Spirit; in a word, with whatever dispositions are holy, are heavenly, or divine. For while thou beholdest with open, uncovered face, (the veil being now taken away,) "the glory of the Lord," his glorious love, and the glorious image wherein thou wast created, thou art "changed into the same image, from glory to glory, by the Spirit of the Lord."

This repentance, this faith, this peace, joy, love, this change from glory to glory, is what the wisdom of the world has voted to be madness, mere enthusiasm, utter distraction. But thou, oh man of God, regard them not; be thou moved by none of these things. Thou knowest in whom thou hast believed. See that no man take thy crown. Whereunto thou hast already attained, hold fast, and follow, till thou attain all the great and precious promises. And thou who hast not yet known him, let not vain men make thee ashamed of the gospel of Christ. Be thou in nothing terrified by those who speak evil of the things which they know not. God will soon turn thy heaviness into joy. Oh let not thy hands hang down. Yet a little longer, and he will take away thy fears, and give thee the spirit of a sound mind. He is nigh "that justifieth: who is he that condemneth? It is Christ that died, yea rather, that rose again, who is even now at the right hand of God, making intercession" for thee.

Now cast thyself on the Lamb of God, with all thy sins, how many soever they be; and "an entrance shall [now] be ministered unto thee, into the kingdom of our Lord and Saviour Jesus Christ!"

## THE DANGER OF RICHES.

[*Arminian Magazine*, 1781. *Works*, ii, 248-58.]

"They that will be rich fall into temptation and a snare, and into many foolish and hurtful desires, which drown men in destruction and perdition."—1 Tim. vi, 9.

How innumerable are the ill consequences which have followed from men's not knowing, or not considering, this great truth! And how few are there even in the Christian world, that either know or duly consider it! Yea, how small is the number of those, even among real Christians, who understand and lay it to heart! Most of these too pass it very lightly over, scarce remembering there is such a text in the Bible. And many put such a construction upon it, as makes it of no manner of effect. "They that will be rich," say they, that is, will be rich at all events; who will be rich, right or wrong; that are resolved to carry their point, to compass this end, whatever means they use to attain it; they *"fall into temptation,"* and into all the evils enumerated by the apostle. But truly if this were all the meaning of the text, it might as well have been out of the Bible.

This is so far from being the whole meaning of the text, that it is no part of its meaning. The apostle does not here speak of gaining riches unjustly, but of quite another thing: his words are to be taken in their plain obvious sense, without any restriction or qualification whatsoever. St. Paul does not say, that they will be rich *by evil means,* by theft, robbery, oppression, or extortion; they that will be rich by fraud or dishonest art; but simply, "they that will be rich:" these, allowing, supposing the means they use to be ever so innocent, "fall into temptation, and a snare, and into many foolish and hurtful desires, which drown men in destruction and perdition."

## The Danger of Riches.

But who believes that? Who receives it as the truth of God? Who is deeply convinced of it? Who preaches this? Great is the company of preachers at this day, regular and irregular; but who of them all, openly and explicitly, preaches this strange doctrine? It is the keen observation of a great man, "The pulpit is the preacher's strong hold." But who even in this strong hold has the courage to declare so unfashionable a truth? I do not remember that in three score years, I have heard one sermon preached upon this subject. And what author, within the same term, has declared it from the press? At least in the English tongue? I do not know one. I have neither seen nor heard of any such author. I have seen two or three who have just touched upon it: but none that treats of it professedly. I have myself frequently touched upon it in preaching, and thrice in what I have published to the world: once in explaining our Lord's sermon on the mount, and once in the discourse on the "mammon of unrighteousness:" but I have never yet either published or preached any sermon expressly upon the subject. It is high time I should;—that I should at length speak as strongly and explicitly as I can, in order to leave a full and clear testimony behind me, whenever it pleases God to call me hence.*

Oh that God would give me to speak right and forcible words, and you to receive them in honest and humble hearts! Let it not be said, "They sit before thee as my people, and they hear thy words: but they will not do them. Thou art unto them as one that hath a pleasant voice, and can play well on an instrument: for they hear thy words, but do them not!" Oh that ye may "not be forgetful hearers, but doers of the word," that ye may be "blessed in your deed!" In this hope I shall endeavour,

---

* [See *The Use of Money, Works*, i, 440-8; *Riches*, ii, 396-401; and the pathetic plea of his last years, *The Danger of Increasing Riches*, ii, 486-91. H. W.]

I. To explain the apostle's words. And,
II. To apply them.

But, oh! "who is sufficient for these things?" Who is able to stem the general torrent? To combat all the prejudices not only of the vulgar, but of the learned and of the religious world? Yet nothing is too hard for God! Still his grace is sufficient for us. In his name then, and by his strength, I will endeavour,

I. To explain the words of the apostle.

And, first, let us consider, what it is to be rich? What does the apostle mean by this expression?

The preceding verse fixes the meaning of that; "Having food and raiment" (literally *coverings;* for the word includes lodging as well as clothes), "let us be therewith content." "But they that will be rich;" that is, who will have more than these; more than food and coverings.— It plainly follows, whatever is more than these, is in the sense of the apostle, *riches;* whatever is above the plain necessaries, or, at most, conveniences of life. Whoever has sufficient food to eat, and raiment to put on, with a place where to lay his head, and something over, is *rich*.

Let us consider, secondly, what is implied in that expression, "they that will be rich." And does not this imply, first, they that desire to be rich; to have more than *food* and *coverings:* they that seriously and deliberately desire more than food to eat, and raiment to put on, and a place where to lay their head; more than the plain necessaries and conveniences of life? All, at least, who allow themselves in this desire, who see no harm in it, desire to be rich.

And so do, secondly, all those that calmly, deliberately, and of set purpose, *endeavour* after more than food and coverings; that aim at and endeavour after, not only so much worldly substance as will procure them the necessaries and conveniences of life, but more than this, whether to lay it up, or lay it out in superfluities. All

## The Danger of Riches.

these undeniably prove their *desire to be rich*, by their endeavours after it.

Must we not, thirdly, rank among those that desire to be rich, all that, in fact, *"lay up treasures on earth?"* a thing as expressly and clearly forbidden by our Lord, as either adultery or murder. It is allowed, 1. That we are to provide necessaries and conveniences for those of our own household: 2. That men in business are to lay up as much as is necessary for the carrying on of that business: 3. That we are to leave our children what will supply them with necessaries and conveniences after we have left the world: and, 4. That we are to provide things honest in the sight of all men, so as to "owe no man any thing:" but to lay up any more when this is done, is what our Lord has flatly forbidden. When it is calmly and deliberately done, it is a clear proof of our desiring to be rich. And thus to lay up money is no more consistent with a good conscience, than to throw it into the sea.

We must rank among them, fourthly, all who *possess* more of this world's goods, than they use according to the will of the donor: I should rather say, of the proprietor; for he only *lends* them to us as stewards; reserving the *property* of them to himself. And, indeed, he cannot possibly do otherwise, seeing they are the work of his hands; he is, and must be, the possessor of heaven and earth. This is his unalienable right; a right he cannot divest himself of. And together with that portion of his goods, which he hath lodged in our hands, he has delivered to us a writing, specifying the purposes for which he has intrusted us with them. If, therefore, we keep more of them in our hands, than is necessary for the preceding purposes, we certainly fall under the charge of "desiring to be rich:" over and above we are guilty of burying our Lord's talent in the earth; and on that account are liable to be pronounced wicked, because unprofitable servants.

Under this imputation of "desiring to be rich," fall, fifthly, all *"lovers of money."* The word properly means, those that *delight in money;* those that take pleasure in it; those that seek their happiness therein; that brood over their gold and silver, bills or bonds. Such was the man described by the fine Roman painter, who broke out in that natural soliloquy;

" Populus me sibilat, at mihi plaudo
Ipse domi quoties nummos contemplor in arcâ.

If there are any vices which are not natural to man, I should imagine this is one: as money of itself does not seem to gratify any natural desire or appetite of the human mind; and as, during an observation of sixty years, I do not remember one instance, of a man given up to the love of money, till he had neglected to employ this precious talent, according to the will of his Master. After this, sin was punished by sin; and this evil spirit was permitted to enter into him.

But besides this gross sort of covetousness, the love of money, there is a more refined species of covetousness, mentioned by the great apostle; πλεονεξία : which literally means, *a desire of having more;* more than we have already. And those also come under the denomination of, "they that will be rich." It is true that this desire, under proper restrictions, is innocent; nay, commendable. But when it exceeds the bounds (and how difficult is it not to exceed them!) then it comes under the present censure.

But who is able to receive these hard sayings? Who can believe that they are the great truths of God? Not many wise, not many noble, not many famed for learning; none, indeed, who are not taught of God. And who are they, whom God teaches? Let our Lord answer: "If any man be willing to do his will, he shall know of the doctrine whether it be of God." Those who are otherwise minded, will be so far from receiving it, that they will not

## The Danger of Riches.

be able to understand it. Two as sensible men as most in England, sat down together, some time since, to read over and consider that plain discourse on, "Lay not up for yourselves treasures upon earth." After much deep consideration, one of them broke out, "Positively, I cannot understand it. Pray do *you* understand it, Mr. L.?" Mr. L. honestly replied, "Indeed, not I. I cannot conceive what Mr. W. means. I can make nothing at all of it." So utterly blind is our natural understanding touching the truth of God!

Having explained the former part of the text, "They that will be rich," and pointed out, in the clearest manner I could, the persons spoken of; I will now endeavour, God being my helper, to explain what is spoken of them: "They fall into temptation, and a snare, and into many foolish and hurtful desires, which drown men in destruction and perdition."

"They fall into *temptation.*" This seems to mean much more than simply, they are tempted. They *enter into the temptation:* they fall plump down into it. The waves of it compass them about, and cover them all over. Of those who thus enter into temptation, very few escape out of it. And the few that do are sorely scorched by it, though not utterly consumed. If they escape at all, it is with the skin of their teeth, and with deep wounds that are not easily healed.

They fall, secondly, into *"a snare,"* the snare of the devil, which he hath purposely set in their way. I believe the Greek word properly means a gin, a steel trap, which shows no appearance of danger. But as soon as any creature touches the spring, it suddenly closes; and either crushes its bones in pieces, or consigns it to inevitable ruin.

They fall thirdly, *"into many foolish and hurtful desires;"* ἀνοήτους: *silly, senseless, fantastic;* as contrary to reason, to sound understanding, as they are to religion:

*hurtful,* both to body and soul, tending to weaken, yea, destroy every gracious and heavenly temper: destructive of that faith which is of the operation of God; of that hope which is full of immortality; of love to God and to our neighbour, and of every good word and work.

But what desires are these? This is a most important question, and deserves the deepest consideration.

In general, they may all be summed up in one, the desiring happiness out of God. This includes, directly or remotely, every foolish and hurtful desire. St. Paul expresses it by "loving the creature more than the Creator;" and by being "lovers of pleasure more than lovers of God." In particular, they are (to use the exact and beautiful enumeration of St. John) "the desire of the flesh, the desire of the eyes, and the pride of life:" all of which, the desire of riches naturally tends both to beget and to increase.

*"The desire of the flesh"* is generally understood in far too narrow a meaning. It does not, as is commonly supposed, refer to one of the senses only; but takes in all the pleasures of sense; the gratification of any of the outward senses. It has reference to the *taste* in particular. How many thousands do we find at this day, in whom the ruling principle is the desire to enlarge the pleasure of tasting? Perhaps they do not gratify this desire in a gross manner, so as to incur the imputation of intemperance; much less so as to violate health, or impair their understanding by gluttony or drunkenness: but they live in a genteel, regular sensuality; in an elegant epicurism, which does not hurt the body, but only destroys the soul; keeping it at a distance from all true religion.

Experience shows, that the imagination is gratified chiefly by means of the eye: therefore, *"the desire of the eyes,"* in its natural sense, is, the desiring and seeking happiness in gratifying the imagination. Now the imagination is gratified either by grandeur, by beauty, or by

## The Danger of Riches.

novelty: chiefly by the last: for neither grand nor beautiful objects please, any longer than they are new.

Seeking happiness in *learning,* of whatever kind, falls under "the desire of the eyes;" whether it be in history, languages, poetry, or any branch of natural or experimental philosophy: yea, we must include the several kinds of learning, such as geometry, algebra, and metaphysics. For if our supreme delight be in any of these, we are herein gratifying "the desire of the eyes."

"*The pride of life*" (whatever else that very uncommon expression, ἡ ἀλαζονεία τοῦ βίου, may mean) seems to imply chiefly, the *desire of honour;* of the esteem, admiration, and applause of men: as nothing more directly tends both to beget and cherish pride than the honour that cometh of men. And as riches attract much admiration, and occasion much applause, they proportionably minister food for pride, and so may also be referred to this head.

*Desire of ease,* is another of these foolish and hurtful desires: desire of avoiding every cross, every degree of trouble, danger, difficulty; a desire of slumbering out life, and going to heaven (as the vulgar say) upon a feather bed. Every one may observe, how riches first beget, and then confirm and increase this desire, making men more and more soft and delicate; more unwilling, and indeed more unable, to "take up their cross daily;" to "endure hardship as good soldiers of Jesus Christ," and to "take the kingdom of heaven by violence."

Riches, either desired or possessed, naturally lead to some or other of these foolish and hurtful desires; and by affording the means of gratifying them all, naturally tend to increase them. And there is a near connection between unholy desires, and every other unholy passion and temper. We easily pass from these to pride, anger, bitterness, envy, malice, revengefulness; to a headstrong, unadvisable, unreprovable spirit; indeed, to every temper that is earthly, sensual, or devilish. All these, the desire or possession of riches naturally tends to create, strengthen, and increase.

And by so doing, in the same proportion as they prevail they "pierce men through with many sorrows:" sorrows from remorse, from a guilty conscience; sorrows flowing from all the evil tempers which they inspire or increase; sorrows inseparable from those desires themselves, as every unholy desire is an uneasy desire; and sorrows from the contrariety of those desires to each other, whence it is impossible to gratify them all. And, in the end, "they drown" the body in pain, disease, "destruction," and the soul in everlasting "perdition."

II. I am, in the second place, to apply what has been said. And this is the principal point. For what avails the clearest knowledge, even of the most excellent things, even of the things of God, if it go no farther than speculation; if it be not reduced to practice? He that hath ears to hear, let him hear! And what he hears, let him instantly put in practice. Oh that God would give me the thing which I long for! That before I go hence and am no more seen, I may see a people wholly devoted to God, crucified to the world, and the world crucified to them! A people truly given up to God, in body, soul, and substance! How cheerfully should I then say, "Now lettest thou thy servant depart in peace!"

I ask then, in the name of God, who of you "desire to be rich?" Which of *you* (ask your own hearts in the sight of God) seriously and deliberately desire (and perhaps applaud yourselves for so doing, as no small instance of your *prudence*) to have more than food to eat, and raiment to put on, and a house to cover you? Who of you desires to have more than the plain necessaries and conveniences of life? Stop! Consider! What are you doing? Evil is before you! Will you rush upon the point of a sword? By the grace of God turn and live!

## The Danger of Riches.

By the same authority I ask, who of you are *endeavouring* to be rich? To procure for yourselves more than the plain necessaries and conveniences of life? Lay, each of you, your hand to your heart, and seriously inquire, Am I of that number? Am I labouring, not only for what I want, but for more than I want? May the Spirit of God say to every one whom it concerns, "Thou art the man!"

I ask, thirdly, who of you are, in fact, *laying up for yourselves treasures upon earth?* Increasing in goods? Adding, as fast as you can, house to house, and field to field?* As long as *thou* thus "doest well unto thyself, men will speak good of thee." They will call thee a wise, a prudent man! A man that *minds the main chance*. Such is, and always has been, the wisdom of the world! But God saith unto thee, "Thou fool!" Art thou not "treasuring up to thyself wrath against the day of wrath, and revelation of the righteous judgment of God?"

Perhaps you will ask, "But do not you yourself advise, to gain all we can, and to save all we can? And is it possible to do this, without both *desiring* and *endeavouring to be rich?* Nay, suppose your endeavours are successful, without actually laying up treasures upon earth?"

---

* "'The ground of a certain rich man brought forth plenteously.' The riches of the ancients consisted chiefly in the fruits of the earth. 'And he said within himself, What shall I do?' . . . What shalt thou do? Why, are not those at the door, whom God hath appointed to receive what thou canst spare? What shalt thou do? Why, *disperse* abroad, and give to the poor. Feed the hungry. Clothe the naked. Be a father to the fatherless, and a husband to the widow. Freely thou hast received; freely give. Oh no! He is wiser than this comes to: he knows better than so.

"'And he said, This will I do;'—without asking God's leave, or thinking about him any more than if there were no God in heaven or on earth;—'I will pull down my barns, and build greater; and there will I bestow all my goods and all my fruits.' *My* fruits! They are as much thine as the clouds that fly over thy head! As much as the winds that blow around thee; which, doubtless, thou canst hold in thy fists! 'And I will say to my soul, Soul, thou hast much goods laid up for many years!' 'Soul, thou hast much goods!' Are then corn, and wine, and oil, the goods of an immortal spirit?"—*Sermon on Worldly Folly*, 1790. *Works*, ii, 452.

I answer, it is possible. You may gain all you can, without hurting either your soul or body; you may save all you can, by carefully avoiding every needless expense, and yet never lay up treasures on earth nor either desire or endeavour so to do.

Permit me to speak as freely of myself, as I would of another man. I *gain all I can* (namely, by writing) without hurting either my soul or body. I *save all I can,* not willingly wasting any thing, not a sheet of paper, not a cup of water. I do not lay out any thing, not a shilling, unless as a sacrifice to God. Yet by *giving all I can,* I am effectually secured from "laying up treasures upon earth." Yea, and I am secured from either desiring or endeavouring it, as long as I give all I can. And that I do this, I call all that know me, both friends and foes, to testify.

But some may say, "Whether you endeavour it or no, you are undeniably *rich*. You have more than the necessaries of life." I have. But the apostle does not fix the charge, barely on *possessing* any quantity of goods, but on possessing more than we employ according to the will of the donor.

Two and forty years ago, having a desire to furnish poor people with cheaper, shorter, and plainer books than any I had seen, I wrote many small tracts, generally a penny a-piece; and afterwards several larger. Some of these had such a sale as I never thought of; and by this means, I unawares became rich. But I never desired or endeavoured after it. And now that it is come upon me unawares, I lay up no treasures upon earth: I lay up nothing at all. My desire and endeavour, in this respect is, to "wind my bottom round the year." I cannot help leaving my books behind me whenever God calls me hence. But in every other respect, my own hands will be my executors.

Herein, my brethren, let you that are rich, be even as I

## The Danger of Riches.

am. Do you that possess more than food and raiment, ask, "What shall we do? Shall we throw into the sea what God hath given us?" God forbid that you should! It is an excellent talent: it may be employed much to the glory of God. Your way lies plain before your face; if you have courage, walk in it. Having *gained,* in a right sense, *all you can,* and *saved all you can:* in spite of nature, and custom, and worldly prudence, *give all you can.* I do not say, Be a good Jew; giving a tenth of all you possess. I do not say, Be a good Pharisee; giving a fifth of all your substance. I dare not advise you, to give half of what you have; no, nor three quarters; but all! Lift up your hearts, and you will see clearly, in what sense this is to be done. If you desire to be "a faithful and a wise steward," out of that portion of your Lord's goods, which he has for the present lodged in your hands, but with the right of resumption whenever it pleaseth him, 1. Provide things needful for yourself; food to eat, raiment to put on; whatever nature moderately requires, for preserving you both in health and strength: 2. Provide these for your wife, your children, your servants, or any others who pertain to your household. If, when this is done, there is an overplus left, then do good to "them that are of the household of faith." If there be an overplus still, "as you have opportunity, do good unto all men." In so doing, you *give all you can:* nay, in a sound sense, all you have. For all that is laid out in this manner, is really given to God. You render unto God the things that are God's, not only by what you give to the poor, but also by that which you expend in providing things needful for yourself and your household.

Oh ye Methodists, hear the word of the Lord! I have a message from God to all men; but to *you* above all. For above forty years I have been a servant to you and to your fathers. And I have not been as a reed shaken with the wind: I have not varied in my testimony. I have testified to you the very same thing, from the first day even until now. But "who hath believed our report?" I fear not many rich. I fear there is need to apply to some of *you* those terrible words of the apostle, "Go to now, ye rich men! weep and howl for the miseries which shall come upon you. Your gold and silver is cankered, and the rust of them shall witness against you, and shall eat your flesh, as it were fire." Certainly it will, unless ye both save all you can, and give all you can. But who of you hath considered this, since you first heard the will of the Lord concerning it? Who is now determined to consider and practise it? By the grace of God, begin to-day!

Oh ye lovers of money, hear the word of the Lord! Suppose ye that money, though multiplied as the sand of the sea, can give happiness? Then you are "given up to a strong delusion, to believe a lie:" a palpable lie, confuted daily by a thousand experiments. Open your eyes! Look all around you! Are the richest men the happiest? Have those the largest share of content, who have the largest possessions? Is not the very reverse true? Is it not a common observation, That the richest of men are, in general, the most discontented, the most miserable? Had not the far greater part of them more content, when they had less money? Look into your own breasts. If you are increased in goods, are you proportionably increased in happiness? You have more substance: but have you more content? You know that in seeking happiness from riches, you are only striving to drink out of empty cups. And let them be painted and gilded ever so finely, they are empty still.

Oh ye that *desire* or *endeavour to be rich,* hear ye the word of the Lord! Why should ye be stricken any more? Will not even experience teach you wisdom? Will ye leap into a pit with your eyes open? Why should you any more *fall into temptation?* It cannot be, but temptation will beset you, as long as you are in the body. But

## The Danger of Riches.

though it should beset you on every side, why will you *enter into* it? There is no necessity for this: it is your own voluntary act and deed. Why should you any more plunge yourselves *into a snare,* into the trap Satan has laid for you, that is ready to break your bones in pieces; to crush your soul to death? After fair warning, why should you sink any more into *foolish and hurtful desires?* Desires as inconsistent with reason, as they are with religion itself. Desires that have done you more hurt already, than all the treasures upon earth can countervail.

Have they not hurt you already, have they not wounded you in the tenderest part, by slackening, if not utterly destroying, your "hunger and thirst after righteousness?" Have you now the same longing that you had once, for the whole image of God? Have you the same vehement desire as you formerly had, of "going on unto perfection?" Have they not hurt you by weakening your *faith?* Have you now faith's "abiding impression, realizing things to come?" Do you endure, in all temptations, from pleasure or pain, "seeing him that is invisible?" Have you every day, and every hour, an uninterrupted sense of his presence? Have they not hurt you with regard to your *hope?* Have you now a hope full of immortality? Are you still big with earnest expectation of all the great and precious promises?" Do you now "taste the powers of the world to come?" Do you "sit in heavenly places with Christ Jesus?"

Have they not so hurt you, as to stab your religion to the heart? Have they not cooled (if not quenched) your *love of God?* This is easily determined. Have you the same delight in God which you once had? Can you now say,

> " I nothing want beneath, above;
> Happy, happy, in thy love!"

I fear not. And if your love of God is in any wise decayed, so is also your love of your neighbour. You are then hurt in the very life and spirit of your religion! If you lose love, you lose all.

Are not you hurt with regard to your *humility?* If you are increased in goods, it cannot well be otherwise. Many will think you a better because you are a richer man; and how can you help thinking so yourself? Especially, considering the commendations which some will give you in simplicity, and many with a design to serve themselves of you.

If you are hurt in your humility, it will appear by this token: you are not so teachable as you were, not so advisable: you are not so easy to be convinced; not so easy to be persuaded: you have a much better opinion of your own judgment, and are more attached to your own will. Formerly one might guide you with a thread: now one cannot turn you with a cart rope. You were glad to be admonished or reproved: but that time is past. And you now account a man your enemy because he tells you the truth. Oh let each of you calmly consider this, and see if it be not your own picture!

Are you not equally hurt, with regard to your *meekness?* You had once learned an excellent lesson of him that was meek as well as lowly in heart. When you were reviled, you reviled not again. You did not return railing for railing, but contrariwise, blessing. Your love was *not provoked,* but enabled you on all occasions to overcome evil with good. Is this your case now? I am afraid not. I fear, you cannot "bear all things." Alas, it may rather be said, you can bear nothing: no injury, nor even affront! How quickly are you ruffled! How readily does that occur, "What! to use *me* so! What insolence is this! How did he dare to do it? I am not now what I was once. Let him know, I am now able to defend myself." You mean, to revenge yourself. And it is much, if you are not willing, as well as able; if you do not take your fellow servant by the throat.

## The Danger of Riches.

And are you not hurt in your *patience* too? Does your love now "endure all things?" Do you still "in patience possess your soul," as when you first believed? Oh what a change is here! You have again learned to be frequently out of humour. You are often fretful: you feel, nay, and give way to peevishness. You find abundance of things go so cross, that you cannot tell how to bear them.

Many years ago I was sitting with a gentleman in London, who feared God greatly; and generally gave away, year by year, nine tenths of his yearly income. A servant came in and threw some coals on the fire. A puff of smoke came out. The baronet threw himself back in his chair and cried out, "Oh Mr. Wesley, these are the crosses I meet with daily!" Would he not have been less impatient, if he had had fifty, instead of five thousand pounds a year?

But to return. Are not you, who have been successful in your endeavours to increase in substance, insensibly sunk into softness of mind, if not of body too? You no longer rejoice to "endure hardship, as good soldiers of Jesus Christ!" You no longer "rush into the kingdom of heaven, and take it as by storm." You do not cheerfully and gladly "deny yourselves, and take up your cross daily." You cannot deny yourself the poor pleasure of a little sleep, or of a soft bed, in order to hear the word that is able to save your souls! Indeed, you "cannot go out so early in the morning: besides it is dark: nay, cold; perhaps rainy too. Cold, darkness, rain: all these together, I can never think of it." You did not say so when you were a poor man. You then regarded none of these things. It is the change of circumstances which has occasioned this melancholy change in your body and mind: you are but the shadow of what you were! What have riches done for you?

"But it cannot be expected I should do as I have done. For I am now grown old." Am not I grown old as well as you? Am not I in my seventy-eighth year? Yet, by the grace of God, I do not slack my pace yet. Neither would *you,* if you were a poor man still.

You are so deeply hurt, that you have nigh lost your zeal for works of mercy, as well as of piety. You once pushed on, through cold or rain, or whatever cross lay in your way, to see the poor, the sick, the distressed. You went about doing good, and found out those who were not able to find you. You cheerfully crept down into their cellars, and climbed up into their garrets,

> " To supply all their wants,
> And spend and be spent in assisting his saints."

You found out every scene of human misery, and assisted, according to your power:

> " Each form of wo your generous pity moved;
> Your Saviour's face you saw, and seeing, loved."

Do you now tread in the same steps? What hinders? Do you fear spoiling your silken coat? Or is there another lion in the way? Are you afraid of catching vermin? And are you not afraid, lest the roaring lion should catch you? Are you not afraid of him that hath said, "Inasmuch as ye have not done it unto the least of these, ye have not done it unto me?" What will follow? "Depart, ye cursed, into everlasting fire, prepared for the devil and his angels!"

In time past how mindful were you of that word, "Thou shalt not hate thy brother in thy heart: thou shalt in any wise reprove thy brother, and not suffer sin upon him!" You *did* reprove, directly or indirectly, all those that sinned in your sight. And happy consequences quickly followed. How good was a word spoken in season! It was often as an arrow from the hand of a giant. Many a heart was pierced. Many of the stout hearted, who scorned to hear a sermon,

> " Fell down before his cross subdued,
> And felt his arrows dipt in blood."

## The Danger of Riches.

But which of you now has that compassion for the ignorant, and for them that are out of the way? They may wander on for *you,* and plunge into the lake of fire, without let or hinderance. Gold hath steeled your hearts. You have something else to do. "Unhelped, unpitied let the wretches fall."

Thus have I given you, oh ye gainers, lovers, possessors of riches, one more (it may be the last) warning. Oh that it may not be in vain! May God write it upon all your hearts! Though "it is easier for a camel to go through the eye of a needle, than for a rich man to enter into the kingdom of heaven," yet the things impossible with men, are possible with God. Lord, speak! And even the rich men, that hear these words, shall enter thy kingdom; shall "take the kingdom of heaven by violence;" shall "sell all for the pearl of great price;" shall be "crucified to the world, and count all things dung, that they may win Christ!"

## THE MORE EXCELLENT WAY.

[*Arminian Magazine*, 1787. *Works*, ii, 266-73.]

'Covet earnestly the best gifts; and yet I show unto you a more excellent way."—1 Cor. xii, 31.

In the preceding verses, St. Paul has been speaking of the extraordinary gifts of the Holy Ghost: such as healing the sick; prophesying, in the proper sense of the word; that is, foretelling things to come; speaking with strange tongues, such as the speaker had never learned; and the miraculous interpretation of tongues. And these gifts, the apostle allows to be desirable: yea, he exhorts the Corinthians, at least the teachers among them (to whom chiefly, if not solely, they were wont to be given in the first ages of the church), to *covet* them *earnestly*, that thereby they might be qualified to be more useful either to Christians or heathens. "And yet," says he, "I show unto you a more excellent way:" far more desirable than all these put together: inasmuch as it will infallibly lead you to happiness, both in this world and in the world to come: whereas you might have all those gifts, yea, in the highest degree, and yet be miserable both in time and eternity.

It does not appear that these extraordinary gifts of the Holy Ghost were common in the church for more than two or three centuries. We seldom hear of them after that fatal period, when the emperor Constantine called himself a Christian; and from a vain imagination of promoting the Christian cause thereby, heaped riches, and power, and honour, upon the Christians in general; but in particular, upon the Christian clergy. From this time they almost totally ceased: very few instances of the kind were found. The cause of this was not (as has been vulgarly supposed) "because there was no more occasion for them," because all the world was become Christians. This is a

## The More Excellent Way. 93

miserable mistake: not a twentieth part of it was then nominally Christians. The real cause was, "the love of many," almost of all Christians, so called, was "waxed cold." The Christians had no more of the Spirit of Christ, than the other heathens. The Son of man, when he came to examine his church, could hardly "find faith upon earth." This was a real cause, why the extraordinary gifts of the Holy Ghost were no longer to be found in the Christian church; because the Christians were turned heathens again, and had only a dead form left.

However, I would not, at present, speak of these, of the extraordinary gifts of the Holy Ghost, but of the ordinary: and these, likewise, we may "covet earnestly," in order to be more useful in our generation. With this view we may covet "the gift of *convincing speech*," in order to "sound the unbelieving heart;" and the gift of *persuasion*, to move the affections, as well as enlighten the understanding. We may covet *knowledge*, both of the word and of the works of God, whether of providence or grace. We may desire a measure of that *faith*, which, on particular occasions, wherein the glory of God or the happiness of men is nearly concerned, goes far beyond the power of natural causes. We may desire an easy elocution, a pleasing address, with resignation to the will of our Lord: yea, whatever would enable us, as we have opportunity, to be useful wherever we are. These gifts we may innocently desire; but there "is a more excellent way."

The way of love; of loving all men for God's sake; of humble, gentle, patient love,—is that which the apostle so admirably describes in the ensuing chapter. And without this he assures us, all eloquence, all knowledge, all faith, all works, and all sufferings, are of no more value in the sight of God, than sounding brass or a rumbling cymbal; and are not of the least avail towards our eternal salvation. Without this, all we know, all we believe, all we do, all we suffer, will profit us nothing in the great day of accounts.

But at present I would take a different view of the text, and point out a "more excellent way," in another sense. It is the observation of an ancient writer, that there have been from the beginning two orders of Christians. The one lived an innocent life, conforming in all things, not sinful, to the customs and fashions of the world; doing many good works, abstaining from gross evils, and attending the ordinances of God. They endeavoured, in general, to have a conscience void of offence in their behaviour, but did not aim at any particular strictness, being in most things like their neighbours. The other Christians not only abstained from all appearance of evil, were zealous of good works in every kind, and attended all the ordinances of God; but likewise used all diligence to attain the whole mind that was in Christ; and laboured to walk, in every point, as their beloved Master. In order to this, they walked in a constant course of universal self denial, trampling on every pleasure which they were not divinely conscious prepared them for taking pleasure in God. They took up their cross daily. They strove, they agonized without intermission, to enter in at the strait gate. This one thing they did, they spared no pains to arrive at the summit of Christian holiness; "leaving the first principles of the doctrine of Christ, to go on to perfection;" to "know all that love of God which passeth knowledge, and to be filled with all the fulness of God."

From long experience and observation I am inclined to think, that whoever finds redemption in the blood of Jesus, whoever is justified, has then the choice of walking in the higher or the lower path. I believe the Holy Spirit at that time sets before him the "more excellent way," and incites him to walk therein; to choose the narrowest path in the narrow way; to aspire after the heights and depths of

## The More Excellent Way.

holiness,—after the entire image of God. But if he does not accept this offer, he insensibly declines into the lower order of Christians. He still goes on in what may be called a good way, serving God in his degree, and finds mercy in the close of life, through the blood of the covenant.

I would be far from quenching the smoking flax; from discouraging those that serve God in a low degree. But I could not wish them to stop here: I would encourage them to come up higher, without thundering hell and damnation in their ears. Without condemning the way wherein they were, telling them it is the way that leads to destruction, I will endeavour to point out to them, what is, in every respect, "a more excellent way."

Let it be well remembered, I do not affirm, that all who do not walk in this way, are in the high road to hell. But this much I must affirm, they will not have so high a place in heaven, as they would have had, if they had chosen the better part. And will this be a small loss— the having so many fewer stars in your crown of glory? Will it be a little thing to have a lower place than you might have had in the kingdom of your Father? Certainly there will be no sorrow in heaven; there all tears will be wiped from our eyes; but if it were possible grief could enter there, we should grieve at that irreparable loss. Irreparable then, but not now. Now, by the grace of God, we may choose the "more excellent way." Let us now compare this in a few particulars, with the way wherein most Christians walk.

I. To begin at the beginning of the day. It is the manner of the generality of Christians, if they are not obliged to work for their living, to rise, particularly in winter, at eight or nine in the morning, after having lain in bed eight or nine, if not more hours. I do not say now (as I should have been very apt to do fifty years ago) that all who indulge themselves in this manner are in the way to hell. But neither can I say, they are in the way to heaven, denying themselves, and taking up their cross daily. Sure I am, there is "a more excellent way" to promote health both of body and mind. From an observation of more than sixty years, I have learned, that men in health require, at an average, from six to seven hours sleep; and healthy women a little more, from seven to eight, in four and twenty hours. I know this quantity of sleep to be most advantageous to the body as well as the soul. It is preferable to any medicine which I have known, both for preventing and removing nervous disorders. It is, therefore, undoubtedly, the most excellent way, in defiance of fashion and custom, to take just so much sleep, as experience proves our nature to require; seeing this is indisputably most conducive both to bodily and spiritual health. And why should you not walk in this way? Because it is difficult? Nay, with men it is impossible. But all things are possible with God; and by his grace, all things will be possible to *you*. Only continue instant in prayer, and you will find this, not only possible, but easy: yea, and it will be far easier, to rise early constantly, than to do it sometimes. But then you must begin at the right end; if you would rise early, you must sleep early. Impose it upon yourself, unless when something extraordinary occurs, to go to bed at a fixed hour. Then the difficulty of it will soon be over; but the advantage of it will remain for ever.

II. The generality of Christians, as soon as they rise, are accustomed to use some kind of *prayer:* and probably to use the same form still, which they learned when they were eight or ten years old. Now I do not condemn those who proceed thus (though many do), as mocking God; though they have used the same form, without any variation, for twenty or thirty years together. But surely there is "a more excellent way" of ordering our private devotions. What if you were to follow the advice given

## The More Excellent Way. 97

by that great and good man, Mr. Law, on this subject? Consider both your outward and inward state, and vary your prayers accordingly. For instance: Suppose your outward state is prosperous; suppose you are in a state of health, ease, and plenty, having your lot cast among kind relations, good neighbours, and agreeable friends, that love you, and you them; then your outward state manifestly calls for praise and thanksgiving to God. On the other hand, if you are in a state of adversity; if God has laid trouble upon your loins; if you are in poverty, in want, in outward distress; if you are in imminent danger; if you are in pain and sickness; then you are clearly called to pour out your soul before God, in such prayer as is suited to your circumstances. In like manner you may suit your devotions to your inward state, the present state of your mind. Is your soul in heaviness, either from a sense of sin, or through manifold temptations? Then let your prayer consist of such confessions, petitions, and supplications, as are agreeable to your distressed situation of mind. On the contrary, is your soul in peace? Are you rejoicing in God? Are his consolations not small with you? Then say with the psalmist, "Thou art my God, and I will love thee: thou art my God, and I will praise thee." You may, likewise, when you have time, add to your other devotions, a little reading and meditation; and perhaps a psalm of praise: the natural effusion of a thankful heart. You must certainly see, that this is "a more excellent way," than the poor, dry form which you used before.

III. The generality of Christians after using some prayer, usually apply themselves to the *business* of their calling. Every man that has any pretence to be a Christian, will not fail to do this: seeing it is impossible that an idle man can be a good man: sloth being inconsistent with religion. But with what view? For what end do you undertake and follow your worldly business? "To provide things necessary for myself and my family." It is a good answer, as far as it goes; but it does not go far enough. For a Turk or a heathen goes so far; does his work for the very same ends. But a Christian may go abundantly farther: his end in all his labour is, to please God; to do, not his own will, but the will of him that sent him into the world; for this very purpose, to do the will of God on earth, as angels do in heaven. He works for eternity. He "labours not for the meat that perisheth" (this is the smallest part of his motive), "but for that which endureth to everlasting life." And is not this "a more excellent way?"

Again: in what *manner* do you transact your worldly business? I trust with diligence; whatever your hand findeth to do, doing it with your might: in justice, rendering to all their due, in every circumstance of life; yea, and in mercy, doing unto every man what you would he should do unto you. This is well: but a Christian is called to go still farther; to add piety to justice; to intermix prayer, especially the prayer of the heart, with all the labour of his hands. Without this, all his diligence and justice only show him to be an honest heathen; and many there are who profess the Christian religion, that go no farther than honest heathenism.

Yet again: in what *spirit* do you go through your business? In the spirit of the world, or in the spirit of Christ? I am afraid thousands of those who are called good Christians, do not understand the question. If you act in the spirit of Christ, you carry the end you at first proposed, through all your work from first to last. You do every thing in the spirit of sacrifice, giving up your will to the will of God; and continually aiming, not at ease, pleasure, or riches, not at any thing "this short-enduring world can give;" but merely at the glory of God. Now can any one deny, that this is the most excellent way of pursuing worldly business?

## The More Excellent Way. 99

IV. But these tenements of clay which we bear about us, require constant reparation, or they will sink into the earth from which they were taken, even sooner than nature requires. Daily food is necessary to prevent this; to repair the decays of nature. It was common in the heathen world, when they were about to use this, to take meat or even drink, *libare pateram Jovi;* to pour out a little to the honour of their god: although the gods of the heathens were but devils, as the apostle justly observes. "It seems" (says a late writer) "there was once some such custom as this in our own country. For we still frequently see a gentleman before he sits down to dinner in his own house, holding his hat before his face, and perhaps seeming to say something: though he generally does it in such a manner, that no one can tell what he says." Now what if, instead of this, every head of a family, before he sat down to eat and drink, either morning, noon, or night (for the reason of the thing is the same at every hour of the day), were seriously to ask a blessing from God, on what he was about to take? Yea, and afterwards, seriously to return thanks to the Giver of all his blessings? Would not this be "a more excellent way," than to use that dull farce, which is worse than nothing; being, in reality, no other than mockery both of God and man?

As to the *quantity* of their food, good sort of men do not usually eat to excess. At least not so far as to make themselves sick with meat, or to intoxicate themselves with drink. And as to the manner of taking it, it is usually innocent, mixed with a little mirth, which is said to help digestion. So far, so good. And provided they take only that measure of plain, cheap, wholesome food, which most promotes health both of body and mind, there will be no cause of blame. Neither can I require you to take that advice of Mr. Herbert, though he was a good man:

> " Take thy meat: think it dust: then eat a bit,
> And say with all, earth to earth I commit."

This is too melancholy: it does not suit with that cheerfulness, which is highly proper at a Christian meal. Permit me to illustrate this subject with a little story. The king of France one day pursuing the chase, outrode all his company, who, after seeking him some time, found him sitting in a cottage eating bread and cheese. Seeing them, he cried out, "Where have I lived all my time? I never before tasted so good food in my life!" "Sire," said one of them, "you never had so *good sauce* before; for you were never hungry." Now it is true, hunger is a good sauce; but there is one that is better still; that is, thankfulness. Sure, that is the most agreeable food, which is seasoned with this. And why should not yours at every meal? You need not then fix your eye on death: but receive every morsel as a pledge of life eternal. The author of your being gives you, in this food, not only a reprieve from death, but an earnest, that, in a little time, "death shall be swallowed up in victory."

The time of taking our food is usually a time of *conversation* also: as it is natural, to refresh our minds while we refresh our bodies. Let us consider a little, in what manner the generality of Christians usually converse together. What are the ordinary subjects of their conversation? If it is harmless (as one would hope it is), if there be nothing in it profane, nothing immodest, nothing untrue, or unkind: if there be no tale bearing, back biting, or evil speaking, they have reason to praise God for his restraining grace. But there is more than this implied, in "ordering our conversation aright." In order to this it is needful, first, that "your communication," that is, discourse or conversation "be good;" that it be materially good; on good subjects; not fluttering about any thing that occurs: for what have you to do with courts and kings? It is not your business to—

## The More Excellent Way.

> "Fight o'er the wars, reform the state;"

unless when some remarkable event calls for the acknowledgment of the justice or mercy of God. You must indeed sometimes talk of worldly things, otherwise we may as well go out of the world. But it should be only so far as is needful: then we should return to a better subject. Secondly, let your conversation be "to the use of edifying;" calculated to edify either the speaker or the hearers, or both: to build them up, as each has particular need, either in faith, or love, or holiness. Thirdly, see that it not only gives entertainment, but in one kind or other, "ministers grace to the hearers." Now is not this "a more excellent way" of conversing, than the harmless way above mentioned?

V. We have seen what is the "more excellent way" of ordering our conversation, as well as our business. But we cannot be always intent upon business: both our bodies and minds require some relaxation. We need intervals of diversion from business. It will be necessary to be very explicit upon this head, as it is a point which has been much misunderstood.

Diversions are of various kinds. Some are almost peculiar to men, as the sports of the field: hunting, shooting, fishing, wherein not many women (I should say ladies) are concerned. Others are indifferently used by persons of both sexes: some of which are of a more public nature; as races, masquerades, plays, assemblies, balls. Others are chiefly used in private houses; as cards, dancing, and music; to which we may add, the reading of plays, novels, romances, newspapers, and fashionable poetry.

Some diversions, indeed, which were formerly in great request, are now fallen into disrepute. The nobility and gentry, in England at least, seem totally to disregard the once fashionable diversion of hawking: and the vulgar themselves are no longer diverted, by men hacking and hewing each other in pieces at broad sword. The noble game of quarter staff, likewise, is now exercised by very few. Yea, cudgelling has lost its honour, even in Wales itself. Bear baiting also is now very seldom seen, and bull baiting not very often. And it seems cock fighting would totally cease in England, were it not for two or three right honourable patrons.

It is not needful to say any thing more of these foul *remains of Gothic barbarity,* than that they are a reproach, not only to all religion, but even to human nature. One would not pass so severe a censure on the sports of the field. Let those who have nothing better to do, still run foxes and hares out of breath. Neither need much be said about horse races, till some man of sense will undertake to defend them. It seems a great deal more may be said in defence of seeing a serious tragedy. I could not do it with a clear conscience; at least not in an English theatre, the sink of all profaneness and debauchery; but possibly others can. I cannot say quite so much for balls or assemblies, which, though more reputable than masquerades, yet must be allowed by all impartial persons to have exactly the same tendency. So undoubtedly have all public dancings. And the same tendency they must have unless the same caution obtained among modern Christians which was observed among the ancient heathens. With them, men and women never danced together; but always in separate rooms. This was always observed in ancient Greece, and for several ages at Rome; where a woman dancing in company with men, would have at once been set down for a prostitute. Of playing at cards, I say the same as of seeing plays. I could not do it with a clear conscience. But I am not obliged to pass any sentence on those that are otherwise minded. I leave them to their own Master: to him let them stand or fall.

But supposing these, as well as the reading of plays, novels, newspapers, and the like, to be quite innocent diversions, yet are there not more excellent ways of diverting themselves for those that love or fear God? Would men of fortune divert themselves in the open air? They may do it by cultivating and improving their lands, by planting their grounds, by laying out, carrying on, and perfecting their gardens and orchards. At other times they may visit and converse with the most serious and sensible of their neighbours: or they may visit the sick, the poor, the widows, and the fatherless in their affliction. Do they desire to divert themselves in the house? They may read useful history, pious and elegant poetry, or several branches of natural philosophy. If you have time, you may divert yourself by music, and perhaps by philosophical experiments. But above all, when you have once learned the use of prayer, you will find, that as

> " That which yields or fills
> All space, the ambient air, wide interfused
> Embraces round this florid earth:"

so will this; till through every space of life it be interfused with all your employments, and wherever you are, whatever you do, embrace you on every side. Then you will be able to say boldly;—

> "With me no melancholy void,
> No moment lingers unemployed
> Or unimproved below;
> My weariness of life is gone,
> Who live to serve my God alone,
> And only Jesus know."

VI. One point only remains to be considered; that is the use of money. What is the way wherein the generality of Christians employ this? And is there not "a more excellent way?"

The generality of Christians usually set apart something yearly, perhaps a tenth or even one eighth part of their income, whether it arise from yearly revenue, or from trade, for charitable uses. A few I have known, who said, like Zaccheus, "Lord, the half of my goods I give to the poor." Oh that it would please God to multiply those friends of mankind, those general benefactors! but,

Besides those who have a stated rule, there are thousands who give large sums to the poor: especially when any striking instance of distress is represented to them in lively colours.

I praise God for all of you who act in this manner. May you never be weary of well doing! May God restore what you give, seven fold into your own bosom! But yet I show unto you "a more excellent way."

You may consider yourself as one, in whose hands the Proprietor of heaven and earth, and all things therein, has lodged a part of his goods, to be disposed of according to his direction. And his direction is, that you should look upon yourself as one of a certain number of indigent persons, who are to be provided for out of that portion of his goods, wherewith you are entrusted. You have two advantages over the rest: the one, that "it is more blessed to give than to receive;" the other, that you are to serve yourself first; and others afterwards. This is the light wherein you are to see yourself and them. But to be more particular. First: If you have no family, after you have provided for yourself, give away all that remains; so that

"Each Christmas your accounts may clear,
And wind your bottom round the year."

This was the practice of all the young men at Oxford, who were called Methodists. For example: one of them had thirty pounds a year. He lived on twenty-eight, and gave away forty shillings. The next year receiving sixty pounds, he still lived on twenty-eight, and gave away two and thirty. The third year he received ninety pounds, and gave away sixty-two. The fourth year he received a hundred and twenty pounds. Still he lived as before on twenty-eight; and gave to the poor ninety-two. Was not this a more excellent way? Secondly: If you have a family, seriously consider before God how much each member of it wants, in order to have what is needful for life and godliness. And in general, do not allow them less, nor much more than you allow yourself. Thirdly: This being done, fix your purpose, to "gain no more." I charge you in the name of God, do not increase your substance! As it comes daily or yearly, so let it go: otherwise you "lay up treasures upon earth." And this our Lord as flatly forbids, as murder and adultery. By doing it therefore, you would, "treasure up to yourselves wrath against the day of wrath, and revelation of the righteous judgment of God."

But suppose it were not forbidden, how can you, on principles of reason, spend your money in a way, which God may *possibly forgive,* instead of spending it in a manner which he will *certainly reward?* You will have no reward in heaven, for what you *lay up:* you will, for what you *lay out:* every pound you put into the earthly bank is sunk: it brings no interest above. But every pound you give to the poor, is put into the bank of heaven. And it will bring glorious interest: yea, and as such will be accumulating to all eternity.

Who then is a wise man, and endued with knowledge among you? Let him resolve this day, this hour, this moment, the Lord assisting him, to choose in all the preceding particulars the "more excellent way:" and let him steadily keep it, both with regard to sleep, prayer, work, food, conversation, and diversions; and particularly, with regard to the employment of that important talent, money. Let *your* heart answer to the call of God, "From this moment, God being my helper, I will lay up no more treasure upon earth: this one thing I will do, I will lay up treasure in heaven: I will render unto God the things that are God's: I will give him all my goods, and all my heart!"

## CATHOLIC SPIRIT.

"And when he was departed thence, he lighted on Jehonadab the son of Rechab coming to meet him: and he saluted him, and said to him, Is thine heart right, as my heart is with thy heart? And Jehonadab answered, It is. If it be, give me thine hand."—2 Kings x, 15.

It is allowed even by those who do not pay this great debt, that love is due to all mankind; the royal law, "Thou shalt love thy neighbour as thyself," carrying its own evidence to all that hear it: and that, not according to the miserable construction put upon it by the zealots of old times, "Thou shalt love thy neighbour," thy relation, acquaintance, friend, and hate thine enemy: "not so; I say unto you," saith our Lord, "Love your enemies, bless them that curse you, do good to them that hate you, and pray for them that despitefully use you, and persecute you; that ye may be the children [may appear so to all mankind] of your Father which is in heaven; who maketh his sun to rise on the evil and on the good, and sendeth rain on the just and on the unjust."

But it is sure, there is a peculiar love which we owe to those that love God. So David: "All my delight is upon the saints that are in the earth, and upon such as excel in virtue." And so a greater than he: "A new commandment I give unto you, that ye love one another: as I have loved you, that ye also love one another. By this shall all men know that ye are my disciples, if ye have love one to another," John xiii, 34, 35. This is that love on which the apostle John so frequently and strongly insists: "This," saith he, "is the message that ye heard from the beginning, that we should love one another," 1 John iii, 11. "Hereby perceive we the love of God, because he laid down his life for us: and we ought [if love should call us thereto] to lay down our lives for the brethren," ver. 16. And again: "Beloved, let us love one another: for love is of God. He that loveth not, knoweth not God; for God is love," chap. iv, 7, 8. "Not that we loved God, but that he loved us, and sent his Son to be the propitiation for our sins. Beloved, if God so loved us, we ought also to love one another," ver. 10, 11.

All men approve of this. But do all men practise it? Daily experience shows the contrary. Where are even the Christians who "love one another, as he hath given us commandment?" How many hinderances lie in the way! The two grand, general hinderances are, first, That they cannot all think alike; and, in consequence of this, secondly, They cannot all walk alike; but in several smaller points their practice must differ, in proportion to the difference of their sentiments.

But although a difference in opinions or modes of worship may prevent an entire external union; yet need it prevent our union in affection? Though we cannot think alike, may we not love alike? May we not be of one heart, though we are not of one opinion? Without all doubt we may. Herein all the children of God may unite, notwithstanding these smaller differences. These remaining as they are, they may forward one another in love and in good works.

Surely in this respect the example of Jehu himself, as mixed a character as he was of, is well worthy both the attention and imitation of every serious Christian. "And when he was departed thence, he lighted on Jehonadab the son of Rechab coming to meet him. And he saluted him, and said to him, Is thine heart right, as my heart is with thy heart? And Jehonadab answered, It is. If it be, give me thine hand."

The text naturally divides itself into two parts, first, A question proposed by Jehu to Jehonadab: "Is thine heart right, as my heart is with thy heart?" Secondly, An offer made on Jehonadab's answering, It is: "If it be, give me thine hand."

## 108        Selections from Wesley.

I. And, first, let us consider the question proposed by Jehu to Jehonadab, "Is thine heart right, as my heart is with thy heart?"

The very first thing we may observe in these words, is, that here is no inquiry concerning Jehonadab's opinions. And yet it is certain, he held some which were very uncommon, indeed quite peculiar to himself; and some which had a close influence upon his practice; on which likewise he laid so great a stress, as to entail them upon his children's children, to their latest posterity. This is evident from the account given by Jeremiah, many years after his death: "I took Jaazaniah and his brethren, and all his sons, and the whole house of the Rechabites,—and set before them pots full of wine and cups, and said unto them, Drink ye wine. But they said, We will drink no wine; for Jonadab [or Jehonadab] the son of Rechab our father" [it would be less ambiguous if the words were placed thus, Jehonadab *our father, the son of* Rechab; out of love and reverence to whom he probably desired his descendants might be called by his name] "commanded us, saying, Ye shall drink no wine, neither ye nor your sons for ever. Neither shall ye build house, nor sow seed, nor plant vineyard, nor have any; but all your days ye shall dwell in tents.—And we have obeyed and done according to all that Jonadab our father commanded us," Jer. xxxv, 3-10.

And yet Jehu (although it seems to have been his manner, both in things secular, and religious, to *drive furiously*) does not concern himself at all with any of these things, but lets Jehonadab abound in his own sense. And neither of them appears to have given the other the least disturbance, touching the opinions which he maintained.

It is very possible, that many good men now also may entertain peculiar opinions; and some of them may be as singular herein, as even Jehonadab was. And it is certain, so long as we know but *in part,* that all men will not see all things alike. It is an unavoidable consequence of the present weakness and shortness of human understanding, that several men will be of several minds in religion as well as in common life. So it has been from the beginning of the world, and so it will be "till the restitution of all things."

Nay farther: Although every man necessarily believes that every particular opinion which he holds is true; (for to believe any opinion is not true, is the same thing as not to hold it); yet can no man be assured that all his own opinions, taken together, are true. Nay, every thinking man is assured they are not; seeing *Humanum est errare et nescire:* to be ignorant of many things, and to mistake in some, is the necessary condition of humanity. This, therefore, he is sensible is his own case. He knows in general, that he himself is mistaken; although in what particulars he mistakes, he does not, perhaps he cannot know.

I say, perhaps he cannot know; for who can tell how far invincible ignorance may extend? Or (that comes to the same thing,) invincible prejudice?—which is often so fixed in tender minds, that it is afterwards impossible to tear up what has taken so deep a root. And who can say, unless he knew every circumstance attending it, how far any mistake is culpable? Seeing all guilt must suppose some concurrence of the will; of which he only can judge who searcheth the heart.

Every wise man, therefore, will allow others the same liberty of thinking, which he desires they should allow him; and will no more insist on their embracing his opinions, than he would have them to insist on his embracing theirs. He bears with those who differ from him, and only asks him, with whom he desires to unite in love, that single question, "is thy heart right, as my heart is with thy heart?"

We may, secondly, observe, that here is no inquiry made concerning Jehonadab's mode of worship; although it is highly probable there was, in this respect also, a very wide difference between them. For we may well believe Jehonadab, as well as all his posterity, worshipped God at Jerusalem: whereas Jehu did not; he had more regard to state policy than religion. And, therefore, although he slew the worshippers of Baal, and destroyed Baal out of Israel; yet from the convenient sin of Jeroboam, the worship of the golden calves, he departed not, 2 Kings x, 29.

But even among men of an upright heart, men who desire to "have a conscience void of offence," it must needs be, that, as long as there are various opinions, there will be various ways of worshipping God; seeing a variety of opinions necessarily implies a variety of practice. And as, in all ages, men have differed in nothing more than in their opinions concerning the Supreme Being, so in nothing have they more differed from each other, than in the manner of worshipping him. Had this been only in the heathen world, it would not have been at all surprising: for we know, these "by [their] wisdom knew not God;" nor, therefore, could they know how to worship him. But is it not strange, that even in the Christian world, although they all agree in the general, "God is a Spirit, and they that worship him must worship him in spirit and in truth," yet the particular modes of worshipping God are almost as various as among the heathens?

And how shall we choose among so much variety? No man can choose for, or prescribe to, another. But every one must follow the dictates of his own conscience, in simplicity and godly sincerity. He must be fully persuaded in his own mind, and then act according to the best light he has. Nor has any creature power to constrain another to walk by his own rule. God has given no right to any of the children of men, thus to lord it

## Catholic Spirit.

over the conscience of his brethren; but every man must judge for himself, as every man must give an account of himself to God.

Although, therefore, every follower of Christ is obliged, by the very nature of the Christian institution, to be a member of some particular congregation or other, some church, as it is usually termed; (which implies a particular manner of worshipping God; for "two cannot walk together unless they be agreed";) yet none can be obliged by any power on earth, but that of his own conscience, to prefer this or that congregation to another, this or that particular manner of worship. I know it is commonly supposed, that the place of our birth fixes the church to which we ought to belong; that one, for instance, who is born in England, ought to be a member of that which is styled the church of England; and, consequently, to worship God in the particular manner which is prescribed by that church. I was once a zealous maintainer of this; but I find many reasons to abate of this zeal. I fear it is attended with such difficulties, as no reasonable man can get over: not the least of which is, that if this rule had taken place, there could have been no reformation from popery; seeing it entirely destroys the right of private judgment, on which that whole reformation stands.

I dare not, therefore, presume to impose my mode of worship on any other. I believe it is truly primitive and apostolical: but my belief is no rule for another. I ask not, therefore, of him with whom I would unite in love, are you of my church? of my congregation? Do you receive the same form of church government, and allow the same church officers with me? Do you join in the same form of prayer, wherein I worship God? I inquire not, do you receive the supper of the Lord in the same posture and manner that I do? Nor, whether, in the administration of baptism, you agree with me in admitting sureties for the baptized; in the manner of administering it; or the age of those to whom it should be administered? Nay, I ask not of you, (as clear as I am in my own mind,) whether you allow baptism and the Lord's supper at all? Let all these things stand by; we will talk of them, if need be, at a more convenient season; my only question at present is this, "Is thine heart right, as my heart is with thy heart?"

But what is properly implied in the question? I do not mean, What did Jehu imply therein? But what should a follower of Christ understand thereby, when he proposes it to any of his brethren?

The first thing implied is this: Is thy heart right with God? Dost thou believe his being, and his perfections? His eternity, immensity, wisdom, power; his justice, mercy, and truth? Dost thou believe, that he now "upholdeth all things by the word of his power?" And that he governs even the most minute, even the most noxious, to his own glory, and the good of them that love him? Hast thou a divine evidence, a supernatural conviction, of the things of God? Dost thou "walk by faith, not by sight?" Looking not at temporal things, but things eternal?

Dost thou believe in the Lord Jesus Christ, "God over all, blessed for ever?" Is he revealed in thy soul? Dost thou know Jesus Christ and him crucified? Does he dwell in thee, and thou in him? Is he formed in thy heart by faith? Having absolutely disclaimed all thy own works, thy own righteousness, hast thou "submitted thyself unto the righteousness of God," which is by faith in Christ Jesus? Art thou "found in him, not having thy own righteousness, but the righteousness which is by faith?" And art thou, through him, "fighting the good fight of faith, and laying hold of eternal life?"

Is thy faith ενεργυμενη δι' αγαπης,—filled with the *energy of love?* Dost thou love God, I do not say, "above

## Catholic Spirit.

all things;" for it is both an unscriptural and an ambiguous expression; but "with all thy heart, and with all thy mind, and with all thy soul, and with all thy strength?" Dost thou seek all thy happiness in him alone? And dost thou find what thou seekest? Does thy soul continually "magnify the Lord, and thy spirit rejoice in God thy Saviour?" Having learned "in every thing to give thanks," dost thou find "it is a joyful and a pleasant thing to be thankful?" Is God the centre of thy soul? The sum of all thy desires? Art thou accordingly laying up thy treasure in heaven, and counting all things else dung and dross? Hath the love of God cast the love of the world out of thy soul? Then thou art "crucified to the world?" thou art dead to all below; and thy "life is hid with Christ in God."

Art thou employed in doing "not thy own will, but the will of him that sent thee?" Of him that sent thee down to sojourn here awhile, to spend a few days in a strange land, till, having finished the work he hath given thee to do, thou return to thy Father's house? Is it thy meat and drink "to do the will of thy Father which is in heaven?" Is thine eye single in all things? Always fixed on him? Always looking unto Jesus? Dost thou point at him in whatsoever thou doest? In all thy labour, thy business, thy conversation? Aiming only at the glory of God in all;—"whatsoever thou doest, either in word or deed, doing it all in the name of the Lord Jesus; giving thanks unto God, even the Father, through him?"

Does the love of God constrain thee to serve him with fear,—to "rejoice unto him with reverence?" Art thou more afraid of displeasing God, than either of death or hell? Is nothing so terrible to thee as the thought of offending the eyes of his glory? Upon this ground, dost thou "hate all evil ways," every transgression of his holy and perfect law; and herein "exercise thyself to have a conscience void of offence towards God, and towards man?"

Is thy heart right towards thy neighbour? Dost thou love, as thyself, all mankind without exception? "If you love those only that love you, what thank have ye?" Do you "love your enemies?" Is your soul full of good will, of tender affection towards them? Do you love even the enemies of God, the unthankful and unholy? Do your bowels yearn over them? Could you "wish yourself [temporally] accursed" for their sake? And do you show this, by "blessing them that curse you, and praying for those that despitefully use you, and persecute you?"

Do you show your love by your works? While you have time, as you have opportunity, do you in fact "do good to all men," neighbours or strangers, friends or enemies, good or bad? Do you do them all the good you can; endeavouring to supply all their wants; assisting them both in body and soul, to the uttermost of your power?—If thou art thus minded, may every Christian say, yea, if thou art but sincerely desirous of it, and following on till thou attain, then "thy heart is right, as my heart is with thy heart."

II. "If it be, give me thy hand." I do not mean, "Be of my opinion." You need not: I do not expect or desire it. Neither do I mean, "I will be of your opinion." I cannot: it does not depend on my choice: I can no more think, than I can see or hear, as I will. Keep you your opinion: I mine; and that as steadily as ever. You need not even endeavour to come over to me, or bring me over to you. I do not desire you to dispute those points, or to hear or speak one word concerning them. Let all opinions alone on one side and the other: only "give me thine hand."

I do not mean, "Embrace my modes of worship: or, I will embrace yours." This also is a thing which does not depend either on your choice or mine. We must both

## Catholic Spirit.

act, as each is fully persuaded in his own mind. Hold you fast that which you believe is most acceptable to God, and I will do the same. I believe the Episcopal form of church government to be scriptural and apostolical. If you think the Presbyterian or Independent is better, think so still, and act accordingly. I believe infants ought to be baptized; and that this may be done either by dipping or sprinkling. If you are otherwise persuaded, be so still, and follow your own persuasion. It appears to me that forms of prayer are of excellent use, particularly in the great congregation. If you judge extemporary prayer to be of more use, act suitably to your own judgment. My sentiment is, that I ought not to forbid water, wherein persons may be baptized; and, that I ought to eat bread and drink wine, as a memorial of my dying Master: however, if you are not convinced of this, act according to the light you have. I have no desire to dispute with you one moment, upon any of the preceding heads. Let all these smaller points stand aside. Let them never come into sight. "If thine heart is as my heart," if thou lovest God and all mankind, I ask no more: "give me thine hand."

I mean, first, love me: and that not only as thou lovest all mankind; not only as thou lovest thine enemies, or the enemies of God, those that hate thee, "that despitefully use thee and persecute thee;" not only as a stranger, as one of whom thou knowest neither good nor evil;—I am not satisfied with this;—no; "If thine heart be right, as mine with thy heart," then love me with a very tender affection, as a friend that is closer than a brother; as a brother in Christ, a fellow citizen of the New Jerusalem, a fellow soldier engaged in the same warfare, under the same Captain of our salvation. Love me as a companion in the kingdom and patience of Jesus, and a joint heir of his glory.

Love me (but in a higher degree than thou dost the bulk of mankind) with the love that is *long suffering and kind;* that is patient; if I am ignorant or out of the way, bearing and not increasing my burden; and is tender, soft, and compassionate still;—that *envieth not,* if at any time it please God to prosper me in his work even more than thee. Love me with the love that *is not provoked,* either at my follies or infirmities; or even at my acting (if it should sometimes so appear to thee) not according to the will of God. Love me so as to *think no evil* of me; to put away all jealousy and evil surmising. Love me with the love that *covereth all things;* that never reveals either my faults or infirmities;—that *believeth all things;* is always willing to think the best, to put the fairest construction on all my words and actions;—that *hopeth all things;* either that the thing related was never done; or not done with such circumstances as are related; or, at least, that it was done with a good intention, or in a sudden stress of temptation. And hope to the end, that whatever is amiss, will, by the grace of God, be corrected; and whatever is wanting, supplied, through the riches of his mercy in Christ Jesus.

I mean, secondly, Commend me to God in all thy prayers; wrestle with him in my behalf, that he would speedily correct what he sees amiss, and supply what is wanting in me. In thy nearest access to the throne of grace, beg of him, who is then very present with thee, that my heart may be more as thy heart, more right both towards God and towards man; that I may have a fuller conviction of things not seen, and a stronger view of the love of God in Christ Jesus; may more steadily walk by faith, not by sight; and more earnestly grasp eternal life. Pray that the love of God, and of all mankind, may be more largely poured into my heart; that I may be more fervent and active in doing the will of my Father which is in heaven; more zealous of good works, and more careful to abstain from all appearance of evil.

I mean, thirdly, Provoke me to love and to good works.

Second thy prayer, as thou hast opportunity, by speaking to me, in love, whatsoever thou believest to be for my soul's health. Quicken me in the work which God has given me to do, and instruct me how to do it more perfectly. Yea, "smite me friendly, and reprove me," wherein soever I appear to thee to be doing rather my own will, than the will of him that sent me. Oh speak and spare not, whatever thou believest may conduce, either to the amending my faults, the strengthening my weakness, the building me up in love, or the making me more fit, in any kind, for the Master's use!

I mean, lastly, Love me not in word only, but in deed and in truth. So far as in conscience thou canst, (retaining still thy own opinions, and thy own manner of worshipping God,) join with me in the work of God, and let us go on hand in hand. And thus far, it is certain, thou mayest go. Speak honourably, wherever thou art, of the work of God, by whomsoever he works, and kindly of his messengers. And if it be in thy power, not only sympathize with them when they are in any difficulty or distress, but give them a cheerful and effectual assistance, that they may glorify God on thy behalf.

Two things should be observed with regard to what has been spoken under this last head: The one, that whatsoever love, whatsoever offices of love, whatsoever spiritual or temporal assistance, I claim from him whose heart is right, as my heart is with his; the same I am ready, by the grace of God, according to my measure, to give him: The other, that I have not made this claim in behalf of myself only, but of all whose heart is right towards God and man, that we may all love one another as Christ hath loved us.

III. One inference we may make from what has been said. We may learn from hence, what is a catholic spirit.

There is scarce any expression which has been more grossly misunderstood, and more dangerously misapplied, than this: but it will be easy for any who calmly consider the preceding observations, to correct any such misapprehensions of it, and to prevent any such misapplication.

From hence we may learn, first, That a catholic spirit is not *speculative* latitudinarianism. It is not an indifference to all opinions: this is the spawn of hell, not the offspring of heaven. This unsettledness of thought, this being "driven to and fro, and tossed about with every wind of doctrine," is a great curse, not a blessing; an irreconcilable enemy, not a friend to true catholicism. A man of a truly catholic spirit, has not now his religion to seek. He is fixed as the sun, in his judgment concerning the main branches of Christian doctrine. It is true, he is always ready to hear and weigh whatsoever can be offered against his principles; but as this does not show any wavering in his own mind, so neither does it occasion any. He does not halt between two opinions, nor vainly endeavour to blend them into one. Observe this, you who know not what spirit ye are of; who call yourselves men of a catholic spirit, only because you are of a muddy understanding; because your mind is all in a mist; because you have no settled, consistent principles, but are for jumbling all opinions together. Be convinced, that you have quite missed your way; you know not where you are. You think you are got into the very spirit of Christ; when, in truth, you are nearer the spirit of antichrist. Go, first, and learn the first elements of the gospel of Christ, and then shall you learn to be of a truly catholic spirit.

From what has been said, we may learn, secondly, that a catholic spirit is not any kind of *practical* latitudinarianism. It is not indifference as to public worship, or as to the outward manner of performing it. This, likewise, would not be a blessing but a curse. Far from being a help thereto, it would, so long as it remained, be an unspeakable hinderance to the worshipping of God in spirit and in truth. But the man of a truly catholic spirit, having weighed all things in the balance of the sanctuary, has no doubt, no scruple at all, concerning that particular mode of worship wherein he joins. He is clearly convinced, that *this* manner of worshipping God is both scriptural and rational. He knows none in the world, which is more scriptural, none which is more rational. Therefore, without rambling hither and thither, he cleaves close thereto, and praises God for the opportunity of so doing.

Hence we may, thirdly, learn, that a catholic spirit is not indifference to all congregations. This is another sort of latitudinarianism, no less absurd and unscriptural than the former. But it is far from a man of a truly catholic spirit. He is fixed in his congregation as well as his principles. He is united to one, not only in spirit, but by all the outward ties of Christian fellowship. There he partakes of all the ordinances of God. There he receives the supper of the Lord. There he pours out his soul in public prayer, and joins in public praise and thanksgiving. There he rejoices to hear the word of reconciliation, the gospel of the grace of God. With these his nearest, his best beloved brethren, on solemn occasions, he seeks God by fasting. These particularly he watches over in love, as they do over his soul; admonishing, exhorting, comforting, reproving, and every way building up each other in the faith. These he regards as his own household; and therefore, according to the ability God has given him, naturally cares for them, and provides that they may have all the things that are needful for life and godliness.

But while he is steadily fixed in his religious principles, in what he believes to be the truth as it is in Jesus; while he firmly adheres to that worship of God which he judges to be most acceptable in his sight; and while he is united, by the tenderest and closest ties, to one particular congregation,—his heart is enlarged towards all mankind, those he knows, and those he does not; he embraces with strong and cordial affection, neighbours and strangers, friends and enemies. This is catholic, or universal love. And he that has this is of a catholic spirit. For love alone gives the title to this character: catholic love is a catholic spirit.

If then we take this word in the strictest sense, a man of a catholic spirit is one who, in the manner above mentioned, gives his hand to all whose hearts are right with his heart: one who knows how to value, and praise God for, all the advantages he enjoys, with regard to the knowledge of the things of God, the true scriptural manner of worshipping him, and, above all, his union with a congregation fearing God and working righteousness: one who, retaining these blessings with the strictest care, keeping them as the apple of his eye, at the same time loves,—as friends, as brethren in the Lord, as members of Christ and children of God, as joint partakers now of the present kingdom of God, and fellow heirs of his eternal kingdom,—all of whatever opinion, or worship, or congregation, who believe in the Lord Jesus Christ; who love God and man; who rejoicing to please, and fearing to offend God, are careful to abstain from evil, and zealous of good works. He is the man of a truly catholic spirit, who bears all these continually upon his heart; who, having an unspeakable tenderness for their persons, and longing for their welfare, does not cease to commend them to God in prayer, as well as to plead their cause before men; who speaks comfortably to them, and labours by all his words, to strengthen their hands in God. He assists them to the uttermost of his power in all things, spiritual and temporal. He is ready "to spend and be spent for them;" yea, to lay down his life for their sake.

Thou, oh man of God, think on these things! If thou

## Catholic Spirit.

art already in this way, go on. If thou hast heretofore mistook the path, bless God who hath brought thee back! And now run the race which is set before thee, in the royal way of universal love. Take heed, lest thou be either wavering in thy judgment, or straitened in thy bowels: but keep an even pace, rooted in the faith once delivered to the saints, and grounded in love, in true catholic love, till thou art swallowed up in love for ever and ever!

## CHARITY.

[*Arminian Magazine,* 1785. *Works,* ii, 279-87.]

"Though I speak with the tongues of men and of angels, and have not charity, I am become as sounding brass, or a tinkling cymbal.

"And though I have the gift of prophecy, and understand all mysteries, and all knowledge; and though I have all faith, so as to remove mountains, and have not charity, I am nothing.

"And though I bestow all my goods to feed the poor, and give my body to be burned, and have not charity, it profiteth me nothing."—1 Cor. xiii, 1-3.

WE know, "all Scripture is given by inspiration of God," and is therefore true and right concerning all things. But we know, likewise, that there are some Scriptures which more immediately commend themselves to every man's conscience. In this rank we may place the passage before us: there are scarce any that object to it. On the contrary, the generality of men very readily appeal to it. Nothing is more common than to find even those who deny the authority of the Holy Scriptures, yet affirming, "this is my religion: that which is described in the thirteenth chapter of the Corinthians." Nay, even a Jew, Dr. Nunes, a Spanish physician, then settled at Savannah, in Georgia, used to say, with great earnestness, "That Paul of Tarsus was one of the finest writers I have ever read. I wish the thirteenth chapter of his first letter to the Corinthians were wrote in letters of gold. And I wish every Jew were to carry it with him wherever he went." He judged (and herein he certainly judged right) that this single chapter contained the whole of true religion. It contains "whatsoever things are just, whatsoever things are pure, whatsoever things are lovely: if there be any virtue, if there be any praise," it is all contained in this.

In order to see this in the clearest light, we may consider,

# Charity

I. What the charity here spoken of is:

II. What those things are which are usually put in the place of it. We may then,

III. Observe, that neither of them, nor all of them put together, can supply the want of it.

I. We are first, to consider, what this charity is. What is the nature, and what are the properties of it?

St. Paul's word is Ἀγάπη, exactly answering to the plain English word *love*. And accordingly it is so rendered in all the old translations of the Bible. So it stood in William Tindale's Bible, which I suppose was the first English translation of the whole Bible. So it was also in the Bible published by the authority of king Henry VIII. So it was likewise, in all the editions of the Bible that were successively published in England during the reign of king Edward VI., queen Elizabeth, and king James I. Nay, so it is found in the Bibles of king Charles the First's reign: I believe, to the period of it. The first Bibles I have seen, wherein the word was changed, were those printed by Roger Daniel and John Field, printers to the parliament, in the year 1649. Hence it seems probable that the alteration was made during the sitting of the long parliament: probably it was then that the Latin word charity was put in place of the English word *love*. It was in an unhappy hour this alteration was made: the ill effects of it remain to this day; and these may be observed, not only among the poor and illiterate; —not only thousands of common men and women, no more understand the word charity, than they do the original Greek;—but the same miserable mistake has diffused itself among men of education and learning. Thousands of these are misled thereby, and imagine that the charity treated of in this chapter refers chiefly, if not wholly, to outward actions, and to mean little more than almsgiving! I have heard many sermons preached upon this chapter; particularly before the University of

Oxford. And I never heard more than one, wherein the meaning of it was not totally misrepresented. But had the old and proper word *love* been retained, there would have been no room for misrepresentation.

But what kind of love is that whereof the apostle is speaking throughout the chapter? Many persons of eminent learning and piety apprehend that it is the love of God. But from reading the whole chapter numberless times, and considering it in every light, I am thoroughly persuaded that what St. Paul is here directly speaking of is the love of our neighbour. I believe whoever carefully weighs the whole tenor of his discourse, will be fully convinced of this. But it must be allowed to be such a love of our neighbour, as can only spring from a love of God. And whence does this love of God flow? Only from that faith which is of the operation of God; which whoever has, has a direct evidence that "God was in Christ reconciling the world unto himself." When this is particularly applied to his heart, so that he can say, with humble boldness, "the life which I now live, I live by faith in the Son of God, who loved me, and gave himself for me;" then, and not till then, "the love of God is shed abroad in his heart." And this love sweetly constrains him to love every child of man with the love which is here spoken of; not with a love of esteem or of complacence; for this can have no place with regard to those who are (if not his personal enemies, yet) enemies to God and their own souls; but with a love of benevolence, —of tender good will to all the souls that God has made.

But it may be asked, "If there be no true love of our neighbour, but that which springs from the love of God: and if the love of God flows from no other fountain than faith in the Son of God; does it not follow, that the whole heathen world is excluded from all possibility of salvation? Seeing they are cut off from faith: for faith cometh by hearing; and how shall they hear without a preacher?"

## Charity.

I answer, St. Paul's words, spoken on another occasion, are applicable to this; "What the law speaketh, it speaketh to them that are under the law." Accordingly, that sentence, "He that believeth not shall be damned," is spoken of them to whom the gospel is preached. Others it does not concern: and we are not required to determine any thing touching their final state. How it will please God, the Judge of all, to deal with *them,* we may leave to God himself. But this we know, that he is not the God of the Christians only, but the God of the heathens also; that he is "rich in mercy to all that call upon him," according to the light they have; and that "in every nation, he that feareth God and worketh righteousness, is accepted of him."

But to return. This is the nature of that love, whereof the apostle is here speaking. But what are the properties of it; the fruits which are inseparable from it? The apostle reckons up many of them; but the principal of them are these.

First, *Love is not puffed up.* As is the measure of love, so is the measure of humility. Nothing humbles the soul so deeply as love: it casts out all "high conceits, engendering pride;" all arrogance and overweening; makes us little, and poor, and base, and vile in our own eyes. It abases us both before God and man; makes us willing to be the least of all, and the servants of all, and teaches us to say, "A mote in the sun beam is little, but I am infinitely less in the presence of God."

Secondly, *Love is not provoked.* Our present English translation renders it, "it is not easily provoked." But how did the word *easily* come in? There is not a tittle of it in the text: the words of the apostle are simply these, οὐ παροξύνεται. Is it not probable, it was inserted by the translators, with a design to excuse St. Paul, for fear his practice should appear to contradict his doctrine? For we read (Acts xv, 36, et seq.), "And some days after,

Paul said unto Barnabas, Let us go again and visit our brethren in every city, where we have preached the word of the LORD, and see how they do. And Barnabas determined to take with them John, whose surname was Mark. But Paul thought not good to take with them one who departed from the work. And the contention was so sharp between them, that they departed asunder one from the other: and so Barnabas took Mark, and sailed unto Cyprus; and Paul chose Silas, and departed; being recommended by the brethren unto the grace of God. And he went through Syria and Cilicia, confirming the churches."

Would not any one think, on reading these words, that they were both equally sharp? That Paul was just as hot as Barnabas, and as much wanting in love as he? But the text says no such thing; as will be plain, if we consider first the occasion. When St. Paul proposed, that they should "again visit the brethren in every city, where they had preached the word," so far they were agreed. "And Barnabas determined to take with them John," because he was his sister's son, without receiving or asking St. Paul's advice. "But Paul thought not good to take him with them who had departed from them from Pamphylia;" whether through sloth or cowardice; "and went not with them to the work." And undoubtedly he thought right: he had reason on his side. The following words are, ἐγένετο οὖν παροξυσμός: literally, "And there was a fit of anger." It does not say in St. Paul: probably it was Barnabas alone; who thus supplied the want of reason with passion: "so that they parted asunder." And Barnabas, resolved to have his own way, did as his nephew had done before; "departed from the work,"—"took Mark with him, and sailed to Cyprus." But Paul went on in his work, "being recommended by the brethren to the grace of God:" which Barnabas seems not to have stayed for. "And he went through Syria and Cilicia, confirming the churches." From the whole account, it does not appear that St. Paul was in any fault: that he either felt any temper, or spoke any word contrary to the law of love. Therefore, not being in any fault, he does not need any excuse.

Certainly he who is full of love is "gentle towards all men." He "in meekness instructs those that oppose themselves;" that oppose what he loves most, even the truth of God, or that holiness without which no man shall see the Lord: not knowing but "God, peradventure, may bring them to the knowledge of the truth." However provoked, he does "not return evil for evil, or railing for railing." Yea, he "blesses those that curse him, and does good to them that despitefully use him and persecute him." He "is not overcome of evil, but" always "overcomes evil with good."

Thirdly, *Love is long suffering*. It endures not a few affronts, reproaches, injuries; but *all things,* which God is pleased to permit either men or devils to inflict. It arms the soul with inviolable patience: not harsh, stoical patience, but yielding as the air, which, making no resistance to the stroke, receives no harm thereby. The lover of mankind remembers him who suffered for us, "leaving us an example that we might tread in his steps." Accordingly, "if his enemy hunger, he feeds him; if he thirst, he gives him drink:" and by so doing, he "heaps coals of fire," of melting love, upon his head. "And many waters cannot quench this love: neither can the floods" of ingratitude "drown it."

II. We are, secondly, to inquire, What those things are, which it is commonly supposed, will supply the place of love? And the first of these is eloquence: a faculty of talking well, particularly on religious subjects. Men are generally inclined to think well of one that talks well. If he speaks properly and fluently of God, and the things of God, who can doubt of his being in God's favour?

And it is very natural for him to think well of himself: to have as favourable an opinion of himself as others have.

But men of reflection are not satisfied with this: they are not content with a flood of words; they prefer thinking before talking; and judge, one that knows much is far preferable to one that talks much. And it is certain, knowledge is an excellent gift of God; particularly knowledge of the Holy Scriptures, in which are contained all the depths of divine knowledge and wisdom. Hence it is generally thought that a man of much knowledge, knowledge of Scripture in particular, must not only be in the favour of God, but likewise enjoy a high degree of it.

But men of deeper reflection are apt to say, "I lay no stress upon any other knowledge, but the knowledge of God by faith. Faith is the only knowledge, which, in the sight of God, is of great price. 'We are saved by faith;' by faith alone: this is the one thing needful. He that believeth, and he alone, shall be saved everlastingly." There is much truth in this: it is unquestionably true, that "we are saved by faith:" consequently, that "he that believeth shall be saved, and he that believeth not shall be damned."

But some men will say, with the apostle James, "Show me thy faith without thy works" (if thou canst; but indeed it is impossible) ; "and I will show thee my faith by my works." And many are induced to think that good works, works of piety and mercy, are of far more consequence than faith itself; and will supply the want of every other qualification for heaven. Indeed, this seems to be the general sentiment, not only of the members of the church of Rome, but of Protestants also; not of the giddy and thoughtless, but the serious members of our own church.

And this cannot be denied, our Lord himself hath said, "Ye shall know them by their fruits:" by their works

ye know them that believe, and them that believe not.
But yet it may be doubted, whether there is not a surer
proof of the sincerity of our faith, than even our works:
that is, our willingly suffering for righteousness' sake:
especially if, after suffering reproach, and pain, and loss
of friends and substance, a man gives up life itself; yea,
by a shameful and painful death, by giving his body to be
burned, rather than he would give up faith and a good
conscience, by neglecting his known duty.

It is proper to observe here, first, What a beautiful
gradation there is, each step rising above the other, in
the enumeration of those several things, which some or
other of those that are called Christians, and are usually
accounted so, really believe will supply the absence of
love.  St. Paul begins at the lowest point, *talking well*,
and advances step by step; every one rising higher than
the preceding, till he comes to the highest of all.  A step
above eloquence is knowledge: faith is a step above this.
Good works are a step above that faith: and even above
this, is suffering for righteousness' sake.  Nothing is
higher than this, but Christian love: the love of our
neighbour, flowing from the love of God.

It may be proper to observe, secondly, That whatever
passes for religion in any part of the Christian world
(whether it be a part of religion, or no part at all, but
either folly, superstition, or wickedness) may with very
little difficulty be reduced to one or other of these heads.
Every thing which is supposed to be religion, either by
Protestants or Romanists, and is not, is contained under
one or another of these five particulars.  Make trial, as
often as you please, with any thing that is called religion,
but improperly so called, and you will find the rule to
hold without any exception.

III. I am now, in the third place, to demonstrate, to all
who have ears to hear, who do not harden themselves
against conviction, that neither any one of these five quali-

fications, nor all of them together, will avail any thing before God, without the love above described.

In order to do this in the clearest manner, we may consider them one by one. And, first, "Though I speak with the tongues of men and of angels;"—with an eloquence such as never was found in men, concerning the nature, attributes, and works of God, whether of creation or providence; though I were not herein a whit behind the chief of the apostles; preaching like St. Peter, and praying like St. John;—yet unless humble, gentle, patient love, be the ruling temper of my soul, I *am* no better in the judgment of God, "than sounding brass, or a rumbling cymbal." The highest eloquence, therefore, either in private conversation, or in public ministrations; the brightest talents either for preaching or prayer; if they were not joined with humble, meek, and patient resignation, might sink me the deeper into hell, but will not bring me one step nearer heaven.

A plain instance may illustrate this. I knew a young man between fifty and sixty years ago, who, during the course of several years, never endeavoured to convince any one of a religious truth, but he *was* convinced: and he never endeavoured to persuade any one to engage in a religious practice, but he was persuaded: what then? All that power of convincing speech, all that force of persuasion, if it was not joined with meekness and lowliness, with resignation and patient love, would no more qualify him for the fruition of God, than a clear voice, or a fine complexion. Nay, it would rather procure him a hotter place in everlasting burnings!

Secondly: "Though I have the gift of prophecy!"—of foretelling those future events which no creature can foresee; and "though I understand all [the] mysteries" of nature, of providence, and the word of God; and "have all knowledge" of things, divine or human, that any mortal ever attained to; though I can explain the most mysterious passages of Daniel, of Ezekiel, and the Revelation;—yet if I have not humility, gentleness, and resignation, "I am nothing" in the sight of God.

A little before the conclusion of the late war in Flanders, one who came from thence gave us a very strange relation. I knew not what judgment to form of this; but waited till John Haime should come over, of whose veracity I could no more doubt, than of his understanding. The account he gave was this:—"Jonathan Pyrah was a member of our society in Flanders. I knew him some years, and knew him to be a man of an unblamable character. One day he was summoned to appear before the board of general officers. One of them said, What is this which we hear of you? We hear you are turned prophet, and that you foretell the downfall of the bloody house of Bourbon, and the haughty house of Austria. We should be glad if you were a real prophet, and if your prophecies came true. But what sign do you give, to convince us you are so; and that your predictions will come to pass? He readily answered, 'Gentlemen, I give you a sign. To morrow at twelve o'clock, you shall have such a storm of thunder and lightning, as you never had before since you came into Flanders. I give you a second sign: as little as any of you expect any such thing, as little appearance of it as there is now, you shall have a general engagement with the French within three days. I give you a third sign: I shall be ordered to advance in the first line. If I am a false prophet, I shall be shot dead at the first discharge. But if I am a true prophet, I shall only receive a musket ball in the calf of my left leg.' At twelve the next day there was such thunder and lightning as they never had before in Flanders. On the third day, contrary to all expectation, was the general battle of Fontenoy. He was ordered to advance in the first line. And at the very first discharge, he did receive a musket ball in the calf of his left leg."

And yet all this profited him nothing, either for temporal or eternal happiness. When the war was over, he returned to England; but the story was got before him: in consequence of which he was sent for by the countess of St——s, and several other persons of quality, who were desirous to receive so surprising an account from his own mouth. He could not bear so much honour. It quite turned his brain. In a little time he ran stark mad. And so he continues to this day, living still, as I apprehend, on Wibsey Mooreside, within a few miles of Leeds.

And what would it profit a man to "have all knowledge," even that which is infinitely preferable to all other, the knowledge of the Holy Scripture? I knew a young man about twenty years ago, who was so thoroughly acquainted with the Bible, that if he was questioned concerning any Hebrew word in the Old, or any Greek word in the New Testament, he would tell, after a little pause, not only how often the one or the other occurred in the Bible, but also what it meant in every place. His name was Thomas Walsh.* Such a master of Biblic knowledge I never saw before, and never expect to see again. Yet if with all his knowledge he had been void of love; if he had been proud, passionate, or impatient: he and all his knowledge would have perished together, as sure as ever he was born.

"And though I have all faith, so that I could remove mountains."—The faith which is able to do this, cannot be the fruit of vain imagination, a mere madman's dream, a system of opinions; but must be a real work of God: otherwise it could not have such an effect. Yet if this faith does not work by love, if it does not produce universal holiness, if it does not bring forth lowliness, meekness, and resignation, it will profit me nothing. This is as

---

* His journal, written by himself, is extant.

## Charity.

certain a truth as any that is delivered in the whole oracles of God. All faith that is, that ever was, or ever can be, separate from tender benevolence to every child of man, friend or foe, Christian, Jew, heretic, or pagan;—separate from gentleness to all men; separate from resignation in all events, and contentedness in all conditions;—is not the faith of a Christian, and will stand us in no stead before the face of God.

Hear ye this, all you that are called Methodists! You, of all men living are most concerned herein. You constantly speak of salvation by faith: and you are in the right for so doing. You maintain (one and all) that a man is justified by faith, without the works of the law. And you cannot do otherwise, without giving up the Bible, and betraying your own souls. You insist upon it, that we are saved by faith: and undoubtedly, so we are. But consider, meantime, that let us have ever so much faith, and be our faith ever so strong, it will never save us from hell, unless it now save us from all unholy tempers; from pride, passion, impatience; from all arrogance of spirit, all haughtiness and over bearing; from wrath, anger, bitterness; from discontent, murmuring, fretfulness, peevishness. We are of all men most inexcusable, if having been so frequently guarded against that strong delusion, we still, while we indulge any of these tempers, bless ourselves, and dream we are in the way to heaven!

Fourthly: "Although I give all my goods to the poor;" —though I divide all my real, and all my personal estate into small portions (so the original word properly signifies); and diligently bestow it on those who, I have reason to believe, are the most proper objects;—yet if I am proud, passionate, or discontented; if I give way to any of these tempers; whatever good I may do to others, I do none to my own soul. Oh how pitiable a case is this! Who would not grieve, that these beneficent men should lose all their labour! It is true, many of them have a reward in this world, if not before, yet after their death. They have costly and pompous funerals. They have marble monuments of the most exquisite workmanship. They have epitaphs wrote in the most elegant strain, which extol their virtues to the skies. Perhaps they have yearly orations spoken over them, to transmit their memory to all generations. So have many founders of religious houses, of colleges, alms houses, and most charitable institutions. And it is an allowed rule, that none can exceed in the praise of the founder of his house, college, or hospital. But still what a poor reward is this! Will it add to their comfort or to their misery, suppose (which must be the case, if they did not die in faith) that they are in the hands of the devil and his angels! What insults, what cutting reproaches, would these occasion, from their infernal companions! Oh that they were wise! that all those who are zealous of good works, would put them in their proper place; would not imagine, they can supply the want of holy tempers; but take care that they may spring from them!

How exceeding strange must this sound in the ears of most of those who are, by the courtesy of England, called Christians! But stranger still is that assertion of the apostle, which comes in the last place: "Although I give my body to be burned, and have not love, it profiteth me nothing." Although rather than deny the faith, rather than commit a known sin, or omit a known duty, I voluntarily submit to a cruel death; "deliver up my body to be burned;" yet if I am under the power of pride, or anger, or fretfulness,—"it profiteth me nothing."

Perhaps this may be illustrated by an example. We have a remarkable account in the tracts of Dr. Geddes (a civilian, who was envoy from queen Anne to the court of Portugal, in the latter end of her reign). He was present at one of those *autos da fé* (acts of faith) wherein the Roman inquisitors burned heretics alive. One of the persons who was then brought out for execution, having been confined in the dungeons of the inquisition, had not seen the sun for many years. It proved a bright sunshiny day. Looking up, he cried out in surprise, "Oh how can any one who sees that glorious luminary, worship any but the God that made it!" A friar standing by, ordered them to run an iron gag through his lips, that he might speak no more. Now what did that poor man feel within when this order was executed? If he said in his heart, though he could not utter it with his lips, "Father, forgive them, for they know not what they do;" undoubtedly the angels of God were ready to carry his soul into Abraham's bosom. But if, instead of this, he cherished the resentment in his heart, which he could not express with his tongue, although his body was consumed by the flames, I will not say his soul went to paradise.

The sum of all that has been observed is this: whatever I speak, whatever I know, whatever I believe, whatever I do, whatever I suffer; if I have not the faith that worketh by love; that produces love to God and all mankind; I am not in the narrow way which leadeth to life; but in the broad road that leadeth to destruction. In other words: whatever eloquence I have; whatever natural or supernatural knowledge; whatever faith I have received from God; whatever works I do, whether of piety or mercy; whatever sufferings I undergo for conscience' sake, even though I resist unto blood: all these things put together, however applauded of men, will avail nothing before God, unless I am meek and lowly in heart, and can say in all things, "Not as I will, but as thou wilt!"

We conclude from the whole (and it can never be too much inculcated, because all the world votes on the other side) that true religion, in the very essence of it, is nothing short of holy tempers. Consequently all other religion, whatever name it bears, whether Pagan, Mohammedan, Jewish, or Christian; and whether Popish or Protestant, Lutheran or Reformed; without these, is lighter than vanity itself.

Let every man, therefore, that has a soul to be saved, see that he secure this one point. With all his eloquence, his knowledge, his faith, works, and sufferings, let him hold fast this "one thing needful." He that through the power of faith, endureth to the end in humble, gentle, patient love; he, and he alone, shall, through the merits of Christ, "inherit the kingdom prepared from the foundation of the world."

London, Oct. 15, 1784.

## SCRIPTURAL CHRISTIANITY.

[*Preached at St. Mary's, Oxford, Before the University, on August 24, 1744.*]

"Whosoever heareth the sound of the trumpet, and taketh not warning; if the sword come, and take him away, his blood shall be upon his own head."—Ezek. xxxiii, 4.

"And they were all filled with the Holy Ghost."—Acts iv, 31.

THE same expression occurs in the second chapter, where we read, "When the day of pentecost was fully come, they were all," (the apostles, with the women, and the mother of Jesus, and his brethren,) "with one accord, in one place. And suddenly there came a sound from heaven, as of a rushing mighty wind. And there appeared unto them cloven tongues, like as of fire, and it sat upon each of them. And they were all filled with the Holy Ghost:" One immediate effect thereof was, "They began to speak with other tongues;" insomuch, that both the Parthians, Medes, Elamites, and the other strangers who "came together, when this was noised abroad, heard them speak, in their several tongues, the wonderful works of God," Acts ii, 1-6.

In this chapter we read, that when the apostles and brethren had been praying, and praising God, "the place was shaken where they were assembled together, and they were all filled with the Holy Ghost," Acts iv, 31. Not that we find any visible appearance here, such as had been in the former instance: nor are we informed that the *extraordinary gifts* of the Holy Ghost were then given to all or any of them; such as the "gift of healing, of working other miracles, of prophecy, of discerning spirits, the speaking with divers kinds of tongues, and the interpretation of tongues," 1 Cor. xii, 9, 10.

Whether these gifts of the Holy Ghost were designed to remain in the church throughout all ages, and whether or no they will be restored at the nearer approach of the "restitution of all things," are questions which it is not needful to decide. But it is needful to observe this, that, even in the infancy of the church, God divided them with a sparing hand. Were all even then prophets? Were all workers of miracles? Had all the gifts of healing? Did all speak with tongues? No, in no wise. Perhaps not one in a thousand. Probably none but the teachers in the church, and only some of them, 1 Cor. xii, 28-30. It was, therefore, for a more excellent purpose than this, that "they were all filled with the Holy Ghost."

It was to give them (what none can deny to be essential to all Christians in all ages) the mind which was in Christ, those holy fruits of the Spirit, which whosoever hath not, is none of his; to fill them with "love, joy, peace, long suffering, gentleness, goodness," Gal. v, 22-24; to endue them with faith, (perhaps it might be rendered, *fidelity*,) with meekness and temperance; to enable them to crucify the flesh, with its affections and lusts, its passions and desires, and, in consequence of that inward change, to fulfil all outward righteousness, to "walk as Christ also walked," "in the work of faith, in the patience of hope, the labour of love," 1 Thess. i, 3.

Without busying ourselves then in curious, needless inquiries, touching those *extraordinary* gifts of the Spirit, let us take a nearer view of these his *ordinary* fruits, which we are assured will remain throughout all ages;—of that great work of God among the children of men, which we are used to express by one word, Christianity; not as it implies a set of opinions, a system of doctrines, but as it refers to men's hearts and lives. And this Christianity it may be useful to consider under three distinct views:

I. As beginning to exist in individuals:

## Scriptural Christianity.

II. As spreading from one to another:

III. As covering the earth.

I design to close these considerations with a plain practical application.

I. And first, let us consider Christianity in its rise, as beginning to exist in individuals.

Suppose, then, one of those who heard the apostle Peter preaching repentance and remission of sins, was pricked to the heart, was convinced of sin, repented, and then believed in Jesus. By this faith of the operation of God, which was the very substance, or subsistence of things hoped for, Heb. xi, 1, the demonstrative evidence of invisible things, he instantly received the spirit of adoption, whereby he now cried, "Abba, Father," Rom. viii, 15. Now first it was that he could call Jesus Lord, by the Holy Ghost, 1 Cor. xii, 3, the Spirit itself bearing witness with his spirit that he was a child of God, Rom. viii, 15. Now it was that he could truly say, "I live not, but Christ liveth in me; and the life which I now live in the flesh, I live by faith in the Son of God, who loved me and gave himself for me," Gal. ii, 20.

This, then, was the very essence of his faith, a divine ελεγχος (*evidence or conviction*) of the love of God the Father, through the Son of his love, to him a sinner, now accepted in the Beloved. And, "being justified by faith, he had peace with God," Rom. v, 1, yea, "the peace of God ruling in his heart;" a peace, which passing all understanding, (παντα νϙν, all barely rational conception) kept his heart and mind from all doubt and fear, through the knowledge of him in whom he had believed. He could not therefore "be afraid of any evil tidings;" for his "heart stood fast believing in the Lord." He feared not what man could do unto him, knowing the very hairs of his head were all numbered. He feared not all the powers of darkness, whom God was daily bruising under his feet. Least of all was he afraid to die; nay, he desired to "depart and to be with Christ," Phil. i, 23; who, "through death, had destroyed him that had the power of death, even the devil, and delivered them who, through fear of death, were all their lifetime (till then) subject to bondage," Heb. ii, 15.

His soul therefore magnified the Lord, and his spirit rejoiced in God his Saviour. "He rejoiced in him with joy unspeakable, who had reconciled him to God, even the Father;" "in whom he had redemption through his blood, the forgiveness of sins." He rejoiced in that witness of God's Spirit with his spirit, that he was a child of God; and more abundantly, "in hope of the glory of God;" in hope of the glorious image of God, and full renewal of his soul in righteousness and true holiness; and in hope of that crown of glory, that "inheritance, incorruptible, undefiled, and that fadeth not away."

"The love of God was also shed abroad in his heart, by the Holy Ghost, which was given unto him," Rom. v, 5. "Because he was a son, God had sent forth the Spirit of his Son into his heart, crying, Abba, Father!" Gal. iv, 6. And that filial love of God was continually increased by the witness he had in himself (1 John v, 10) of God's pardoning love to him; by "beholding what manner of love it was, which the Father had bestowed upon him, that he should be called a child of God," 1 John iii, 1. So that God was the desire of his eyes, and the joy of his heart; his portion in time and in eternity.

He that thus *loved* God, could not but love his brother also; and "not in word only, but in deed and in truth." "If God," said he, "so loved us, we ought also to love one another," 1 John iv, 11; yea, every soul of man, as "the mercy of God is over all his works," Psa. cxlv, 9. Agreeably hereto, the affection of this lover of God embraced all mankind for his sake; not excepting those whom he had never seen in the flesh, or those of whom he knew nothing more than that they were "the offspring of God,"

## Scriptural Christianity. 141

for whose souls his Son had died; not excepting the *evil* and *unthankful,* and least of all his enemies, those who hated, or persecuted, or despitefully used him for his Master's sake. These had a peculiar place, both in his heart and in his prayers. He loved them "even as Christ loved us."

And "love is not puffed up," 1 Cor. xiii, 4. It abases to the dust every soul wherein it dwells: accordingly, he was lowly of heart, little, mean, and vile in his own eyes. He neither sought, nor received the praise of men, but that which cometh of God only. He was meek and long suffering, gentle to all, and easy to be entreated. Faithfulness and truth never forsook him; they were "bound about his neck, and wrote on the table of his heart." By the same Spirit he was enabled to be temperate in all things, refraining his soul even as a weaned child. He was "crucified to the world, and the world crucified to him;" superior to "the desire of the flesh, the desire of the eye, and the pride of life." By the same almighty love was he saved, both from passion and pride; from lust and vanity; from ambition and covetousness; and from every temper which was not in Christ.

It may easily be believed, he who had this love in his heart, would work no evil to his neighbour. It was impossible for him, knowingly and designedly, to do harm to any man. He was at the greatest distance from cruelty and wrong, from any unjust or unkind action. With the same care did he "set a watch before his mouth, and keep the door of his lips," lest he should offend in tongue, either against justice, or against mercy or truth. He put away all lying, falsehood, and fraud; neither was guile found in his mouth. He spake evil of no man; nor did an unkind word ever come out of his lips.

And, as he was deeply sensible of the truth of that word, "without me ye can do nothing," and, consequently, of the need he had to be watered of God every moment;

so he continued daily in all the ordinances of God, the stated channels of his grace to man: "in the apostles' doctrine," or teaching, receiving that food of the soul with all readiness of heart; in "the breaking of bread," which he found to be the communion of the body of Christ; and "in the prayers" and praises offered up by the great congregation. And thus, he daily "grew in grace," increasing in strength, in the knowledge and love of God.

But it did not satisfy him, barely to abstain from doing evil. His soul was athirst to do good. The language of his heart continually was, "My Father worketh hitherto, and I work." My Lord went about doing good; and shall not I tread in his steps? As he had opportunity, therefore, if he could do no good of a higher kind, he fed the hungry, clothed the naked, helped the fatherless or stranger, visited and assisted them that were sick or in prison. He gave all his goods to feed the poor. He rejoiced to labour or to suffer for them; and wherein soever he might profit another, there especially to "deny himself." He counted nothing too dear to part with for them, as well remembering the word of his Lord, "Inasmuch as ye have done it unto one of the least of these my brethren, ye have done it unto me," Matt. xxv, 40.

Such was Christianity in its rise. Such was a Christian in ancient days. Such was every one of those, who, when they heard the threatenings of the chief priests and elders, "lifted up their voice to God with one accord, and were all filled with the Holy Ghost. The multitude of them that believed were of one heart and of one soul." (So did the love of him in whom they had believed, constrain them to love one another!) "Neither said any of them that aught of the things which he possessed was his own; but they had all things common." So fully were they crucified to the world, and the world crucified to them! "And they continued steadfastly with one accord

## Scriptural Christianity. 143

in the apostles' doctrine, and in the breaking of bread, and in prayer," Acts ii, 42. "And great grace was upon them all; neither was there any among them that lacked: for as many as were possessors of lands or houses, sold them, and brought the prices of the things that were sold, and laid them down at the apostles' feet: and distribution was made unto every man according as he had need," Acts iv, 31-35.

II. Let us take a view, in the second place, of this Christianity, as spreading from one to another, and so gradually making its way into the world: for such was the will of God concerning it, who did not "light a candle to put it under a bushel, but that it might give light to all that were in the house." And this our Lord had declared to his first disciples, "Ye are the salt of the earth," "the light of the world;" at the same time that he gave that general command, "Let your light so shine before men, that they may see your good works, and glorify your Father which is in heaven," Matt. v, 13-16.

And, indeed, supposing a few of these lovers of mankind to see "the whole world lying in wickedness," can we believe they would be unconcerned at the sight, at the misery of those for whom their Lord died? Would not their bowels yearn over them, and their hearts melt away for very trouble? Could they then stand idle all the day long, even were there no command from him whom they loved? Rather would they not labour, by all possible means, to pluck some of these brands out of the burning? Undoubtedly they would: they would spare no pains to bring back whomsoever they could of those poor "sheep that had gone astray, to the great Shepherd and Bishop of their souls," 1 Pet. ii, 25.

So the Christians of old did. They laboured, having opportunity, "to do good unto all men," Gal. vi, 10, warning them to flee from the wrath to come; now, now to escape the damnation of hell. They declared, "The times

of ignorance God winked at; but now he calleth all men
every where to repent," Acts xvii, 30. They cried aloud,
Turn ye, turn ye from your evil ways; "so iniquity shall
not be your ruin," Ezek. xviii, 30. They reasoned with
them of temperance and righteousness, or justice, of the
virtues opposite to their reigning sins, and of judgment
to come; of the wrath of God, which would surely be
executed on evil doers in that day when he should judge
the world, Acts xxiv, 25.

They endeavoured herein to speak to every man severally
as he had need. To the careless, to those who lay
unconcerned in darkness and in the shadow of death, they
thundered, "Awake, thou that sleepest: arise from the
dead, and Christ shall give thee light:" but to those who
were already awakened out of sleep, and groaning under
a sense of the wrath of God, their language was, "We
have an Advocate with the Father; he is the propitiation
for our sins." Meantime, those who had believed, they
provoked to love and to good works; to patient continuance
in well doing; and to abound more and more in that
holiness without which no man can see the Lord, Heb.
xii, 14.

And their labour was not in vain in the Lord. His
word ran, and was glorified. It grew mightily and prevailed.
But so much the more did offences prevail also.
The world in general were offended, "because they testified
of it, that the works thereof were evil," John vii, 7.
The men of pleasure were offended, not only because
these men were made as it were, to reprove their
thoughts:—"He professeth," said they, "to have the
knowledge of God; he calleth himself the child of the
Lord; his life is not like other men's; his ways are of
another fashion; he abstaineth from our ways, as from
filthiness; he maketh his boast, that God is his Father,"
Wisd. ii, 13-16:—but much more, because so many of
their companions were taken away, and would no more

run with them to the same excess of riot, 1 Pet. iv, 4.
The men of reputation were offended, because, as the
gospel spread, they declined in the esteem of the people;
and because many no longer dared to give them flattering
titles, or to pay man the homage due to God only. The
men of trade called one another together, and said, "Sirs,
ye know that by this craft we have our wealth. But ye
see and hear that these men have persuaded and turned
away much people. So that this our craft is in danger to
be set at nought," Acts xix, 25, &c. Above all, the men
of religion, so called, the men of *outside* religion, "the
saints of the world," were offended, and ready at every
opportunity to cry out, "Men of Israel, help! we have
found these men pestilent fellows, movers of sedition
throughout the world," Acts xxiv, 5. "These are the
men that teach all men, every where, against the people,
and against the law," Acts xxi, 28.

Thus it was that the heavens grew black with clouds,
and the storm gathered amain. For the more Christianity spread, the more hurt was done, in the account of
those who received it not; and the number increased of
those who were more and more enraged at these "men
who thus turned the world upside down," Acts xvii, 6;
insomuch that more and more cried out, "Away with such
fellows from the earth; it is not fit that they should live;"
yea, and sincerely believed, that whosoever should kill
them would do God service.

Meanwhile they did not fail to cast out their name as
evil, Luke vi, 22; so that this "sect was every where
spoken against," Acts xxviii, 22. Men said all manner of
evil of them, even as had been done of the prophets that
were before them, Matt. v, 11. And whatsoever any
would affirm, others would believe. So that offences
grew as the stars of heaven for multitude. And hence
arose, at the time foreordained of the Father, persecution
in all its forms. Some, for a season, suffered only shame

and reproach; some, "the spoiling of their goods;" "some had trial of mocking and scourging; some of bonds and imprisonment;" and others "resisted unto blood," Heb. x, 34, xi, 36, &c.

Now it was that the pillars of hell were shaken, and the kingdom of God spread more and more. Sinners were every where "turned from darkness to light, and from the power of Satan unto God." He gave his children "such a mouth, and such wisdom, as all their adversaries could not resist:" and their lives were of equal force with their words. But above all, their sufferings spake to all the world. They "approved themselves the servants of God, in afflictions, in necessities, in distresses, in stripes, in imprisonments, in tumults, in labours; in perils in the sea, in perils in the wilderness, in weariness and painfulness, in hunger and in thirst, in cold and nakedness," 2 Cor. vi, 4, &c. And when, having fought the good fight, they were led as sheep to the slaughter, and offered up on the sacrifice and service of their faith, then the blood of each found a voice, and the heathen owned, "He being dead yet speaketh."

Thus did Christianity spread itself in the earth. But how soon did the tares appear with the wheat, and the *mystery of iniquity* work as well as the *mystery of godliness!* How soon did Satan find a seat, even *in the temple of God,* "till the woman fled into the wilderness," and "the faithful were again minished from the children of men!" Here we tread a beaten path: the still increasing corruptions of the succeeding generations have been largely described from time to time, by those witnesses God raised up, to show that he had "built his church upon a Rock, and the gates of hell should not (wholly) prevail against her," Matt. xvi, 18.

III. But shall we not see greater things than these? Yea, greater than have been yet from the beginning of the World. Can Satan cause the truth of God to fail, or

## Scriptural Christianity. 147

his promises to be of none effect? If not, the time will come when Christianity will prevail over all, and cover the earth. Let us stand a little, and survey (the third thing which was proposed) this strange sight, a *Christian World*. Of this the prophets of old inquired and searched diligently, 1 Pet. i, 10, 11, &c: of this the Spirit which was in them testified: "It shall come to pass in the last days, that the mountain of the Lord's house shall be established on the top of the mountains, and shall be exalted above the hills, and all nations shall flow unto it. And they shall beat their swords into ploughshares, and their spears into pruning hooks. Nation shall not lift up sword against nation; neither shall they learn war any more," Isa. ii, 1-4. "In that day there shall be a root of Jesse, which shall stand for an ensign of the people. To it shall the Gentiles seek, and his rest shall be glorious. And it shall come to pass in that day, that the Lord shall set his hand again to recover the remnant of his people; and he shall set up an ensign for the nations, and shall assemble the outcasts of Israel, and gather together the dispersed of Judah, from the four corners of the earth," Isa. xi, 10-12. "The wolf shall then dwell with the lamb, and the leopard shall lie down with the kid, and the calf, and the young lion, and the fatling together; and a little child shall lead them. They shall not hurt nor destroy, saith the Lord, in all my holy mountain. For the earth shall be full of the knowledge of the Lord, as the waters cover the sea," Isa. xi, 6-9.

To the same effect are the words of the great apostle, which it is evident have never yet been fulfilled. "Hath God cast away his people? God forbid." "But through their fall salvation is come to the Gentiles." "And if the diminishing of them be the riches of the Gentiles, how much more their fulness?" "For I would not, brethren, that ye should be ignorant of this mystery, That blindness in part is happened to Israel, until the fulness of the

Gentiles be come in; and so all Israel shall be saved," Rom. xi, 1, 11, 25, 26.

Suppose now the fulness of time to be come, and the prophecies to be accomplished. What a prospect is this! All is "peace, quietness and assurance for ever." Here is no din of arms, no "confused noise," no "garments rolled in blood." "Destructions are come to a perpetual end:" wars are ceased from the earth. Neither are there any intestine jars remaining; no brother rising up against brother; no country or city divided against itself, and tearing out its own bowels. Civil discord is at an end for evermore, and none is left either to destroy or hurt his neighbour. Here is no oppression to make even the wise man mad; no extortion to grind the face of the poor; no robbery or wrong; no rapine or injustice; for all are "content with such things as they possess." Thus "righteousness and peace have kissed each other," Psa. lxxxv, 10; they have "taken root and filled the land:" "righteousness flourishing out of the earth," and "peace looking down from heaven."

And with righteousness or justice, mercy is also found. The earth is no longer full of cruel habitations. The Lord hath destroyed both the blood-thirsty and malicious, the envious and revengeful man. Were there any provocation, there is none that now knoweth to return evil for evil; but indeed there is none that doeth evil, no, not one; for all are harmless as doves. And being filled with peace and joy in believing, and united in one body, by one spirit, they all love as brethren, they are all of one heart, and of one soul. "Neither saith any of them, that aught of the things which he possesseth is his own." There is none among them that lacketh; for every man loveth his neighbour as himself. And all walk by one rule, "Whatever ye would that men should do unto you even so do unto them."

It follows, that no unkind word can ever be heard

among them, no strife of tongues, no contention of any kind, no railing or evil speaking; but every one "opens his mouth with wisdom, and in his tongue there is the law of kindness." Equally incapable are they of fraud or guile; their love is without dissimulation: their words are always the just expression of their thoughts, opening a window into their breast, that whosoever desires may look into their hearts, and see that only love and God are there.

Thus, where the Lord omnipotent taketh to himself his mighty power and reigneth, doth he "subdue all things to himself," cause every heart to overflow with love, and fill every mouth with praise. "Happy are the people that are in such a case: yea, blessed are the people who have the Lord for their God," Psa. cxliv, 15. "Arise, shine, (saith the Lord,) for thy light is come, and the glory of the Lord is risen upon thee." "Thou hast known that I, the Lord, am thy Saviour, and thy Redeemer, the mighty God of Jacob. I have made thy officers peace, and thy exacters righteousness. Violence shall no more be heard in the land, wasting nor destruction within thy borders; but thou shalt call thy walls, salvation, and thy gates, praise." "Thy people are all righteous; they shall inherit the land for ever; the branch of my planting, the work of my hands, that I may be glorified." "The sun shall be no more thy light by day; neither for brightness shall the moon give light unto thee: but the Lord shall be unto thee an everlasting light and thy God thy glory," Isa. lx, 1, 16-19.

IV. Having thus briefly considered Christianity, as beginning, as going on, and as covering the earth; it remains only that I should close the whole with a plain, practical application.

And first, I would ask, Where does this Christianity now exist? Where, I pray, do the Christians live? Which is the country, the inhabitants whereof are all thus filled with the Holy Ghost? Are all of one heart and of one soul? Cannot suffer one among them to lack anything, but continually give to every man as he hath need? Who, one and all, have the love of God filling their hearts, and constraining them to love their neighbour as themselves? Who have all "put on bowels of mercy, humbleness of mind, gentleness, long suffering?" Who offend not in any kind, either by word or deed, against justice, mercy, or truth; but in every point do unto all men, as they would these should do unto them. With what propriety can we term any a Christian country, which does not answer this description? Why then, let us confess we have never yet seen a Christian country upon earth.

I beseech you, brethren, by the mercies of God, if ye do account me a madman or a fool, yet, *as a fool bear with me.* It is utterly needful that some one should use great plainness of speech towards you. It is more especially needful at *this* time; for who knoweth but it is the *last?* Who knoweth how soon the righteous Judge may say, "I will no more be intreated for this people." "Though Noah, Daniel, and Job, were in this land, they should but deliver their own souls." And who will use this plainness, if I do not? Therefore I, even I, will speak. And I adjure you, by the living God, that ye steel not your breasts against receiving a blessing at *my* hands. Do not say in your hearts, *Non persuadebis, etiamsi persuaseris:* or in other words, Lord, thou shalt not *send by whom thou wilt send;* let me rather perish in my blood, than be saved by this man!

Brethren, "I am persuaded better things of you, though I thus speak." Let me ask you then, in tender love, and in the spirit of meekness, Is this city a Christian city? Is Christianity, scriptural Christianity, found here? Are we, considered as a community of men, so "filled with the Holy Ghost," as to enjoy in our hearts, and show forth in our lives, the genuine fruits of that Spirit? Are all

## Scriptural Christianity. 151

the magistrates, all heads and governors of colleges and halls, and their respective societies, (not to speak of the inhabitants of the town,) "of one heart and one soul?" Is "the love of God shed abroad in our hearts?" Are our tempers the same that were in him? And are our lives agreeable thereto? Are we "holy as He who hath called us is holy, in all manner of conversation?"

I intreat you to observe, that here are no peculiar notions now under consideration: that the question moved is not concerning *doubtful opinions,* of one kind or another, but concerning the undoubted, fundamental branches (if there be any such) of our common Christianity. And for the decision thereof, I appeal to your own consciences, guided by the word of God. He therefore that is not condemned by his own heart let him go free.

In the fear, then, and in the presence of the great God before whom both you and I shall shortly appear, I pray you that are in authority over us, whom I reverence for your office' sake, to consider, (and not after the manner of dissemblers with God,) are you "filled with the Holy Ghost?" Are you lively portraitures of Him whom ye are appointed to represent among men? "I have said ye are gods," ye magistrates and rulers; ye are by office so nearly allied to the God of heaven! In your several stations and degrees, ye are to show forth unto us "the Lord our governor." Are all the thoughts of your hearts, all your tempers and desires suitable to your high calling? Are all your words like unto those which come out of the mouth of God? Is there in all your actions, dignity and love? A greatness which words cannot express, which can flow only from a heart full of God; and yet consistent with the character of "man that is a worm, and the son of man that is a worm!"

Ye venerable men, who are more especially called to form the tender minds of youth, to dispel thence the shades of ignorance and error and train them up to be wise unto salvation, are you "filled with the Holy Ghost?" With all those "fruits of the Spirit," which your important office so indispensably requires? Is your heart whole with God? Full of love and zeal to set up his kingdom on earth? Do you continually remind those under your care, that the one rational end of all our studies, is to know, love, and serve "the only true God, and Jesus Christ whom he hath sent?" Do you inculcate upon them day by day, that love alone never faileth: (whereas, whether there be tongues, they shall fail, or philosophical knowledge, it shall vanish away;) and that without love, all learning is but splendid ignorance, pompous folly, vexation of spirit? Has all you teach an actual tendency to the love of God, and of all mankind for his sake? Have you an eye to this end in whatever you prescribe, touching the kind, the manner, and the measure of their studies; desiring and labouring that, wherever the lot of these young soldiers of Christ is cast, they may be so many burning and shining lights, adorning the gospel of Christ in all things? And permit me to ask, Do you put forth all your strength in the vast work you have undertaken? Do you labour herein with all your might? Exerting every faculty of your soul? Using every talent which God hath lent you, and that to the uttermost of your power?

Let it not be said, that I speak here, as if all under your care were intended to be clergymen. Not so: I only speak as if they were all intended to be Christians. But what example is set them by us who enjoy the beneficence of our forefathers? by fellows, students, scholars; more especially those who are of some rank and eminence? Do ye, brethren, abound in the fruits of the Spirit, in lowliness of mind, in self denial and mortification, in seriousness and composure of spirit, in patience, meekness, sobriety, temperance; and in unwearied, restless endeavours to do good in every kind unto all men, to relieve their

## Scriptural Christianity. 153

outward wants, and to bring their souls to the true knowledge and love of God? Is this the general character of fellows of colleges? I fear it is not. Rather, have not pride and haughtiness of spirit, impatience and peevishness, sloth and indolence, gluttony and sensuality, and even proverbial uselessness, been objected to us, perhaps not always by our enemies, nor wholly without ground? Oh that God would roll away this reproach from us, that the very memory of it might perish for ever!

Many of us are more immediately consecrated to God, called to minister in holy things. Are we then patterns to the rest, "in word, in conversation, in charity, in spirit, in faith, in purity?" 2 Cor. iv, 2. Is there written on our forehead and on our heart, "Holiness to the Lord?" From what motives did we enter upon this office? Was it indeed with a single eye "to serve God, trusting that we were inwardly moved by the Holy Ghost, to take upon us this ministration, for the promoting of his glory, and the edifying of his people?" And have we "clearly determined, by God's grace, to give ourselves wholly to this office?" Do we forsake and set aside, as much as in us lies, all worldly cares and studies? Do we apply ourselves wholly to this one thing, and draw all our cares and studies this way? Are we apt to teach? Are we taught of God, that we may be able to teach others also? Do we know God? Do we know Jesus Christ? Hath "God revealed his Son in us?" And hath he made us "able ministers of the new covenant?" Where then are the "seals of our apostleship?" Who, that were dead in trespasses and sins, have been quickened by our word? Have we a burning zeal to save souls from death, so that for their sake we often forget even to eat our bread? Do we speak plainly, "by manifestation of the truth commending ourselves to every man's conscience in the sight of God?" 2 Cor. iv, 2. Are we dead to the world and the things of the world, "laying up all our treasure in heaven?" Do we lord over God's heritage? Or are we the least, the servants of all? When we bear the reproach of Christ, does it sit heavy upon us? Or do we rejoice therein? When we are smitten on the one cheek, do we resent it? Are we impatient of affronts? Or do we turn the other also; not resisting the evil, but overcoming evil with good? Have we a bitter zeal, inciting us to strive sharply and passionately with them that are out of the way? Or is our zeal the flame of love, so as to direct all our words with sweetness, lowliness, and meekness of wisdom?

Once more, What shall we say concerning the youth of this place? Have you either the form or the power of Christian godliness? Are you humble, teachable, advisable; or stubborn, self-willed, heady, and high minded? Are you obedient to your superiors as to parents? Or do you despise those to whom you owe the tenderest reverence? Are you diligent in your easy business, pursuing your studies with all your strength? Do you redeem the time, crowding as much work into every day as it can contain? Rather, are ye not conscious to yourselves, that you waste away day after day, either in reading what has no tendency to Christianity, or in gaming, or in—you know not what? Are you better managers of your fortune than of your time? Do you, out of principle, take care to owe no man any thing? Do you "remember the sabbath day to keep it holy;" to spend it in the more immediate worship of God? When you are in his house, do you consider that God is there? Do you behave, "as seeing him that is invisible?" Do you know how to possess your bodies in sanctification and honour? Are not drunkenness and uncleanness found among you? Yea, are there not of you who "glory in their shame?" Do not many of you "take the name of God in vain," perhaps habitually, without either remorse or fear? Yea, are there not a multitude of you that are forsworn? I fear, a swiftly increasing multitude. Be not surprised, brethren. Before God and this congregation, I own myself to have been of the number, solemnly swearing to observe all those customs, which I knew nothing of; and those statutes, which I did not so much as read over, either then, or for some years after. What is perjury, if this is not? But if it be, oh what a weight of sin, yea, sin of no common dye, lieth upon us! And doth not the Most High regard it?

May it not be one of the consequences of this, that so many of you are a generation of triflers; triflers with God, with one another, and with your own souls? For, how few of you spend, from one week to another, a single hour in private prayer! How few have any thought of God in the general tenor of your conversation! Who of you is, in any degree, acquainted with the work of his Spirit, his supernatural work in the souls of men? Can you bear, unless now and then, in a church, any talk of the Holy Ghost? Would not you take it for granted, if one began such a conversation, that it was either hypocrisy or enthusiasm? In the name of the Lord God Almighty, I ask, What religion are you of? Even the talk of Christianity, ye cannot, will not bear. Oh, my brethren! what a Christian city is this! "It is time for thee, Lord, to lay to thine hand!"

For, indeed, what probability, what possibility rather, (speaking after the manner of men,) is there that Christianity, scriptural Christianity, should be again the religion of this place? That all orders of men among us should speak and live as men "filled with the Holy Ghost?" By whom should this Christianity be restored? By those of you that are in authority? Are you convinced then that this is scriptural Christianity? Are you desirous it should be restored? And do ye not count your fortune, liberty, life, dear unto yourselves, so ye may be instrumental in the restoring of it? But, suppose ye have this desire, who hath any power proportioned to the effect? Perhaps some of you have made a few faint attempts, but with how small success! Shall Christianity then be restored by young, unknown, inconsiderable men? I know not whether ye yourselves could suffer it. Would not some of you cry out, "Young man, in so doing thou reproachest us?" But there is no danger of your being put to the proof; so hath iniquity overspread us like a flood. Whom then shall God send? The famine, the pestilence, (the last messengers of God to a guilty land,) or the sword? The armies of the Romish aliens to reform us into our first love? Nay, "rather let us fall into thy hand, oh Lord, and let us not fall into the hand of man."

Lord, save, or we perish! Take us out of the mire that we sink not! Oh help us against these enemies! for vain is the help of man. Unto thee all things are possible. According to the greatness of thy power, preserve thou those that are appointed to die; and preserve us in the manner that seemeth to thee good; not as we will, but as thou wilt!

## THE GENERAL SPREAD OF THE GOSPEL.

"The earth shall be full of the knowledge of the Lord, as the waters cover the sea."—Isa. xi, 9.

In what a condition is the world at present! How does darkness, intellectual darkness, ignorance, with vice and misery attendant upon it, cover the face of the earth! From the accurate inquiry, made with indefatigable pains by our ingenious countryman, Mr. Brerewood; (who travelled himself over a great part of the known world, in order to form the more exact judgment;) supposing the world to be divided into thirty parts, nineteen of them are professed heathens, altogether as ignorant of Christ, as if he had never come into the world: six of the remaining parts are professed Mohammedans: so that only five in thirty are so much as nominally Christians!

And let it be remembered, that since this computation was made, many new nations have been discovered; numberless islands, particularly in the South sea, large and well inhabited: but by whom? By heathens of the basest sort; many of them inferior to the beasts of the field. Whether they eat men or no, (which indeed I cannot find any sufficient ground to believe,) they certainly kill all that fall into their hands. They are, therefore, more savage than lions; who kill no more creatures than are necessary to satisfy their present hunger. See the real dignity of human nature! Here it appears in its genuine purity, not polluted either by those "general corrupters, kings," or by the least tincture of religion! What will Abbé Raynal (that determined enemy to monarchy and revelation) say to this?

A little, and but a little, above the heathens in religion, are the Mohammedans. But how far and wide has this miserable delusion spread over the face of the earth! Insomuch that the Mohammedans are considerably more in number (as six to five) than Christians. And by all the accounts which have any pretence to authenticity, these are also, in general, as utter strangers to all true religion as their four footed brethren; as void of mercy as lions and tigers; as much given up to brutal lusts as bulls or goats: so that they are in truth a disgrace to human nature, and a plague to all that are under the iron yoke.

It is true, a celebrated writer (Lady Mary Wortley Montague,) gives a very different character of them. With the finest flow of words, in the most elegant language, she labours to wash the Æthiop white. She represents them as many degrees above the Christians; as some of the most amiable people in the world; as possessed of all the social virtues; as some of the most accomplished of men. But I can in no wise receive her report: I cannot rely upon her authority. I believe those round about her had just as much religion as their admirer had, when she was admitted into the interior parts of the grand Seignior's seraglio. Notwithstanding, therefore, all that such a witness does or can say in their favour, I believe the Turks in general are little, if at all better, than the generality of the heathens.

And little if at all better than the Turks, are the Christians in the Turkish dominions; even the best of them; those that live in the Morea, or are scattered up and down in Asia. The more numerous bodies of Georgian, Circassian, Mengrelian Christians, are a proverb of reproach to the Turks themselves; not only for their deplorable ignorance, but for their total, stupid, barbarous irreligion.

From the most authentic accounts we can obtain of the southern Christians, those in Abyssinia, and of the northern churches, under the jurisdiction of the patriarch of Moscow, we have reason to fear they are much in the same condition, both with regard to knowledge and religion, as those in Turkey. Or if those in Abyssinia are more civilized, and have a larger share of knowledge, yet they do not appear to have any more religion than either the Mohammedans or Pagans.

The western churches seem to have the pre-eminence over all these in many respects. They have abundantly more knowledge: they have more scriptural and more rational modes of worship. Yet two thirds of them are still involved in the corruptions of the church of Rome; and most of these are entirely unacquainted with either the theory or practice of religion. And as to those who are called Protestants or reformed, what acquaintance with it have they? Put Papist and Protestants, French and English together, the bulk of one, and of the other nation; and what manner of Christians are they? Are they "holy as He that hath called them is holy?" Are they filled with "righteousness, and peace, and joy in the Holy Ghost?" Is there "that mind in them which was also in Christ Jesus?" And do they "walk as Christ also walked?" Nay, they are as far from it as hell is from heaven!

Such is the present state of mankind in all parts of the world! But how astonishing is this, if there is a God in heaven; and if his eyes are over all the earth! Can he despise the work of his own hand? Surely this is one of the greatest mysteries under heaven! How is it possible to reconcile this with either the wisdom or goodness of God? And what can give ease to a thoughtful mind under so melancholy a prospect? What but the consideration, that things will not always be so; that another scene will soon be opened? God will be jealous of his honour; he will arise and maintain his own cause. He will judge the prince of this world, and spoil him of his usurped dominion. He will give his Son "the heathen for his inheritance, and the uttermost parts of the earth for his possession." "The earth shall be filled with the knowledge of the Lord, as the waters cover the sea." The loving knowledge of God, producing uniform, uninterrupted holiness and happiness, shall cover the earth; shall fill every soul of man.

"Impossible," will some men say, "yea, the greatest of all impossibilities, that we should see a Christian world; yea, a Christian nation, or city! How can these things be?" On one supposition, indeed, not only all impossibility, but all difficulty vanishes away. Only suppose the Almighty to act *irresistibly,* and the thing is done; yea, with just the same ease as when "God said, Let there be light; and there was light." But then, man would be man no longer: his inmost nature would be changed. He would no longer be a moral agent, any more than the sun or the wind; as he would no longer be endued with liberty,—a power of choosing, or self determination: consequently, he would no longer be capable of virtue or vice; of reward or punishment.

But setting aside this clumsy way of cutting the knot which we are not able to untie; how can all men be made holy and happy, while they continue men? While they still enjoy both the understanding, the affections, and the liberty, which are essential to a moral agent? There seems to be a plain, simple way of removing this difficulty, without entangling ourselves in any subtle, metaphysical disquisitions. As God is one, so the work of God is uniform in all ages. May we not then conceive how he *will* work on the souls of men in times to come, by considering how he *does* work *now,* and how he *has* wrought in times past?

Take one instance of this, and such an instance as you cannot easily be deceived in. You know how God wrought in *your own* soul, when he first enabled you to say, "The life I now live, I live by faith in the Son of God, who loved me, and gave himself for me." He did not take away your understanding; but enlightened and strengthened it. He did not destroy any of your affections: rather they were more vigorous than before.

Least of all did he take away your liberty; your power of choosing good or evil: he did not *force* you: but, being *assisted* by his grace, you, like Mary, *chose* the better part. Just so has he *assisted* five in one house to make that happy *choice;* fifty or five hundred in one city; and many thousands in a nation;—without depriving any of them of that liberty which is essential to a moral agent.

Not that I deny, that there are exempt cases, wherein

"The overwhelming power of saving grace"

does, for a time, work as irresistibly as lightning falling from heaven. But I speak of God's general manner of working, of which I have known innumerable instances; perhaps more within fifty years last past, than any one in England or in Europe. And with regard even to these exempt cases; although God does work irresistibly *for the time,* yet I do not believe that there is any human soul, in which God works irresistibly *at all times.* Nay, I am fully persuaded there is not. I am persuaded there are no men living that have not many times "resisted the Holy Ghost," and made void "the counsel of God against themselves." Yea, I am persuaded, every child of God has had, at some time, "life and death set before him," eternal life and eternal death; and has in himself the casting voice. So true is that well known saying of St. Austin; (one of the noblest he ever uttered;) *"Qui fecit nos sine nobis, non salvabit nos sine nobis:"* He that made us without ourselves, will not save us without ourselves. Now in the same manner as God *has* converted so many to himself, without destroying their liberty; he *can* undoubtedly convert whole nations, or the whole world: and it is as easy to him to convert a world, as one individual soul.

Let us observe what God has done already. Between fifty and sixty years ago, God raised up a few young men, in the university of Oxford, to testify those grand truths, which were then little attended to:—That without holiness no man shall see the Lord;—that this holiness is the work of God, who worketh in us both to will and to do;—that he doeth it of his own good pleasure, merely for the merits of Christ;—that this holiness is the mind that was in Christ; enabling us to walk as he also walked;—that no man can be thus sanctified till he be justified;—and, that we are justified by faith alone. These great truths they declared on all occasions, in private and in public; having no design but to promote the glory of God, and no desire but to save souls from death.

From Oxford, where it first appeared, the little leaven spread wider and wider. More and more saw the truth as it is in Jesus, and received it in the love thereof. More and more found "redemption through the blood of Jesus, even the forgiveness of sins." They were born again of his Spirit, and filled with righteousness, and peace, and joy in the Holy Ghost. It afterwards spread to every part of the land, and a little one became a thousand. It then spread into North Britain, and Ireland; and a few years after, into New York, Pennsylvania, and many other provinces in America, even as high as Newfoundland and Nova Scotia. So that, although at first this "grain of mustard seed" was "the least of all the seeds;" yet, in a few years, it grew into a "large tree, and put forth great branches."

Generally, when these truths, justification by faith in particular, were declared in any large town, after a few days or weeks, there came suddenly on the great congregation,—not in a corner, at London, Bristol, Newcastle-upon-Tyne, in particular,—a violent and impetuous power, which,

"Like mighty winds or torrents fierce,
Did then opposers all o'erturn."

And this frequently continued, with shorter or longer

## The General Spread of the Gospel. 163

intervals, for several weeks or months. But it gradually subsided, and then the work of God was carried on by gentle degrees; while that Spirit, in watering the seed that had been sown, in confirming and strengthening them that had believed,

> "Deign'd his influence to infuse,
> Secret, refreshing as the silent dews."

And this difference in his usual manner of working, was observable, not only in Great Britain and Ireland, but in every part of America, from south to north, wherever the word of God came with power.

Is it not then highly probable, that God will carry on his work in the same manner as he has begun it? That he *will* carry it on, I cannot doubt; however Luther may affirm, that a revival of religion never lasts above a generation,—that is, thirty years; (whereas the present revival has already continued above fifty;) or however prophets of evil may say, "All will be at an end when the first instruments are removed." There will then, very probably, be a great shaking; but I cannot induce myself to think, that God has wrought so glorious a work, to let it sink and die away in a few years: no, I trust, this is only the beginning of a far greater work, the dawn of "the latter day glory."

And is it not probable, I say, that he will carry it on, in the same manner as he has begun? At the first breaking out of this work in this or that place, there may be a shower, a torrent of grace; and so at some other particular seasons, which "the Father has reserved in his own power:" but in general, it seems, the kingdom of God will not "come with observation;" but will silently increase, wherever it is set up, and spread from heart to heart, from house to house, from town to town, from one kingdom to another. May it not spread, first, through the remaining provinces; then, through the isles of North

America; and, at the same time, from England to Holland, where there is already a blessed work in Utrecht, Haerlem, and many other cities? Probably it will spread from these to the Protestants in France, to those in Germany, and those in Switzerland; then to Sweden, Denmark, Russia, and all the other Protestant nations in Europe.

May we not suppose, that the same leaven of pure and undefiled religion, of the experimental knowledge and love of God, of inward and outward holiness, will afterwards spread to the Roman Catholics in Great Britain, Ireland, Holland; in Germany, France, Switzerland; and in all other countries, where Romanists and Protestants live intermixed, and familiarly converse with each other? Will it not then be easy for the wisdom of God to make a way for religion, in the life and power thereof, into those countries that are merely Popish; as Italy, Spain, Portugal? And may it not be gradually diffused from thence to all that name the name of Christ, in the various provinces of Turkey, in Abyssinia, yea, and in the remotest parts, not only of Europe, but of Asia, Africa, and America?

And in every nation under heaven, we may reasonably believe, God will observe the same order which he hath done from the beginning of Christianity. "They shall all know me, saith the Lord;" not from the greatest to the least; (this is that wisdom of the world, which is foolishness with God;) but, "from the least to the greatest;" that the praise may not be of men, but of God? Before the end, even the rich shall enter into the kingdom of God. Together with them will enter in the great, the noble, the honourable; yea, the rulers, the princes, the kings of the earth. Last of all, the wise and learned, the men of genius, the philosophers, will be convinced that they are fools: will be "converted, and become as little children," and "enter into the kingdom of God."

Then shall be fully accomplished to the house of Israel, the spiritual Israel, of whatever people or nation, that gracious promise; "I will put my laws in their minds, and write them in their hearts: and I will be to them a God, and they shall be to me a people. And they shall not teach every man his neighbour, and every man his brother; saying, Know the Lord: for they shall all know me, from the least to the greatest. For I will be merciful to their unrighteousness, and their sins and their iniquities will I remember no more." Then shall "the times of [universal] refreshment come from the presence of the Lord." The grand "pentecost" shall "fully come," and "devout men in every nation under heaven," however distant in place from each other, shall "all be filled with the Holy Ghost;" and they will "continue steadfast in the apostles' doctrine, and in the fellowship, and in the breaking of bread, and in prayers;" they will "eat their meat," and do all that they have to do, "with gladness and singleness of heart. Great grace will be upon them all;" and they will be "all of one heart and of one soul." The natural, necessary consequence of this will be the same as it was in the beginning of the Christian church: "None of them will say, that aught of the things which he possesses is his own; but they will have all things common. Neither will there be any among them that want: for as many as are possessed of lands or houses, will sell them; and distribution will be made to every man, according as he has need." All their desires, meantime, and passions, and tempers, will be cast in one mould; while all are doing the will of God on earth, as it is done in heaven. All their "conversation will be seasoned with salt," and will "minister grace to the hearers;" seeing it will not be so much they that speak, "as the Spirit of their Father that speaketh in them." And there will be no "root of bitterness springing up," either to defile or trouble them: there will be no

Ananias or Sapphira, to bring back the cursed love of money among them; there will be no partiality; no "widows neglected in the daily ministration:" Consequently, there will be no temptation to any murmuring thought, or unkind word of one against another; while,

> "They all are of one heart and soul,
> And only love inspires the whole."

The grand stumbling block being thus happily removed out of the way, namely, the lives of the Christians; the Mohammedans will look upon them with other eyes, and begin to give attention to their words. And as their words will be clothed with divine energy, attended with the demonstration of the Spirit and power, those of them that fear God will soon take knowledge of the spirit whereby the Christians speak. They will "receive with meekness the engrafted word," and will bring forth fruit with patience. From them the leaven will soon spread to those who, till then, had no fear of God before their eyes. Observing the *Christian dogs,* as they used to term them, to have changed their nature; to be sober, temperate, just, benevolent; and that, in spite of all provocations to the contrary; from admiring their lives, they will surely be led to consider and embrace their doctrine. And then the Saviour of sinners will say, "The hour is come; I will glorify my Father: I will seek and save the sheep that were wandering on the dark mountains. Now will I avenge myself of my enemy, and pluck the prey out of the lion's teeth. I will resume my own, for ages lost: I will claim the purchase of my blood." So he will go forth in the greatness of his strength, and all his enemies shall flee before him. All the prophets of lies shall vanish away, and all the nations that had followed them shall acknowledge the great Prophet of the Lord, "mighty in word and deed;" and "shall honour the Son, even as they honour the Father."

## The General Spread of the Gospel. 167

And then the grand stumbling block being removed from the heathen nations also; the same Spirit will be poured out upon them, even those that remain in the uttermost parts of the sea. The poor American savage will no more ask, "What are the Christians better than us?"—when they see their steady practice of universal temperance, and of justice, mercy, and truth. The Malabarian heathen will have no more room to say, "Christian man take my wife: Christian man much drunk: Christian man kill man! *Devil-Christian!* Me no Christian." Rather, seeing how far the Christians exceed their own countrymen in whatsoever things are lovely and of good report, they will adopt a very different language, and say, *Angel-Christian!* The holy lives of the Christians will be an argument they will not know how to resist: seeing the Christians steadily and uniformly practise what is agreeable to the law written in their own hearts, their prejudices will quickly die away, and they will gladly receive "the truth as it is in Jesus."

We may reasonably believe, that the heathen nations which are mingled with the Christians, and those that, bordering upon Christian nations, have constant and familiar intercourse with them, will be some of the first who learn to worship God in spirit and in truth; those, for instance, that live on the continent of America, or in the islands that have received colonies from Europe. Such are likewise all those inhabitants of the East Indies, that adjoin to any of the Christian settlements. To these may be added, numerous tribes of Tartars, the heathen parts of the Russias, and the inhabitants of Norway, Finland, and Lapland. Probably these will be followed by those more distant nations with whom the Christians trade; to whom they will impart what is of infinitely more value than earthly pearls, or gold and silver. The God of love will then prepare his messengers, and make a way into the polar regions; into the deepest recesses of America, and into the interior parts of Africa; yea, into the heart of China and Japan, with the countries adjoining them. And "their sound" will then "go forth into all lands, and their voice to the ends of the earth!"

But one considerable difficulty still remains: there are very many heathen nations in the world that have no intercourse, either by trade or any other means, with Christians of any kind. Such are the inhabitants of the numerous islands in the South sea, and probably in all large branches of the ocean. Now what shall be done for these poor outcasts of men? "How shall they believe," saith the apostle, "in him of whom they have not heard? And how shall they hear without a preacher?" You may add, "And how shall they preach, unless they be sent?" Yea, but is not God able to send them? Cannot he raise them up, as it were, out of the stones? And can he ever want means of sending them? No: were there no other means, he can "take them by his Spirit," as he did Ezekiel, chap. iii, 12, or by his angel, as he did Philip, Acts viii, and set them down wheresoever it pleaseth him. Yea, he can find out a thousand ways, to foolish man unknown. And he surely will: for heaven and earth may pass away; but his word shall not pass away: he will give his Son "the uttermost parts of the earth for his possession."

And so all Israel too shall be saved. For "blindness has happened to Israel," as the great apostle observes, Rom. xi, 25, &c, till the fulness of the "Gentiles be come in." Then "the Deliverer that cometh out of Sion shall turn away iniquity from Jacob." "God hath now concluded them all in unbelief, that he may have mercy upon all." Yea, and he will so have mercy upon all Israel, as to give them all temporal, with all spiritual blessings. For this is the promise: "For the Lord thy God will gather thee from all nations, whither the Lord thy God hath scattered thee. And the Lord thy God will bring thee into the land which thy fathers possessed, and thou shalt

## The General Spread of the Gospel. 169

possess it. And the Lord thy God will circumcise thine heart, and the heart of thy seed, to love the Lord thy God with all thine heart, and with all thy soul," Deut. xxx, 3. Again: "I will gather them out of all countries, whither I have driven them: and I will bring them again unto this place, and I will cause them to dwell safely: and I will give them one heart, and one way, that they may fear me for ever. I will put my fear in their hearts, that they shall not depart from me. And I will plant them in this land assuredly, with my whole heart and with my whole soul," Jer. xxxii, 37, &c. Yet again: "I will take you from among the heathen, and gather you out of all countries, and will bring you into your own land. Then will I sprinkle clean water upon you, and ye shall be clean: from all your filthiness, and from all your idols, will I cleanse you. And ye shall dwell in the land that I gave to your fathers; and ye shall be my people, and I will be your God," Ezek. xxxvi, 24, &c.

At that time will be accomplished all those glorious promises made to the Christian church, which will not then be confined to this or that nation, but will include all the inhabitants of the earth. "They shall not hurt nor destroy in all my holy mountain," Isa. xi, 9. "Violence shall no more be heard in thy land, wasting nor destruction within thy borders; but thou shalt call thy walls Salvation, and thy gates Praise." Thou shalt be encompassed on every side with salvation, and all that go through thy gates shall praise God. "The sun shall be no more thy light by day; neither for brightness shall the moon give light unto thee: but the Lord shall be unto thee an everlasting light, and thy God thy glory." The light of the sun and moon shall be swallowed up in the light of his countenance, shining upon thee. "Thy people also shall be all righteous, . . . the work of my hands, that I may be glorified." "As the earth bringeth forth her bud, and the garden causeth the things that are sown in it to spring forth; so the Lord God will cause righteousness and praise to spring forth before all the nations," Isa. lx, 14, &c, and lxi, 11.

This I apprehend to be the answer, yea, the only full and satisfactory answer that can be given, to the objection against the wisdom and goodness of God, taken from the present state of the world. It will not always be thus: these things are only permitted for a season by the great Governor of the world, that he may draw immense, eternal good out of this temporary evil. This is the very key which the apostle himself gives us in the words above recited: "God hath concluded them all in unbelief, that he might have mercy upon all." In view of this glorious event, how well may we cry out; "Oh the depth of the riches both of the wisdom and knowledge of God!" although for a season "his judgments were unsearchable, and his ways past finding out," Rom. xi, 32, 33. It is enough, that we are assured of this one point that all these transient evils will issue well, will have a happy conclusion; and that "mercy first and last will reign." All unprejudiced persons may see with their eyes, that he is already renewing the face of the earth: and we have strong reason to hope that the work he hath begun, he will carry on unto the day of the Lord Jesus; that he will never intermit this blessed work of his Spirit, until he has fulfilled all his promises, until he hath put a period to sin, and misery, and infirmity, and death, and re-established universal holiness and happiness, and caused all the inhabitants of the earth to sing together, "Hallelujah, the Lord God Omnipotent reigneth!" "Blessing, and glory, and wisdom, and honour, and power, and might, be unto our God for ever and ever!" Rev. vii, 12.

# TREATISES.

### A PLAIN ACCOUNT
#### OF
## THE PEOPLE CALLED METHODISTS,*
#### IN A LETTER TO
### THE REV. MR. PERRONET,
##### VICAR OF SHOREHAM, IN KENT.

##### Written in the year 1748.

[1749. *Works*, v, 176-90.]

REVEREND AND DEAR SIR,—Some time since, you desired an account of the whole economy of the people commonly called *Methodists*. And you received a true (as far as it went) but not a full account. To supply what I think was wanting in that, I send you this account, that you may know, not only their practice on every head, but likewise the reasons whereon it is grounded, the occasion of every step they have taken, and the advantages reaped thereby.

But I must premise, that as they had not the least expectation, at first, of any thing like what has since followed, so they had no previous design or plan at all; but every thing arose just as the occasion offered. They saw or felt some impending or pressing evil, or some

---

\* "In that little tract, 'A Plain Account of the People called Methodists,' you see our whole plan. We have but one point in view; to be altogether Christians, Scriptural, rational Christians."—*Letter to Miss Bishop*, 1767. *Works*, vii, 159.

good end necessary to be pursued. And many times they fell unawares on the very thing which secured the good, or removed the evil. At other times, they consulted on the most probable means, following only common sense and Scripture: though they generally found, in looking back, something in Christian antiquity likewise, very nearly parallel thereto.

I. About ten years ago, my brother and I were desired to preach in many parts of London. We had no view therein, but so far as we were able, (and we knew God could work by whomsoever it pleased him,) to convince those who would hear what true Christianity was, and to persuade them to embrace it.

The points we chiefly insisted upon were four: First, that orthodoxy, or right opinions, is, at best, but a very slender part of religion, if it can be allowed to be any part of it at all;* that neither does religion consist in negatives, in bare harmlessness of any kind; nor merely in externals, in doing good, or using the means of grace, in works of piety (so called) or of charity; that it is nothing short of, or different from, "the mind that was in Christ;" the image of God stamped upon the heart; inward righteousness, attended with the peace of God; and "joy in the Holy Ghost." Secondly, that the only way under heaven to this religion is, to "repent and

---

* "Indeed it is not a little sin, to represent trifles as necessary to salvation; such as going of pilgrimages, or any thing that is not expressly enjoined in the holy Scripture. Among these we may undoubtedly rank orthodoxy, or right opinions. We know indeed that wrong opinions in religion naturally lead to wrong tempers, or wrong practices; and that, consequently, it is our bounden duty to pray that we may have a right judgment in all things. But still a man may judge as accurately as the devil, and yet be as wicked as he."—From one of the last sermons, *On the Wedding Garment*, 1790. *Works*, ii, 459.

"Though right tempers cannot subsist without right opinion, yet right opinion may subsist without right tempers. There may be a right opinion of God, without either love, or one right temper toward him. Satan is a proof of it."—*Remarks on "A Defense of Aspasio Vindicated,"* 1766. *Works*, vi, 126.

believe the Gospel;" or (as the Apostle words it) "repentance toward God, and faith in our Lord Jesus Christ." Thirdly, that by this faith, "he that worketh not, but believeth on him that justifieth the ungodly, is justified freely by his grace, through the redemption which is in Jesus Christ." And, Lastly, that "being justified by faith," we taste of the heaven to which we are going; we are holy and happy; we tread down sin and fear, and "sit in heavenly places with Christ Jesus."

Many of those who heard this began to cry out that we brought "strange things to their ears; that this was doctrine which they never heard before, or at least never regarded. They "searched the Scriptures whether these things were so," and acknowledged "the truth as it is in Jesus." Their hearts also were influenced as well as their understandings, and they determined to follow "Jesus Christ, and him crucified."

Immediately they were surrounded with difficulties;— all the world rose up against them; neighbours, strangers, acquaintance, relations, friends, began to cry out amain, "Be not righteous overmuch; why shouldest thou destroy thyself?" Let not "much religion make thee mad."

One, and another, and another came to us, asking, what they should do, being distressed on every side; as every one strove to weaken, and none to strengthen, their hands in God. We advised them, "Strengthen you one another. Talk together as often as you can. And pray earnestly with and for one another, that you may 'endure to the end, and be saved.'" Against this advice we presumed there could be no objection; as being grounded on the plainest reason, and on so many scriptures both of the Old Testament and New, that it would be tedious to recite them.

They said, "But we want you likewise to talk with us often, to direct and quicken us in our way, to give us the advices which you well know we need, and to pray with us, as well as for us." I asked, Which of you desire this?

Let me know your names and places of abode. They did so. But I soon found they were too many for me to talk with severally so often as they wanted it. So I told them, "If you will all of you come together every Thursday, in the evening, I will gladly spend some time with you in prayer, and give you the best advice I can."

Thus arose, without any previous design on either side, what was afterward called *a Society;*\* a very innocent name, and very common in London, for any number of people associating themselves together. The thing proposed in their associating themselves together was obvious to every one. They wanted to "flee from the wrath to come," and to assist each other in so doing. They therefore united themselves "in order to pray together, to receive the word of exhortation, and to watch over one another in love, that they might help each other to work out their salvation."

There is one only condition previously required in those

---

\* " I now advised the serious part of the congregation to form themselves into a sort of little society, and to meet once or twice a week, in order to instruct, exhort, and reprove one another. And out of these I selected a smaller number, for a more intimate union with each other ; in order to which I met them together at my house every Sunday in the afternoon. [Savannah, Ga., 1736.] . . .

"After the evening service, as many of my parishioners as desire it, meet at my house (as they do also on Wednesday evening), and spend about an hour in prayer, singing, and mutual exhortation. A small number (mostly those who design to communicate the next day) meet here on Saturday evening ; and a few of these come to me on the other evenings, and pass half an hour in the same employment.

"I cannot but observe that these were the first rudiments of the Methodist societies. But who could then have even formed a conjecture whereto they would grow ? . . .

" On Monday, May 1 [1738], our little society began in London. But it may be observed, the first rise of Methodism, so called, was in November, 1729, when four of us met together at Oxford ; the second was at Savannah, in April, 1736, when twenty or thirty persons met at my house ; the last was at London, on this day, when forty or fifty of us agreed to meet together every Wednesday evening, in order to a free conversation, begun and ended with singing and prayer."—*A Short History of the People Called Methodists*, 1781. *Works*, vii, 347-8.

who desire admission into this society,—"a desire to flee from the wrath to come, to be saved from their sins."\* (See the Rules of the United Societies.) They now likewise agreed, that as many of them as had an opportunity would meet together every Friday, and spend the dinner hour in crying to God, both for each other, and for all mankind.

It quickly appeared, that their thus uniting together answered the end proposed therein. In a few months, the far greater part of those who had begun to "fear God, and work righteousness," but were not united together, grew faint in their minds, and fell back into what they were before. Meanwhile the far greater part of those who were thus united together continued "striving to enter in at the strait gate," and to "lay hold on eternal life."

On reflection, I could not but observe, This is the very thing which was from the beginning of Christianity. In the earliest times, those whom God had sent forth "preached the Gospel to every creature." And the οἱ ἀκροαταί, "the body of hearers," were mostly either Jews or

---

\*"One circumstance more is quite peculiar to the people called Methodists; that is, the terms upon which any person may be admitted into their society. They do not impose, in order to their admission, any opinions whatever. Let them hold particular or general redemption, absolute or conditional decrees; let them be Churchmen or Dissenters, Presbyterians or Independents, it is no obstacle. Let them choose one mode of baptism or another, it is no bar to their admission. The Presbyterian may be a Presbyterian still; the Independent or Anabaptist use his own mode of worship. So may the Quaker; and none will contend with him about it. They think, and let think. One condition and one only, is required,—A real desire to save their soul. Where this is, it is enough: they desire no more: they lay stress upon nothing else: they ask only, 'Is thy heart herein as my heart? If it be, give me thy hand.'

"Is there any other society in Great Britain or Ireland that is so remote from bigotry? that is so truly of a catholic spirit? so ready to admit all serious persons without distinction? Where, then, is there such another society in Europe? in the habitable world? I know none. Let any man show it me that can. Till then let no one talk of the bigotry of the Methodists."—*Thoughts upon a Late Phenomenon*, 1788. *Works*, vii, 321.

Heathens. But as soon as any of these were so convinced of the truth, as to forsake sin and seek the Gospel salvation, they immediately joined them together, took an account of their names, advised them to watch over each other, and met these κατηχούμενοι, "catechumens" (as they were then called), apart from the great congregation, that they might instruct, rebuke, exhort, and pray with them, and for them, according to their several necessities.

But it was not long before an objection was made to this, which had not once entered into my thought:— "Is not this making a schism? Is not the joining these people together, gathering churches out of churches?"

It was easily answered, If you mean only gathering people out of buildings called churches, it is. But if you mean, dividing Christians from Christians, and so destroying Christian fellowship, it is not. For (1.) These were not Christians before they were thus joined. Most of them were barefaced Heathens. (2.) Neither are they Christians, from whom you suppose them to be divided. You will not look me in the face and say they are. What! drunken Christians! cursing and swearing Christians! lying Christians! cheating Christians! If these are Christians at all, they are devil Christians, as the poor Malabarians term them. (3.) Neither are they divided any more than they were before, even from these wretched devil Christians. They are as ready as ever to assist them, and to perform every office of real kindness toward them. (4.) If it be said, "But there are some true Christians in the parish, and you destroy the Christian fellowship between these and them;" I answer, That which never existed, cannot be destroyed. But the fellowship you speak of never existed. Therefore it cannot be destroyed. Which of those true Christians had any such fellowship with these? Who watched over them in love? Who marked their growth in grace? Who advised and exhorted them from time to time? Who prayed with them and for them, as they had need? This, and this alone is Christian fellowship: but, alas! where is it to be found? Look east or west, north or south; name what parish you please: is this Christian fellowship there? Rather, are not the bulk of the parishioners a mere rope of sand? What Christian connection is there between them? What intercourse in spiritual things? What watching over each other's souls? What bearing of one another's burdens? What a mere jest is it then, to talk so gravely of destroying what never was! The real truth is just the reverse of this: we introduce Christian fellowship where it was utterly destroyed. And the fruits of it have been peace, joy, love, and zeal for every good word and work.

II. But as much as we endeavoured to watch over each other, we soon found some who did not live the Gospel. I do not know that any hypocrites were crept in; for indeed there was no temptation: but several grew cold, and gave way to the sins which had long easily beset them. We quickly perceived there were many ill consequences of suffering these to remain among us. It was dangerous to others; inasmuch as all sin is of an infectious nature. It brought such a scandal on their brethren as exposed them to what was not properly the reproach of Christ. It laid a stumbling block in the way of others, and caused the truth to be evil spoken of.

We groaned under these inconveniences long, before a remedy could be found. The people were scattered so wide in all parts of the town, from Wapping to Westminster, that I could not easily see what the behaviour of each person in his own neighbourhood was: so that several disorderly walkers did much hurt before I was apprized of it.

At length, while we were thinking of quite another thing, we struck upon a method for which we have cause to bless God ever since. I was talking with several of the society in Bristol concerning the means of paying the debts there, when one stood up and said, "Let every member of the society give a penny a week till all are paid." Another answered, "But many of them are poor, and cannot afford to do it." "Then," said he, "put eleven of the poorest with me; and if they can give any thing, well: I will call on them weekly; and if they can give nothing, I will give for them as well as for myself. And each of you call on eleven of your neighbours weekly; receive what they give, and make up what is wanting." It was done. In a while, some of these informed me, they found such and such a one did not live as he ought. It struck me immediately, "This is the thing; the very thing we have wanted so long." I called together all the leaders of the classes (so we used to term them and their companies), and desired, that each would make a particular inquiry into the behaviour of those whom he saw weekly. They did so. Many disorderly walkers were detected. Some turned from the evil of their ways. Some were put away from us. Many saw it with fear, and rejoiced unto God with reverence.

As soon as possible, the same method was used in London and all other places. Evil men were detected and reproved. They were borne with for a season. If they forsook their sins, we received them gladly; if they obstinately persisted therein, it was openly declared that they were not of us. The rest mourned and prayed for them, and yet rejoiced, that, as far as in us lay, the scandal was rolled away from the society.

It is the business of a leader,

(1.) To see each person in his class, once a week at the least, in order to inquire how their souls prosper; to advise, reprove, comfort, or exhort, as occasion may require; to receive what they are willing to give, toward the relief of the poor.

(2.) To meet the minister and the stewards of the society, in order to inform the minister of any that are sick, or of any that are disorderly and will not be reproved; to pay to the stewards what they have received of their several classes in the week preceding.

At first they visited each person at his own house; but this was soon found not so expedient. And that on many accounts: (1.) It took up more time than most of the leaders had to spare. (2.) Many persons lived with masters, mistresses, or relations, who would not suffer them to be thus visited. (3.) At the houses of those who were not so averse, they often had no opportunity of speaking to them but in company. And this did not at all answer the end proposed, of exhorting, comforting, or reproving. (4.) It frequently happened that one affirmed what another denied. And this could not be cleared up without seeing them together. (5.) Little misunderstandings and quarrels of various kinds frequently arose among relations or neighbours; effectually to remove which, it was needful to see them all face to face. Upon all these considerations it was agreed, that those of each class should meet all together. And by this means, a more full inquiry was made into the behaviour of every person. Those who could not be visited at home, or no otherwise than in company, had the same advantage with others. Advice or reproof was given as need required, quarrels made up, misunderstandings removed: and after an hour or two spent in this labour of love, they concluded with prayer and thanksgiving.

It can scarce be conceived what advantages have been reaped from this little prudential regulation. Many now happily experienced that Christian fellowship of which they had not so much as an idea before. They began to "bear one another's burdens," and naturally to "care for each other." As they had daily a more intimate acquaintance with, so they had a more endeared affection for, each other. And "speaking the truth in love, they grew up into him in all things, who is the Head, even

Christ; from whom the whole body, fitly joined together, and compacted by that which every joint supplied, according to the effectual working in the measure of every part, increased unto the edifying itself in love."

But notwithstanding all these advantages, many were at first extremely averse to meeting thus. Some, viewing it in a wrong point of light, not as a privilege (indeed an invaluable one), but rather a restraint, disliked it on that account, because they did not love to be restrained in any thing. Some were ashamed to speak before company. Others honestly said, "I do not know why; but I do not like it."

Some objected, "There were no such meetings when I came into the society first: and why should there now? I do not understand these things, and this changing one thing after another continually." It was easily answered: It is pity but they had been at first. But we knew not then either the need or the benefit of them. Why we use them, you will readily understand, if you read over the rules of the society. That with regard to these little prudential helps we are continually changing one thing after another, is not a weakness or fault, as you imagine, but a peculiar advantage which we enjoy. By this means we declare them all to be merely prudential, not essential, not of divine institution. We prevent, so far as in us lies, their growing formal or dead. We are always open to instruction; willing to be wiser every day than we were before, and to change whatever we can change for the better.

Another objection was, "There is no Scripture for this, for classes and I know not what." I answer (1.) There is no Scripture against it. You cannot show one text that forbids them. (2.) There is much Scripture for it, even all those texts which enjoin the substance of those various duties whereof this is only an indifferent circumstance, to be determined by reason and experience. (3.) You seem not to have observed, that the Scripture, in most points, gives only general rules; and leaves the particular circumstances to be adjusted by the common sense of mankind. The Scripture, for instance, gives that general rule, "Let all things be done decently and in order." But common sense is to determine, on particular occasions, what order and decency require. So, in another instance, the Scripture lays it down as a general, standing direction: "Whether ye eat or drink, or whatsoever ye do, do all to the glory of God." But it is common prudence which is to make the application of this, in a thousand particular cases.

"But these," said another, "are all man's inventions." This is but the same objection in another form. And the same answer will suffice for any reasonable person. These are man's inventions. And what then? That is, they are methods which men have found, by reason and common sense, for the more effectually applying several Scripture rules, couched in general terms, to particular occasions.

They spoke far more plausibly than these, who said, "The thing is well enough in itself. But the leaders are insufficient for the work: they have neither gifts nor graces for such an employment." I answer (1.) Yet such leaders as they are, it is plain God has blessed their labour. (2) If any of these is remarkably wanting in gifts or grace, he is soon taken notice of and removed. (3.) If you know any such, tell it to me, not to others, and I will endeavour to exchange him for a better. (4.) It may be hoped they will all be better than they are, both by experience and observation, and by the advices given them by the minister every Tuesday night, and the prayers (then in particular) offered up for them.

III. About this time, I was informed that several persons in Kingswood frequently met together at the school; and, when they could spare the time, spent the greater part of the night in prayer, and praise, and thanksgiving.

Some advised me to put an end to this; but, upon weighing the thing thoroughly, and comparing it with the practice of the ancient Christians, I could see no cause to forbid it. Rather, I believed it might be made of more general use. So I sent them word, I designed to watch with them on the Friday nearest the full moon, that we might have light thither and back again. I gave public notice of this the Sunday before, and, withal, that I intended to preach; desiring they, and they only, would meet me there, who could do it without prejudice to their business or families. On Friday abundance of people came. I began preaching between eight and nine; and we continued till a little beyond the noon of night, singing, praying, and praising God.

This we have continued to do once a month ever since, in Bristol, London, and Newcastle, as well as Kingswood; and exceeding great are the blessings we have found therein: it has generally been an extremely solemn season; when the word of God sunk deep into the heart, even of those who till then knew him not. If it be said, "This was only owing to the novelty of the thing (the circumstance which still draws such multitudes together at those seasons), or perhaps to the awful silence of the night:" I am not careful to answer in this matter. Be it so: however, the impression then made on many souls has never since been effaced. Now, allowing that God did make use either of the novelty or any other indifferent circumstance, in order to bring sinners to repentance, yet they are brought. And herein let us rejoice together.

Nay, may I not put the case farther yet? If I can probably conjecture that, either by the novelty of this ancient custom, or by any other indifferent circumstance, it is in my power to "save a soul from death, and hide a multitude of sins," am I clear before God if I do it not, if I do not snatch that brand out of the burning?

IV. As the society increased, I found it required still

greater care to separate the precious from the vile. In order to this, I determined, at least once in three months, to talk with every member myself, and to inquire at their own mouths, as well as of their leaders and neighbours, whether they grew in grace and in the knowledge of our Lord Jesus Christ. At these seasons I likewise particularly inquire whether there be any misunderstanding or difference among them; that every hinderance of peace and brotherly love may be taken out of the way.

To each of those of whose seriousness and good conversation I found no reason to doubt, I gave a testimony under my own hand, by writing their name on a ticket prepared for that purpose; every ticket implying as strong a recommendation of the person to whom it was given as if I had wrote at length, "I believe the bearer hereof to be one that fears God, and works righteousness."

Those who bore these tickets (these σύμβολα or *tesseræ*, as the ancients termed them, being of just the same force with the ἐπιστολαὶ συστατικαί, *commendatory letters,* mentioned by the Apostle), wherever they came, were acknowledged by their brethren, and received with all cheerfulness. These were likewise of use in other respects. By these it was easily distinguished, when the society were to meet apart, who were members of it, and who not. These also supplied us with a quiet and inoffensive method of removing any disorderly member. He has no new ticket at the quarterly visitation (for so often the tickets are changed); and hereby it is immediately known that he is no longer of the community.

V. The thing which I was greatly afraid of all this time, and which I resolved to use every possible method of preventing, was, a narrowness of spirit, a party zeal, a being straitened in our own bowels; that miserable bigotry which makes many so unready to believe that there is any work of God but among themselves. I thought it might be a help against this, frequently to read, to all who were willing to hear, the accounts I received from time to time of the work which God is carrying on in the earth, both in our own and other countries, not among us alone, but among those of various opinions and denominations. For this I allotted one evening in every month; and I find no cause to repent my labour. It is generally a time of strong consolation to those who love God, and all mankind for his sake; as well as of breaking down the partition walls which either the craft of the devil or the folly of men has built up; and of encouraging every child of God to say, (O when shall it once be!) "Whosoever doeth the will of my Father which is in heaven, the same is my brother, and sister, and mother."

VI. By the blessing of God upon their endeavours to help one another, many found the pearl of great price. Being justified by faith they had "peace with God, through our Lord Jesus Christ." These felt a more tender affection than before, to those who were partakers of like precious faith; and hence arose such a confidence in each other, that they poured out their souls into each other's bosom. Indeed they had great need so to do; for the war was not over, as they had supposed; but they had still to wrestle both with flesh and blood, and with principalities and powers: so that temptations were on every side; and often temptations of such a kind, as they knew not how to speak in a class; in which persons of every sort, young and old, men and women, met together.

These, therefore, wanted some means of closer union; they wanted to pour out their hearts without reserve, particularly with regard to the sin which did still easily beset them, and the temptations which were most apt to prevail over them. And they were the more desirous of this, when they observed it was the express advice of an inspired writer: "Confess your faults one to another, and pray one for another, that ye may be healed."

In compliance with their desire, I divided them into

smaller companies; putting the married or single men, and married or single women, together. The chief rules of these bands (that is, little companies; so that old English word signifies) run thus:—

"In order to 'confess our faults one to another,' and pray one for another that we may be healed, we intend (1.) To meet once a week, at the least. (2.) To come punctually at the hour appointed. (3.) To begin with singing or prayer. (4.) To speak each of us in order, freely and plainly, the true state of our souls, with the faults we have committed in thought, word, or deed, and the temptations we have felt since our last meeting. (5.) To desire some person among us (thence called a leader) to speak his own state first, and then to ask the rest, in order, as many and as searching questions as may be, concerning their state, sins, and temptations."

That their design in meeting might be the more effectually answered, I desired all the men-bands, to meet me together every Wednesday evening, and the women on Sunday, that they might receive such particular instructions and exhortations as, from time to time, might appear to be most needful for them; that such prayers might be offered up to God, as their necessities should require; and praise returned to the Giver of every good gift, for whatever mercies they had received.

In order to increase in them a grateful sense of all his mercies, I desired that, one evening in a quarter, all the men in band; on a second, all the women would meet; and on a third, both men and women together; that we might together "eat bread," as the ancient Christians did, "with gladness and singleness of heart." At these love-feasts (so we termed them, retaining the name, as well as the thing, which was in use from the beginning) our food is only a little plain cake and water. But we seldom return from them without being fed, not only with the "meat which perisheth," but with "that which endureth to everlasting life."

Great and many are the advantages which have ever since flowed from this closer union of the believers with each other. They prayed for one another, that they might be healed of the faults they had confessed; and it was so. The chains were broken, the bands were burst in sunder, and sin had no more dominion over them. Many were delivered from the temptations out of which, till then, they found no way to escape. They were built up in our most holy faith. They rejoiced in the Lord more abundantly. They were strengthened in love, and more effectually provoked to abound in every good work.

But it was soon objected to the bands (as to the classes before), "These were not at first. There is no Scripture for them. These are man's works, man's building, man's invention." I reply, as before, these are also prudential helps, grounded on reason and experience, in order to apply the general rules given in Scripture according to particular circumstances.

An objection much more boldly and frequently urged, is, that "all these bands are mere Popery." I hope I need not pass a harder censure on those (most of them at least) who affirm this, than that they talk of they know not what; they betray in themselves the most gross and shameful ignorance. Do not they yet know, that the only Popish confession is, the confession made by a single person to a priest?—and this itself is in nowise condemned by our Church; nay, she recommends it in some cases. Whereas, that we practise is, the confession of several persons conjointly, not to a priest, but to each other. Consequently, it has no analogy at all to Popish confession. But the truth is, this is a stale objection, which many people make against any thing they do not like. It is all Popery out of hand.

VII. And yet while most of these who were thus intimately joined together, went on daily from faith to faith; some fell from the faith, either all at once, by falling into known wilful sin; or gradually, and almost insensibly, by giving way in what they called little things; by sins of omission, by yielding to heart sins, or by not watching unto prayer. The exhortations and prayers used among the believers did no longer profit these. They wanted advice and instruction suited to their case; which as soon as I observed, I separated them from the rest, and desired them to meet me apart on Saturday evenings.

At this hour, all the hymns, exhortations, and prayers are adapted to their circumstances; being wholly suited to those who *did* see God, but have now lost sight of the light of his countenance; and who mourn after him, and refuse to be comforted till they know he has healed their backsliding.

By applying both the threats and promises of God to these real, not nominal, penitents, and by crying to God in their behalf, we endeavoured to bring them back to the great "Shepherd and Bishop of their souls;" not by any of the fopperies of the Roman Church, although, in some measure, countenanced by antiquity. In prescribing hair shirts, and bodily austerities, we durst not follow even the ancient Church; although we had unawares, both in dividing οἱ πιστοί, the believers, from the rest of the society, and in separating the penitents from them, and appointing a peculiar service for them.

VIII. Many of these soon recovered the ground they had lost. Yea, they rose higher than before; being more watchful than ever, and more meek and lowly, as well as stronger in the faith that worketh by love. They now outran the greater part of their brethren, continually walking in the light of God, and having fellowship with the Father, and with his Son Jesus Christ.

I saw it might be useful to give some advices to all those who continued in the light of God's countenance, which the rest of their brethren did not want, and probably could not receive. So I desired a small number of such as appeared to be in this state, to spend an hour with me every Monday morning. My design was, not only to direct them how to press after perfection; to exercise their every grace, and improve every talent they had received; and to incite them to love one another more, and to watch more carefully over each other; but also to have a select company, to whom I might unbosom myself on all occasions, without reserve; and whom I could propose to all their brethren as a pattern of love, of holiness, and of good works.

They had no need of being incumbered with many rules; having the best rule of all in their hearts. No peculiar directions were therefore given to them, excepting only these three:—

First. Let nothing spoken in this society be spoken again. (Hereby we had the more full confidence in each other.)

Secondly. Every member agrees to submit to his minister in all indifferent things.

Thirdly. Every member will bring, once a week, all he can spare toward a common stock.

Every one here has an equal liberty of speaking, there being none greater or less than another. I could say freely to these, when they were met together, "Ye may all prophesy one by one" (taking that word in its lowest sense), "that all may learn, and all may be comforted." And I often found the advantage of such a free conversation, and that "in the multitude of counsellors there is safety." Any who is inclined so to do is likewise encouraged to pour out his soul to God. And here especially we have found, that "the effectual fervent prayer of a righteous man availeth much."

IX. This is the plainest and clearest account I can give of the people commonly called *Methodists*. It remains only to give you a short account of those who serve their brethren in love. These are leaders of classes and bands (spoken of before), assistants, stewards, visiters of the sick, and schoolmasters.

In the third part of the "Appeal," I have mentioned how we were led to accept of lay assistants.* Their office is, in the absence of the minister,

---

* " It pleased God, by two or three ministers of the Church of England, to call many sinners to repentance; who, in several parts were undeniably turned from a course of sin, to a course of holiness.

" The ministers of the places where this was done ought to have received those ministers with open arms; and to have taken them who had just begun to serve God into their peculiar care; watching over them in tender love, lest they should fall back into the snare of the devil.

" Instead of this, the greater part spoke of those ministers as if the devil, not God, had sent them. Some repelled them from the Lord's table; others stirred up the people against them, representing them, even in their public discourses, as fellows not fit to live; Papists, heretics, traitors; conspirators against their king and country.

"And how did they watch over the sinners lately reformed? Even as a leopard watcheth over his prey. They drove some of them also from the Lord's table; to which till now they had no desire to approach. They preached all manner of evil concerning them, openly cursing them in the name of the Lord. They turned many out of their work; persuaded others to do so too, and harassed them all manner of ways.

" The event was, that some were wearied out, and so turned back to their vomit again. And then these good pastors gloried over them, and endeavoured to shake others by their example.

" When the ministers by whom God had helped them before came again to those places, great part of their work was to begin again (if it could be begun again); but the relapsers were often so hardened in sin, that no impression could be made upon them.

" What could they do in a case of so extreme necessity, where many souls lay at stake?

" No clergyman would assist at all. The expedient that remained was, to find some one among themselves, who was upright of heart, and of sound judgment in the things of God; and to desire him to meet the rest as often as he could, in order to confirm them, as he was able, in the ways of God, either by reading to them, or by prayer, or by exhortation.

" God immediately gave a blessing hereto. In several places, by means of these plain men, not only those who had already begun to run well were hindered from drawing back to perdition; but other sinners also, from time to time, were converted from the error of their ways.

" This plain account of the whole proceeding I take to be the best defence of it. I know no scripture which forbids making use of such help, in a case of such necessity. And I praise God who has given even this help to those poor sheep, when ' their own shepherds pitied them not.' "—*A Farther Appeal to Men of Reason and Religion*, Part iii, 1745. *Works*, v, 158-9.

(1.) To expound every morning and evening. (2.) To meet the united society, the bands, the select society, and the penitents, once a week. (3.) To visit the classes once a quarter. (4.) To hear and decide all differences. (5.) To put the disorderly back on trial, and to receive on trial for the bands or society. (6.) To see that the stewards, the leaders, and the schoolmasters faithfully discharge their several offices. (7.) To meet the leaders of the bands and classes weekly, and the stewards, and to overlook their accounts.

X. But, long before this, I felt the weight of a far different care, namely, care of temporal things. The quarterly subscriptions amounted, at a mean computation, to above three hundred pounds a year. This was to be laid out, partly in repairs, partly in other necessary expenses, and partly in paying debts. The weekly contributions fell little short of eight pounds a week; which was to be distributed as every one had need. And I was expected to take thought for all these things: but it was a burden I was not able to bear; so I chose out first one, then four, and after a time, seven, as prudent men as I knew, and desired them to take charge of these things upon themselves, that I might have no incumbrance of this kind.

The business of these stewards is,

To manage the temporal things of the society. To receive the subscriptions and contributions. To expend what is needful from time to time. To send relief to the poor. To keep an exact account of all receipts and expenses. To inform the minister if any of the rules of the society are not punctually observed. To tell the preachers in love, if they think any thing amiss, either in their doctrine or life.

The rules of the stewards are,

(1.) Be frugal. Save every thing that can be saved honestly. (2.) Spend no more than you receive. Contract no debts. (3.) Have no long accounts. Pay every thing within the week. (4.) Give none that asks relief, either an ill word or an ill look. Do not hurt them, if you cannot help. (5.) Expect no thanks from man.

They met together at six every Thursday morning; consulted on the business which came before them; sent relief to the sick, as every one had need; and gave the remainder of what had been contributed each week to those who appeared to be in the most pressing want. So that all was concluded within the week; what was brought on Tuesday being constantly expended on Thursday. I soon had the pleasure to find, that all these temporal things were done with the utmost faithfulness and exactness; so that my cares of this kind were at an end. I had only to revise the accounts, to tell them if I thought any thing might be amended, and to consult how deficiencies might be supplied from time to time; for these were frequent and large (so far were we from abundance), the income by no means answering the expenses. But that we might not faint, sometimes we had unforeseen helps in times of the greatest perplexity. At other times we borrowed larger or smaller sums: of which the greatest part has since been repaid. But I owe some hundred pounds to this day. So much have I gained by preaching the Gospel!

XI. But it was not long before the stewards found a great difficulty with regard to the sick. Some were ready to perish before they knew of their illness; and when they did know, it was not in their power (being persons generally employed in trade) to visit them so often as they desired.

When I was apprized of this, I laid the case at large before the whole society; showed how impossible it was for the stewards to attend all that were sick in all parts of the town; desired the leaders of classes would more carefully inquire, and more constantly inform them, who were sick; and asked, "Who among you is willing, as well as able, to supply this lack of service?"

The next morning many willingly offered themselves. I chose six-and-forty of them, whom I judged to be of the most tender, loving spirit; divided the town into twenty-three parts, and desired two of them to visit the sick in each division.

It is the business of a visiter of the sick,

To see every sick person within his district thrice a week. To inquire into the state of their souls, and to advise them as occasion may require. To inquire into their disorders, and procure advice for them. To relieve them, if they are in want. To do any thing for them, which he (or she) can do. To bring in his accounts weekly to the stewards. (The leaders now do this.) Upon reflection, I saw how exactly, in this also, we had copied after the primitive Church. What were the ancient deacons? What was Phebe the deaconess, but such a visiter of the sick?

I did not think it needful to give them any particular rules beside these that follow:—

(1.) Be plain and open in dealing with souls. (2.) Be mild, tender, patient. (3.) Be cleanly in all you do for the sick. (4.) Be not nice.

We have ever since had great reason to praise God for his continued blessing on this undertaking. Many lives have been saved, many sicknesses healed, much pain and want prevented or removed. Many heavy hearts have been made glad, many mourners comforted: and the visiters have found, from Him whom they serve, a present reward for all their labour.

XII. But I was still in pain for many of the poor that were sick; there was so great expense, and so little profit. And first, I resolved to try, whether they might not receive more benefit in the hospitals. Upon the trial, we found there was indeed less expense, but no more good done, than before. I then asked the advice of several physicians for them; but still it profited not. I saw the poor people pining away, and several families ruined, and that without remedy.

At length I thought of a kind of desperate expedient. "I will prepare, and give them physic myself." For six or seven-and-twenty years, I had made anatomy and physic the diversion of my leisure hours; though I never properly studied them, unless for a few months when I was going to America, where I imagined I might be of some service to those who had no regular physician among them. I applied to it again. I took into my assistance an apothecary, and an experienced surgeon; resolving, at the same time, not to go out of my depth, but to leave all difficult and complicated cases to such physicians as the patients should choose.

I gave notice of this to the society; telling them, that all who were ill of chronical distempers (for I did not care to venture upon acute) might, if they pleased, come to me at such a time, and I would give them the best advice I could, and the best medicines I had.

Many came (and so every Friday since): among the rest was one William Kirkman, a weaver, near Old Nichol-street. I asked him, "What complaint have you?" "O sir," said he, "a cough, a very sore cough. I can get no rest day nor night."

I asked, "How long have you had it?" He replied, "About three-score years: it began when I was eleven years old." I was nothing glad that this man should come first, fearing our not curing him might discourage others. However, I looked up to God and said, "Take this three or four times a day. If it does you no good, it will do you no harm." He took it two or three days. His cough was cured, and has not returned to this day.

Now, let candid men judge, does humility require me to deny a notorious fact? If not, which is vanity? to say, I by my own skill restored this man to health; or to say, God did it by his own almighty power? By what figure of speech this is called boasting, I know not. But I will put no name to such a fact as this. I leave that to the Rev. Dr. Middleton.

In five months, medicines were occasionally given to above five hundred persons. Several of these I never saw before; for I did not regard whether they were of the society or not. In that time seventy-one of these, regularly taking their medicines, and following the regimen prescribed (which three in four would not do), were entirely cured of distempers long thought to be incurable. The whole expense of the medicines during this time, was nearly forty pounds. We continued this ever since, and, by the blessing of God, with more and more success.

XIII. But I had for some years observed many, who, although not sick, were not able to provide for themselves, and had none who took care to provide for them: these were chiefly feeble, aged widows. I consulted with the stewards, how they might be relieved. They all agreed, if we could keep them in one house, it would not only be far less expensive to us, but also far more comfortable for them. Indeed we had no money to begin; but we believed He would provide, "who defendeth the cause of the widow:" so we took a lease of two little houses near; we fitted them up, so as to be warm and clean. We took in as many widows as we had room for, and provided them with things needful for the body; toward the expense of which I set aside, first, the weekly contributions of the bands, and then all that was collected at the Lord's Supper. It is true, this does not suffice: so that we are considerably in debt, on this account also. But we are persuaded, it will not always be so; seeing "the earth is the Lord's, and the fulness thereof."

In this (commonly called the Poor House) we have now nine widows, one blind woman, two poor children, two upper servants, a maid and a man. I might add, four or five preachers; for I myself, as well as the other preachers who are in town, diet with the poor, on the same food, and at the same table; and we rejoice herein, as a comfortable earnest of our eating bread together in our Father's kingdom.

I have blessed God for this house ever since it began; but lately much more than ever. I honour these widows; for they "are widows indeed." So that it is not in vain, that, without any design of so doing, we have copied after another of the institutions of the apostolic age. I can now say to all the world, "Come and see how these Christians love one another!" (This has been since dropped for want of support.)

XIV. Another thing which had given me frequent concern was, the case of abundance of children. Some their parents could not afford to put to school: so they remained like "a wild ass's colt." Others were sent to school, and learned, at least, to read and write; but they learned all kind of vice at the same time: so that it had been better for them to have been without their knowledge, than to have bought it at so dear a price.

At length I determined to have them taught in my own house, that they might have an opportunity of learning to read, write, and cast accounts (if no more), without being under almost a necessity of learning Heathenism at the same time: and after several unsuccessful trials, I found two such schoolmasters as I wanted; men of honesty and of sufficient knowledge, who had talents for, and their hearts in, the work.

They have now under their care near sixty children: the parents of some pay for their schooling; but the greater part, being very poor, do not; so that the expense is chiefly defrayed by voluntary contributions. We have of late clothed them too, as many as wanted. The rules of the school are these that follow: (This also has been dropped for some time, 1772.)

First. No child is admitted under six years of age.

Secondly. All the children are to be present at the morning sermon. Thirdly. They are at school from six to twelve, and from one to five. Fourthly. They have no play-days. Fifthly. No child is to speak in school, but to the masters. Sixthly. The child who misses two days in one week, without leave, is excluded the school.

We appointed two stewards for the school also. The business of these is, to receive the school subscriptions, and expend what is needful; to talk with each of the masters weekly; to pray with and exhort the children twice a week; to inquire diligently, whether they grow in grace and in learning, and whether the rules are punctually observed; every Tuesday morning, in conjunction with the masters, to exclude those children that do not observe the rules; every Wednesday morning to meet with and exhort their parents, to train them up at home in the ways of God.

A happy change was soon observed in the children, both with regard to their tempers and behaviour. They learned reading, writing, and arithmetic swiftly; and at the same time they were diligently instructed in the sound principles of religion, and earnestly exhorted to fear God, and work out their own salvation.

XV. A year or two ago, I observed among many a distress of another kind. They frequently wanted, perhaps in order to carry on their business, a present supply of money. They scrupled to make use of a pawnbroker; but where to borrow it they knew not. I resolved to try if we could not find a remedy for this also. I went, in a few days, from one end of the town to the other, and exhorted those who had this world's goods, to assist their needy brethren. Fifty pounds were contributed. This was immediately lodged in the hands of two stewards; who attended every Tuesday morning, in order to lend to those who wanted any small sum, not exceeding twenty shillings, to be repaid within three months. (We now, 1772, lend any sum not exceeding five pounds.)

It is almost incredible, but it manifestly appears from their accounts, that, with this inconsiderable sum, two hundred and fifty have been assisted, within the space of one year. Will not God put it into the heart of some lover of mankind to increase this little stock? If this is not "lending unto the Lord," what is? O confer not with flesh and blood, but immediately

> " Join hands with God, to make a poor man live !"

I think, sir, now you know all that I know of this people. You see the nature, occasion, and design of whatever is practised among them. And, I trust, you may be pretty well able to answer any questions which may be asked concerning them; particularly by those who inquire concerning my revenue, and what I do with it all.

Some have supposed this was no greater than that of the bishop of London. But others computed that I received eight hundred a year from Yorkshire only. Now, if so, it cannot be so little as ten thousand pounds a year which I receive out of all England!

Accordingly, a gentleman in Cornwall (the rector of Redruth) extends the calculation pretty considerably. "Let me see," said he: "Two millions of Methodists; and each of these paying two-pence a week." If so, I must have eight hundred and sixty thousand pounds, with some odd shillings and pence, a year.

A tolerable competence! But be it more or less, it is nothing at all to me. All that is contributed or collected in every place is both received and expended by others; nor have I so much as the "beholding thereof with my eyes." And so it will be, till I turn Turk or Pagan. For I look upon all this revenue, be it what it may, as sacred to God and the poor; out of which, if I want any thing, I am relieved, even as another poor man. So were originally all ecclesiastical revenues, as every man of learning knows: and the bishops and priests used them only as such. If any use them otherwise now, God help them!

I doubt not, but if I err in this, or any other point, you will pray God to show me his truth. To have "a conscience void of offence toward God and toward man" is the desire of,

   Reverend and dear sir,
    Your affectionate brother and servant,
      JOHN WESLEY.

WESLEY'S HOUSE, CITY ROAD, LONDON

## A SHORT HISTORY OF METHODISM.*
[*Works*, v, 246-8.]

It is not easy to reckon up the various accounts which have been given of the people called Methodists; very many of them as far remote from truth as that given by the good gentleman in Ireland: *"Methodists!* Ay, they are the people who place all religion in *wearing long beards."*

Abundance of the mistakes which are current concerning them have undoubtedly sprung from this: Men lump together, under this general name, many who have no manner of connection with each other; and then whatever any of these speaks or does is of course imputed to all.

The following short account may prevent persons of a calm and candid disposition from doing this; although men of a warm or prejudiced spirit will do just as they did before. But let it be observed, this is not designed for a defence of the Methodists (so called), or any part of them. It is a bare relation of a series of naked facts, which alone may remove abundance of misunderstandings.

In November, 1729, four young gentlemen of Oxford, —Mr. John Wesley, fellow of Lincoln College; Mr. Charles Wesley, student of Christ Church; Mr. Morgan, commoner of Christ Church; and Mr. Kirkham, of Merton College,—began to spend some evenings in a week together, in reading, chiefly, the Greek Testament. The next year two or three of Mr. John Wesley's pupils desired the liberty of meeting with them; and afterward one of Mr. Charles Wesley's pupils. It was in 1732, that Mr.

---

* I have not been able to ascertain the precise time at which this tract was written. . . . It appears to have been first published some time about 1764; and was probably intended to screen Mr. Wesley and his friends from the reproach attached to the conduct of those who separated from him.—EDIT.

Ingham, of Queen's College, and Mr. Broughton, of Exeter, were added to their number. To these, in April, was joined Mr. Clayton, of Brazennose, with two or three of his pupils. About the same time Mr. James Hervey was permitted to meet with them, and in 1735, Mr. Whitefield.*

The exact regularity of their lives, as well as studies, occasioned a young gentleman of Christ Church to say, "Here is a new set of Methodists sprung up;" alluding to some ancient physicians who were so called. The name was new and quaint; so it took immediately, and the Methodists were known all over the university.

They were all zealous members of the Church of England; not only tenacious of all her doctrines, so far as they knew them, but of all her discipline, to the minutest circumstance. They were likewise zealous observers of all the university statutes, and that for conscience' sake. But they observed neither these nor any thing else any farther than they conceived it was bound upon them by their one book, the Bible; it being their one desire and design to be downright Bible Christians; taking the Bible, as interpreted by the primitive Church and our own, for their whole and sole rule.

The one charge then advanced against them was, that they were "righteous overmuch;" that they were abundantly too scrupulous, and too strict, carrying things to great extremes: in particular, that they laid too much stress upon the rubrics and canons of the Church; that they insisted too much on observing the statutes of the university; and that they took the Scriptures in too strict and literal a sense; so that if they were right, few indeed would be saved.

---

* "Having now obtained what I had long desired, a company of friends that were as my own soul, I set up my rest, being fully determined to live and die in this sweet retirement."—*A Short History of the People Called Methodists*, 1781. *Works*, vii, 346.

In October, 1735, Mr. John and Charles Wesley, and Mr. Ingham, left England,* with a design to go and preach to the Indians in Georgia: but the rest of the gentlemen continued to meet, till one and another was ordained and left the university. By which means, in about two years' time, scarce any of them were left.

In February, 1738, Mr. Whitefield went over to Georgia, with a design to assist Mr. John Wesley; but Mr. Wesley just then returned to England. Soon after he had a meeting with Messrs. Ingham, Stonehouse, Hall, Hutchings, Kinchin, and a few other clergymen, who all appeared to be of one heart, as well as of one judgment, resolved to be Bible Christians at all events; and, wherever they were, to preach with all their might plain, old, Bible Christianity.

They were hitherto perfectly regular in all things, and zealously attached to the Church of England. Meantime, they began to be convinced, that "by grace we are saved through faith;" that justification by faith was the doctrine of the Church, as well as of the Bible. As soon as they believed, they spake; salvation by faith being now their

---

* "We were above three months on board, during which time our common way of living was this: From four in the morning till five, each of us used private prayer. From five to seven, we read the Bible together. At seven, we breakfasted. At eight was the public service. From nine to twelve, I learned German; Mr. Delamotte, Greek; my brother wrote sermons; and Mr. Ingham instructed the children. At twelve, we met together. About one, we dined. The time from dinner to four, we spent in reading to those of whom each of us had taken charge, or in speaking to them severally, as need required. At four, were the evening prayers; when either the Second lesson was explained (as it always was in the morning), or the children were catechised and instructed before the congregation. From five to six, we again used private prayer. From six to seven, I read in our cabin to two or three of the passengers (we had eighty English on board); and each of my brethren to a few more in theirs. At seven, I joined with the Germans (of whom we had twenty-six on board) in their public service, while Mr. Ingham was reading between the decks to as many as desired to hear. At eight, we met again, to instruct and exhort each other; and between nine and ten went to bed."—*A Short History of the People Called Methodists*, 1781. *Works*, vii, 346-7.

standing topic. Indeed this implied three things: (1.) That men are all, by nature, "dead in sin," and, consequently, "children of wrath." (2.) That they are "justified by faith alone." (3.) That faith produces inward and outward holiness: and these points they insisted on day and night. In a short time they became popular preachers. The congregations were large wherever they preached. The former name was then revived; and all these gentlemen, with their followers, were entitled Methodists.

In March, 1741, Mr. Whitefield, being returned to England, entirely separated from Mr. Wesley and his friends, because he did not hold the decrees. Here was the first breach, which warm men persuaded Mr. Whitefield to make merely for a difference of opinion. Those, indeed, who believed universal redemption had no desire at all to separate; but those who held particular redemption would not hear of any accommodation, being determined to have no fellowship with men that "were in so dangerous errors." So there were now two sorts of Methodists, so called; those for particular, and those for general, redemption.

Not many years passed, before William Cudworth and James Relly separated from Mr. Whitefield. These were properly Antinomians, absolute, avowed enemies to the law of God, which they never preached or professed to preach, but termed all legalists who did. With them, "preaching the law" was an abomination. They had "nothing to do" with the law. They would "preach Christ," as they called it, but without one word either of holiness or good works. Yet these were still denominated Methodists, although differing from Mr. Whitefield, both in judgment and practice, abundantly more than Mr. Whitefield did from Mr. Wesley.

In the mean time, Mr. Venn and Mr. Romaine began to be spoken of; and not long after, Mr. Madan and Mr.

## A Short History of Methodism.

Berridge, with a few other clergymen, who, although they had no connection with each other, yet preaching salvation by faith, and endeavouring to live accordingly, to be Bible Christians, were soon included in the general name of Methodists. And so indeed were all others who preached salvation by faith, and appeared more serious than their neighbours. Some of these were quite regular in their manner of preaching; some were quite irregular (though not by choice; but necessity was laid upon them; they must preach irregularly, or not at all); and others were between both, regular in most, though not in all, particulars.

In 1762, George Bell, and a few other persons, began to speak great words. In the latter end of the year, they foretold that the world would be at an end on the 28th of February. Mr. Wesley, with whom they were then connected, withstood them both in public and private. This they would not endure; so, in January and February, 1763, they separated from him. Soon after, Mr. Maxfield, one of Mr. Wesley's preachers, and several of the people, left Mr. Wesley; but still Mr. Maxfield and his adherents go under the general name of Methodists.

At present those who remain with Mr. Wesley are mostly Church-of-England men. They love her Articles, her Homilies, her Liturgy, her discipline, and unwillingly vary from it in any instance. Meantime, all who preach among them declare, "We are all by nature children of wrath:" but "by grace we are saved through faith;" saved both from the guilt and from the power of sin. They endeavour to live according to what they preach, to be plain Bible Christians. And they meet together, at convenient times, to encourage one another therein. They tenderly love many that are Calvinists, though they do not love their opinions. Yea, they love the Antinomians themselves; but it is with a love of compassion only: for they hate their doctrines with a perfect hatred; they abhor them as they do hell fire; being convinced nothing can so effectually destroy all faith, all holiness, and all good works.

With regard to these, Mr. Relly and his adherents, it would not be strange if they should grow into reputation. For they will never shock the world, either by the harshness of their doctrine, or the singularity of their behaviour. But let those who determine both to preach and to live the Gospel expect that men will "say all manner of evil of them." "The servant is not above his Master, nor the disciple above his Lord. If, then, they have called the Master of the house, Beelzebub, how much more them of his household?" It is their duty, indeed, "as much as lieth in them, to live peaceably with all men." But when they labour after peace, the world will "make themselves ready for battle." It is their constant endeavour to "please all men, for their good, to edification." But yet they know it cannot be done: they remember the word of the Apostle, "If I yet please men, I am not the servant of Christ." They go on, therefore, "through honour and dishonour, through evil report and good report;" desiring only, that their Master may say in that day, "Servants of God, well done!"

# THOUGHTS UPON METHODISM.

[*Arminian Magazine*, 1787.  *Works*, vii, 315-7.]

I AM not afraid that the people called Methodists should ever cease to exist either in Europe or America. But I am afraid, lest they should only exist as a dead sect, having the form of religion without the power. And this undoubtedly will be the case, unless they hold fast both the doctrine, spirit, and discipline with which they first set out.

What was their fundamental doctrine? That the Bible is the whole and sole rule both of Christian faith and practice. Hence they learned (1.) That religion is an inward principle; that it is no other than the mind that was in Christ; or, in other words, the renewal of the soul after the image of God, in righteousness and true holiness.* (2.) That this can never be wrought in us, but by the power of the Holy Ghost. (3.) That we receive this, and every other blessing, merely for the sake of Christ: and (4.) That whosoever hath the mind that was in Christ, the same is our brother, and sister, and mother.

In the year 1729, four young students in Oxford agreed to spend their evenings together. They were all zealous members of the Church of England, and had no peculiar opinions, but were distinguished only by their constant attendance on the church and sacrament. In 1735 they were increased to fifteen; when the chief of them embarked for America, intending to preach to the Heathen Indians. Methodism then seemed to die away; but it

---

\* " ' What then is religion?' It is happiness in God, or in the knowledge and love of God. It is 'faith working by love;' producing 'righteousness, and peace, and joy in the Holy Ghost.' In other words, it is a heart and life devoted to God ; or, communion with God the Father and the Son ; or, the mind which was in Christ Jesus, enabling us to walk as he walked."—*Letter to Mr. C.*, 1786. *Works*, vii, 223.

revived again in the year 1738; especially after Mr. Wesley (not being allowed to preach in the churches) began to preach in the fields. One and another then coming to inquire what they must do to be saved, he desired them to meet him all together; which they did, and increased continually in number. In November, a large building, the Foundery, being offered him, he began preaching therein, morning and evening; at five in the morning, and seven in the evening, that the people's labour might not be hindered.

From the beginning the men and women sat apart, as they always did in the primitive church; and none were suffered to call any place their own, but the first comers sat down first. They had no pews; and all the benches for rich and poor were of the same construction. Mr. Wesley began the service with a short prayer; then sung a hymn and preached (usually about half an hour), then sung a few verses of another hymn, and concluded with prayer. His constant doctrine was, salvation by faith, preceded by repentance, and followed by holiness.

But when a large number of people was joined, the great difficulty was, to keep them together. For they were continually scattering hither and thither, and we knew no way to help it. But God provided for this also, when we thought not of it. A year or two after, Mr. Wesley met the chief of the society in Bristol, and inquired, "How shall we pay the debt upon the preaching house?" Captain Foy stood up and said, "Let every one in the society give a penny a week, and it will easily be done." "But many of them," said one, "have not a penny to give." "True," said the Captain; "then put ten or twelve of them to me. Let each of these give what they can weekly, and I will supply what is wanting." Many others made the same offer. So Mr. Wesley divided the societies among them; assigning a class of about twelve persons to each of these, who were termed leaders.

Not long after, one of these informed Mr. Wesley that, calling on such a one in his house, he found him quarrelling with his wife. Another was found in drink. It immediately struck into Mr. Wesley's mind, "This is the very thing we wanted. The leaders are the persons who may not only receive the contributions, but also watch over the souls of their brethren." The society in London, being informed of this, willingly followed the example of that in Bristol; as did every society from that time, whether in Europe or America. By this means, it was easily found if any grew weary or faint, and help was speedily administered. And if any walked disorderly, they were quickly discovered, and either amended or dismissed.

For those who knew in whom they had believed, there was another help provided. Five or six, either married or single men, met together at such an hour as was convenient, according to the direction of St. James, "Confess your faults one to another, and pray one for another, and ye shall be healed." And five or six of the married or single women met together for the same purpose. Innumerable blessings have attended this institution, especially in those who were going on to perfection. When any seemed to have attained this, they were allowed to meet with a select number, who appeared, so far as man could judge, to be partakers of the same "great salvation."

From this short sketch of Methodism (so called), any man of understanding may easily discern, that it is only plain, Scriptural religion, guarded by a few prudential regulations. The essence of it is holiness of heart and life; the circumstantials all point to this. And as long as they are joined together in the people called Methodists, no weapon formed against them shall prosper. But if even the circumstantial parts are despised, the essential will soon be lost. And if ever the essential parts should evaporate, what remains will be dung and dross.

It nearly concerns us to understand how the case stands with us at present. I fear, wherever riches have increased, (exceeding few are the exceptions,) the essence of religion, the mind that was in Christ, has decreased in the same proportion. Therefore do I not see how it is possible, in the nature of things, for any revival of true religion to continue long. For religion must necessarily produce both industry and frugality; and these cannot but produce riches. But as riches increase, so will pride, anger, and love of the world in all its branches.

How, then, is it possible that Methodism, that is, the religion of the heart, though it flourishes now as a green bay tree, should continue in this state? For the Methodists in every place grow diligent and frugal; consequently, they increase in goods. Hence they proportionably increase in pride, in anger, in the desire of the flesh, the desire of the eyes, and the pride of life. So, although the form of religion remains, the spirit is swiftly vanishing away.

Is there no way to prevent this? this continual declension of pure religion? We ought not to forbid people to be diligent and frugal: we must exhort all Christians to gain all they can, and to save all they can; that is, in effect, to grow rich! What way then (I ask again), can we take, that our money may not sink us to the nethermost hell? There is one way, and there is no other under heaven. If those who "gain all they can," and "save all they can," will likewise "give all they can;" then, the more they gain, the more they will grow in grace, and the more treasure they will lay up in heaven.

London, August 4, 1786.

## AN EARNEST APPEAL

TO

MEN OF REASON AND RELIGION.

[1743. *Works*, v, 5-33.]

Doth our law judge any man, before it hear him, and know what he doeth?—John vii, 51.

ALTHOUGH it is with us a "very small thing to be judged of you or of man's judgment," seeing we know God will "make our innocency as clear as the light, and our just dealing as the noon-day;" yet are we ready to give any that are willing to hear a plain account, both of our principles and actions; as having "renounced the hidden things of shame," and desiring nothing more, "than by manifestation of the truth to commend ourselves to every man's conscience in the sight of God."

We see (and who does not?) the numberless follies and miseries of our fellow creatures. We see, on every side, either men of no religion at all, or men of a lifeless, formal religion. We are grieved at the sight; and should greatly rejoice, if by any means we might convince some that there is a better religion to be attained,—a religion worthy of God that gave it. And this we conceive to be no other than love; the love of God and of all mankind; the loving God with all our heart, and soul, and strength, as having first loved *us,* as the fountain of all the good we have received, and of all we ever hope to enjoy; and the loving every soul which God hath made, every man on earth, as our own soul.

This love we believe to be the medicine of life, the never-failing remedy for all the evils of a disordered world, for all the miseries and vices of men. Wherever this is, there are virtue and happiness going hand in hand. There is humbleness of mind, gentleness, long suffering, the whole image of God; and at the same time a peace that passeth all understanding, and joy unspeakable and full of glory.

> "Eternal sunshine of the spotless mind;
> Each prayer accepted, and each wish resign'd;
> Desires composed, affections ever even,
> Tears that delight, and sighs that waft to heaven."

This religion we long to see established in the world, a religion of love, and joy, and peace, having its seat in the inmost soul, but ever showing itself by its fruits, continually springing forth, not only in all innocence (for love worketh no ill to his neighbour), but likewise in every kind of beneficence, spreading virtue and happiness all around it.

This religion have we been following after for many years, as many know, if they would testify: but all this time, seeking wisdom, we found it not; we were spending our strength in vain. And being now under full conviction of this, we declare it to all mankind; for we desire not that others should wander out of the way as we have done before them; but rather that they may profit by our loss, that they may go (though we did not, having then no man to guide us) the straight way to the religion of love, even by faith.

Now, faith (supposing the Scripture to be of God) is πραγμάτων ἔλεγχος οὐ βλεπομένων, "the demonstrative evidence of things unseen," the supernatural evidence of things invisible, not perceivable by eyes of flesh, or by any of our natural senses or faculties. Faith is that divine evidence whereby the spiritual man discerneth God, and the things of God. It is with regard to the spiritual world, what sense is with regard to the natural. It is the spiritual sensation of every soul that is born of God.

Perhaps you have not considered it in this view. I will, then, explain it a little further.

## An Earnest Appeal.

Faith, according to the scriptural account, is the eye of the new-born soul. Hereby every true believer in God "seeth him who is invisible." Hereby (in a more particular manner, since life and immortality have been brought to light by the Gospel) he "seeth the light of the glory of God in the face of Jesus Christ;" and "beholdeth what manner of love it is which the Father hath bestowed upon us, that we," who are born of the Spirit, "should be called the sons of God."

It is the ear of the soul, whereby a sinner "hears the voice of the Son of God, and lives;" even that voice which alone wakes the dead, "Son, thy sins are forgiven thee."

It is (if I may be allowed the expression) the palate of the soul; for hereby a believer "tastes the good word, and the powers of the world to come;" and "hereby he both tastes and sees that God is gracious," yea, "and merciful to him a sinner."

It is the feeling of the soul, whereby a believer perceives, through the "power of the Highest overshadowing him," both the existence and the presence of Him in whom "he lives, moves, and has his being;" and indeed the whole invisible world, the entire system of things eternal. And hereby, in particular, he feels "the love of God shed abroad in his heart."

By this faith we are saved from all uneasiness of mind, from the anguish of a wounded spirit, from discontent, from fear and sorrow of heart, and from that inexpressible listlessness and weariness, both of the world and of ourselves, which we had so helplessly laboured under for many years; especially when we were out of the hurry of the world, and sunk into calm reflection. In this we find that love of God, and of all mankind, which we had elsewhere sought in vain. This we know and feel, and therefore cannot but declare, saves every one that partakes of it, both from sin and misery, from every unhappy and every unholy temper.

> "Soft peace she brings, wherever she arrives;
> She builds our quiet, as she forms our lives;
> Lays the rough paths of peevish nature even,
> And opens in each breast a little heaven."

If you ask, "Why then have not all men this faith? all, at least, who conceive it to be so happy a thing? Why do they not believe immediately?"

We answer (on the Scripture hypothesis), "It is the gift of God." No man is able to work it in himself. It is a work of omnipotence. It requires no less power thus to quicken a dead soul, than to raise a body that lies in the grave. It is a new creation; and none can create a soul anew, but He who at first created the heavens and the earth.

May not your own experience teach you this? Can you give yourself this faith? Is it now in your power to see, or hear, or taste, or feel God? Have you already, or can you raise in yourself, any perception of God, or of an invisible world? I suppose you do not deny that there is an invisible world; you will not charge it in poor old Hesiod to Christian prejudice of education, when he says, in those well-known words,

> "Millions of spiritual creatures walk the earth
> Unseen, whether we wake, or if we sleep."

Now, is there any power in your soul whereby you discern either these, or Him that created them? Or, can all your wisdom and strength open an intercourse between yourself and the world of spirits? Is it in your power to burst the veil that is on your heart, and let in the light of eternity? You know it is not. You not only do not, but cannot, by your own strength, thus believe. The more you labour so to do, the more you will be convinced "it is the gift of God."

It is the free gift of God, which he bestows, not on those who are worthy of his favour, not on such as are previously holy, and so fit to be crowned with all the

## An Earnest Appeal.

blessings of his goodness; but on the ungodly and unholy; on those who till that hour were fit only for everlasting destruction; those in whom was no good thing, and whose only plea was, "God be merciful to me, a sinner!" No merit, no goodness in man precedes the forgiving love of God. His pardoning mercy supposes nothing in us but a sense of mere sin and misery; and to all who see, and feel, and own their wants, and their utter inability to remove them, God freely gives faith, for the sake of Him in whom he is always "well pleased."

This is a short, rude sketch of the doctrine we teach. These are our fundamental principles; and we spend our lives in confirming others herein, and in a behaviour suitable to them.

Now, if you are a reasonable man, although you do not believe the Christian system to be of God, lay your hand upon your breast, and calmly consider what it is that you can here condemn? What evil have we done to *you*, that you should join the common cry against us? Why should *you* say, "Away with such fellows from the earth; it is not fit that they should live?"

It is true, your judgment does not fall in with ours. We believe the Scripture to be of God. This you do not believe. And how do you defend yourselves against them who urge you with the guilt of unbelief? Do you not say, "Every man *must* judge according to the light he has," and that "if he be true to this, he ought not to be condemned?" Keep then to this, and turn the tables. *Must* not *we* also judge according to the light we have? You can in no wise condemn us without involving yourselves in the same condemnation. According to the light *we* have, we cannot but believe the Scripture is of God; and while we believe this, we dare not turn aside from it, to the right hand or to the left.

Let us consider this point a little further. You yourself believe there is a God. You have the witness of this in your own breast. Perhaps sometimes you tremble before him. You believe there is such a thing as right and wrong; that there is a difference between moral good and evil. Of consequence you must allow, there is such a thing as conscience: I mean, that every person, capable of reflection, is conscious to himself when he looks back on any thing he has done, whether it be good or evil. You must likewise allow, that every man is to be guided by his own conscience, not another's. Thus far, doubtless, you may go, without any danger of being a volunteer in faith.

Now then, be consistent with yourself. If there be a God, who, being just and good (attributes inseparable from the very idea of God), is "a rewarder of them that diligently seek him," ought we not to do whatever we believe will be acceptable to so good a Master? Observe: If we believe, if we are fully persuaded of this in our mind ought we not thus to seek him, and that with all diligence? Else, how should we expect any reward at his hands?

Again: Ought we not to do what we believe is morally good, and to abstain from what we judge is evil? By good I mean, conducive to the good of mankind, tending to advance peace and good will among men, promotive of the happiness of our fellow creatures; and by evil, what is contrary thereto. Then surely you cannot condemn our endeavouring, after our power, to make mankind happy (I now speak only with regard to the present world); our striving, as we can, to lessen their sorrows, and to teach them, in whatsoever state they are, therewith to be content.

Yet again: Are we to be guided by our own conscience, or by that of other men? You surely will not say that any man's conscience can preclude mine. You, at least, will not plead for robbing us of what you so strongly claim for yourselves: I mean the right of private judgment,

## An Earnest Appeal.

which is indeed unalienable from reasonable creatures. You well know, that, unless we faithfully follow the dictates of our own mind, we cannot have a conscience void of offence toward God and toward man.

Upon your own principles, therefore, you must allow us to be, at least, innocent. Do you find any difficulty in this? You speak much of prepossession and prejudice; beware you are not entangled therein yourselves! Are you not prejudiced against us, because we believe and strenuously defend that system of doctrines which you oppose? Are you not enemies to us, because you take it for granted we are so to you? Nay, God forbid! I once saw one, who, from a plentiful fortune, was reduced to the lowest extremity. He was lying on a sick bed, in violent pain, without even convenient food, or one friend to comfort him: so that when his merciful landlord, to complete all, sent one to take his bed from under him, I was not surprised at his attempt to put an end to so miserable a life. Now, when I saw that poor man weltering in his blood, could I be angry at him? Surely, no. No more can I at you. I can no more hate, than I can envy, you. I can only lift up my heart to God for you (as I did then for him), and, with silent tears, beseech the Father of mercies, that he would look on you in your blood, and say unto you, "Live."

"Sir," said that unhappy man, at my first interview with him, "I scorn to deceive you or any man. You must not tell me of your Bible, for I do not believe one word of it. I know there is a God; and believe he is all in all, the *Anima mundi* (the soul of the world), the

"*Totam
Mens agitans molem, et magno se corpore miscens.*
(The all-informing soul,
Which spreads through the vast mass, and moves the whole.)"

But further than this I believe not: all is dark; my thought is lost. But I hear," added he, "you preach to a great number of people every night and morning. Pray, what would you do with them? Whither would you lead them? What religion do you preach? What is it good for?" I replied, "I do preach to as many as desire to hear, every night and morning. You ask, what I would do with them: I would make them virtuous and happy, easy in themselves, and useful to others. Whither would I lead them? To heaven; to God the Judge, the lover of all, and to Jesus the Mediator of the new covenant. What religion do I preach? The religion of love; the law of kindness brought to light by the Gospel. What is this good for? To make all who receive it enjoy God and themselves: to make them like God; lovers of all; contented in their lives; and crying out at their death, in calm assurance, 'O grave, where is thy victory! Thanks be unto God, who giveth me the victory, through my Lord Jesus Christ.'"

Will you object to such a religion as this, that it is not reasonable? Is it not reasonable then to love God? Hath he not given you life, and breath, and all things? Does he not continue his love to you, filling your heart with food and gladness? What have you which you have not received of him? And does not love demand a return of love? Whether, therefore, you do love God or no, you cannot but own it is reasonable so to do; nay, seeing he is the Parent of all good, to love him with all your heart.

Is it not reasonable also to love our neighbour, every man whom God hath made? Are we not brethren, the children of one Father? Ought we not, then, to love one another? And should we only love them that love us? Is that acting like our Father which is in heaven? He causeth his sun to shine on the evil and on the good, and sendeth rain on the just and on the unjust. And can there be a more equitable rule than this: "Thou shalt love thy neighbour as thyself?" You will plead for the reasonableness of this; as also for that golden rule (the only adequate measure of brotherly love, in all our words and actions), "Whatsoever ye would that men should do unto you, even so do unto them?"

Is it not reasonable then, that, as we have opportunity, we should do good unto all men; not only friends but enemies; not only to the deserving, but likewise to the evil and unthankful? Is it not right that all our life should be one continued labour of love? If a day passes without doing good, may one not well say, with Titus, *Amici, diem perdidi!* (My friends, I have lost a day!) And is it enough, to feed the hungry, to clothe the naked, to visit those who are sick or in prison? Should we have no pity for those

> " Who sigh beneath guilt's horrid stain,
> The worst confinement, and the heaviest chain? "

Should we shut up our compassion toward those who are of all men most miserable, because they are miserable by their own fault? If we have found a medicine to heal even that sickness, should we not, as we have freely received it, freely give? Should we not pluck them as brands out of the fire? the fire of lust, anger, malice, revenge? Your inmost soul answers, "It should be done; it is reasonable in the highest degree." Well, this is the sum of our preaching, and of our lives, our enemies themselves being the judges. If therefore you allow, that it is reasonable to love God, to love mankind, and to do good to all men, you cannot but allow that religion which we preach and live to be agreeable to the highest reason.

Perhaps, all this you can bear. It is tolerable enough; and if we spoke only of being saved by love, you should have no great objection: but you do not comprehend what we say of being saved by faith. I know you do not. You do not in any degree comprehend what we mean by that expression: have patience then, and I will tell you yet again. By those words, "We are saved by faith," we mean, that the moment a man receives that faith which is above described, he is saved from doubt and fear, and sorrow of heart, by a peace that passes all understanding; from the heaviness of a wounded spirit, by joy unspeakable; and from his sins, of whatsoever kind they were, from his vicious desires, as well as words and actions, by the love of God, and of all mankind, then shed abroad in his heart.

We grant, nothing is more unreasonable, than to imagine that such mighty effects as these can be wrought by that poor, empty, insignificant thing, which the world calls faith, and you among them. But supposing there be such a faith on the earth as that which the Apostle speaks of, such an intercourse between God and the soul, what is too hard for such a faith? You yourselves may conceive that "all things are possible to him that" thus "believeth;" to him that thus "walketh with God," that is now a citizen of heaven, an inhabitant of eternity. If therefore you will contend with us, you must change the ground of your attack. You must flatly deny there is any faith upon earth: but perhaps this you might think too large a step. You cannot do this without a secret condemnation in your own breast. O that you would at length cry to God for that heavenly gift! whereby alone this truly reasonable religion, this beneficent love of God and man, can be planted in your heart.

If you say, "But those that profess this faith are the most unreasonable of all men;" I ask, Who are those that profess this faith? Perhaps you do not personally know such a man in the world. Who are they that so much as profess to have this "evidence of things not seen?" that profess to "see Him that is invisible," to hear the voice of God, and to have his Spirit ever "witnessing with their spirits, that they are the children of God?" I fear you will find few that even profess this faith, among the large numbers of those who are called believers.

## An Earnest Appeal.

"However, there are enough that profess themselves Christians." Yea, too many, God knoweth; too many that confute their vain professions, by the whole tenor of their lives. I will allow all you can say on this head, and perhaps more than all. It is now some years since I was engaged unawares in a conversation with a strong reasoner, who at first urged the wickedness of the American Indians, as a bar to our hope of converting them to Christianity. But when I mentioned their temperance, justice, and veracity (according to the accounts I had then received), it was asked, "Why, if those Heathens are such men as these, what will they gain by being made Christians? What would they gain by being such Christians as we see every where round about us?" I could not deny they would lose, not gain, by such a Christianity as this. Upon which she added, "Why, what else do you mean by Christianity?" My plain answer was, "What do you apprehend to be more valuable than good sense, good nature, and good manners? All these are contained, and that in the highest degree, in what I mean by Christianity. Good sense (so called) is but a poor, dim shadow of what Christians call faith. Good nature is only a faint, distant resemblance of Christian charity. And good manners, if of the most finished kind that nature, assisted by art, can attain to, is but a dead picture of that holiness of conversation which is the image of God visibly expressed. All these, put together by the art of God, I call Christianity." "Sir, if this be Christianity," said my opponent, in amaze, "I never saw a Christian in my life."

Perhaps it is the same case with *you*. If so, I am grieved for you, and can only wish, till you do see a living proof of this, that you would not say you see a Christian. For this is scriptural Christianity, and this alone. Whenever, therefore, you see an unreasonable man, you see one who perhaps calls himself by that name, but is no more a Christian than he is an angel. So far as he departs from true, genuine reason, so far he departs from Christianity. Do not say, "This is only asserted, not proved." It is undeniably proved by the original charter of Christianity. We appeal to this, to the written word. If any man's temper, or words, or actions, are contradictory to right reason, it is evident, to a demonstration, they are contradictory to this. Produce any possible or conceivable instance, and you will find the fact is so. The lives, therefore, of those who are *called* Christians, is no just objection to Christianity.

We join with you then in desiring a religion founded on reason, and every way agreeable thereto. But one question still remains to be asked, What do you mean by *reason?* I suppose you mean the eternal reason, or the nature of things; the nature of God, and the nature of man, with the relations necessarily subsisting between them. Why, this is the very religion *we* preach; a religion evidently founded on, and every way agreeable to, eternal reason, to the essential nature of things. Its foundation stands on the nature of God and the nature of man, together with their mutual relations. And it is every way suitable thereto; to the nature of God; for it begins in knowing him: and where, but in the true knowledge of God, can you conceive true religion to begin? It goes on in loving him and all mankind; for you cannot but imitate whom you love: it ends in serving him; in doing his will; in obeying him whom we know and love.

It is every way suited to the nature of man; for it begins in a man's knowing himself; knowing himself to be what he really is,—foolish, vicious, miserable. It goes on to point out the remedy for this, to make him truly wise, virtuous, and happy; as every thinking mind (perhaps from some implicit remembrance of what it originally was) longs to be. It finishes all, by restoring the due relations between God and man; by uniting for ever the tender Father, and the grateful, obedient son; the great Lord of all, and the faithful servant; doing not his own will, but the will of him that sent him.

But perhaps by reason you mean the faculty of reasoning, of inferring one thing from another. There are many, it is confessed (particularly those who are styled Mystic divines), that utterly decry the use of reason, thus understood, in religion; nay, that condemn all reasoning concerning the things of God, as utterly destructive of true religion.

But we can in no wise agree with this. We find no authority for it in holy writ. So far from it, that we find there both our Lord and his Apostles continually reasoning with their opposers. Neither do we know, in all the productions of ancient and modern times, such a chain of reasoning or argumentation, so close, so solid, so regularly connected, as the Epistle to the Hebrews. And the strongest reasoner whom we have ever observed (excepting only Jesus of Nazareth) was that Paul of Tarsus; the same who has left that plain direction for all Christians: "In malice," or wickedness, "be ye children; but in understanding," or reason, "be ye men."

We therefore not only allow, but earnestly exhort, all who seek after true religion, to use all the reason which God hath given them, in searching out the things of God. But your reasoning justly, not only on this, but on any subject whatsoever, pre-supposes true judgments already formed, whereon to ground your argumentation. Else, you know, you will stumble at every step; because *ex falso non sequitur verum,* "it is impossible, if your premises are false, to infer from them true conclusions."

You know, likewise, that before it is possible for you to form a true judgment of them, it is absolutely necessary that you have a clear apprehension of the things of God, and that your ideas thereof be all fixed, distinct, and determinate. And seeing our ideas are not innate, but must all originally come from our senses, it is certainly necessary that you have senses capable of discerning objects of this kind: not those only which are called natural senses, which in this respect profit nothing, as being altogether incapable of discerning objects of a spiritual kind; but spiritual senses, exercised to discern spiritual good and evil. It is necessary that you have *the hearing ear,* and the *seeing eye,* emphatically so called; that you have a new class of senses opened in your soul, not depending on organs of flesh and blood, to be "the evidence of things not seen," as your bodily senses are of visible things; to be the avenues to the invisible world, to discern spiritual objects, and to furnish you with ideas of what the outward "eye hath not seen, neither the ear heard."

And till you have these internal senses, till the eyes of your understanding are opened, you can have no apprehension of divine things, no idea of them at all. Nor, consequently, till then, can you either judge truly, or reason justly, concerning them; seeing your reason has no ground whereon to stand, no materials to work upon.

To use the trite instance: as you cannot reason concerning colours, if you have no natural sight, because all the ideas received by your other senses are of a different kind; so that neither your hearing, nor any other sense, can supply your want of sight, or furnish your reason in this respect with matter to work upon: so you cannot reason concerning spiritual things, if you have no spiritual sight; because all your ideas received by your outward senses are of a different kind; yea, far more different from those received by faith or internal sensation, than the idea of colour from that of sound. These are only different species of one genus, namely, sensible ideas, received by external sensation: whereas the ideas of faith differ *toto genere* [entirely] from those of external sensation. So that it is not conceivable, that external sensation should

## An Earnest Appeal.

supply the want of internal senses; or furnish your reason in this respect with matter to work upon.

What then will your reason do here? How will it pass from things natural to spiritual; from the things that are seen to those that are not seen; from the visible to the invisible world? What a gulf is here! By what art will reason get over the immense chasm? This cannot be, till the Almighty come in to your succour, and give you that faith you have hitherto despised. Then upborne, as it were, on eagles' wings, you shall soar away into the regions of eternity; and your enlightened reason shall explore even "the deep things of God;" God himself "revealing them to you by his Spirit." . . .

Perhaps the first thing that now occurs to your mind relates to the doctrine which we teach. You have heard that we say, "Men may live without sin." And have you not heard that the Scripture says the same;—we mean, without committing sin? . . .

Have you not another objection nearly allied to this, namely, that we preach perfection? True; but what perfection? The term you cannot object to; because it is scriptural. All the difficulty is, to fix the meaning of it according to the word of God. And this we have done again and again, declaring to all the world, that Christian perfection does not imply an exemption from ignorance, or mistake, or infirmities, or temptations; but that it does imply the being so crucified with Christ, as to be able to testify, "I live not, but Christ liveth in me," Gal. ii, 20, and hath "purified my heart by faith," Acts xv, 9. It does imply "the casting down every high thing that exalteth itself against the knowledge of God, and bringing into captivity every thought to the obedience of Christ." It does imply "the being holy, as he that hath called us is holy, in all manner of conversation," 2 Cor. x, 5; 1 Peter i, 15; and, in a word, "the loving the Lord our God with all our heart, and serving him with all our strength."

Now, is it possible for any who believe the Scripture to deny one tittle of this? You cannot. You dare not. You would not for the world. You know it is the pure word of God. And this is the whole of what we preach; this is the height and depth of what we (with St. Paul) call perfection,—a state of soul devoutly to be wished by all who have tasted of the love of God. O pray for it without ceasing! It is the one thing you want. Come with boldness to the throne of grace, and be assured that when you ask this of God, you shall have the petition you ask of him. We know indeed that to man, to the natural man, this is impossible. But we know also, that as no word is impossible with God, so "all things are possible to him that believeth."

For "we are saved by faith." But have you not heard this urged as another objection against us, that we preach salvation by faith alone? And does not St. Paul do the same thing? "By grace," saith he, "ye are saved through faith." Can any words be more express? And elsewhere, "Believe in the Lord Jesus, and thou shalt be saved," Acts xvi, 31.

What we mean by this (if it has not been sufficiently explained already) is, that we are saved from our sins, only by a confidence in the love of God. As soon as we "behold what manner of love it is which the Father hath bestowed upon us, we love him" (as the Apostle observes), "because he first loved us." And then is that commandment written in our heart, "That he who loveth God love his brother also;" from which love of God and man, meekness, humbleness of mind, and all holy tempers, spring. Now, these are the very essence of salvation, of Christian salvation, salvation from sin; and from these outward salvation flows, that is, holiness of life and conversation. Well, and are not these things so? If you know in whom you have believed, you need no further witnesses. . . .

"But by talking thus you encourage sinners." I do encourage them—to repent; and do not you? Do not you know how many heap sin upon sin, purely for want of such encouragement; because they think they can never be forgiven, there is no place for repentance left? Does not your heart also bleed for them? What would you think too dear to part with? What would you not do, what would you not suffer, to bring one such sinner to repentance? Could not your love "endure all things" for them? Yes,—if you believed it would do them good; if you had any hope that they would be better. Why do you not believe it would do them good? Why have you not a hope that they will be better? Plainly, because you do not love them enough; because you have not that charity which not only endureth, but at the same time believeth and hopeth all things. . . .

This only we confess, that we preach inward salvation, now attainable by faith. And for preaching this (for no other crime was then so much as pretended) we were forbid to preach any more in those churches, where, till then, we were gladly received. This is a notorious fact. Being thus hindered from preaching in the places we should first have chosen, we now declare the "grace of God which bringeth salvation, in all places of his dominion;" as well knowing, that God dwelleth not only in temples made with hands. This is the real, and it is the only real, ground of complaint against us. And this we avow before all mankind, we do preach this salvation by faith. And not being suffered to preach it in the usual places, we declare it wherever a door is opened, either on a mountain, or a plain, or by a river side (for all which we conceive we have sufficient precedent), or in prison, or, as it were, in the house of Justus, or the school of one Tyrannus. Nor dare we refrain. "A dispensation of the Gospel is committed to me; and wo is me, if I preach not the Gospel."

Here we allow the fact, but deny the guilt. But in every other point alleged, we deny the fact, and call upon the world to prove it, if they can. More especially, we call upon those who for many years saw our manner of life at Oxford. These well know that "after the straitest sect of our religion we lived Pharisees;" and that the grand objection to us for all those years was, the being righteous overmuch; the reading, fasting, praying, denying ourselves,—the going to church, and to the Lord's table,—the relieving the poor, visiting those that were sick and in prison, instructing the ignorant, and labouring to reclaim the wicked,—more than was necessary for salvation. These were our open, flagrant crimes, from the year 1729 to the year 1737; touching which our Lord shall judge in that day.

But, waiving the things that are past, which of you now convinceth us of sin? Which of you (I here more especially appeal to my brethren the clergy) can personally convict us of any ungodliness or unholiness of conversation? Ye know in your own hearts (all that are candid men, all that are not utterly blinded with prejudice), that we "labour to have a conscience void of offence both toward God and toward man." Brethren, I would to God that in this ye were even as we. But indeed (with grief I speak it) ye are not. There are among yourselves ungodly and unholy men; openly, undeniably such; drunkards, gluttons, returners of evil for evil, liars, swearers, profaners of the day of the Lord. Proof hereof is not wanting, if ye require it. Where then is your zeal against these? A clergyman, so drunk he can scarce stand or speak, may, in the presence of a thousand people (at Epworth, in Lincolnshire), set upon another clergyman of the same Church, both with abusive words and open violence. And what follows? Why, the one is still allowed to dispense the sacred signs of the body and blood of Christ: but the other is not allowed to receive them,— because he is a field preacher.

O ye pillars and fathers of the Church, are these things well pleasing to Him who hath made you overseers over that flock which he hath purchased with his own blood? O that ye would suffer me to boast myself a little! Is there not a cause? Have ye not compelled me? Which of your clergy are more unspotted in their lives, which more unwearied in their labours, than those whose "names ye cast out as evil," whom ye count "as the filth and off-scouring of the world?" Which of them is more zealous to spend and be spent, for the lost sheep of the house of Israel? Or who among them is more ready to be offered up for their flock "upon the sacrifice and service of their faith?"

Will ye say (as the historian of Catiline), *Si sic pro patriâ!* [If thus for your country!] "If this were done in defence of the Church, and not in order to undermine and destroy it!" That is the very proposition I undertake to prove,—that we are now defending the Church, even the Church of England, in opposition to all those who either secretly undermine or more openly attempt to destroy it.

That we are Papists (we who are daily and hourly preaching that very doctrine which is so solemnly anathematized by the whole Church of Rome), is such a charge that I dare not waste my time in industriously confuting it. Let any man of common sense only look on the title pages of the sermons we have lately preached at Oxford, and he will need nothing more to show him the weight of this senseless, shameless accusation;—unless he can suppose the governors both of Christ Church and Lincoln College, nay, and all the university, to be Papists too.

You yourself can easily acquit us of this; but not of the other part of the charge. You still think we are secretly undermining, if not openly destroying, the Church. What do you mean by the Church? A visible Church (as our article defines it) is a company of faithful or believing people;—*cœtus credentium*. This is the essence of a church; and the properties thereof are (as they are described in the words that follow), "among whom the pure word of God is preached, and the sacraments duly administered."* Now then (according to this authentic account), what is the Church of England? What is it indeed, but the faithful people, the true believers in England? It is true, if these are scattered abroad, they come under another consideration: but when they are visibly joined, by assembling together to hear the pure word of God preached, and to eat of one bread, and drink of one cup, they are then properly the visible Church of England.

It were well if this were a little more considered by those who so vehemently cry out, "The Church! the Church!" (as those of old, "The temple of the Lord! the temple of the Lord!") not knowing what they speak, nor whereof they affirm. A provincial or national Church, according to our article, is the true believers of that province or nation. If these are dispersed up and down, they are only a part of the invisible Church of Christ.

---

* "According to this definition, those congregations in which the pure word of God (a strong expression) is not preached are no parts either of the church of England, or the church catholic: as neither are those in which the sacraments are not duly administered.

"I will not undertake to defend the accuracy of this definition. I dare not exclude from the church catholic, all those congregations in which any unscriptural doctrines, which cannot be affirmed to be 'the pure word of God,' are sometimes, yea, frequently preached; neither all those congregations in which the sacraments are not 'duly administered.' Certainly if these things are so, the church of Rome is not so much as a part of the catholic church: seeing therein neither is 'the pure word of God' preached, nor the sacraments 'duly administered.' Whoever they are that have 'one spirit, one hope, one Lord, one faith, one God and Father of all;' I can easily bear with their holding wrong opinions, yea, and superstitious modes of worship; nor would I, on these accounts, scruple still to include them within the pale of the catholic church: neither would I have any objection to receive them, if they desired it, as members of the church of England."—*Sermon of the Church*, 1786. *Works*, ii, 158.

## An Earnest Appeal.

But if they are visibly joined by assembling together to hear his word and partake of his supper, they are then a visible Church, such as the Church of England, France, or any other.

This being premised, I ask, How do we undermine or destroy the Church,—the provincial, visible Church of England? The article mentions three things as essential to a visible Church. First: Living faith; without which, indeed, there can be no Church at all, neither visible nor invisible. Secondly: Preaching, and consequently hearing, the pure word of God, else that faith would languish and die. And, Thirdly, a due administration of the sacraments,—the ordinary means whereby God increaseth faith. Now come close to the question: In which of these points do we undermine or destroy the Church? . . .

But perhaps you have heard that we in truth regard no Church at all; that gain is the true spring of all our actions; that I, in particular, am well paid for my work, having thirteen hundred pounds a year (as a reverend author accurately computes it) at the Foundery alone, over and above what I receive from Bristol, Kingswood, Newcastle, and other places; and that whoever survives me will see I have made good use of my time; for I shall not die a beggar. . . .

Inform yourself a little better, and you will find that both at Newcastle, Bristol, and Kingswood, and all other places, where any collection is made, the money collected is both received and expended by the stewards of those several societies, and never comes into my hands at all,— neither first nor last. And you, or any who desire it, shall read over the accounts kept by any of those stewards, and see with your own eyes, that by all these societies I gain just as much as you do. . . .

You can never reconcile it with any degree of common sense, that a man who wants nothing, who has already all the necessaries, all the conveniences, nay, and

many of the superfluities, of life, and these not only
independent on any one, but less liable to contingencies
than even a gentleman's freehold estate; that such a one
should calmly and deliberately throw up his ease, most
of his friends, his reputation, and that way of life which
of all others is most agreeable both to his natural temper,
and education; that he should toil day and night, spend all
his time and strength, knowingly destroy a firm constitu-
tion, and hasten into weakness, pain, diseases, death,—to
gain a debt of six or seven hundred pounds!*

But suppose the balance on the other side, let me ask
you one plain question, For what gain (setting conscience
aside) will *you* be obliged to act thus? to live exactly as
I do? For what price will you preach (and that with all
your might, not in an easy, indolent, fashionable way)
eighteen or nineteen times every week; and this throughout the year? What shall I give you to travel seven or
eight hundred miles, in all weathers, every two or three
months? For what salary will you abstain from all other
diversions, than the doing good, and the praising God?
I am mistaken if you would not prefer strangling to such
a life, even with thousands of gold and silver.†

---

* " I am, to this day, ashamed before God, that I do so little to what
I ought to do. But this you call 'overdone humility,' and suppose it to
be inconsistent with what occurs in the ninety-third and ninety-fourth
paragraphs of the 'Earnest Appeal.' I believe it is not at all inconsistent therewith ; only one expression there is too strong,—' all his time
and strength ; '—for this very cause, 'I am ashamed before God.' I do
not spend all my time so profitably as I might, nor all my strength ;
at least, not all I might have, if it were not for my own lukewarmness
and remissness ; if I wrestled with God in constant and fervent prayer."
—*Letter to Mr. John Smith*, 1747. *Works*, vi. 640.

† " But suppose field preaching to be, in a case of this kind, ever so
expedient, or even necessary, yet who will contest with us for this province ? May we not enjoy this quiet and unmolested ? Unmolested, I
mean, by any competitors : for who is there among you, brethren, that
is willing (examine your own hearts) even to save souls from death at
this price ? Would not you let a thousand souls perish, rather than you
would be the instruments of rescuing them thus? I do not speak now
with regard to conscience, but to the inconveniences that must accom-

And what is the comfort you have found out for me in these circumstances? Why, that I shall not die a beggar. So now I am supposed to be heaping up riches, that I may leave them behind me. *Leave them behind me!* For whom? my wife and children? Who are they? They are yet unborn. Unless thou meanest the children of faith whom God hath given me. But my heavenly Father feedeth them. Indeed, if I lay up riches at all, it must be to leave behind me; seeing my fellowship is a provision for life. But I cannot understand this. What comfort would it be to my soul, now launched into eternity, that I had left behind me gold as the dust, and silver as the sand of the sea? Will it follow me over the great gulf? or can I go back to it? Thou that liftest up thy eyes in hell, what do thy riches profit thee now? Will all thou once hadst under the sun gain thee a drop of water to cool thy tongue? O the comfort of riches left behind to one who is tormented in that flame! You put me in mind of those celebrated lines (which I once exceeding admired), addressed by way of consolation to the soul of a poor self-murderer:—

> " Yet shall thy grave with rising flowers be dress'd,
> And the green turf lie light upon thy breast!
> Here shall the year its earliest beauties show:
> Here the first roses of the spring shall blow:
> While angels with their silver wings o'ershade
> The place now sacred by thy relics made."

---

pany it. Can you sustain them, if you would? Can you bear the summer sun to beat upon your naked head? Can you suffer the wintry rain or wind, from whatever quarter it blows? Are you able to stand in the open air without any covering or defence when God casteth abroad his snow like wool, or scattereth his hoar frost like ashes? And yet these are some of the smallest inconveniencies which accompany field preaching. Far beyond all these, are the contradiction of sinners, the scoffs both of the great vulgar and the small; contempt and reproach of every kind; often more than verbal affronts, stupid, brutal violence, sometimes to the hazard of health, or limbs, or life. Brethren, do you envy us this honour? What, I pray, would buy you to be a field preacher? Or what, think you, could induce any man of common sense to continue therein one year, unless he had a full conviction in himself that it was the will of God concerning him?"—*A Farther Appeal to Men of Reason and Religion*, Part iii, 1745. *Works*, v, 163.

I will now simply tell you my sense of these matters, whether you will hear, or whether you will forbear. Food and raiment I have; such food as I choose to eat, and such raiment as I choose to put on. I have a place where to lay my head. I have what is needful for life and godliness. And I apprehend this is all the world can afford. The kings of the earth can give me no more. For as to gold and silver, I count it dung and dross; I trample it under my feet. I (yet not I, but the grace of God that is in me) esteem it just as the mire in the streets. I desire it not; I seek it not; I only fear lest any of it should cleave to me, and I should not be able to shake it off before my spirit returns to God. It must indeed pass through my hands; but I will take care (God being my helper) that the mammon of unrighteousness shall only pass through; it shall not rest there. None of the accursed thing shall be found in my tents when the Lord calleth me hence. And hear ye this, all you who have discovered the treasures which I am to leave behind me: If I leave behind me ten pounds (above my debts, and my books, or what may happen to be due on account of them), you and all mankind bear witness against me, that I lived and died a thief and a robber.

Before I conclude, I cannot but entreat you who know God to review the whole matter from the foundation. Call to mind what the state of religion was in our nation a few years since. In whom did you find the holy tempers that were in Christ? bowels of mercies, lowliness, meekness, gentleness, contempt of the world, patience, temperance, long-suffering? a burning love to God, rejoicing evermore, and in every thing giving thanks; and a tender love to all mankind, covering, believing, hoping, enduring all things? Perhaps you did not know one such man in the world. But how many that had all unholy tempers? What vanity and pride, what stubbornness and self-will, what anger, fretfulness, discontent, what suspicion and resentment, what inordinate affections, what irregular passions, what foolish and hurtful desires, might you find in those who were called the *best* of men, in those who made the strictest profession of religion? And how few did you know who went so far as the profession of religion, who had even the "form of godliness!" Did you not frequently bewail, wherever your lot was cast, the general want of even outward religion? How few were seen at the public worship of God! how much fewer at the Lord's table! And was even this little flock zealous of good works, careful, as they had time, to do good to all men? On the other hand, did you not with grief observe outward irreligion in every place? Where could you be for one week without being an eye or an ear witness of cursing, swearing, or profaneness, of Sabbath breaking or drunkenness, of quarrelling or brawling, of revenge or obscenity? Were these things done in a corner? Did not gross iniquity of all kinds overspread our land as a flood? yea, and daily increase, in spite of all the opposition which the children of God did or could make against it?

If you had been then told that the jealous God would soon arise and maintain his own cause; that he would pour down his Spirit from on high, and renew the face of the earth; that he would shed abroad his love in the hearts of the outcasts of men, producing all holy and heavenly tempers, expelling anger, and pride, and evil desire, and all unholy and earthly tempers; causing outward religion, the work of faith, the patience of hope, the labour of love, to flourish and abound; and, wherever it spread, abolishing outward irreligion, destroying all the works of the devil: if you had been told that this living knowledge of the Lord would in a short space of time overspread our land; yea, and daily increase, in spite of all the opposition which the devil and his children did or could make against it; would you not have vehemently desired to see that day, that you might bless God and rejoice therein?

Behold, the day of the Lord is come! He is again visiting and redeeming his people. Having eyes, see ye not? Having ears, do ye not hear, neither understand with your hearts? At this hour the Lord is rolling away our reproach. Already his standard is set up. His Spirit is poured forth on the outcasts of men, and his love shed abroad in their hearts. Love of all mankind, meekness, gentleness, humbleness of mind, holy and heavenly affections, do take place of hate, anger, pride, revenge, and vile or vain affections. Hence, wherever the power of the Lord spreads, springs outward religion in all its forms. The houses of God are filled; the table of the Lord is thronged on every side. And those who thus show their love of God, show they love their neighbour also, by being careful to maintain good works, by doing all manner of good, as they have time, to all men. They are likewise careful to abstain from all evil. Cursing, Sabbath breaking, drunkenness, with all other (however fashionable) works of the devil, are not once named among them. All this is plain, demonstrable fact. For this also is not done in a corner. Now, do you acknowledge the day of your visitation? Do you bless God and rejoice therein?

What hinders? Is it this,—that men say all manner of evil of those whom God is pleased to use as instruments in his work? O ye fools, did ye suppose the devil was dead? or that he would not fight for his kingdom? And what weapons shall he fight with, if not with lies? Is he not a liar, and the father of it? Suffer ye then thus far. Let the devil and his children say all manner of evil of us. And let them go on deceiving each other, and being deceived. But ye need not be deceived also; or if you are, if you will believe all they say, be it so,—that we are weak, silly, wicked men; without sense, without learning, without even a desire or design of doing good; yet I insist upon the fact: Christ is preached, and sinners are converted to God. This none but a madman can deny. We

## An Earnest Appeal. 235

are ready to prove it by a cloud of witnesses. Neither, therefore, can the inference be denied, that God is now visiting his people. O that all men may know, in this their day, the things that make for their peace!

Upon the whole, to men of the world I would still recommend the known advice of Gamaliel: "Refrain from these men, and let them alone: for if this work be of men, it will come to nought; but if it be of God, ye cannot overthrow it; lest haply ye be found even to fight against God." But unto you whom God hath chosen out of the world, I say, Ye are our brethren, and of our father's house; it behoveth you, in whatsoever manner ye are able, "to strengthen our hands in God." And this ye are all able to do; to wish us good luck in the name of the Lord, and to pray continually that none of "these things may move us," and that "we may not count our lives dear unto ourselves, so that we may finish our course with joy, and the ministry which we have received of the Lord Jesus!"

## A LETTER TO
### THE REV. MR. DOWNES, RECTOR OF ST. MICHAEL'S,
#### WOOD-STREET:
#### OCCASIONED BY HIS LATE TRACT,
### ENTITLED "METHODISM EXAMINED AND EXPOSED."

[*Works*, v, 428-37.]

LONDON, November 17, 1759.

REVEREND SIR,—In the Tract which you have just published concerning the people called Methodists, you very properly say, "Our first care should be, candidly and fairly to examine their doctrines. For, as to censure them unexamined would be unjust; so to do the same without a fair and impartial examination would be ungenerous." And again: "We should, in the first place, carefully and candidly examine their doctrines." (p. 68.) This is undoubtedly true. But have you done it? Have you ever examined their doctrines yet? Have you examined them fairly? fairly and candidly? candidly and carefully? Have you read over so much as the Sermons they have published, or the "Appeal to Men of Reason and Religion?" I hope you have not; for I would fain make some little excuse for your uttering so many senseless, shameless falsehoods. I hope you know nothing about the Methodists, no more than I do about the Cham of Tartary; that you are ignorant of the whole affair, and are so bold, only because you are blind. *Bold* enough! Throughout your whole Tract, you speak *satis pro imperio* [sufficiently authoritatively],—as authoritatively as if you was, not an archbishop only, but apostolic vicar also; as if you had the full papal power in your hands, and fire and faggot at your beck! And *blind* enough; so that you blunder on, through thick and thin, bespattering

## A Letter to the Rev. Mr. Downes.

all that come in your way, according to the old, laudable maxim, "Throw dirt enough, and some will stick."

I hope, I say, that this is the case, and that you do not knowingly assert so many palpable falsehoods. You say, "If I am mistaken, I shall always be ready and desirous to retract my error." (p. 56.) A little candour and care might have prevented those mistakes; this is the first thing one would have desired. The next is, that they may be removed; that you may see wherein you have been mistaken, and be more wary for the time to come.

You undertake to give an account, First, of the rise and principles, Then, of the practices, of the Methodists.

On the former head you say, "Our Church has long been infested with these grievous wolves, who, though no more than two when they entered in, and they so young they might rather be called wolflings" (that is lively and pretty!), "have yet spread their ravenous kind through every part of this kingdom. Where, what havoc they have made, how many of the sheep they have torn, I need not say." (pp. 4, 5.) "About twenty-five years ago, these two bold though beardless divines" (pity, sir, that you had not taught me, twenty-five years ago, *sapientem pascere barbam* [to cherish a sapient beard], and thereby to avoid some part of your displeasure), "being lifted with spiritual pride, were presumptuous enough to become founders of the sect called Methodists." (p. 6.) "A couple of young, raw, aspiring twigs of the ministry dreamed of a special and supernatural call to this." (p. 25.) No, sir; it was you dreamed of this, not we. We dreamed of nothing twenty-five years ago, but instructing our pupils in religion and learning, and a few prisoners in the common principles of Christianity. You go on: "They were ambitious of being accounted missionaries, immediately delegated by Heaven to correct the errors of bishops and archbishops, and reform their abuses; to instruct the clergy in the true nature of

Christianity, and to caution the laity not to venture their souls in any such unhallowed hands as refused to be initiated in all the mysteries of Methodism." (pp. 20, 21.) Well *asserted* indeed; but where is the *proof* of any one of these propositions? I must insist upon this; clear, cogent proof: else they must be set down for so many glaring falsehoods.

"The Church of Rome (to which on so many accounts they were much obliged, and as gratefully returned the obligation) taught them to set up for infallible interpreters of Scripture." (p. 54.) Pray, on what accounts are we "obliged to the Church of Rome?" And how have we "returned the obligation?" I beg you would please (1.) To explain this; and (2.) To prove that we ever yet (whoever taught us) "set up for infallible interpreters of Scripture." So far from it, that we have over and over declared, in print as well as in public preaching, "We are no more to expect any living man to be infallible than to be omniscient." (Vol. i, p. 357.)

"As to other extraordinary gifts, influences, and operations of the Holy Ghost, no man who has but once dipped into their Journals, and other ostentatious trash of the same kind, can doubt their looking upon themselves as not coming one whit behind the greatest of the Apostles." (*Methodism Examined,* p. 21.)

I acquit you, sir, of ever having "once dipped into that ostentatious trash." I do not accuse you of having read so much as the titles of my Journals. I say, *my* Journals; for (as little as you seem to know it) my brother has published none. I therefore look upon this as simple ignorance. You talk thus, because you know no better. You do not know, that in these very Journals I utterly disclaim the "extraordinary gifts of the Spirit," and all other "influences and operations of the Holy Ghost" than those that are common to all real Christians.

And yet I will not say, this ignorance is blameless. For

ought you not to have known better? Ought you not to have taken the pains of procuring better information, when it might so easily have been had? Ought you to have publicly advanced so heavy charges as these, without knowing whether they were true or no?

You proceed to give as punctual an account of us, *tanquam intus et in cute nosses* [as if you had known us in heart and life]: "They outstripped, if possible, even Montanus, for external sanctity and severity of discipline." (p. 22.) "They condemned all regard for temporal concerns. They encouraged their devotees to take no thought for any one thing upon earth; the consequence of which was, a total neglect of their affairs, and impoverishment of their families." (p. 23.) Blunder all over! We had no room for any discipline, severe or not, five-and-twenty years ago, unless college discipline; my brother then residing at Christ Church, and I at Lincoln College. And as to our "sanctity" (were it more or less), how do you know it was only external? Was you intimately acquainted with us? I do not remember where I had the honour of conversing with you. Or could you (as the legend says of St. Pabomius) "smell a heretic ten miles" off? And how came you to dream, again, that we "condemned all regard for temporal concerns, and encouraged men to take no thought for any one thing upon earth?" Vain dream! We on the contrary, severely condemn all who neglect their temporal concerns, and who do not take care of every thing on earth wherewith God hath entrusted them. The consequence of this is, that the Methodists, so called, do not "neglect their affairs and impoverish their families;" but, by diligence in business, "provide things honest in the sight of all men." Insomuch, that multitudes of them, who, in time past, had scarce food to eat or raiment to put on, have now "all things needful for life and godliness;" and that for their families, as well as themselves.

Hitherto you have been giving an account of two wolflings only; but now they are grown into perfect wolves. Let us see what a picture you draw of them in this state, both as to their principles and practice.

You begin with a home stroke: "In the Montanist you may behold the bold lineaments and bloated countenance of the Methodist." (p. 17.) I wish you do not squint at the honest countenance of Mr. Venn, who is indeed as far from fear as he is from guile. But if it is somewhat "bloated," that is not his fault; sickness may have the same effect on yours or mine.

But to come closer to the point: "They have darkened religion with many ridiculous fancies, tending to confound the head, and to corrupt the heart." (p. 13.) "A thorough knowledge of them would work, in every rightly-disposed mind, an abhorrence of those doctrines which directly tend to distract the head, and to debauch the heart, by turning faith into frenzy, and the grace of God into wantonness." (pp. 101, 102.) "These doctrines are unreasonable and ridiculous, clashing with our natural ideas of the divine perfections, with the end of religion, with the honour of God, and man's both present and future happiness. Therefore we pronounce them 'filthy dreamers,' turning faith into fancy, the Gospel into farce; thus adding blasphemy to enthusiasm." (pp. 66, 68.)

Take breath, sir; there is a long paragraph behind. "The abettors of these wild and whimsical notions are (1.) Close friends to the Church of Rome, agreeing with her in almost everything but the doctrine of merit: (2.) They are no less kind to infidelity, by making the Christian religion a mere creature of the imagination: (3.) They cut up Christianity by the roots, frustrating the very end for which Christ died, which was, that by holiness we might be 'made meet for the inheritance of the saints:' (4.) They are enemies not only to Christianity, but to 'every religion whatsoever,' by labouring to subvert or overturn the whole system of morality: (5.) Consequently, they must be enemies of society, dissolving the band by which it is united and knit together." In a word: "All ancient heresies have in a manner concentred in the Methodists; particularly those of the Simonians, Gnostics, Antinomians," (as widely distant from each other as Predestinarians from Calvinists!) "Valentinians, Donatists, and Montanists." (pp. 101, 102.) While your hand was in, you might as well have added, Carpocratians, Eutychians, Nestorians, Sabellians. If you say, "I never heard of them;" no matter for that; you may find them, as well as the rest, in Bishop Pearson's index.

Well, all this is mere flourish; raising a dust, to blind the eyes of the spectators. Generals, you know, prove nothing. Leaving this as it is, let us come to particulars.

But, first, give me leave to transcribe a few words from a tract published some years ago. "Your lordship premises, 'It is not at all needful to charge the particular tenets upon the particular persons among them.' Indeed, it is needful in the highest degree. Just as needful as it is not to put a stumbling block in the way of our brethren; not to lay them under an almost insuperable temptation of condemning the innocent with the guilty." (*Letter to the Bishop of London,* vol. v, pp. 340, 341.)

And it is now far more needful than it was then; as that title of reproach, *Methodist,* is now affixed to many people who are not under my care, nor ever had any connection with me. And what have I to do with these? If you give me a nick-name, and then give it to others whom I know not, does this make me accountable for them? either for their principles or practice? In nowise. I am to answer for myself, and for those that are in connection with me. This is all that a man of common sense can undertake, or a man of common humanity require.

Let us begin then upon even ground; and if you can
prove upon me, John Wesley, any one of the charges
which you have advanced, call me not only a wolf, but
an otter, if you please.

Your First particular charge (which, indeed, runs
through your book, and is repeated in twenty different
places) is, that we make the way to heaven too broad,
teaching, men may be saved by faith without works.
Some of your words are, "They set out with forming a
fair and tempting model of religion, so flattering the
follies of degenerate man, that it could not fail to gain
the hearts of multitudes, especially of the loose and
vicious, the lazy and indolent. They want to get to
heaven the shortest way, and with the least trouble: now,
a reliance on Christ, and a disclaiming of good works,
are terms as easy as the merest libertine can ask. They
persuade their people that they may be saved by the
righteousness of Christ, without any holiness of their
own; nay, that good works are not only unnecessary, but
also dangerous; that we may be saved by faith, without
any other requisite, such as Gospel obedience, and a holy
life. Lastly: The Valentinians pretended, that if good
works were necessary to salvation, it was only to animal
men, that is, to all who were not of their clan; and that,
although sin might damn others, it could not hurt them.
In consequence of which they lived in all lust and impurity, and wallowed in the most unheard-of bestialities.
The Methodists distinguish much after the same manner."
(*Methodism Examined*, pp. 52, 31, 38, 14.)

Sir, you are not awake yet. You are dreaming still,
and fighting with shadows of your own raising. The
"model of religion with which the Methodists set out"
is perfectly well known; if not to you, yet to many thousands in England who are no Methodists. I laid it before the university of Oxford, at St. Mary's, on January
1, 1733. You may read it when you are at leisure; for

## A Letter to the Rev. Mr. Downes. 243

it is in print, entitled, "The Circumcision of the Heart." And whoever reads only that one discourse, with any tolerable share of attention, will easily judge, whether that "model of religion flatters the follies of degenerate man," or is likely to "gain the hearts of multitudes, especially of the loose and vicious, the lazy and indolent!" Will a man choose this, as "the shortest way to heaven, and with the least trouble?" Are these "as easy terms as any libertine" or infidel "can desire?" The truth is, we have been these thirty years continually reproached for just the contrary to what you dream of; with making the way to heaven too strait; with being ourselves "righteous overmuch," and teaching others, they could not be saved without so many works as it was impossible for them to perform. And to this day, instead of teaching men that they may be saved by a faith which is without good works, without "Gospel obedience and holiness of life," we teach exactly the reverse, continually insisting on all outward as well as all inward holiness.* For the

---

* "Is not the whole dispute of salvation by faith or by works a mere strife of words?

"A. In asserting salvation by faith, we mean this: (1.) That pardon (salvation begun) is received by faith producing works. (2.) That holiness (salvation continued) is faith working by love. (3.) That heaven (salvation finished) is the reward of this faith.

"If you who assert salvation by works, or by faith and works, mean the same thing (understanding by faith, the revelation of Christ in us,—by salvation, pardon, holiness, glory), we will not strive with you at all. If you do not, this is not a strife of words; but the very vitals, the essence of Christianity is the thing in question."—*Minutes of Some Late Conversations* ("*The Doctrinal Minutes*" for 1746). *Works*, v, 205.

"We said in 1744, 'We have leaned too much toward Calvinism.' Wherein? . . . (2.) With regard to 'working for life,' which our Lord expressly commands us to do. 'Labour,' ἐργάζεσθε, literally, '*work*, for the meat that endureth to everlasting life.' And in fact, every believer, till he comes to glory, works *for* as well as *from* life. (3.) We have received it as a maxim, that 'a man is to do nothing in order to justification.' Nothing can be more false. Whoever desires to find favour with God, should 'cease from evil, and learn to do well.' So God himself teaches by the prophet Isaiah. Whoever repents, should 'do works meet for repentance.' And if this is not in order to find favour, what does he do them for?

notorious truth of this we appeal to the whole tenor of our sermons, printed and unprinted; in particular to those upon "Our Lord's Sermon on the Mount," wherein every branch of Gospel obedience is both asserted and proved to be indispensably necessary to eternal salvation.

Therefore, as to the rest of the "Antinomian trash" which you have so carefully gathered up, as, "that the regenerate are as pure as Christ himself; that it would be criminal for them to pray for pardon; that the greatest crimes are no crimes in the saints" &c, &c (p. 17), I have no concern therewith at all, no more than with any that teach it. Indeed I have confuted it over and over, in tracts published many years ago.

A Second charge which you advance is, that "we suppose every man's final doom to depend on God's sovereign will and pleasure" (I presume you mean, on his absolute, unconditional decree); that we "consider man as a mere machine;" that we suppose believers "cannot fall from grace." (p. 31.) Nay, I suppose none of these things. Let those who do, answer for themselves. I suppose just the contrary in "Predestination Calmly Considered," a tract published ten years ago. . . .

---

"Once more review the whole affair:

"(1.) Who of us is now accepted of God?

"He that now believes in Christ with a loving, obedient heart.

"(2.) But who among those that never heard of Christ?

"He that, according to the light he has, 'feareth God and worketh righteousness.'

"(3.) Is this the same with 'he that is sincere?'

"Nearly, if not quite.

"(4.) Is not this salvation by works?

"Not by the merit of works, but by works as a condition.

"(5.) What have we then been disputing about for these thirty years?

"I am afraid about words, namely, in some of the foregoing instances.

"(6.) As to merit itself, of which we have been so dreadfully afraid: we are rewarded according to our works, yea, because of our works. How does this differ from 'for the sake of our works?' And how differs this from *secundum merita operum?* which is no more than, 'as our works deserve.' Can you split this hair? I doubt I cannot."—*Minutes of Several Conversations*, 1744-1789 (" *The Large Minutes*," 1789). *Works*, v, 238-9.

A Sixth charge is: "They treat Christianity as a wild, enthusiastic scheme, which will bear no examination." (p. 30.) Where, or when? In what sermon? In what tract, practical or polemical? I wholly deny the charge. I have myself closely and carefully examined every part of it, every verse of the New Testament, in the original, as well as in our own and other translations.

Nearly allied to this is the threadbare charge of enthusiasm, with which you frequently and largely compliment us. But as this also is asserted only, and not proved, it falls to the ground of itself. Meantime, your asserting it is a plain proof that you know nothing of the men you talk of. Because you know them not, you so boldly say, "One advantage we have over them, and that is reason." Nay, that is the very question. I appeal to all mankind, whether you have it or no. However, you are sure we have it not, and are never likely to have. For "reason," you say, "cannot do much with an enthusiast, whose first principle is, to have nothing to do with reason, but resolve all his religious opinions and notions into immediate inspiration." Then, by your own account, I am no enthusiast; for I resolve none of my notions into immediate inspiration. I have something to do with reason; perhaps as much as many of those who make no account of my labours. And I am ready to give up every opinion which I cannot by calm, clear reason defend. Whenever, therefore, you will try what you can do by argument, which you have not done yet, I wait your leisure, and will follow you step by step, which way soever you lead.

"But is not this plain proof of the enthusiasm of the Methodists, that they despise human learning, and make a loud and terrible outcry against it?" Pray, sir, when and where was this done? Be so good as to point out the time and place; for I am quite a stranger to it. I believe, indeed, and so do you, that many men make an ill use of their learning. But so they do of their Bibles: therefore

this is no reason for despising or crying out against it. I
would use it just as far as it will go; how far I apprehend
it may be of use, how far I judge it to be expedient at
least, if not necessary, for a clergyman, you might have
seen in the "Earnest Address to the Clergy." But, in the
meantime, I bless God that there is a more excellent gift
that either the knowledge of languages or philosophy.
For tongues, and knowledge, and learning, will vanish
away; but love never faileth.

I think this is all you have said which is any way
material concerning the doctrines of the Methodists. The
charges you bring concerning their spirit or practice may
be despatched in fewer words.

And, First, you charge them with pride and uncharitableness: "They talk as proudly as the Donatists, of their
being the only true preachers of the Gospel, and esteem
themselves, in contradistinction to others, as the regenerate, the children of God, and as having arrived at sinless
perfection." (p. 15.)

All of a piece. We neither talk nor think so. We
doubt not but there are many true preachers of the
Gospel, both in England and elsewhere, who have no
connection with, no knowledge of, us. Neither can we
doubt but that there are many thousand children of God
who never heard our voice or saw our face. And this
may suffice for an answer to all the assertions of the same
kind which are scattered up and down your work. Of
sinless perfection, here brought in by head and shoulders,
I have nothing to say at present.

You charge them, Secondly, "with boldness and blasphemy, who, triumphing in their train of credulous and
crazy followers, the spurious" (should it not be rather
*the genuine?*) "offspring of their insidious craft, ascribe
the glorious event to divine grace, and, in almost every
page of their paltry harangues, invoke the blessed Spirit
to go along with them in their soul-awakening work;

that is, to continue to assist them in seducing the simple and unwary." (p. 41.)

What we ascribe to divine grace is this: the convincing sinners of the errors of their ways, and the "turning them from darkness to light, from the power of Satan to God." Do not you yourself ascribe this to grace? And do not you too invoke the blessed Spirit to go along with you in every part of your work? If you do not, you lose all your labour. Whether we "seduce men into sin," or by his grace save them from it, is another question.

You charge us, Thirdly, with "requiring a blind and implicit trust from our disciples;" (p. 10;) who, accordingly, "trust as implicitly in their preachers, as the Papists in their Pope, Councils, or Church." (p. 51.) Far from it: neither do we require it; nor do they that hear us place any such trust in any creature. They "search the Scriptures," and hereby try every doctrine whether it be of God: and what is agreeable to Scripture, they embrace; what is contrary to it they reject.

You charge us, Fourthly, with injuring the clergy in various ways: (1.) "They are very industrious to dissolve or break off that spiritual intercourse which the relation wherein we stand requires should be preserved betwixt us and our people." But can that spiritual intercourse be either preserved or broke off, which never existed? What spiritual intercourse exists between you, the rector of St. Michael's, and the people of your parish? I suppose you preach to them once a week, and now and then read prayers. Perhaps you visit one in ten of the sick. And is this all the spiritual intercourse which you have with those over whom the Holy Ghost hath made you an overseer? In how poor a sense then do you watch over the souls for whom you are to give an account to God! Sir, I wish to God there were a truly spiritual intercourse between you and all your people! I wish you "knew all your flock by name, not excepting the men-servants and women-servants!" Then you might cherish each, "as a nurse her own children," and "train them up in the nurture and admonition of the Lord." Then might you "warn every one, and exhort every one," till you should "present every one perfect in Christ Jesus." . . .

If you fall upon people that meddle not with you, without either fear or wit, you may possibly find they have a little more to say for themselves than you was aware of. I "follow peace with all men;" but if a man set upon me without either rhyme or reason, I think it my duty to defend myself, so far as truth and justice permit. Yet still I am (if a poor enthusiast may not be so bold as to style himself your brother),

Reverend Sir, your servant for Christ's sake,
JOHN WESLEY.

## A LETTER TO A CLERGYMAN.
[*Works*, v, 349-52.]

TULLAMORE, May 4, 1748.

REVEREND SIR,—I have at present neither leisure nor inclination to enter into a formal controversy; but you will give me leave just to offer a few loose hints relating to the subject of last night's conversation:—

I. 1. Seeing life and health are things of so great importance, it is, without question, highly expedient that physicians should have all possible advantages of learning and education.

2. That trial should be made of them, by competent judges, before they practise publicly.

3. That after such trial, they be authorized to practise by those who are empowered to convey that authority.

4. And that, while they are preserving the lives of others, they should have what is sufficient to sustain their own.

5. But supposing a gentleman, bred at the university in Dublin, with all the advantages of education, after he has undergone all the usual trials, and then been regularly authorized to practise:

6. Suppose, I say, this physician settles at ———, for some years, and yet makes no cures at all; but, after trying his skill on five hundred persons, cannot show that he has healed one; many of his patients dying under his hands, and the rest remaining just as they were before he came:

7. Will you condemn a man who, having some little skill in physic, and a tender compassion for those who are sick or dying all around him, cures many of those, without fee or reward, whom the doctor *could* not cure?

8. At least *did* not (which is the same thing as to the

case in hand), were it only for this reason, because he did not go to them, and they would not come to him?

9. Will you condemn him because he has not learning, or has not had a university education?

What then? He cures those whom the man of learning and education cannot cure!

10. Will you object, that he is no physician, nor has any authority to practise?

I cannot come into your opinion. I think, *Medicus est qui medetur,* "He is a physician who heals;" and that every man has authority to save the life of a dying man.

But if you only mean, he has no authority to take fees, I contend not; for he takes none at all.

11. Nay, and I am afraid it will hold, on the other hand, *Medicus non est qui non medetur;* I am afraid, if we use propriety of speech, "He is no physician who works no cure."

12. "O, but he has taken his degree of doctor of physic, and therefore has authority."

Authority to do what? "Why, to heal all the sick that will employ him." But (to waive the case of those who will not employ him; and would you have even their lives thrown away?) he does not heal those that do employ him. He that was sick before, is sick still; or else he is gone hence, and is no more seen.

Therefore, his authority is not worth a rush; for it serves not the end for which it was given.

13. And surely he has no authority to kill them, by hindering another from saving their lives!

14. If he either attempts or desires to hinder him, if he condemns or dislikes him for it, it is plain to all thinking men, he regards his own fees more than the lives of his patients.

II. Now, to apply: 1. Seeing life everlasting, and holiness, or health of soul, are things of so great importance, it is highly expedient that ministers, being physicians

## A Letter to a Clergyman.

of the soul, should have all advantages of education and learning.

2. That full trial should be made of them in all respects, and that by the most competent judges, before they enter on the public exercise of their office, the saving souls from death.

3. That after such trial, they be authorized to exercise that office by those who are empowered to convey that authority. (I believe bishops are empowered to do this, and have been so from the apostolic age.)

4. And that those whose souls they save ought, meantime, to provide them what is needful for the body.

5. But suppose a gentleman bred at the university in Dublin, with all the advantages of education, after he has undergone the usual trials, and been regularly authorized to save souls from death:

6. Suppose, I say, this minister settles at ——, for some years, and yet saves no soul at all, saves no sinners from their sins; but after he has preached all this time to five or six hundred persons, cannot show that he has converted one from the error of his ways; many of his parishioners dying as they lived, and the rest remaining just as they were before he came:

7. Will you condemn a man, who, having compassion on dying souls, and some knowledge of the Gospel of Christ, without any temporal reward, saves them from their sins whom the minister *could* not save?

8. At least *did* not; nor ever was likely to do it; for he did not go to them, and they would not come to him.

9. Will you condemn such a preacher because he has not learning, or has not had a university education?

What then? He saves those sinners from their sins whom the man of learning and education cannot save.

A peasant being brought before the college of physicians, at Paris, a learned doctor accosted him, "What, friend, do you pretend to prescribe to people that have agues? Dost thou know what an ague is?"

He replied, "Yes, sir; an ague is what I can cure, and you cannot."

Will you object, "But he is no minister, nor has any authority to save souls?"

10. I must beg leave to dissent from you in this. I think he is a true, evangelical minister, διάκονος, "servant" of Christ and his church, who οὕτω διακονεῖ, "so ministers," as to save souls from death, to reclaim sinners from their sins; and that every Christian, if he is able to do it, has authority to save a dying soul.

But if you only mean, "He has no authority to take tithes," I grant it. He takes none: as he has freely received, so he freely gives.

11. But, to carry the matter a little farther: I am afraid it will hold, on the other hand, with regard to the soul as well as the body, *Medicus non est qui non medetur.* [He who cures none is no physician.] I am afraid, reasonable men will be much inclined to think, he that saves no souls is no minister of Christ.

12. "O, but he is ordained, and therefore has authority."

Authority to do what? "To save all the souls that will put themselves under his care." True; but (to waive the case of them that will not; and would you desire that even those should perish?) he does not, in fact, save them that are under his care: therefore, what end does his authority serve? He that was a drunkard is a drunkard still. The same is true of the Sabbath breaker, the thief, the common swearer. This is the best of the case; for many have died in their iniquity, and their blood will God require at the watchman's hand.

13. For surely he has no authority to murder souls, either by his neglect, by his smooth, if not false, doctrine, or by hindering another from plucking them out of the fire, and bringing them to life everlasting.

14. If he either attempts or desires to hinder him, if

## A Letter to a Clergyman.

he condemns or is displeased with him for it, how great reason is there to fear that he regards his own profit more than the salvation of souls! I am,

Reverend Sir, your affectionate brother,
JOHN WESLEY.

## A LETTER ON PREACHING CHRIST.

[*Arminian Magazine*, 1779. *Works*, vi, 555-9.]

LONDON, December 20, 1751.

MY DEAR FRIEND,—The point you speak of in your letter of September 21, is of a very important nature. I have had many serious thoughts concerning it, particularly for some months last past; therefore, I was not willing to speak hastily or slightly of it, but rather delayed till I could consider it thoroughly.

I mean by *preaching the Gospel,* preaching the love of God to sinners, preaching the life, death, resurrection, and intercession of Christ, with all the blessings which, in consequence thereof, are freely given to true believers.

By *preaching the law,* I mean, explaining and enforcing the commands of Christ, briefly comprised in the Sermon on the Mount.

Now, it is certain, preaching the Gospel to penitent sinners "begets faith;" that it "sustains and increases spiritual life in true believers."

Nay, sometimes it "teaches and guides" them that believe; yea, and "convinces them that believe not."

So far all are agreed. But what is the stated means of feeding and comforting believers? What is the means, as of begetting spiritual life where it is not, so of sustaining and increasing it where it is?

Here they divide. Some think, preaching the law only; others, preaching the Gospel only. I think, neither the one nor the other; but duly mixing both, in every place, if not in every sermon.

I think, the right method of preaching is this: at our first beginning to preach at any place, after a general declaration of the love of God to sinners, and his willingness that they should be saved, to preach the law, in the strongest, the closest, the most searching manner possible;

only intermixing the Gospel here and there, and showing it, as it were, afar off.

After more and more persons are convinced of sin, we may mix more and more of the Gospel, in order to "beget faith," to raise into spiritual life those whom the law hath slain; but this is not to be done too hastily neither. Therefore, it is not expedient wholly to omit the law; not only because we may well suppose that many of our hearers are still unconvinced; but because otherwise there is danger, that many who are convinced will heal their own wounds slightly; therefore, it is only in private converse with a thoroughly convinced sinner, that we should preach nothing but the Gospel.

If, indeed, we could suppose a whole congregation to be thus convinced, we should need to preach only the Gospel: and the same we might do, if our whole congregation were supposed to be newly justified. But when these grow in grace, and in the knowledge of Christ, a wise builder would preach the law to them again; only taking particular care to place every part of it in a Gospel light, as not only a command, but a privilege also, as a branch of the glorious liberty of the sons of God. He would take equal care to remind them, that this is not the cause, but the fruit, of their acceptance with God; that other cause, "other foundation can no man lay, than that which is laid, even Jesus Christ;" that we are still forgiven and accepted, only for the sake of what he hath done and suffered for us; and that all true obedience springs from love to him, grounded on his first loving us. He would labour, therefore, in preaching any part of the law, to keep the love of Christ continually before their eyes; that thence they might draw fresh life, vigour, and strength, to run the way of his commandments.

Thus would he preach the law even to those who were pressing on to the mark. But to those who were careless, or drawing back, he would preach it in another manner, nearly as he did before they were convinced of sin. To those, meanwhile, who were earnest, but feeble-minded, he would preach the Gospel chiefly; yet variously intermixing more or less of the law, according to their various necessities.

By preaching the law in the manner above described, he would teach them how to walk in Him whom they had received. Yea, and the same means (the main point wherein, it seems, your mistake lies) would both sustain and increase their spiritual life. For the commands are food, as well as the promises; food equally wholesome, equally substantial. These, also, duly applied, not only direct, but likewise nourish and strengthen the soul.

Of this you appear not to have the least conception; therefore, I will endeavour to explain it. I ask, then, Do not all the children of God experience, that when God gives them to see deeper into his blessed law, whenever he gives a new degree of light, he gives, likewise, a new degree of strength? Now I see, he that loves me, bids me do this; and now I feel I can do it, through Christ strengthening me.

Thus light and strength are given by the same means, and frequently in the same moment; although sometimes there is a space between. For instance: I hear the command, "Let your communication be always in grace, meet to minister grace to the hearers." God gives me more light into this command. I see the exceeding height and depth of it. At the same time I see (by the same light from above) how far I have fallen short. I am ashamed; I am humbled before God. I earnestly desire to keep it better; I pray to him that hath loved me for more strength, and I have the petition I ask of him. Thus the law not only convicts the unbeliever, and enlightens the believing soul, but also conveys food to a believer; sustains and increases his spiritual life and strength.

And if it increases his spiritual life and strength, it

cannot but increase his comfort also. For, doubtless, the more we are alive to God, the more we shall rejoice in him; the greater measure of his strength we receive, the greater will be our consolation also.

And all this, I conceive, is clearly declared in one single passage of Scripture:—

"The law of the Lord is perfect, converting the soul; the testimony of the Lord is sure, making wise the simple; the statutes of the Lord are right, rejoicing the heart; the commandment of the Lord is pure, enlightening the eyes. More to be desired are they than gold, yea, than much find gold; sweeter also than honey, and the honey-comb." They are both food and medicine; they both refresh, strengthen, and nourish the soul.

Not that I would advise to preach the law without the Gospel, any more than the Gospel without the law. Undoubtedly, both should be preached in their turns; yea, both at once, or both in one: all the conditional promises are instances of this. They are law and Gospel mixed together.

According to this model, I should advise every preacher continually to preach the law; the law grafted upon, tempered by, and animated with, the spirit of the Gospel. I advise him to declare, explain, and enforce every command of God; but, meantime, to declare, in every sermon (and the more explicitly the better), that the first and great command to a Christian is, "Believe in the Lord Jesus Christ;" that Christ is all in all, our "wisdom, righteousness, sanctification, and redemption;" that all life, love, strength, are from him alone, and all freely given to us through faith. And it will ever be found, that the law thus preached both enlightens and strengthens the soul; that it both nourishes and teaches; that it is the guide, "food, medicine, and stay," of the believing soul.

Thus all the Apostles built up believers; witness all

the Epistles of St. Paul, James, Peter, and John. And upon this plan all the Methodists first set out. . . . From the beginning they had been taught both the law and the Gospel. "God loves you; therefore, love and obey him. Christ died for you; therefore, die to sin. Christ is risen; therefore, rise in the image of God. Christ liveth evermore; therefore live to God, till you live with him in glory."

So we preached; and so you believed. This is the Scriptural way, the Methodist way, the true way. God grant we may never turn therefrom, to the right hand or to the left! I am, my dear friend,

Your ever affectionate brother,
JOHN WESLEY.

## THOUGHTS CONCERNING GOSPEL MINISTERS.

[*Arminian Magazine*, 1784. *Works*, vi, 199, 200.]

How frequently do we hear this expression from the mouths of rich and poor, learned and unlearned! Many lament that they have not a Gospel minister in their church, and therefore are constrained to seek one at the meeting. Many rejoice that they have a Gospel minister, and that there are many such in their neighbourhood. Meantime, they generally speak with much displeasure, if not contempt, of those who they say are not Gospel ministers.

But it is to be feared, few of these understand what they say. Few understand what that expression means. Most that use it have only crude, confused notions concerning Gospel ministers. And hence many inconveniences arise; yea, much hurt to the souls of men. They contract prejudices in favour of very worthless men, who are indeed blind leaders of the blind; not knowing what the real Gospel is, and therefore incapable of preaching it to others. Meantime, from the same cause, they contract prejudices against other ministers, who, in reality, both live and preach the Gospel; and therefore are well able to instruct them in all those truths that accompany salvation.

But what then is the meaning of the expression? Who is a Gospel minister? Let us consider this important question calmly, in the fear and in the presence of God.

Not every one that preaches the eternal decrees (although many suppose this is the very thing); that talks much of the sovereignty of God, of free, distinguishing grace, of dear electing love, of irresistible grace, and of the infallible perseverance of the saints. A man may speak of all these by the hour together; yea, with all his heart, and with all his voice; and yet have no right at all to the title of a Gospel minister.*

Not every one that talks largely and earnestly on those precious subjects,—the righteousness and blood of Christ. Let a man descant upon these in ever so lively a manner, let him describe his sufferings ever so pathetically; if he stops there, if he does not show man's duty, as well as Christ's sufferings; if he does not apply all to the consciences of the hearers; he will never lead them to life, either here or hereafter, and therefore is no Gospel minister.†

Not every one who deals in the promises only, without ever showing the terrors of the law; that slides over "the wrath of God revealed from heaven against all ungodliness and unrighteousness," and endeavours to heal those that never were wounded. These promise-mongers are no Gospel ministers.

Not every one (very nearly allied to the former) who bends all his strength to coax sinners to Christ. Such soft, tender expressions, as "My dear hearers, My dear lambs," though repeated a thousand times, do not prove a Gospel minister.

---

* "Calvinism is not the Gospel."—*Letter to Miss Bishop*, 1778. *Works*, vii, 242.

† "But to speak freely; I myself find more life in the Church prayers, than in any formal extemporary prayers of Dissenters. Nay, I find more profit in sermons on either good tempers, or good works, than in what are vulgarly called *Gospel sermons*. That term has now become a mere cant word: I wish none of our society would use it. It has no determinate meaning. Let but a pert, self-sufficient animal, that has neither sense nor grace, bawl out something about Christ, or his blood, or justification by faith, and his hearers cry out, ' What a fine Gospel sermon!' Surely the Methodists have not so learned Christ! We know no Gospel without salvation from sin."—*Ibid*. *Works*, vii, 242. "But of all preaching, what is usually called Gospel preaching is the most useless, if not the most mischievous: a dull, yea, or lively, harangue on the sufferings of Christ, or salvation by faith, without strongly inculcating holiness. I see, more and more, that this naturally tends to drive holiness out of the world."—*Letter to his Brother Charles*, 1772. *Works*, vi, 674-5.

Lastly. Not every one that preaches justification by faith; he that goes no farther than this, that does not insist upon sanctification also, upon all the fruits of faith, upon universal holiness, does not declare the whole counsel of God, and consequently is not a Gospel minister.

Who then is such? Who is a Gospel minister, in the full, Scriptural sense of the word? He, and he alone, of whatever denomination, that does declare the whole counsel of God; that does preach the whole Gospel, even justification and sanctification, preparatory to glory. He that does not put asunder what God has joined, but publishes alike, "Christ dying for us, and Christ living in us." He that constantly applies all this to the hearts of the hearers, being willing to spend and be spent for them; having himself the mind which was in Christ, and steadily walking as Christ also walked; he, and he alone, can with propriety be termed a Gospel minister.

Let it be particularly observed, if the Gospel be "glad tidings of great salvation which shall be unto all people," then those only are, in the full sense, Gospel ministers who proclaim the "great salvation;" that is, salvation from all (both inward and outward) sin, into "all the mind that was in Christ Jesus;" and likewise proclaim offers of this salvation to every child of man. This honourable title is therefore vilely prostituted, when it is given to any but those who testify "that God willeth all men to be saved," and "to be perfect as their Father which is in heaven is perfect."

## AN ADDRESS TO THE CLERGY.

[1756. *Works*, vi, 217-31.]

LONDON, February 6, 1756.

BRETHREN AND FATHERS,—Let it not be imputed to forwardness, vanity, or presumption, that one who is of little esteem in the Church takes upon him thus to address a body of people, to many of whom he owes the highest reverence. I owe a still higher regard to Him who I believe requires this at my hands; to the great Bishop of our souls; before whom both you and I must shortly give an account of our stewardship. It is a debt I owe to love, to real, disinterested affection, to declare what has long been the burden of my soul. And may the God of love enable you to read these lines in the same spirit wherewith they were wrote! It will easily appear to an unprejudiced reader, that I do not speak from a spirit of anger or resentment. I know well, "the wrath of man worketh not the righteousness of God." Much less would I utter one word out of contempt; a spirit justly abhorred by God and man. Neither of these can consist with that earnest, tender love, which is the motive of my present undertaking. In this spirit I desire to cast my bread upon the waters; it is enough if I find it again after many days.

Meantime, you are sensible, love does not forbid, but rather require, plainness of speech. Has it not often constrained you, as well as me, to lay aside, not only disguise, but reserve also; and "by manifestation of the truth to commend ourselves to every man's conscience in the sight of God?" And while I endeavour to do this, let me earnestly entreat you, for the love of God, for the love of your own soul, for the love of the souls committed to your charge, yea, and of the whole Church of Christ, do not bias your mind, by thinking *who* it is that speaks; but impartially consider *what* is spoken. And

## An Address to the Clergy.

if it be false or foolish, reject it; but do not reject "the words of truth and soberness."

My first design was, to offer a few plain thoughts to the clergy of our own Church only. But upon farther reflection, I see no cause for being so "straitened in my own bowels." I am a debtor to all; and therefore, though I primarily speak to them with whom I am more immediately connected, yet I would not be understood to exclude any, of whatsoever denomination, whom God has called to "watch over the souls of others, as they that must give account."

In order to our giving this account with joy, are there not two things which it highly imports us to consider: First, What manner of men ought we to be? Secondly, Are we such, or are we not?

I. And, First, if we are "overseers over the Church of God, which he hath bought with his own blood," what manner of men ought we to be, in gifts as well as in grace?

To begin with gifts; and, 1. With those that are from nature. Ought not a minister to have, First, a good understanding, a clear apprehension, a sound judgment, and a capacity of reasoning with some closeness? Is not this necessary in a high degree for the work of the ministry? Otherwise, how will he be able to understand the various states of those under his care; or to steer them through a thousand difficulties and dangers, to the haven where they would be? Is it not necessary, with respect to the numerous enemies whom he has to encounter? Can a fool cope with all the men that know not God, and with all the spirits of darkness? Nay, he will neither be aware of the devices of Satan, nor the craftiness of his children.

Secondly. Is it not highly expedient that a guide of souls should have likewise some liveliness and readiness of thought? Or how will he be able, when need requires, to "answer a fool according to his folly?" How frequent is this need! seeing we almost everywhere meet with those empty, yet petulant creatures, who are far "wiser in their own eyes, than seven men that can render a reason." Reasoning, therefore, is not the weapon to be used with them. You cannot deal with them thus. They scorn being convinced; nor can they be silenced but in their own way.

Thirdly. To a sound understanding, and a lively turn of thought, should be joined a good memory; if it may be ready, that you may make whatever occurs in reading or conversation your own; but, however, retentive, lest we be "ever learning, and never able to come to the knowledge of the truth." On the contrary, "every scribe instructed unto the kingdom of heaven," every teacher fitted for his work, "is like a householder, who bringeth out of his treasures things new and old."

2. And as to acquired endowments, can he take one step aright, without first a competent share of knowledge? a knowledge, First, of his own office; of the high trust in which he stands, the important work to which he is called? Is there any hope that a man should discharge his office well, if he knows not what it is? that he should acquit himself faithfully of a trust, the very nature whereof he does not understand? Nay, if he knows not the work God has given him to do, he cannot finish it.

Secondly. No less necessary is a knowledge of the Scriptures, which teach us how to teach others; yea, a knowledge of all the Scriptures; seeing scripture interprets scripture; one part fixing the sense of another. So that, whether it be true or not, that every good textuary is a good divine, it is certain none can be a good divine who is not a good textuary. None else can be mighty in the Scriptures; able both to instruct and to stop the mouths of gainsayers.

In order to do this accurately, ought he not to know the literal meaning of every word, verse, and chapter; with-

## An Address to the Clergy.

out which there can be no firm foundation on which the spiritual meaning can be built? Should he not likewise be able to deduce the proper corollaries, speculative and practical, from each text; to solve the difficulties which arise, and answer the objections which are or may be raised against it; and to make a suitable application of all to the consciences of his hearers?

Thirdly. But can he do this, in the most effectual manner, without a knowledge of the original tongues? Without this, will he not frequently be at a stand, even as to texts which regard practice only? But he will be under still greater difficulties, with respect to controverted scriptures. He will be ill able to rescue these out of the hands of any man of learning that would pervert them: for whenever an appeal is made to the original, his mouth is stopped at once.

Fourthly. Is not a knowledge of profane history, likewise, of ancient customs, of chronology and geography, though not absolutely necessary yet highly expedient, for him that would thoroughly understand the Scriptures; since the want even of this knowledge is but poorly supplied by reading the comments of other men?

Fifthly. Some knowledge of the sciences also, is, to say the least, equally expedient. Nay, may we not say, that the knowledge of one (whether art or science), although now quite unfashionable, is even necessary next, and in order to, the knowledge of the Scripture itself? I mean logic. For what is this, if rightly understood, but the art of good sense? of apprehending things clearly, judging truly, and reasoning conclusively? What is it, viewed in another light, but the art of learning and teaching; whether by convincing or persuading? What is there, then, in the whole compass of science, to be desired in comparison of it?

Is not some acquaintance with what has been termed the second part of logic (metaphysics), if not so necessary as this, yet highly expedient (1.) In order to clear our apprehension (without which it is impossible either to judge correctly, or to reason closely or conclusively), by ranging our ideas under general heads? And (2.) In order to understand many useful writers, who can very hardly be understood without it?

Should not a minister be acquainted too with at least the general grounds of natural philosophy? Is not this a great help to the accurate understanding several passages of Scripture? Assisted by this, he may himself comprehend, and on proper occasions explain to others, how the invisible things of God are seen from the creation of the world; how "the heavens declare the glory of God, and the firmament showeth his handiwork;" till they cry out, "O Lord, how manifold are thy works! In wisdom hast thou made them all."

But how far can he go in this, without some knowledge of geometry? which is likewise useful, not barely on this account, but to give clearness of apprehension, and a habit of thinking closely and connectedly.

It must be allowed indeed, that some of these branches of knowledge are not so indispensably necessary as the rest; and therefore no thinking man will condemn the Fathers of the Church, for having, in all ages and nations, appointed some to the ministry, who, suppose they had the capacity, yet had not had the opportunity of attaining them. But what excuse is this for one who has the opportunity, and makes no use of it? What can be urged for a person who has had a university education, if he does not understand them all? Certainly, supposing him to have any capacity, to have common understanding, he is inexcusable before God and man.

Sixthly. Can any who spend several years in those seats of learning, be excused if they do not add to that of the languages and sciences, the knowledge of the Fathers? the most authentic commentators on Scripture, as being both nearest the fountain, and eminently endued with that Spirit by whom all Scripture was given. It will be easily perceived, I speak chiefly of those who wrote before the Council of Nice. But who would not likewise desire to have some acquaintance with those that followed them? with St. Chrysostom, Basil, Jerome, Austin; and, above all, the man of a broken heart, Ephraem Syrus?

Seventhly. There is yet another branch of knowledge highly necessary for a clergyman, and that is, knowledge of the world; a knowledge of men, of their maxims, tempers, and manners, such as they occur in real life. Without this he will be liable to receive much hurt, and capable of doing little good; as he will not know, either how to deal with men according to the vast variety of their characters, or to preserve himself from those who almost in every place lie in wait to deceive.

How nearly allied to this is the discernment of spirits! so far as it may be acquired by diligent observation. And can a guide of souls be without it? If he is, is he not liable to stumble at every step?

Eighthly. Can he be without an eminent share of prudence? that most uncommon thing which is usually called common sense? But how shall we define it? Shall we say, with the Schools, that it is *recta ratio rerum agibilium particularium* [a right regard of particular things which may be done]? Or is it an habitual consideration of all the circumstances of a thing,—

*Quis, quid, ubi, quibus auxiliis, cur, quomodo, quando* [Who, what, where, with what helps, why, how, when], and a facility of adapting our behaviour to the various combinations of them? However it be defined, should it not be studied with all care, and pursued with all earnestness of application? For what terrible inconveniences ensue, whenever it is remarkably wanting.

Ninthly. Next to prudence or common sense (if it be not included therein), a clergyman ought certainly to have some degree of good breeding; I mean address, easiness, and propriety of behaviour, wherever his lot is cast: perhaps one might add, he should have (though not the stateliness; for he is "the servant of all," yet) all the courtesy of a gentleman, joined with the correctness of a scholar. Do we want a pattern of this? We have one in St. Paul, even before Felix, Festus, King Agrippa. One can scarce help thinking he was one of the best bred men, one of the finest gentlemen in the world. O that we likewise had the skill to "please all men for their good unto edification!"

In order to this, especially in our public ministrations, would not one wish for a strong, clear, musical voice, and a good delivery, both with regard to pronunciation and action? I name these here, because they are far more acquirable than has been commonly imagined. A remarkably weak and untunable voice has by steady application become strong and agreeable. Those who stammered almost at every word, have learned to speak clearly and plainly. And many who were eminently ungraceful in their pronunciation and awkward in their gesture, have in some time, by art and labour, not only corrected that awkwardness of action and ungracefulness of utterance, but have become excellent in both, and in these respects likewise the ornaments of their profession.

What may greatly encourage those who give themselves up to the work, with regard to all these endowments, many of which cannot be attained without considerable labour, is this: They are assured of being assisted in all their labour by Him who teacheth man knowledge. And who teaches like him? Who, like him, giveth wisdom to the simple? How easy it is for him (if we desire it, and believe that he is both able and willing to do this), by the powerful, though secret, influences of his Spirit, to open and enlarge our understanding; to strengthen all our faculties; to bring to our remembrance whatsoever things

## An Address to the Clergy.

are needful, and to fix and sharpen our attention to them; so that we may profit above all who depend wholly on themselves, in whatever may qualify us for our Master's work!

3. But all these things, however great they may be in themselves, are little in comparison of those that follow. For what are all other gifts, whether natural or acquired, when compared to the grace of God? And how ought this to animate and govern the whole intention, affection, and practice of a minister of Christ?

(1.) As to his intention, both in undertaking this important office, and in executing every part of it, ought it not to be singly this, to glorify God, and to save souls from death? Is not this absolutely and indispensably necessary, before all and above all things? "If his eye be single, his whole body," his whole soul, his whole work, "will be full of light." "God who commanded light to shine out of darkness," will shine on his heart; will direct him in all his ways, will give him to see the travail of his soul, and be satisfied. But if his eye, his intention, be not single, if there be any mixture of meaner motives, (how much more, if those were or are his leading motives in undertaking or exercising this high office!) his "whole body," his whole soul, "will be full of darkness," even such as issues from the bottomless pit: Let not such a man think that he shall have any blessing from the Lord. No; the curse of God abideth on him. Let him not expect to enjoy any settled peace, any solid comfort, in his own breast; neither can he hope there will be any fruit of his labours, any sinners converted to God.

(2.) As to his affections. Ought not a "steward of the mysteries of God," a shepherd of the souls for whom Christ died, to be endued with an eminent measure of love to God, and love to all his brethren? a love the same in kind, but in degree far beyond that of ordinary Christians? Can he otherwise answer the high character he bears, and the relation wherein he stands? Without this, how can he go through all the toils and difficulties which necessarily attend the faithful execution of his office? Would it be possible for a parent to go through the pain and fatigue of bearing and bringing up even one child, were it not for that vehement affection, that inexpressible στοργή, which the Creator has given for that very end? How much less will it be possible for any pastor, any spiritual parent, to go through the pain and labour of "travailing in birth for," and bringing up, many children to the measure of the full stature of Christ, without a large measure of that inexpressible affection which "a stranger intermeddleth not with!"

He therefore must be utterly void of understanding, must be a madman of the highest order, who, on any consideration whatever, undertakes this office, while he is a stranger to this affection. Nay, I have often wondered that any man in his senses does not rather dig or thresh for a livelihood, than continue therein, unless he feels at least (which is *extremâ lineâ amare*) [to love in the highest degree] such an earnest concern for the glory of God, and such a thirst after the salvation of souls, that he is ready to do any thing, to lose any thing, or to suffer any thing, rather than one should perish for whom Christ died.

And is not even this degree of love to God and man utterly inconsistent with the love of the world; with the love of money or praise; with the very lowest degree of either ambition or sensuality? How much less can it consist with that poor, low, irrational, childish principle, the love of diversions? (Surely even a man, were he neither a minister nor a Christian, should "put away childish things.") Not only this, but the love of pleasure, and, what lies still deeper in the soul, the love of ease, flees before it.

(3.) As to his practice: "Unto the ungodly saith God, Why dost thou preach my laws?" What is a minister of Christ, a shepherd of souls, unless he is all devoted to God? unless he abstain, with the utmost care and diligence, from every evil word and work; from all appearance of evil; yea, from the most innocent things, whereby any might be offended or made weak? Is he not called, above others, to be an example to the flock, in his private as well as public character? an example of all holy and heavenly tempers, filling the heart so as to shine through the life? Consequently, is not his whole life, if he walks worthy of his calling, one incessant labour of love; one continued tract of praising God, and helping man; one series of thankfulness and beneficence? Is he not always humble, always serious, though rejoicing evermore; mild, gentle, patient, abstinent? May you not resemble him to a guardian angel, ministering to those "who shall be heirs of salvation?" Is he not one sent forth from God, to stand between God and man, to guard and assist the poor, helpless children of men, to supply them both with light and strength, to guide them through a thousand known and unknown dangers, till at the appointed time he returns, with those committed to his charge, to his and their Father who is in heaven?

O who is able to describe such a messenger of God, faithfully executing his high office! working together with God, with the great Author both of the old and of the new creation! See his Lord, the eternal Son of God, going forth on that work of omnipotence, and creating heaven and earth by the breath of his mouth! See the servant whom he delighteth to honour, fulfilling the counsel of his will, and in his name speaking the word whereby is raised a new spiritual creation. Empowered by him, he says to the dark, unformed void of nature, "Let there be light; and there is light. Old things are passed away; behold, all things are become new." He is continually employed, in what the angels of God have not the honour to do,—cooperating with the Redeemer of men in "bringing many children to glory."

Such is a true minister of Christ; and such, beyond all possibility of dispute, ought both you and I to be.

II. But are we such? What are we in the respects above named? It is a melancholy but necessary consideration. It is true, many have wrote upon this subject; and some of them admirably well: yet few, if any, at least in our nation, have carried their inquiry through all these particulars. Neither have they always spoken so plain and home as the nature of the thing required. But why did they not? Was it because they were unwilling to give pain to those whom they loved? Or were they hindered by fear of disobliging, or of incurring any temporal inconvenience? Miserable fear! Is any temporal inconvenience whatever to be laid in the balance with the souls of our brethren? Or were they prevented by shame, arising from a consciousness of their own many and great defects? Undoubtedly this might extenuate the fault, but not altogether remove it. For is it not a wise advice, "Be not ashamed when it concerneth thy soul," especially when it concerns the souls of thousands also? In such a case may God

> "Set as a flint our steady face,
> Harden to adamant our brow!"

But is there not another hinderance? Should not compassion, should not tenderness hinder us from giving pain? Yes, from giving unnecessary pain. But what manner of tenderness is this? It is like that of a surgeon who lets his patient be lost because he is too compassionate to probe his wounds. Cruel compassion! Let me give pain, so I may save life. Let me probe, that God may heal.

1. Are we then such as we are sensible we should be,

First, with regard to natural endowments? I am afraid not. If we were, how many stumbling blocks would be removed out of the way of serious Infidels? Alas, what terrible effects do we continually see of that common though senseless imagination, "The boy, if he is fit for nothing else, will do well enough for a parson!" Hence it is, that we see (I would to God there were no such instance in all Great Britain, or Ireland!) dull, heavy, blockish ministers; men of no life, no spirit, no readiness of thought; who are consequently the jest of every pert fool, every lively, airy coxcomb they meet. We see others whose memory can retain nothing; therefore they can never be men of considerable knowledge; they can never know much even of those things which they are most nearly concerned to know. Alas, they are pouring the water into a leaky vessel; and the broken cistern can hold no water! I do not say, with Plato, that "all human knowledge is nothing but remembering." Yet certain it is, that, without remembering, we can have but a small share of knowledge. And even those who enjoy the most retentive memory, find great reason still to complain,

> "Skill comes so slow, and life so fast does fly;
> We learn so little, and forget so much!"

And yet we see and bewail a still greater defect in some that are in the ministry. They want sense, they are defective in understanding, their capacity is low and shallow, their apprehension is muddy and confused; of consequence, they are utterly incapable either of forming a true judgment of things, or of reasoning justly upon any thing. O how can these who themselves know nothing aright, impart knowledge to others? how instruct them in all the variety of duty, to God, their neighbour, and themselves? How will they guide them through all the mazes of error, through all the entanglements of sin and temptation? How will they apprize them of the devices of Satan, and guard them against all the wisdom of the world?

It is easy to perceive, I do not speak this for their sake (for they are incorrigible); but for the sake of parents, that they may open their eyes and see, a blockhead can never "do well enough for a parson." He may do well enough for a tradesman; so well as to gain fifty or a hundred thousand pounds. He may do well enough for a soldier; nay (if you pay well for it), for a very well-dressed and well-mounted officer. He may do well enough for a sailor, and may shine on the quarter-deck of a man-of-war. He may do so well, in the capacity of a lawyer or physician, as to ride in his gilt chariot. But O! think not of his being a minister, unless you would bring a blot upon your family, a scandal upon our Church, and a reproach on the Gospel, which he may murder, but cannot teach.

2. Are we such as we are sensible we should be, Secondly, with regard to acquired endowments? Here the matter (suppose we have common understanding) lies more directly within our own power. But under this, as well as the following heads, methinks, I would not consider at all, how many or how few are either excellent or defective. I would only desire every person who reads this to apply it to himself. Certainly some one in the nation is defective. Am not I the man?

Let us each seriously examine himself. Have I (1.) Such a knowledge of Scripture, as becomes him who undertakes so to explain it to others, that it may be a light in all their paths? Have I a full and clear view of the analogy of faith, which is the clue to guide me through the whole? Am I acquainted with the several parts of Scripture; with all parts of the Old Testament and the New? Upon the mention of any text, do I know the context, and the parallel places? Have I that point at least of a good divine, the being a good textuary? Do

## An Address to the Clergy.

I know the grammatical construction of the four Gospels; of the Acts; of the Epistles; and am I a master of the spiritual sense (as well as the literal) of what I read? Do I understand the scope of each book, and how every part of it tends thereto? Have I skill to draw the natural inferences deducible from each text? Do I know the objections raised to them or from them by Jews, Deists, Papists, Arians, Socinians, and all other sectaries, who more or less corrupt or cauponize the word of God? Am I ready to give a satisfactory answer to each of these objections? And have I learned to apply every part of the sacred writings, as the various states of my hearers require?

(2.) Do I understand Greek and Hebrew? Otherwise, how can I undertake (as every minister does), not only to explain books which are written therein, but to defend them against all opponents? Am I not at the mercy of every one who does understand, or even pretends to understand, the original? For which way can I confute his pretence? Do I understand the language of the Old Testament? critically? at all? Can I read into English one of David's Psalms; or even the first chapter of Genesis? Do I understand the language of the New Testament? Am I a critical master of it? Have I enough of it even to read into English the first chapter of St. Luke? If not, how many years did I spend at school? How many at the university? And what was I doing all those years? Ought not shame to cover my face?

(3.) Do I understand my own office? Have I deeply considered before God the character which I bear? What is it to be an ambassador of Christ, an envoy from the King of heaven? And do I know and feel what is implied in "watching over the souls" of men "as he that must give account?"

(4.) Do I understand so much of profane history as tends to confirm and illustrate the sacred? Am I acquainted with the ancient customs of the Jews and other nations mentioned in Scripture? Have I a competent knowledge of chronology, that at least which refers to the sacred writings? And am I so far (if no farther) skilled in geography, as to know the situation, and give some account, of all the considerable places mentioned therein?

(5.) Am I a tolerable master of the sciences? Have I gone through the very gate of them, logic? If not, I am not likely to go much farther when I stumble at the threshold. Do I understand it so as to be ever the better for it? to have it always ready for use; so as to apply every rule of it, when occasion is, almost as naturally as I turn my hand? Do I understand it at all? Are not even the moods and figures above my comprehension? Do not I poorly endeavour to cover my ignorance, by affecting to laugh at their barbarous names? Can I even reduce an indirect mood to a direct; an hypothetic to a categorical syllogism? Rather, have not my stupid indolence and laziness made me very ready to believe, what the little wits and pretty gentlemen affirm, "that logic is good for nothing?" It is good for this at least (wherever it is understood), to make people talk less; by showing them both what is, and what is not, to the point; and how extremely hard it is to prove any thing. Do I understand metaphysics; if not the depths of the Schoolmen, the subtleties of Scotus or Aquinas, yet the first rudiments, the general principles, of that useful science? Have I conquered so much of it, as to clear my apprehension and range my ideas under proper heads; so much as enables me to read with ease and pleasure, as well as profit, Dr. Henry Moore's Works, Malebranche's "Search after Truth," and Dr. Clarke's "Demonstration of the Being and Attributes of God?" Do I understand natural philosophy? If I have not gone deep therein, have I digested the general grounds of it? Have I mastered Gravesande, Keill, Sir Isaac Newton's Principia, with his

## An Address to the Clergy.

"Theory of Light and Colours?" In order thereto, have I laid in some stock of mathematical knowledge? Am I master of the mathematical A B C of Euclid's Elements? If I have not gone thus far, if I am such a novice still, what have I been about ever since I came from school?

(6.) Am I acquainted with the Fathers; at least with those venerable men who lived in the earliest ages of the Church? Have I read over and over the golden remains of Clemens Romanus, of Ignatius and Polycarp; and have I given one reading, at least, to the works of Justin Martyr, Tertullian, Origen, Clemens Alexandrinus, and Cyprian?

(7.) Have I any knowledge of the world? Have I studied men (as well as books), and observed their tempers, maxims, and manners? Have I learned to beware of men; to add the wisdom of the serpent to the innocence of the dove? Has God given me by nature, or have I acquired, any measure of the discernment of spirits; or of its near ally, prudence, enabling me on all occasions to consider all circumstances, and to suit and vary my behaviour according to the various combinations of them? Do I labour never to be rude or ill mannered; not to be remarkably wanting in good breeding? Do I endeavour to copy after those who are eminent for address and easiness of behaviour? Am I (though never light or trifling, either in word or action, yet) affable and courteous to all men? And do I omit no means which is in my power, and consistent with my character, of "pleasing all men" with whom I converse, "for their good to edification?"

If I am wanting even in these lowest endowments, shall I not frequently regret the want? How often shall I move heavily and be far less useful than I might have been! How much more shall I suffer in my usefulness, if I have wasted the opportunities I once had of acquainting myself with the great lights of antiquity, the Ante-

Nicene Fathers; or if I have droned away those precious hours wherein I might have made myself master of the sciences! How poorly must I many times drag on, for want of the helps which I have vilely cast away! But is not my case still worse, if I have loitered away the time wherein I should have perfected myself in Greek and Hebrew? I might before this have been critically acquainted with these treasuries of sacred knowledge. But they are now hid from my eyes; they are close locked up, and I have no key to open them. However, have I used all possible diligence to supply that grievous defect (so far as it can be supplied now), by the most accurate knowledge of the English Scriptures? Do I meditate therein day and night? Do I think (and consequently speak) thereof, "when I sit in the house, and when I walk by the way; when I lie down, and when I rise up?" By this means have I at length attained a thorough knowledge, as of the sacred text, so of its literal and spiritual meaning? Otherwise how can I attempt to instruct others therein? Without this, I am a blind guide indeed! I am absolutely incapable of teaching my flock what I have never learned myself; no more fit to lead souls to God, than I am to govern the world.

3. And yet there is a higher consideration than that of gifts; higher than any or all of these joined together; a consideration in view of which all external and all intellectual endowments vanish into nothing. Am I such as I ought to be, with regard to the grace of God? The Lord God enable me to judge aright of this!

And, (1.) What was my intention in taking upon me this office and ministry? What was it, in taking charge of this parish, either as minister or curate? Was it always, and is it now, wholly and solely to glorify God, and save souls? Has my eye been singly fixed on this, from the beginning hitherto? Had I never, have I not now, any mixture in my intention; any alloy of baser

## An Address to the Clergy.

metal? Had I, or have I, no thought of worldly gain; "filthy lucre," as the Apostle terms it? Had I at first, have I now, no secular view? no eye to honour or preferment? to a plentiful income; or, at least, a competency? a warm and comfortable livelihood?

Alas! my brother! "If the light that is in thee be darkness, how great is that darkness!" Was a comfortable livelihood, then, your motive for entering into the ministry? And do you avow this in the face of the sun, and without one blush upon your cheek? I cannot compare you with Simon Magus; you are many degrees beneath him. He offered to give money for the gift of God, the power of conferring the Holy Ghost. Hereby, however, he showed that he set a higher value on the gift, than on the money which he would have parted with for it. But you do not; you set a far higher value on the money than on the gift; insomuch that you do not desire, you will not accept of, the gift, unless the money accompany it! The Bishop said, when you was ordained, "Receive thou the Holy Ghost." But that was the least of your care. Let who will receive this, so you receive the money, the revenue of a good benefice. While you minister the word and sacraments before God, he gives the Holy Ghost to those who duly receive them: So that, "through your hands,," likewise, "the Holy Ghost is," in this sense, "given" now. But you have little concern whether he be or not; so little, that you will minister no longer, he shall be given no more either through your lips or hands, if you have no more money for your labour. O Simon, Simon! what a saint wert thou, compared to many of the most honourable men now in Christendom!

Let not any either ignorantly or wilfully mistake me. I would not "muzzle the ox that treadeth out the corn." I know the spiritual "labourer," too, "is worthy of his reward;" and, that, if "we sow unto" our flock "spiritual things," it is meet that we "reap of their carnal things."

I do not therefore blame, no, not in any degree, a minister's taking a yearly salary; but I blame his seeking it. The thing blamable is the having it in his view, as the motive, or any part of the motive, for entering into this sacred office.

> *" Hic nigræ succus loliginis, hæc est
> Ærugo mera."*
> [" This is fell poison's blackest juice."—BOSCAWEN.]

If preferment, or honour, or profit, was in his eye, his eye was not single. And our Lord knew no medium between a single and an evil eye. The eye, therefore, which is not single is evil. It is a plain, adjudged case. He then that has any other design in undertaking or executing the office of a minister than purely this, to glorify God and save souls, his eye is not single. Of consequence, it is evil; and therefore his "whole body" must be "full of darkness." "The light which is in" him "is" very "darkness;" darkness covers his whole soul; he has no solid peace; he has no blessing from God; and there is no fruit of his labours.

It is no wonder that they who see no harm in this, see no harm in adding one living to another, and, if they can, another to that; yet still wiping their mouth, and saying, they have done no evil. In the very first step, their eye was not single; therefore their mind was filled with darkness. So they stumble on still in the same mire, till their feet "stumble on the dark mountains."

It is pleaded, indeed, that "a small living will not maintain a large family." *Maintain!* How? It will not clothe them "in purple and fine linen;" nor enable them to fare "sumptuously every day:" But will not the living you have now afford you and yours the plain necessaries, yea, and conveniences, of life? Will it not maintain you in the frugal, Christian simplicity which becomes a minister of Christ? It will not maintain you in pomp and grandeur, in elegant luxury, in fashionable sensuality.

So much the better. If your eyes were open, whatever your income was, you would flee from these as from hellfire.

It has been pleaded, Secondly, "By having a larger income, I am able to do more good." But dare you aver, in the presence of God, that it was singly with this view, only for this end, that you sought a larger income? If not, you are still condemned before God; your eye was not single. Do not therefore quibble and evade. This was not your motive of acting. It was not the desire of doing more good, whether to the souls or bodies of men; it was not the love of God (you know it was not; your own conscience is as a thousand witnesses): but it was "the love of money," and "the desire of other things," which animated you in this pursuit. If then, the word of God is true, you are in darkness still: it fills and covers your soul.

I might add, a larger income does not necessarily imply a capacity of doing more spiritual good. And this is the highest kind of good. It is good to feed the hungry, to clothe the naked: But it is a far nobler good to "save souls from death," to "pluck" poor "brands out of the burning." And it is that to which you are peculiarly called, and to which you have solemnly promised to "bend all your studies and endeavours." But you are by no means sure, that, by adding a second living to your first, you shall be more capable of doing good in this kind than you would have been had you laid out all your time, and all your strength, on your first flock.

"However, I shall be able to do more temporal good." You are not sure even of this. "If riches increase, they are increased that eat them." Perhaps your expenses may rise proportionably with your income. But if not, if you have a greater ability, shall you have a greater willingness, to do good? You have no reason in the world to believe this. There are a thousand instances of the contrary. How many have less will when they have more power! Now they have more money, they love it more; when they had little, they did their "diligence gladly to give of that little;" but since they have had much, they are so far from "giving plenteously," that they can hardly afford to give at all.

"But by my having another living, I maintain a valuable man, who might otherwise want the necessaries of life." I answer (1.) Was this your whole and sole motive in seeking that other living? If not, this plea will not clear you from the charge; your eye was not single. (2.) If it was, you may put it beyond dispute; you may prove at once the purity of your intention:— Make that valuable man rector of one of your parishes, and you are clear before God and man.

But what can be pleaded for those who have two or more flocks, and take care of none of them? who just look at them now and then for a few days, and then remove to a convenient distance, and say, "Soul, thou hast much goods laid up for many years; take thine ease; eat, drink, and be merry?"

Some years ago I was asking a plain man, "Ought not he who feeds the flock, to eat of the milk of the flock?" He answered: "Friend, I have no objection to that. But what is that to him who does not feed the flock? He stands on the far side of the hedge, and feeds himself. It is another who feeds the flock; and ought he to have the milk of the flock? What canst thou say for him?" Truly, nothing at all; and he will have nothing to say for himself, when the great Shepherd shall pronounce that just sentence, "Bind" the unprofitable servant "hand and foot, and cast him into outer darkness."

I have dwelt the longer on this head, because a right intention is the first point of all, and the most necessary of all; inasmuch as the want of this cannot be supplied by any thing else whatsoever. It is the setting out wrong;

a fault never to be amended, unless you return to the place whence you came, and set out right. It is impossible therefore to lay too great stress upon a single eye, a pure intention; without which, all our sacrifice, our prayers, sermons, and sacraments, are an abomination to the Lord.

I cannot dismiss this important article, without touching upon one thing more. How many are directly concerned therein, I leave to the Searcher of hearts.

You have been settled in a living or a curacy for some time. You are now going to exchange it for another. Why do you this? For what reason do you prefer this before your former living or curacy? "Why, I had but fifty pounds a year where I was before, and now I shall have a hundred." And is this your real motive of acting —the true reason why you make the exchange? "It is: and is it not a sufficient reason?" Yes, for a Heathen; but not for one who calls himself a Christian.

Perhaps a more gross infatuation than this was never yet known upon earth. There goes one who is commissioned to be an ambassador of Christ, a shepherd of never dying souls, a watchman over the Israel of God, a steward of the mysteries which "angels desire to look into." Where is he going? "To London, to Bristol, to Northampton." Why does he go thither? "To get more money." A tolerable reason for driving a herd of bullocks to one market rather than the other; though if a drover does this without any farther view, he acts as a Heathen, not a Christian. But what a reason for leaving the immortal souls over whom the Holy Ghost had made you overseer! And yet this is the motive which not only influences in secret, but is acknowledged openly and without a blush! Nay, it is excused, justified, defended; and that not by a few, here and there, who are apparently void both of piety and shame; but by numbers of seemingly religious men, from one end of England to the other!

(2.) Am I, Secondly, such as I ought to be, with regard to my affections? I am taken from among, and ordained for, men, in things pertaining to God. I stand between God and man, by the authority of the great Mediator, in the nearest and most endearing relation both to my Creator and to my fellow creatures. Have I accordingly given my heart to God, and to my brethren for his sake? Do I love God with all my soul and strength? and my neighbour, every man, as myself? Does this love swallow me up, possess me whole, constitute my supreme happiness? Does it animate all my passions and tempers, and regulate all my powers and faculties? Is it the spring which gives rise to all my thoughts, and governs all my words and actions? If it does, not unto me, but unto God be the praise! If it does not, "God be merciful to me a sinner!"

At least, do I feel such a concern for the glory of God, and such a thirst after the salvation of men, that I am ready to do any thing, however contrary to my natural inclination, to part with any thing, however agreeable to me, to suffer any thing, however grievous to flesh and blood, so I may save one soul from hell? Is this my ruling temper at all times and in all places? Does it make all my labour light? If not, what a weariness is it! what a drudgery! Had I not far better hold the plough?

But is it possible this should be my ruling temper, if I still love the world? No, certainly, if I "love the world, the love of the Father is not in" me. The love of God is not in me, if I love money, if I love pleasure, so called, or diversion. Neither is it in me, if I am a lover of honour or praise, or of dress, or of good eating and drinking. Nay, even indolence, or the love of ease, is inconsistent with the love of God.

What a creature then is a covetous, an ambitious, a luxurious, an indolent, a diversion-loving clergyman! Is it any wonder that infidelity should increase, where any of

## An Address to the Clergy.

these are to be found? that many, comparing their spirit with their profession, should blaspheme that worthy name whereby they are called? But "wo be unto him by whom the offence cometh! It were good for that man if he had never been born." It were good for him now, rather than he should continue to turn the lame out of the way, "that a millstone were hanged about his neck, and he were cast into the depth of the sea!"

(3.) May not you, who are of a better spirit, consider, Thirdly, Am I such as I ought to be, with regard to my practice? Am I, in my private life, wholly devoted to God? Am I intent upon this one thing, to do in every point "not my own will, but the will of him that sent me?" Do I carefully and resolutely abstain from every evil word and work? "from all appearance of evil?" from all indifferent things, which might lay a stumbling block in the way of the weak? Am I zealous of good works? As I have time, do I do good to all men? and that in every kind, and in as high a degree as I am capable?

How do I behave in the public work whereunto I am called,—in my pastoral character? Am I "a pattern" to my "flock, in word, in behaviour, in love, in spirit, in faith, in purity?" Is my "word," my daily conversation, "always in grace," always "meet to minister grace to the hearers?" Is my behaviour suitable to the dignity of my calling? Do I walk as Christ also walked? Does the love of God and man not only fill my heart, but shine through my whole conversation? Is the spirit, the temper which appears in all my words and actions, such as allows me to say with humble boldness, Herein, "be ye followers of me, as I am of Christ?" Do all who have spiritual discernment take knowledge (judging of the tree by its fruits) that "the life which I now live, I live by faith in the Son of God;" and that in all "simplicity and godly sincerity I have my conversation in the world?" Am I exemplarily pure from all worldly desire, from all vile and vain affections? Is my life one continued labour of love, one tract of praising God and helping man? Do I in every thing see "Him who is invisible?" And "beholding with open face the glory of the Lord," am I "changed into the same image from glory to glory, by the Spirit of the Lord?"

Brethren, is not this our calling, even as we are Christians; but more eminently as we are ministers of Christ? And why (I will not say, do we fall short, but why) are we satisfied with falling so short of it? Is there any necessity laid upon us, of sinking so infinitely below our calling? Who hath required this at our hands? Certainly, not He by whose authority we minister. Is not his will the same with regard to us, as with regard to his first ambassadors? Is not his love, and is not his power still the same, as they were in the ancient days? Know we not, that Jesus Christ "is the same yesterday, to-day, and for ever?" Why then may not you be as "burning and as shining lights," as those that shone seventeen hundred years ago? Do you desire to partake of the same burning love, of the same shining holiness? Surely you do. You cannot but be sensible it is the greatest blessing which can be bestowed on any child of man. Do you design it; aim at it; "press on to" this "mark of the prize of the high calling of God in Christ Jesus?" Do you constantly and earnestly pray for it? Then, as the Lord liveth, ye shall attain. Only let us pray on, and "tarry at Jerusalem, till we be endued with power from on high." Let us continue in all the ordinances of God, particularly in meditating on his word, "in denying ourselves, and taking up our cross daily," and, "as we have time, doing good to all men;" and then assuredly "the great Shepherd" of us and our flocks will "make us perfect in every good work to do his will, and work in us all that is well pleasing in his sight!" This is the desire and prayer of

Your Brother and Servant, in our common Lord,
JOHN WESLEY.

# FARTHER THOUGHTS
## ON SEPARATION FROM THE CHURCH.
[*Arminian Magazine*, 1790. *Works*, vii, 325-6.]

FROM a child I was taught to love and reverence the Scripture, the oracles of God; and, next to these, to esteem the primitive Fathers, the writers of the three first centuries. Next after the primitive Church, I esteemed our own, the Church of England, as the most Scriptural National Church in the world.* I therefore not only assented to all the doctrines, but observed all the Rubric in the Liturgy; and that with all possible exactness, even at the peril of my life.†

---

* "Having had an opportunity of seeing several of the churches abroad, and having deeply considered the several sorts of Dissenters at home, I am fully convinced that our own Church, with all her blemishes, is nearer the Scriptural plan than any other in Europe."—*Letter to Sir Harry Trelawney. Works*, vii, 233.

† "I hold all the doctrines of the Church of England. I love her liturgy. I approve her plan of discipline, and only wish it could be put in execution. I do not knowingly vary from any rule of the Church, unless in those few instances, where I judge, and as far as I judge, there is an absolute necessity.

"For instance, (1.) As few clergymen open their churches to me, I am under the necessity of *preaching abroad*.

"(2.) As I know no forms that will suit all occasions, I am often under a necessity of *praying extempore*.

"(3.) In order to build up the flock of Christ in faith and love, I am under a necessity of uniting them together, and of dividing them into little companies, that they may provoke one another to love and good works.

"(4.) That my fellow labourers and I may more effectually assist each other, to save our own souls and those that hear us, I judge it necessary to meet the preachers, or at least, the greater part of them, once a year.

"(5.) In those conferences we fix the stations of all the preachers for the ensuing year.

"But all this is not separating from the Church. So far from it, that, whenever I have opportunity, I attend the Church service myself, and advise all our societies so to do."—*Sermon on the Ministerial Office*, 1789. *Works*, ii, 542-3.

"Dr. Coke made two or three little alterations in the prayer book without my knowledge. I took particular care throughout, to alter nothing merely for altering' sake. In religion, I am for as few innovations as possible. I love the old wine best."—*Letter to Mr. Walter Churchey*, 1789. *Works*, vii, 86.

In this judgment, and with this spirit, I went to America, strongly attached to the Bible, the primitive Church, and the Church of England, from which I would not vary in one jot or tittle on any account whatever. In this spirit I returned as regular a clergyman as any in the three kingdoms; till, after not being permitted to preach in the churches, I was constrained to preach in the open air.*

Here was my first irregularity; and it was not voluntary, but constrained. The second was extemporary prayer. This, likewise, I believed to be my bounden duty, for the sake of those who desired me to watch over their souls. I could not in conscience refrain from it; neither from accepting those who desired to serve me as sons in the Gospel.

When the people joined together, simply to help each other to heaven, increased by hundreds and thousands,

---

\* "Being thus excluded from the churches, and not daring to be silent, it remained only to preach in the open air; which I did at first, not out of choice, but necessity; but I have since seen abundant reason to adore the wise providence of God herein, making a way for myriads of people, who never troubled any church, nor were likely so to do, to hear that word which they soon found to be the power of God unto salvation."—*A Short History of the People Called Methodists*, 1781. *Works*, vii, 349.

"I never 'attempted to deny,' that the novelty of our manner of preaching has induced thousands and ten thousands to hear us, who would otherwise never have heard us at all, nor perhaps any other preacher. But I utterly deny, that 'the effects wrought on many of them that heard were owing to novelty, and that only.' The particular effects wrought at Epworth, were these: many drunkards, many unjust and profane men, on whom both my father and I had for several years spent our strength in vain, from that time began to live, and continue so to do, a sober, righteous, and godly life. Now, I deny that this effect can be owing to novelty, or to any principle but the power of God.

"If it be asked, But were there not 'the same hearers, the same preachers, and the same God to influence, in the church, as on the tomb stone?' I answer (1.) There were not all the same hearers in the church; not above one third of them. (2.) There was the same preacher in the church, but he did not then preach the same doctrine; and therefore (3.) Though there was the same God, there was not the same influence, or blessing from him."—*Letter to Mr. John Smith*, 1747. *Works*, vi, 646.

still they had no more thought of leaving the Church than of leaving the kingdom. Nay, I continually and earnestly cautioned them against it; reminding them that we were a part of the Church of England, whom God had raised up, not only to save our own souls, but to enliven our neighbours, those of the Church in particular. And at the first meeting of all our preachers in conference, in June, 1744, I exhorted them to keep to the Church; observing, that this was our peculiar glory,—not to form any new sect, but, abiding in our own Church, to do all men all the good we possibly could.*

But as more Dissenters joined with us, many of whom were much prejudiced against the Church, these, with or without design, were continually infusing their own prejudices into their brethren. I saw this, and gave warning of it from time to time, both in private and in public; and in the year 1758, I resolved to bring the matter to a fair issue. So I desired the point might be considered at large, whether it was expedient for the Methodists to leave the Church. The arguments on both sides were discussed for several days; and at length we agreed, without a dissenting voice, "It is by no means expedient that the Methodists should leave the Church of England."

Nevertheless, the same leaven continued to work in various parts of the kingdom. The grand argument (which in some particular cases must be acknowledged to have weight) was this: "The minister of the parish wherein we dwell neither lives nor preaches the Gospel. He walks in the way to hell himself, and teaches his flock to do the same. Can you advise them to attend

---

* "We look upon ourselves, not as the authors or ringleaders of a particular sect or party (it is the farthest thing from our thoughts); but as messengers of God to those who are Christians in name, but Heathens in heart and in life, to call them back to that from which they are fallen, to real genuine Christianity."—*Reasons against a Separation from the Church of England*, 1758. *Works*, vii, 295.

his preaching?" I cannot advise them to it. "What, then, can they do on the Lord's day, suppose no other church be near? Do you advise them to go to a Dissenting meeting? Or to meet in their own preaching house?" Where this is really the case, I cannot blame them if they do. Although, therefore, I earnestly oppose the general separation of the Methodists from the Church, yet I cannot condemn such a partial separation in this particular case. I believe, to separate thus far from these miserable wretches, who are the scandal of our Church and nation, would be for the honour of our Church, as well as to the glory of God.

And this is no way contrary to the profession which I have made above these fifty years. I never had any design of separating from the Church: I have no such design now. I do not believe the Methodists in general design it, when I am no more seen. I do, and will do, all that is in my power to prevent such an event. Nevertheless, in spite of all that I can do, many of them will separate from it: although I am apt to think, not one half, perhaps not a third, of them. These will be so bold and injudicious as to form a separate party, which, consequently, will dwindle away into a dry, dull, separate party.* In flat opposition to these, I declare once more, that I live and die a member of the Church of England; and that none who regard my judgment or advice will ever separate from it.

JOHN WESLEY.

LONDON, Dec. 11, 1789.

---

* "I still think, when the Methodists leave the Church of England, God will leave them. Every year more and more of the clergy are convinced of the truth, and grow well-affected toward us. It would be contrary to all common sense, as well as to good conscience, to make a separation now."—*Letter to Mr. Samuel Bardsley*, 1787. *Works*, vii, 132.

# THE CHARACTER OF A METHODIST.*

[1742 (*Green*). *Works*, v, 240-5.]

*Not as though I had already attained.*

## TO THE READER.

SINCE the name first came abroad into the world, many have been at a loss to know what a Methodist is; what are the principles and the practice of those who are commonly called by that name; and what the distinguishing marks of this sect, "which is every where spoken against."

And it being generally believed, that I was able to give the clearest account of these things (as having been one of the first to whom that name was given, and the person by whom the rest were supposed to be directed), I have been called upon, in all manner of ways, and with the utmost earnestness, so to do. I yield at last to the continued importunity both of friends and enemies; and do now give the clearest account I can, in the presence of the Lord and Judge of heaven and earth, of the principles and practice whereby those who are called Methodists are distinguished from other men.

I say those who are called Methodists; for, let it be well observed, that this is not a name which they take to themselves, but one fixed upon them by way of reproach, without their approbation or consent. It was first given to three or four young men at Oxford, by a student of Christ Church; either in allusion to the ancient sect of

---

* "The first tract I ever wrote expressly on this subject [Christian perfection] was published in the latter end of this year [1739]. That none might be prejudiced before they read it, I gave it the indifferent title of 'The Character of a Methodist.' In this I described a perfect Christian, placing in the front, 'Not as though I had already attained.'" —*A Plain Account of Christian Perfection*, 1777. *Works*, vi, 486.
"The tract you refer to (as is expressly declared in the preface) does not describe what the Methodists are already; but what they desire to be, and what they will be then when they fully practise the doctrine they hear."—*A Second Letter to Bishop Lavington*, 1750. *Works*, v, 383.

physicians so called, from their teaching, that almost all diseases might be cured by a specific *method* of diet and exercise, or from their observing a more regular *method* of study and behaviour than was usual with those of their age and station.

I should rejoice (so little ambitious am I to be at the head of any sect or party) if the very name might never be mentioned more, but be buried in eternal oblivion.\* But if that cannot be, at least let those who will use it, know the meaning of the word they use. Let us not always be fighting in the dark. Come, and let us look one another in the face. And perhaps some of you who hate what I am *called,* may love what I *am* by the grace of God; or rather, what "I follow after, if that I may apprehend that for which also I am apprehended of Christ Jesus."

## THE CHARACTER OF A METHODIST.

The distinguishing marks of a Methodist are not his opinions of any sort. His assenting to this or that scheme of religion, his embracing any particular set of notions, his espousing the judgment of one man or of another, are all quite wide of the point. Whosoever, therefore, imagines that a Methodist is a man of such or such an opinion, is grossly ignorant of the whole affair; he mistakes the truth totally. We believe, indeed, that "all Scripture is given by the inspiration of God;" and herein we are distinguished from Jews, Turks, and Infidels. We believe the written word of God to be the only and sufficient rule both of Christian faith and practice; and herein we are fundamentally distinguished from those

---

\* "Would to God that all the party names, and unscriptural phrases and forms, which have divided the Christian world, were forgot; and that we might all agree to sit down together, as humble, loving disciples, at the feet of our common Master, to hear his word, to imbibe his Spirit, and to transcribe his life in our own!"—*Preface to Explanatory Notes upon the New Testament*, 1755. *Works*, vii, 536.

## The Character of a Methodist.

of the Romish Church. We believe Christ to be the eternal, supreme God; and herein we are distinguished from the Socinians and Arians. But as to all opinions which do not strike at the root of Christianity, we think and let think.* So that, whatsoever they are, whether right or wrong, they are no distinguishing marks of a Methodist.

Neither are words or phrases of any sort. We do not place our religion, or any part of it, in being attached to any peculiar mode of speaking, any quaint or uncommon set of expressions. The most obvious, easy, common words, wherein our meaning can be conveyed, we prefer before others, both on ordinary occasions, and when we

---

* "If you say, 'Because you hold opinions which I cannot believe are true:' I answer, Believe them true or false; I will not quarrel with you about any opinion. Only see that your heart be right toward God, that you know and love the Lord Jesus Christ; that you love your neighbour, and walk as your Master walked; and I desire no more. I am sick of opinions: I am weary to bear them. My soul loathes this frothy food. Give me solid and substantial religion; give me an humble, gentle lover of God and man; a man full of mercy and good fruits, without partiality and without hypocrisy; a man laying himself out in the work of faith, the patience of hope, the labour of love. Let my soul be with these Christians, wheresoever they are, and whatsoever opinion they are of. 'Whosoever' thus 'doeth the will of my Father which is in heaven, the same is my brother, and sister, and mother.'"—*A Farther Appeal to Men of Reason and Religion*, Part iii, 1745. *Works*, v, 173. "Be true also to your principles touching opinions and the externals of religion. Use every ordinance which you believe is of God; but beware of narrowness of spirit toward those who use them not. Conform yourself to those modes of worship which you approve; yet love as brethren those who cannot conform. Lay so much stress on opinions, that all your own, if it be possible, may agree with truth and reason; but have a care of anger, dislike, or contempt toward those whose opinions differ from yours. You are daily accused of this (and, indeed, what is it whereof you are not accused?); but beware of giving any ground for such an accusation. Condemn no man for not thinking as you think: let every one enjoy the full and free liberty of thinking for himself; let every man use his own judgment, since every man must give an account of himself to God. Abhor every approach, in any kind or degree, to the spirit of persecution. If you cannot reason or persuade a man into the truth, never attempt to force him into it. If love will not compel him to come in, leave him to God, the Judge of all."—*Advice to the People Called Methodists*, 1745. *Works*, v, 253.

speak of the things of God. We never, therefore, willingly or designedly, deviate from the most usual way of speaking; unless when we express Scripture truths in Scripture words, which, we presume, no Christian will condemn. Neither do we affect to use any particular expressions of Scripture more frequently than others, unless they are such as are more frequently used by the inspired writers themselves. It is as gross an error to place the marks of a Methodist in his words, as in opinions of any sort.

Nor do we desire to be distinguished by actions, customs, or usages, of an indifferent nature. Our religion does not lie in doing what God has not enjoined, or abstaining from what he hath not forbidden. It does not lie in the form of our apparel, in the posture of our body, or the covering of our heads; nor yet in abstaining from marriage, or from meats and drinks, which are all good if received with thanksgiving. Therefore, neither will any man, who knows whereof he affirms, fix the mark of a Methodist here,—in any actions or customs purely indifferent, undetermined by the word of God.

Nor, lastly, is he distinguished by laying the whole stress of religion on any single part of it. If you say, "Yes, he is; for he thinks 'we are saved by faith alone:'" I answer, You do not understand the terms. By salvation he means holiness of heart and life.* And this he affirms

---

* " By salvation I mean, not barely, according to the vulgar notion, deliverance from hell, or going to heaven; but a present deliverance from sin, a restoration of the soul to its primitive health, its original purity; a recovery of the divine nature; the renewal of our souls after the image of God, in righteousness and true holiness, in justice, mercy, and truth. This implies all holy and heavenly tempers, and, by consequence, all holiness of conversation.

" Now, if by salvation we mean a present salvation from sin, we cannot say, holiness is the condition of it; for it is the thing itself. Salvation, in this sense, and holiness, are synonymous terms. We must therefore say, 'We are saved by faith.' Faith is the sole condition of this salvation. For without faith we cannot be thus saved. But whosoever believeth is saved already."—*A Farther Appeal to Men of Reason and Religion*, Part i, 1745. *Works*, v, 35.

## The Character of a Methodist.

to spring from true faith alone. Can even a nominal Christian deny it? Is this placing a part of religion for the whole? "Do we then make void the law through faith? God forbid! Yea, we establish the law." We do not place the whole of religion (as too many do, God knoweth) either in doing no harm, or in doing good, or in using the ordinances of God. No, not in all of them together; wherein we know by experience a man may labour many years, and at the end have no religion at all, no more than he had at the beginning. Much less in any one of these; or, it may be, in a scrap of one of them: like her who fancies herself a virtuous woman, only because she is not a prostitute; or him who dreams he is an honest man, merely because he does not rob or steal. May the Lord God of my fathers preserve me from such a poor, starved religion as this! Were this the mark of a Methodist, I would sooner choose to be a sincere Jew, Turk, or Pagan.

"What then is the mark? Who is a Methodist, according to your own account?"[*] I answer: A Methodist is one who has "the love of God shed abroad in his heart by the Holy Ghost given unto him;" one who "loves the Lord his God with all his heart, and with all his soul, and with all his mind, and with all his strength." God is the joy of his heart, and the desire of his soul; which is constantly crying out, "Whom have I in heaven but thee? and there is none upon earth that I desire beside thee! My God and my all! Thou art the strength of my heart, and my portion for ever!"

He is therefore happy in God, yea, always happy, as having in him "a well of water springing up into everlasting life," and overflowing his soul with peace and joy.

---

[*] " Mr. Wesley's explanation of the word *Methodist*, in this Dictionary, is worthy of notice. It is, 'One that lives according to the method laid down in the Bible.'—EDIT."—*Note to The Complete English Dictionary*, 1753. *Works*, vii, 534.

"Perfect love" having now "cast out fear," he "rejoices evermore." He "rejoices in the Lord always," even "in God his Saviour;" and in the Father, "through our Lord Jesus Christ, by whom he hath now received the atonement." "Having" found "redemption through his blood, the forgiveness of his sins," he cannot but rejoice, whenever he looks back on the horrible pit out of which he is delivered; when he sees "all his transgressions blotted out as a cloud, and his iniquities as a thick cloud." He cannot but rejoice, whenever he looks on the state wherein he now is; "being justified freely, and having peace with God through our Lord Jesus Christ." For "he that believeth, hath the witness" of this "in himself;" being now the son of God by faith. "Because he is a son, God hath sent forth the Spirit of his Son into his heart, crying, Abba, Father!" And "the Spirit itself beareth witness with his spirit, that he is a child of God." He rejoices also, whenever he looks forward, "in hope of the glory that shall be revealed;" yea, this his joy is full, and all his bones cry out, "Blessed be the God and Father of our Lord Jesus Christ, who, according to his abundant mercy, hath begotten me again to a living hope—of an inheritance incorruptible, undefiled, and that fadeth not away, reserved in heaven for me!"

And he who hath this hope, thus "full of immortality, in every thing giveth thanks;" as knowing that this (whatsoever it is) "is the will of God in Christ Jesus concerning him." From him, therefore, he cheerfully receives all, saying, "Good is the will of the Lord;" and whether the Lord giveth or taketh away, equally "blessing the name of the Lord." For he hath "learned, in whatsoever state he is, therewith to be content." He knoweth "both how to be abased, and how to abound. Every where and in all things he is instructed both to be full and to be hungry, both to abound and suffer need." Whether in ease or pain, whether in sickness or health,

## The Character of a Methodist. 297

whether in life or death, he giveth thanks from the ground of his heart to Him who orders it for good; knowing that as "every good gift cometh from above," so none but good can come from the Father of lights, into whose hand he has wholly committed his body and soul, as into the hands of a faithful Creator. He is therefore "careful" (anxiously or uneasily) "for nothing;" as having "cast all his care on Him that careth for him," and "in all things" resting on him, after "making his request known to him with thanksgiving."

For indeed he "prays without ceasing." It is given him "always to pray, and not to faint." Not that he is always in the house of prayer; though he neglects no opportunity of being there. Neither is he always on his knees, although he often is, or on his face, before the Lord his God. Nor yet is he always crying aloud to God, or calling upon him in words: for many times "the Spirit maketh intercession for him with groans that cannot be uttered." But at all times the language of his heart is this: "Thou brightness of the eternal glory, unto thee is my heart, though without a voice, and my silence speaketh unto thee." And this is true prayer, and this alone. But his heart is ever lifted up to God, at all times and in all places. In this he is never hindered, much less interrupted, by any person or thing. In retirement or company, in leisure, business, or conversation, his heart is ever with the Lord. Whether he lie down or rise up, God is in all his thoughts; he walks with God continually, having the loving eye of his mind still fixed upon him, and every where "seeing him that is invisible."

And while he thus always exercises his love to God, by praying without ceasing, rejoicing evermore, and in every thing giving thanks, this commandment is written in his heart, "That he who loveth God, love his brother also." And he accordingly loves his neighbour as himself; he loves every man as his own soul. His heart is full of love to all mankind, to every child of "the Father of the spirits of all flesh." That a man is not personally known to him, is no bar to his love; no, nor that he is known to be such as he approves not, that he repays hatred for his good will. For he "loves his enemies;" yea, and the enemies of God, "the evil and the unthankful." And if it be not in his power to "do good to them that hate him," yet he ceases not to pray for them, though they continue to spurn his love, and still "despitefully use him and persecute him."

For he is "pure in heart." The love of God has purified his heart from all revengeful passions, from envy, malice, and wrath, from every unkind temper or malign affection. It hath cleansed him from pride and haughtiness of spirit, whereof alone cometh contention. And he hath now "put on bowels of mercies, kindness, humbleness of mind, meekness, long suffering:" so that he "forbears and forgives, if he had a quarrel against any; even as God in Christ hath forgiven him." And indeed all possible ground for contention, on his part, is utterly cut off. For none can take from him what he desires; seeing he "loves not the world, nor" any of "the things of the world;" being now "crucified to the world, and the world crucified to him;" being dead to all that is in the world, both to "the lust of the flesh, the lust of the eye, and the pride of life." For "all his desire is unto God, and to the remembrance of his name."

Agreeable to this his one desire, is the one design of his life, namely, "not to do his own will, but the will of Him that sent him." His one intention at all times and in all things is, not to please himself, but Him whom his soul loveth. He has a single eye. And because "his eye is single, his whole body is full of light." Indeed, where the loving eye of the soul is continually fixed upon God, there can be no darkness at all, "but the whole is light; as when the bright shining of a candle doth enlighten the house." God then reigns alone. All that is in the soul is holiness to the Lord. There is not a motion in his heart, but is according to his will. Every thought that arises points to Him, and is in obedience to the law of Christ.

And the tree is known by its fruits. For as he loves God, so he keeps his commandments; not only some, or most of them, but all, from the least to the greatest. He is not content to "keep the whole law, and offend in one point;" but has in all points, "a conscience void of offence toward God and toward man." Whatever God has forbidden, he avoids; whatever God hath enjoined, he doeth; and that whether it be little or great, hard or easy, joyous or grievous to the flesh. He "runs the way of God's commandments," now he hath set his heart at liberty. It is his glory so to do; it is his daily crown of rejoicing, "to do the will of God on earth, as it is done in heaven;" knowing it is the highest privilege of "the angels of God, of those that excel in strength, to fulfill his commandments, and hearken to the voice of his word."

All the commandments of God he accordingly keeps, and that with all his might. For his obedience is in proportion to his love, the source from whence it flows. And therefore, loving God with all his heart, he serves him with all his strength. He continually presents his soul and body a living sacrifice, holy, acceptable to God; entirely and without reserve devoting himself, all he has, and all he is, to his glory. All the talents he has received, he constantly employs according to his Master's will; every power and faculty of his soul, every member of his body. Once he "yielded" them "unto sin" and the devil, "as instruments of unrighteousness;" but now, "being alive from the dead, he yields" them all "as instruments of righteousness unto God."

By consequence, whatsoever he doeth, it is all to the glory of God. In all his employments of every kind, he not only aims at this (which is implied in having a single eye), but actually attains it. His business and refreshments, as well as his prayers, all serve this great end. Whether he sit in his house or walk by the way, whether he lie down or rise up, he is promoting, in all he speaks or does, the one business of his life; whether he put on his apparel, or labour, or eat and drink, or divert himself from too wasting labour, it all tends to advance the glory of God, by peace and good will among men. His one invariable rule is this, "Whatsoever ye do, in word or deed, do it all in the name of the Lord Jesus, giving thanks to God and the Father by him."

Nor do the customs of the world at all hinder his "running the race that is set before him." He knows that vice does not lose its nature, though it becomes ever so fashionable; and remembers, that "every man is to give an account of himself to God." He cannot, therefore, "follow" even "a multitude to do evil." He cannot "fare sumptuously every day," or "make provision for the flesh to fulfil the lusts thereof." He cannot "lay up treasures upon earth," any more than he can take fire into his bosom. He cannot "adorn himself," on any pretence, "with gold or costly apparel." He cannot join in or countenance any diversion which has the least tendency to vice of any kind. He cannot "speak evil" of his neighbour, any more than he can lie either for God or man. He cannot utter an unkind word of any one; for love keeps the door of his lips. He cannot speak "idle words;" "no corrupt communication" ever "comes out of his mouth," as is all that "which is" not "good to the use of edifying," not "fit to minister grace to the hearers." But "whatsoever things are pure, whatsoever things are lovely, whatsoever things are" justly "of good report," he thinks and speaks, and acts, "adorning the Gospel of our Lord Jesus Christ in all things."

Lastly. As he has time, he "does good unto all men;" unto neighbours and strangers, friends and enemies: and

## The Character of a Methodist.

that in every possible kind; not only to their bodies, by "feeding the hungry, clothing the naked, visiting those that are sick or in prison;" but much more does he labour to do good to their souls, as of the ability which God giveth; to awaken those that sleep in death; to bring those who are awakened to the atoning blood, that, "being justified by faith, they may have peace with God;" and to provoke those who have peace with God to abound more in love and in good works. And he is willing to "spend and be spent herein," even "to be offered up on the sacrifice and service of their faith," so they may "all come unto the measure of the stature of the fulness of Christ."

These are the principles and practices of our sect; these are the marks of a true Methodist. By these alone do those who are in derision so called, desire to be distinguished from other men. If any man say, "Why, these are only the common, fundamental principles of Christianity!" Thou hast said; so I mean; this is the very truth; I know they are no other; and I would to God both thou and all men knew, that I, and all who follow my judgment, do vehemently refuse to be distinguished from other men, by any but the common principles of Christianity,—the plain, old Christianity that I teach, renouncing and detesting all other marks of distinction. And whosoever is what I preach (let him be called what he will, for names change not the nature of things), he is a Christian, not in name only, but in heart and in life. He is inwardly and outwardly conformed to the will of God, as revealed in the written word. He thinks, speaks, and lives, according to the method laid down in the revelation of Jesus Christ. His soul is renewed after the image of God, in righteousness and in all true holiness. And having the mind that was in Christ, he so walks as Christ also walked.

By these marks, by these fruits of a living faith, do

we labour to distinguish ourselves from the unbelieving world, from all those whose minds or lives are not according to the Gospel of Christ. But from real Christians, of whatsoever denomination they be, we earnestly desire not to be distinguished at all; not from any who sincerely follow after what they know they have not yet attained. No: "Whosoever doeth the will of my Father which is in heaven, the same is my brother, and sister, and mother." And I beseech you, brethren, by the mercies of God, that we be in no wise divided among ourselves. Is thy heart right, as my heart is with thine? I ask no farther question. If it be, give me thy hand. For opinions, or terms, let us not destroy the work of God. Dost thou love and serve God? It is enough. I give thee the right hand of fellowship. If there be any consolation in Christ, if any comfort of love, if any fellowship of the Spirit, if any bowels and mercies; let us strive together for the faith of the Gospel; walking worthy of the vocation wherewith we are called; with all lowliness and meekness, with long suffering, forbearing one another in love, endeavouring to keep the unity of the Spirit in the bond of peace; remembering, there is one body, and one Spirit, even as we are called with one hope of our calling; "one Lord, one faith, one baptism; one God and Father of all, who is above all, and through all, and in you all."

FACSIMILE OF A PAGE OF JOHN WESLEY'S MS.
JOURNAL IN GEORGIA

## A LETTER TO A ROMAN CATHOLIC.
[*Works*, v, 761-6.]

DUBLIN, July 18, 1749.

You have heard ten thousand stories of us who are commonly called Protestants, of which, if you believe only one in a thousand, you must think very hardly of us. But this is quite contrary to our Lord's rule, "Judge not, that ye be not judged;" and has many ill consequences; particularly this,—it inclines us to think as hardly of you. Hence we are on both sides less willing to help one another, and more ready to hurt each other. Hence brotherly love is utterly destroyed; and each side looking on the other as monsters, gives way to anger, hatred, malice, to every unkind affection; which have frequently broke out in such inhuman barbarities as are scarce named among the Heathens.

Now, can nothing be done, even allowing us on both sides to retain our own opinions, for the softening our hearts toward each other, the giving a check to this flood of unkindness, and restoring at least some small degree of love among our neighbours and countrymen? Do not you wish for this? Are you not fully convinced, that malice, hatred, revenge, bitterness, whether in us or in you, in our hearts or yours, are an abomination to the Lord? Be our opinions right, or be they wrong, these tempers are undeniably wrong. They are the broad road that leads to destruction, to the nethermost hell.

I do not suppose all the bitterness is on your side. I know there is too much on our side also; so much, that I fear many Protestants (so called) will be angry at me too, for writing to you in this manner; and will say, "It is showing you too much favour; you deserve no such treatment at our hands."

But I think you do. I think you deserve the tenderest

regard I can show, were it only because the same God hath raised you and me from the dust of the earth, and has made us both capable of loving and enjoying him to eternity; were it only because the Son of God has bought you and me with his own blood. How much more, if you are a person fearing God (as without question many of you are), and studying to have a conscience void of offence toward God and toward man?

I shall therefore endeavour, as mildly and inoffensively as I can, to remove in some measure the ground of your unkindness, by plainly declaring what our belief and what our practice is; that you may see, we are not altogether such monsters as perhaps you imagined us to be.

A true Protestant may express his belief in these or the like words:—

As I am assured that there is an infinite and independent Being, and that it is impossible there should be more than one; so I believe, that this One God is the Father of all things, especially of angels and men; that he is in a peculiar manner the Father of those whom he regenerates by his Spirit, whom he adopts in his Son, as co-heirs with him, and crowns with an eternal inheritance; but in a still higher sense, the Father of his only Son, whom he hath begotten from eternity.

I believe this Father of all, not only to be able to do whatsoever pleaseth him, but also to have an eternal right of making what and when and how he pleaseth, and of possessing and disposing of all that he has made; and that he of his own goodness created heaven and earth, and all that is therein.

I believe that Jesus of Nazareth was the Saviour of the world, the Messiah so long foretold; that, being anointed with the Holy Ghost, he was a Prophet, revealing to us the whole will of God; that he was a Priest, who gave himself a sacrifice for sin, and still makes intercession for transgressors; that he is a King, who has all power in heaven and in earth, and will reign till he has subdued all things to himself.

I believe he is the proper, natural Son of God, God of God, very God of very God; and that he is the Lord of all, having absolute, supreme, universal dominion over all things; but more peculiarly our Lord, who believe in him, both by conquest, purchase, and voluntary obligation.

I believe that he was made man, joining the human nature with the divine in one person; being conceived by the singular operation of the Holy Ghost, and born of the blessed Virgin Mary, who, as well after as before she brought him forth, continued a pure and unspotted virgin.

I believe he suffered inexpressible pains both of body and soul, and at last, death, even the death of the cross, at the time that Pontius Pilate governed Judea, under the Roman emperor; that his body was then laid in the grave, and his soul went to the place of separate spirits; that the third day he rose again from the dead; that he ascended into heaven; where he remains in the midst of the throne of God, in the highest power and glory, as Mediator till the end of the world, as God to all eternity; that, in the end, he will come down from heaven, to judge every man according to his works; both those who shall be then alive, and all who have died before that day.

I believe the infinite and eternal Spirit of God, equal with the Father and the Son, to be not only perfectly holy in himself, but the immediate cause of all holiness in us; enlightening our understandings, rectifying our wills and affections, renewing our natures, uniting our persons to Christ, assuring us of the adoption of sons, leading us in our actions; purifying and sanctifying our souls and bodies, to a full and eternal enjoyment of God.

I believe that Christ by his Apostles gathered unto himself a church, to which he has continually added such as shall be saved; that this catholic, that is, universal, church, extending to all nations and all ages, is holy in all its members, who have fellowship with God the Father, Son, and Holy Ghost; that they have fellowship with the holy angels, who constantly minister to these heirs of salvation; and with all the living members of Christ on earth, as well as all who are departed in his faith and fear.

I believe God forgives all the sins of them that truly repent and unfeignedly believe his holy Gospel; and that, at the last day, all men shall rise again, every one with his own body.

I believe, that as the unjust shall, after their resurrection, be tormented in hell for ever, so the just shall enjoy inconceivable happiness in the presence of God to all eternity.

Now, is there any thing wrong in this? is there any one point which you do not believe as well as we?

But you think we ought to believe more. We will not now enter into the dispute. Only let me ask, If a man sincerely believes thus much, and practises accordingly, can any one possibly persuade you to think that such a man shall perish everlastingly?

"But does he practise accordingly?" If he does not, we grant all his faith will not save him. And this leads me to show you, in few and plain words, what the practice of a true Protestant is.

I say, *a true Protestant;* for I disclaim all common swearers, Sabbath breakers, drunkards; all whoremongers, liars, cheats, extortioners; in a word, all that live in open sin. These are no Protestants; they are no Christians at all. Give them their own name; they are open Heathens. They are the curse of the nation, the bane of society, the shame of mankind, the scum of the earth.

A true Protestant believes in God, has a full confidence in his mercy, fears him with a filial fear, and loves him with all his soul. He worships God in spirit and in truth, in every thing gives him thanks; calls upon him with his heart as well as his lips, at all times and in all places; honors his holy name and his word, and serves him truly all the days of his life.

Now, do not you yourself approve of this? Is there any one point you can condemn? Do not you practise as well as approve of it? Can you ever be happy if you do not? Can you ever expect true peace in this, or glory in the world to come, if you do not believe in God through Christ? if you do not thus fear and love God? My dear friend, consider, I am not persuading you to leave or change your religion,* but to follow after that fear and love of God without which all religion is vain. I say not a word to you about your opinions or outward manner of worship. But I say, all worship is an abomination to the Lord, unless you worship him in spirit and in truth; with your heart, as well as your lips; with your spirit, and with your understanding also. Be your form of worship what it will, but in every thing give him thanks; else it is all but lost labour. Use whatever outward observances you please, but put your whole trust in him; but honour his holy name and his word, and serve him truly all the days of your life.

Again: A true Protestant loves his neighbour, that is, every man, friend or enemy, good or bad, as himself, as he loves his own soul, as Christ loved us. And as Christ laid down his life for us, so is he ready to lay down his life for his brethren. He shows this love, by doing to all men, in all points, as he would they should do unto him.

---

* "It is true, that, for thirty years last past, I have 'gradually put on a more catholic spirit;' finding more and more tenderness for those who differed from me either in opinions or modes of worship. But it is not true, that I 'reject any design of converting others from any communion.' I have, by the blessing of God, converted several from Popery, who are now alive and ready to testify it."—*Second Letter to Bishop Lavington,* 1750. *Works,* v, 400.

He loves, honours, and obeys his father and mother, and helps them to the uttermost of his power. He honours and obeys the king, and all that are put in authority under him. He cheerfully submits to all his governors, teachers, spiritual pastors, and masters. He behaves lowly and reverently to all his betters. He hurts nobody, by word or deed. He is true and just in all his dealings. He bears no malice or hatred in his heart. He abstains from all evil speaking, lying, and slandering; neither is guile found in his mouth. Knowing his body to be the temple of the Holy Ghost, he keeps it in sobriety, temperance, and chastity. He does not desire other men's goods; but is content with that he hath; labours to get his own living, and to do the whole will of God in that state of life unto which it has pleased God to call him.

Have you anything to reprove in this? Are you not herein even as he? If not (tell the truth) are you not condemned both by God and your own conscience? Can you fall short of any one point hereof without falling short of being a Christian?

Come, my brother, and let us reason together. Are you right if you only love your friend and hate your enemy? Do not even the Heathens and publicans so? You are called to love your enemies; to bless them that curse you, and to pray for them that despitefully use you and persecute you. But are you not disobedient to the heavenly calling? Does your tender love to all men, not only the good, but also the evil and unthankful, approve you the child of your Father which is in heaven? Otherwise, whatever you believe and whatever you practise, you are of your father the devil. Are you ready to lay down your life for your brethren? And do you do unto all as you would they should do unto you? If not, do not deceive your own soul: You are but a Heathen still. Do you love, honour, and obey your father and mother, and help them to the utmost of your power? Do you honour and obey

## A Letter to a Roman Catholic.

all in authority? all your governors, spiritual pastors, and masters? Do you behave lowly and reverently to all your betters? Do you hurt nobody, by word or deed? Are you true and just in all your dealings? Do you take care to pay whatever you owe? Do you feel no malice, or envy, or revenge, no hatred or bitterness to any man? If you do, it is plain you are not of God: For all these are the tempers of the devil. Do you speak the truth from your heart to all men, and that in tenderness and love? Are you "an Israelite indeed, in whom is no guile?" Do you keep your body in sobriety, temperance, and chastity, as knowing it is the temple of the Holy Ghost, and that, if any man defile the temple of God, him will God destroy? Have you learned, in every state wherein you are, therewith to be content? Do you labour to get your own living, abhorring idleness as you abhor hell-fire? The devil tempts other men; but an idle man tempts the devil. An idle man's brain is the devil's shop, where he is continually working mischief. Are you not slothful in business? Whatever your hand finds to do, do you do it with your might? And do you do all as unto the Lord, as a sacrifice unto God, acceptable in Christ Jesus?

This, and this alone, is the old religion. This is true, primitive Christianity. O when shall it spread over all the earth! When shall it be found both in us and you? Without waiting for others, let each of us, by the grace of God, amend one.

Are we not thus far agreed? Let us thank God for this, and receive it as a fresh token of his love. But if God still loveth us, we ought also to love one another. We ought, without this endless jangling about opinions, to provoke one another to love and to good works. Let the points wherein we differ stand aside; here are enough wherein we agree, enough to be the ground of every Christian temper, and of every Christian action.

O brethren, let us not still fall out by the way! I hope

to see you in heaven. And if I practise the religion above decribed, you dare not say I shall go to hell. You cannot think so. None can persuade you to it. Your own conscience tells you the contrary. Then if we cannot as yet think alike in all things, at least we may love alike. Herein we cannot possibly do amiss. For one point none can doubt a moment,—"God is love; and he that dwelleth in love, dwelleth in God, and God in him."

In the name, then, and in the strength, of God, let us resolve, First, not to hurt one another; to do nothing unkind or unfriendly to each other, nothing which we would not have done to ourselves. Rather let us endeavour after every instance of a kind, friendly, and Christian behaviour toward each other.

Let us resolve, Secondly, God being our helper, to speak nothing harsh or unkind to each other. The sure way to avoid this, is to say all the good we can, both of and to one another: In all our conversation, either with or concerning each other, to use only the language of love; to speak with all softness and tenderness; with the most endearing expression, which is consistent with truth and sincerity.

Let us, Thirdly, resolve to harbour no unkind thought, no unfriendly temper, toward each other. Let us lay the axe to the root of the tree: let us examine all that rises in our heart, and suffer no disposition there which is contrary to tender affection. Then shall we easily refrain from unkind actions and words, when the very root of bitterness is cut up.

Let us, Fourthly, endeavour to help each other on in whatever we are agreed leads to the kingdom. So far as we can, let us always rejoice to strengthen each other's hands in God. Above all, let us each take heed to himself (since each must give an account of himself to God) that he fall not short of the religion of love; that he be not condemned in that he himself approveth. O let you and

# A Letter to a Roman Catholic. 311

I (whatever others do) press on to the prize of our high calling! that, being justified by faith, we may have peace with God through our Lord Jesus Christ; that we may rejoice in God through Jesus Christ, by whom we have received the atonement; that the love of God may be shed abroad in our hearts by the Holy Ghost which is given unto us. Let us count all things but loss for the excellency of the knowledge of Jesus Christ our Lord; being ready for him to suffer the loss of all things, and counting them but dung, that we may win Christ.

I am your affectionate servant, for Christ's sake.

## A PLAIN ACCOUNT OF GENUINE CHRISTIANITY.*

[Printed separately, 1753. Originally the conclusion of *A Letter to the Rev. Dr. Conyers Middleton*, 1749. *Works*, v, 752-61.]

WE have been long disputing about Christians, about Christianity, and the evidence whereby it is supported. But what do these terms mean? Who is a Christian indeed? What is real, genuine Christianity? And what is the surest and most accessible evidence (if I may so speak) whereby I may know that it is of God? May the God of the Christians enable me to speak on these heads, in a manner suitable to the importance of them!

Section I. I would consider, First, Who is a Christian indeed? What does that term properly imply? It has been so long abused, I fear, not only to mean nothing at all, but, what was far worse than nothing, to be a cloak for the vilest hypocrisy, for the grossest abominations and immoralities of every kind, that it is high time to rescue it out of the hands of wretches that are a reproach to human nature; to show determinately what manner of man he is, to whom this name of right belongs.

A Christian cannot think of the Author of his being without abasing himself before him; without a deep sense of the distance between a worm of earth, and him that sitteth on the circle of the heavens. In his presence he sinks into the dust, knowing himself to be less than nothing in his eye; and being conscious, in a manner words cannot express, of his own littleness, ignorance, foolishness. So that he can only cry out, from the fulness of his heart, "O God! what is man? what am I?"

He has a continual sense of his dependence on the Parent of good for his being, and all the bless-

---

* Perhaps the most beautiful of all Mr. Wesley's tracts.—EDIT. *Works*, i, xiv.

## Genuine Christianity.

ings that attend it. To him he refers every natural and every moral endowment; with all that is commonly ascribed either to fortune, or to the wisdom, courage, or merit of the possessor. And hence he acquiesces in whatsoever appears to be his will, not only with patience, but with thankfulness. He willingly resigns all he is, all he has, to his wise and gracious disposal. The ruling temper of his heart is the most absolute submission, and the tenderest gratitude, to his sovereign Benefactor. And this grateful love creates filial fear; an awful reverence toward him, and an earnest care not to give place to any disposition, not to admit an action, word, or thought, which might in any degree displease that indulgent Power to whom he owes his life, breath, and all things.

And as he has the strongest affection for the Fountain of all good, so he has the firmest confidence in him; a confidence which neither pleasure nor pain, neither life nor death, can shake. But yet this, far from creating sloth or indolence, pushes him on to the most vigorous industry. It causes him to put forth all his strength, in obeying him in whom he confides. So that he is never faint in his mind, never weary of doing whatever he believes to be his will. And as he knows the most acceptable worship of God is to imitate him he worships, so he is continually labouring to transcribe into himself all his imitable perfections; in particular, his justice, mercy, and truth, so eminently displayed in all his creatures.

Above all, remembering that God is love, he is conformed to the same likeness. He is full of love to his neighbour; of universal love; not confined to one sect or party; not restrained to those who agree with him in opinions, or in outward modes of worship; or to those who are allied to him by blood, or recommended by nearness of place. Neither does he love those only that love him, or that are endeared to him by intimacy of acquaintance. But his love resembles that of him whose mercy is over all his works. It soars above all these scanty bounds, embracing neighbours and strangers, friends and enemies; yea, not only the good and gentle, but also the froward, the evil and unthankful. For he loves every soul that God has made; every child of man, of whatever place or nation. And yet this universal benevolence does in no wise interfere with a peculiar regard for his relations, friends, and benefactors; a fervent love for his country; and the most endeared affection to all men of integrity, of clear and generous virtue.

His love, as to these, so to all mankind, is in itself generous and disinterested; springing from no view of advantage to himself, from no regard to profit or praise; no, nor even the pleasure of loving. This is the daughter, not the parent, of his affection. By experience he knows that social love, if it mean the love of our neighbour, is absolutely different from self-love, even of the most allowable kind; just as different as the objects at which they point. And yet it is sure, that, if they are under due regulations, each will give additional force to the other, till they mix together never to be divided.

And this universal, disinterested love is productive of all right affections. It is fruitful of gentleness, tenderness, sweetness; of humanity, courtesy, and affability. It makes a Christian rejoice in the virtues of all, and bear a part in their happiness; at the same time that he sympathizes with their pains, and compassionates their infirmities. It creates modesty, condescension, prudence, together with calmness and evenness of temper. It is the parent of generosity, openness, and frankness, void of jealousy and suspicion. It begets candour, and willingness to believe and hope whatever is kind and friendly

## Genuine Christianity.

of every man; and invincible patience, never overcome of evil, but overcoming evil with good.*

The same love constrains him to converse, not only with a strict regard to truth, but with artless sincerity and genuine simplicity, as one in whom there is no guile. And, not content with abstaining from all such expressions as are contrary to justice or truth, he endeavours to refrain from every unloving word, either to a present or of an absent person; in all his conversation aiming at this, either to improve himself in knowledge or virtue, or to make those with whom he converses some way wiser, or better, or happier than they were before.

The same love is productive of all right actions. It leads him into an earnest and steady discharge of all social offices, of whatever is due to relations of every kind; to his friends, to his country, and to any particular community whereof he is a member.† It prevents his

---

* "You seem to apprehend, that I believe religion to be inconsistent with cheerfulness, and with a sociable, friendly temper. So far from it, that I am convinced, as true religion or holiness cannot be without cheerfulness, so steady cheerfulness, on the other hand, cannot be without holiness or true religion. And I am equally convinced, that religion has nothing sour, austere, unsociable, unfriendly in it; but, on the contrary, implies the most winning sweetness, the most amiable softness and gentleness. Are you for having as much cheerfulness as you can? So am I. Do you endeavour to keep alive your taste for all the truly innocent pleasures of life? So do I likewise. Do you refuse no pleasure but what is a hinderance to some greater good, or has a tendency to some evil? It is my very rule; and I know no other by which a sincere reasonable Christian can be guided."—*Letter to Mrs. Chapman*, 1737. *Works*, vi, 615.

† "In every age and country Satan has whispered to those who began to taste the powers of the world to come, 'To the desert!' 'To the wilderness!' Most of our little flock at Oxford were tried with this; my brother and I in particular. Nay, but I say, 'To the Bible! To the Bible!' And there you will learn, 'as you have time, to do good unto all men;' to warn every man, to exhort every man as you have opportunity. Although the greatest part of your care and labour should be laid out on those that are of the household of faith, certainly you may do good to others without any ways endangering your own salvation. What at present you much want is simplicity, in the archbishop of Cambray's sense of the word: That grace 'whereby the soul casts off all unnecessary reflections upon itself.'"—*Letter to Miss Bishop*, 1774. *Works*, vii, 167.

willingly hurting or grieving any man. It guides him into a uniform practice of justice and mercy, equally extensive with the principle whence it flows. It constrains him to do all possible good, of every possible kind, to all men; and makes him invariably resolved, in every circumstance of life, to do that, and that only, to others, which, supposing he were himself in the same situation, he would desire they should do to him.

And as he is easy to others, so he is easy in himself. He is free from the painful swellings of pride, from the flames of anger, from the impetuous gusts of irregular self-will. He is no longer tortured with envy or malice, or with unreasonable and hurtful desire. He is no more enslaved to the pleasures of sense, but has the full power both over his mind and body, in a continued cheerful course of sobriety, of temperance and chastity. He knows how to use all things in their place, and yet is superior to them all. He stands above those low pleasures of imagination which captivate vulgar minds, whether arising from what mortals term greatness, or from novelty, or beauty. All these too he can taste, and still look upward; still aspire to nobler enjoyments. Neither is he a slave to fame; popular breath affects not him; he stands steady and collected in himself.

And he who seeks no praise, cannot fear dispraise. Censure gives him no uneasiness, being conscious to himself that he would not willingly offend, and that he has the approbation of the Lord of all. He cannot fear want, knowing in whose hand is the earth and the fulness thereof, and that it is impossible for him to withhold from one that fears him any manner of thing that is good. He cannot fear pain, knowing it will never be sent, unless it be for his real advantage; and that then his strength will be proportioned to it, as it has always been in times past. He cannot fear death; being able to trust Him he loves with his soul as well as his body; yea, glad

## Genuine Christianity.

to leave the corruptible body in the dust, till it is raised incorruptible and immortal. So that, in honour or shame, in abundance or want, in ease or pain, in life or in death, always, and in all things, he has learned to be content, to be easy, thankful, happy.

He is happy in knowing there is a God, an intelligent Cause and Lord of all, and that he is not the produce either of blind chance or inexorable necessity. He is happy in the full assurance he has that this Creator and End of all things is a Being of boundless wisdom, of infinite power to execute all the designs of his wisdom, and of no less infinite goodness to direct all his power to the advantage of all his creatures. Nay, even the consideration of his immutable justice, rendering to all their due, of his unspotted holiness, of his all-sufficiency in himself, and of that immense ocean of all perfections which centre in God from eternity to eternity, is a continual addition to the happiness of a Christian.

A farther addition is made thereto, while, in contemplating even the things that surround him, that thought strikes warmly upon his heart,—

"These are thy glorious works, Parent of Good!"

while he takes knowledge of the invisible things of God, even his eternal power and wisdom in the things that are seen, the heavens, the earth, the fowls of the air, the lilies of the field. How much more, while, rejoicing in the constant care which he still takes of the work of his own hand, he breaks out, in a transport of love and praise, "O Lord our Governor, how excellent are thy ways in all the earth! Thou that hast set thy glory above the heavens!" While he, as it were, sees the Lord sitting upon his throne, and ruling all things well; while he observes the general providence of God, coextended with his whole creation, and surveys all the effects of it in the heavens and earth, as a well-pleased spectator; while he sees the wisdom and goodness of his general government descending to every particular, so presiding over the whole universe as over a single person, so watching over every single person as if he were the whole universe; how does he exult when he reviews the various traces of the Almighty goodness, in what has befallen himself in the several circumstances and changes of his own life! all which he now sees have been allotted to him, and dealt out in number, weight, and measure. With what triumph of soul, in surveying either the general or particular providence of God, does he observe every line pointing out a hereafter, every scene opening into eternity!

He is peculiarly and inexpressibly happy, in the clearest and fullest conviction, "This all powerful, all wise, all gracious Being, this Governor of all loves me. This Lover of my soul is always with me, is never absent, no, not for a moment. And I love him: there is none in heaven but thee, none on earth that I desire beside thee! And he has given me to resemble himself; he has stamped his image on my heart. And I live unto him; I do only his will; I glorify him with my body and my spirit. And it will not be long before I shall die unto him; I shall die into the arms of God. And then farewell sin and pain; then it only remains that I should live with him for ever."

This is the plain, naked portraiture of a Christian. But be not prejudiced against him for his name. Forgive his particularities of opinion, and (what you think) superstitious modes of worship. These are circumstances but of small concern, and do not enter into the essence of his character. Cover them with a veil of love, and look at the substance,—his tempers, his holiness, his happiness.

Can calm reason conceive either a more amiable or a more desirable character?

Is it your own? Away with names! Away with opinions! I care not what you are called. I ask not (it does not deserve a thought) what opinion you are of, so you are conscious to yourself, that you are the man whom I have been (however faintly) describing.

Do not you know, you ought to be such? Is the Governor of the world well pleased that you are not?

Do you (at least) desire it? I would to God that desire may penetrate your inmost soul; and that you may have no rest in your spirit till you are, not only almost, but altogether, a Christian!

Section II. The second point to be considered is, What is real, genuine Christianity? whether we speak of it as a principle in the soul, or as a scheme or system of doctrine.

Christianity, taken in the latter sense, is that system of doctrine which describes the character above recited, which promises, it shall be mine (provided I will not rest till I attain), and which tells me how I may attain it.

First. It describes this character in all its parts, and that in the most lively and affecting manner. The main lines of this picture are beautifully drawn in many passages of the Old Testament. These are filled up in the New, retouched and finished with all the art of God.

The same we have in miniature more than once; particularly in the thirteenth chapter of the former Epistle to the Corinthians, and in that discourse which St. Matthew records as delivered by our Lord at his entrance upon his public ministry.

Secondly. Christianity promises this character shall be mine, if I will not rest till I attain it. This is promised both in the Old Testament and the New. Indeed the New is, in effect, all a promise; seeing every description of the servants of God mentioned therein has the nature of a command; in consequence of those general injunctions: "Be ye followers of me, as I am of Christ," 1 Cor. xi, 1: "Be ye followers of them who through faith and patience inherit the promises," Heb. vi, 12. And every command has the force of a promise, in virtue of those general promises: "A new heart will I give you, and I will put my Spirit within you, and cause you to walk in my statutes, and ye shall keep my judgments and do them," Ezek. xxxvi, 26, 27. "This is the covenant that I will make after those days, saith the Lord; I will put my laws into their minds, and write them in their hearts," Heb. viii, 10. Accordingly, when it is said, "Thou shalt love the Lord thy God with all thy heart, and with all thy soul, and with all thy mind," Matt. xxii, 37; it is not only a direction what I shall do, but a promise of what God will do in me; exactly equivalent with what is written elsewhere: "The Lord thy God will circumcise thy heart and the heart of thy seed" (alluding to the custom then in use), "to love the Lord thy God with all thy heart, and with all thy soul," Deut. xxx, 6.

This being observed, it will readily appear to every serious person, who reads the New Testament with that care which the importance of the subject demands, that every particular branch of the preceding character is manifestly promised therein; either explicitly, under the very form of a promise, or virtually, under that of description or command.

Christianity tells me, in the Third place, how I may attain the promise; namely, by faith.

But what is faith? Not an opinion, no more than it is a form of words; not any number of opinions put together, be they ever so true. A string of opinions is no more Christian faith, than a string of beads is Christian holiness.

It is not an assent to any opinion, or any number of opinions. A man may assent to three, or three-and-twenty creeds: he may assent to all the Old and New Testament (at least, as far as he understands them), and yet have no Christian faith at all.

The faith by which the promise is attained is represented by Christianity, as a power wrought by the Almighty in an immortal spirit, inhabiting a house of clay, to see through that veil into the world of spirits, into things invisible and eternal; a power to discern those things which with eyes of flesh and blood no man hath seen or can see, either by reason of their nature, which (though they surround us on every side) is not perceivable by these gross senses; or by reason of their distance, as being yet afar off in the bosom of eternity.

This is Christian faith in the general notion of it. In its more particular notion, it is a divine evidence or conviction wrought in the heart, that God is reconciled to me through his Son; inseparably joined with a confidence in him, as a gracious reconciled Father, as for all things, so especially for all those good things which are invisible and eternal.

To believe (in the Christian sense) is, then, to walk in the light of eternity; and to have a clear sight of, and confidence in, the Most High, reconciled to me through the Son of his love.

Now, how highly desirable is such a faith, were it only on its own account! For how little does the wisest of men know of any thing more than he can see with his eyes! What clouds and darkness cover the whole scene of things invisible and eternal! What does he know even of himself as to his invisible part? what of his future manner of existence? How melancholy an account does the prying, learned philosopher (perhaps the wisest and best of all Heathens), the great, the venerable Marcus Antoninus, give of these things! What was the result of all his serious researches, of his high and deep contemplations? "Either dissipation (of the soul as well as the body, into the common, unthinking mass) or reabsorption into the universal fire, the unintelligent source of all things; or some unknown manner of conscious existence, after the body sinks to rise no more." One of these three he supposed must succeed death; but which, he had no light to determine. Poor Antoninus! with all his wealth, his honour, his power! with all his wisdom and philosophy,

> "What points of knowledge did he gain?
> That life is sacred all,—and vain!
> Sacred, how high, and vain, how low,
> He could not tell; but died to know."

"He died to know!" and so must you, unless you are now a partaker of Christian faith. O consider this! Nay, and consider, not only how little you know of the immensity of the things that are beyond sense and time, but how uncertainly do you know even that little! How faintly glimmering a light is that you have! Can you properly be said to know any of these things? Is that knowledge any more than bare conjecture? And the reason is plain. You have no senses suitable to invisible or eternal objects. What desiderata then, especially to the rational, the reflecting, part of mankind are these? A more extensive knowledge of things invisible and eternal; a greater certainty in whatever knowledge of them we have; and, in order to both, faculties capable of discerning things invisible.

Is it not so? Let impartial reason speak. Does not every thinking man want a window, not so much in his neighbour's, as in his own, breast? He wants an opening there, of whatever kind, that might let in light from eternity. He is pained to be thus feeling after God so darkly, so uncertainly; to know so little of God, and indeed so little of any beside material objects. He is concerned that he must see even that little, not directly, but in the dim, sullied glass of sense; and consequently so imperfectly and obscurely, that it is all a mere enigma still.

Now, these very desiderata faith supplies. It gives a more extensive knowledge of things invisible, showing what eye had not seen, nor ear heard, neither could it before enter into our heart to conceive. And all these it shows in the clearest light, with the fullest certainty and evidence. For it does not leave us to receive our notices of them by mere reflection from the dull glass of sense; but resolves a thousand enigmas of the highest concern by giving faculties suited to things invisible. O who would not wish for such a faith, were it only on these accounts! How much more, if by this I may receive the promise, I may attain all that holiness and happiness!

So Christianity tells me; and so I find it, may every real Christian say. I now am assured that these things are so: I experience them in my own breast. What Christianity (considered as a doctrine) promised, is accomplished in my soul. And Christianity, considered as an inward principle, is the completion of all those promises. It is holiness and happiness, the image of God impressed on a created spirit; a fountain of peace and love springing up into everlasting life.

Section III. And this I conceive to be the strongest evidence of the truth of Christianity. I do not undervalue traditional evidence. Let it have its place and its due honour. It is highly serviceable in its kind, and in its degree. And yet I cannot set it on a level with this.

It is generally supposed, that traditional evidence is weakened by length of time; as it must necessarily pass through so many hands, in a continued succession of ages. But no length of time can possibly affect the strength of this internal evidence. It is equally strong, equally new, through the course of seventeen hundred years. It passes now, even as it has done from the beginning, directly from God into the believing soul. Do you suppose time will ever dry up this stream? O no! It shall never be cut off:

"*Labitur et labetur in omne volubilis ævum.*
(It flows on, and will for ever flow.)"

Traditional evidence is of an extremely complicated

nature, necessarily including so many and so various considerations, that only men of a strong and clear understanding can be sensible of its full force. On the contrary, how plain and simple is this; and how level to the lowest capacity! Is not this the sum: "One thing I know; I was blind, but now I see?" An argument so plain, that a peasant, a woman, a child, may feel all its force.

The traditional evidence of Christianity stands, as it were, a great way off; and therefore, although it speaks loud and clear, yet makes a less lively impression. It gives us an account of what was transacted long ago, in far distant times as well as places. Whereas the inward evidence is intimately present to all persons, at all times, and in all places. It is nigh thee, in thy mouth and in thy heart, if thou believest in the Lord Jesus Christ. "This," then, "is the record," this is the evidence, emphatically so called, "that God hath given unto us eternal life; and this life is in his Son."

If, then, it were possible (which I conceive it is not) to shake the traditional evidence of Christianity, still he that has the internal evidence (and every true believer hath the witness or evidence in himself) would stand firm and unshaken. Still he could say to those who were striking at the external evidence, "Beat on the sack of Anaxagoras." But you can no more hurt my evidence of Christianity, than the tyrant could hurt the spirit of that wise man.

I have sometimes been almost inclined to believe, that the wisdom of God has, in most later ages, permitted the external evidence of Christianity to be more or less clogged and incumbered for this very end, that men (of reflection especially) might not altogether rest there, but be constrained to look into themselves also, and attend to the light shining in their hearts.

Nay, it seems (if it may be allowed for us to pry so far into the reasons of the divine dispensations) that, particularly in this age, God suffers all kind of objections to be raised against the traditional evidence of Christianity, that men of understanding, though unwilling to give it up, yet, at the same time they defend this evidence, may not rest the whole strength of their cause thereon, but seek a deeper and firmer support for it.

Without this I cannot but doubt, whether they can long maintain their cause; whether, if they do not obey the loud call of God, and lay far more stress than they have hitherto done on this internal evidence of Christianity, they will not, one after another, give up the external, and (in heart at least) go over to those whom they are now contending with; so that in a century or two the people of England will be fairly divided into real Deists and real Christians.

And I apprehend this would be no loss at all, but rather an advantage to the Christian cause; nay, perhaps it would be the speediest, yea, the only effectual, way of bringing all reasonable Deists to be Christians.

May I be permitted to speak freely? May I, without offence, ask of you that are called Christians, what real loss would you sustain in giving up your present opinion, that the Christian system is of God? Though you bear the name, you are not Christians: you have neither Christian faith nor love. You have no divine evidence of things unseen; you have not entered into the holiest by the blood of Jesus. You do not love God with all your heart; neither do you love your neighbour as yourself. You are neither happy nor holy. You have not learned in every state therewith to be content; to rejoice evermore, even in want, pain, death; and in every thing to give thanks. You are not holy in heart; superior to pride, to anger, to foolish desires. Neither are you holy in life; you do not walk as Christ also walked. Does not the main of your Christianity lie in your opinion, decked with a few outward observances? For as to morality, even honest,

Heathen morality (O let me utter a melancholy truth!), many of those whom you style Deists, there is reason to fear, have far more of it than you.

Go on, gentlemen, and prosper. Shame these nominal Christians out of that poor superstition which they call Christianity. Reason, rally, laugh them out of their dead, empty forms, void of spirit, of faith, of love. Convince them, that such mean pageantry (for such it manifestly is, if there is nothing in the heart correspondent with the outward show) is absolutely unworthy, you need not say of God, but even of any man that is endued with common understanding. Show them, that while they are endeavouring to please God thus, they are only beating the air. Know your time; press on; push your victories, till you have conquered all that know not God. And then He, whom neither they nor you know now, shall rise and gird himself with strength, and go forth in his almighty love, and sweetly conquer you all together.

O that the time were come! How do I long for you to be partakers of the exceeding great and precious promise! How am I pained when I hear any of you using those silly terms, which the men of form have taught you, calling the mention of the only thing you want, *cant!* the deepest wisdom, the highest happiness, *enthusiasm!* What ignorance is this! How extremely despicable would it make you in the eyes of any but a Christian! But he cannot despise you, who loves you as his own soul, who is ready to lay down his life for your sake.

Perhaps you will say, "But this internal evidence of Christianity affects only those in whom the promise is fulfilled. It is no evidence to me." There is truth in this objection. It does affect them chiefly, but it does not affect them only. It cannot, in the nature of things, be so strong an evidence to others as it is to them. And yet it may bring a degree of evidence, it may reflect some light on you also.

## Genuine Christianity.   327

For, First, you see the beauty and loveliness of Christianity, when it is rightly understood; and you are sure there is nothing to be desired in comparison of it.

Secondly. You know the Scripture promises this, and says, it is attained by faith, and by no other way.

Thirdly. You see clearly how desirable Christian faith is, even on account of its own intrinsic value.

Fourthly. You are a witness, that the holiness and happiness above described can be attained no other way. The more you have laboured after virtue and happiness, the more convinced you are of this. Thus far then you need not lean upon other men; thus far you have personal experience.

Fifthly. What reasonable assurance can you have of things whereof you have not personal experience? Suppose the question were, Can the blind be restored to sight? This you have not yourself experienced. How then will you know that such a thing ever was? Can there be an easier or surer way than to talk with one or some number of men who were blind, but are now restored to sight? They cannot be deceived as to the fact in question; the nature of the thing leaves no room for this. And if they are honest men (which you may learn from other circumstances), they will not deceive you.

Now, transfer this to the case before us: And those who were blind, but now see,—those who were sick many years, but now are healed,—those who were miserable, but now are happy,—will afford you also a very strong evidence of the truth of Christianity; as strong as can be in the nature of things, till you experience it in your own soul: and this, though it be allowed they are but plain men, and, in general, of weak understanding; nay, though some of them should be mistaken in other points, and hold opinions which cannot be defended.

## THOUGHTS CONCERNING THE ORIGIN OF POWER.

[1772. *Works*, vi, 269-74.]

By power, I here mean supreme power, the power over life and death, and consequently over our liberty and property, and all things of an inferior nature.

In many nations this power has in all ages been lodged in a single person. This has been the case in almost the whole eastern world, from the earliest antiquity; as in the celebrated empires of Assyria, of Babylon, of Media, Persia, and many others. And so it remains to this day, from Constantinople to the farthest India. The same form of government obtained very early in very many parts of Afric, and remains in most of them still, as well as in the empires of Morocco and Abyssinia. The first adventurers to America found absolute monarchy established there also; the whole power being lodged in the emperor of Mexico, and the yncas of Peru. Nay, and many of the ancient nations of Europe were governed by single persons; as Spain, France, the Russias, and several other nations are at this day.

But in others, the power has been lodged in a few, chiefly the rich and noble. This kind of government, usually styled aristocracy, obtained in Greece and in Rome, after many struggles with the people, during the later ages of the republic. And this is the government which at present subsists in various parts of Europe. In Venice indeed, as well as in Genoa, the supreme power is nominally lodged in one, namely, the doge; but in fact, he is only a royal shade; it is really lodged in a few of the nobles.

Where the people have the supreme power, it is termed a democracy. This seems to have been the ancient form of government in several of the Grecian states. And so it was at Rome for some ages after the expulsion of the kings. From the earliest authentic records, there is reason to believe it was for espousing the cause of the people, and defending their rights against the illegal encroachments of the nobles, that Marcus Coriolanus was driven into banishment, and Manlius Capitolinus, as well as Tiberius and Caius Gracchus, murdered. Perhaps formerly the popular government subsisted in several states. But it is scarce now to be found, being every where swallowed up either in monarchy or aristocracy.

But the grand question is, not in whom this power is lodged, but from whom it is ultimately derived. What is the origin of power? What is its primary source? This has been long a subject of debate. And it has been debated with the utmost warmth, by a variety of disputants. But as earnest as they have been on each side of the question, they have seldom come to any good conclusion; but have left the point undecided still, to be a ball of contention to the next generation.

But is it impossible, in the nature of things, to throw any light on this obscure subject? Let us make the experiment; let us (without pretending to dictate, but desiring every one to use his own judgment) try to find out some ground whereon to stand, and go as far as we can toward answering the question. And let not any man be angry on the account, suppose we should not exactly agree. Let every one enjoy his own opinion, and give others the same liberty.

Now, I cannot but acknowledge, I believe an old book, commonly called the Bible, to be true. Therefore I believe, "there is no power but from God: the powers that be are ordained of God," Rom. xiii, 1. There is no subordinate power in any nation, but what is derived from the supreme power therein. So in England the king, in the United Provinces the states are the fountain of all power. And there is no supreme power, no power of the sword, of life and death, but what is derived from God, the Sovereign of all.

But have not the people, in every age and nation, the right of disposing of this power; of investing therewith whom they please, either one or more persons; and that, in what proportion they see good, and upon what conditions? Consequently, if those conditions are not observed, have they not a right to take away the power they gave? And does not this imply, that they are the judges whether those conditions are observed or not? Otherwise, if the receivers were judges of their own cause, this right would fall into nothing.

To prove this, that the people in every country are the source of power, it is argued thus: "All men living upon earth are naturally equal; none is above another; and all are naturally free, masters of their own actions. It manifestly follows, no man can have any power over another, unless by his own consent. The power therefore which the governors in any nation enjoy, must be originally derived from the people, and presupposes an original compact between them and their first governors."\*

This seems to be the opinion which is now generally

---

\* "That 'every freeman is governed by laws to which he has consented:' as confidently as it has been asserted, it is absolutely false. In wide-extended dominions, a very small part of the people are concerned in making laws. This, as all public business, must be done by delegation; the delegates are chosen by a select number. And those that are not electors, who are far the greater part, stand by, idle and helpless spectators.

"The case of electors is little better. When they are near equally divided, in the choice of their delegates to represent them in the parliament or national assembly, almost half of them must be governed, not only without, but even against, their own consent.

"And how has any man consented to those laws which were made before he was born? Our consent to these, nay, and to the laws now made even in England, is purely passive. And in every place, as all men are born the subjects of some state or other, so they are born, passively, as it were, consenting to the laws of that state. Any other than this kind of consent, the condition of civil life does not allow."—*A Calm Address to Our American Colonies*, 1775. *Works*, vi, 295.

## The Origin of Power. 331

espoused by men of understanding and education; and that (if I do not mistake) not in England alone, but almost in every civilized nation. And it is usually espoused with the fullest and strongest persuasion, as a truth little less than self evident, as what is clear beyond all possibility of doubt, what commands the assent of all reasonable men. Hence if any man affected to deny it, he would in most companies be rather hooted at than argued with; it being so absurd to oppose what is confirmed by the general suffrage of mankind.

But still (suppose it to need no proof) it may need a little explaining; for every one does not understand the term. Some will ask, "Who are the people? Are they every man, woman, and child?" Why not? Is it not allowed, is it not affirmed, is it not our fundamental principle, our incontestable, self-evident axiom, that "all persons living upon earth are naturally equal; that all human creatures are naturally free; masters of their own actions; that none can have any power over others, but by their own consent?" Why then should not every man, woman, and child, have a voice in placing their governors; in fixing the measure of power to be entrusted with them, and the conditions on which it is entrusted? And why should not every one have a voice in displacing them too; seeing it is undeniable, they that gave the power have a right to take it away? Do not quibble or shuffle. Do not evade the question; but come close to the point. I ask, By what argument do you prove that women are not naturally as free as men? And, if they are, why have they not as good a right as we have to choose their own governors? Who can have any power over free, rational creatures, but by their own consent? And are they not free by nature, as well as we? Are they not rational creatures?

But suppose we exclude women from using their natural right, by might overcoming right, by main strength (for it is sure that we are stronger than they; I mean that we have stronger limbs, if we have not stronger reason), what pretence have we for excluding men like ourselves, yea, thousands, and tens of thousands, barely because they have not lived one-and-twenty years? "Why, they have not wisdom or experience to judge concerning the qualifications necessary for governors." I answer, (1.) Who has? How many of the voters in Great Britain? one in twenty? one in a hundred? If you exclude all who have not this wisdom, you will leave few behind. But (2.) Wisdom and experience are nothing to the purpose. You have put the matter upon another issue. Are they men? That is enough. Are they human creatures? Then they have a right to choose their own governors; an indefeasible right; a right inherent, inseparable from human nature. "But in England, at least, they are excluded by law." But did they consent to the making of that law? If not, by your original supposition, it can have no power over them. I therefore utterly deny that we can consistently with that supposition, debar either women or minors from choosing their own governors.

But suppose we exclude these by main force (which it is certain we are able to do, since though they have most votes they have least strength), are all that remain, all men of full age, the people? Are all males, then, that have lived one-and-twenty years allowed to choose their own governors? "Not at all; not in England, unless they are freeholders, unless they have forty shillings a year." Worse and worse. After depriving half the human species of their natural right for want of a beard; after depriving myriads more for want of a stiff beard, for not having lived one-and-twenty years; you rob others (probably some hundred thousands) of their birthright for want of money! Yet not altogether on this account neither; if so, it might be more tolerable. But here is an Englishman who has money enough to buy the estates of fifty freeholders, and yet he must not be numbered among the people because he has not two or three acres of land! How is this? By what right do you exclude a man from being one of the people because he has not forty shillings a year; yea, or not a groat? Is he not a man, whether he be rich or poor? Has he not a soul and a body? Has he not the nature of a man; consequently, all the rights of a man, all that flow from human nature; and, among the rest, that of not being controlled by any but by his own consent?

"But he is excluded by law." By what law? by a law of his own making? Did he consent to the making of it? Before this law was passed, was his consent either obtained or asked? If not, what is that law to him? No man, you aver, has any power over another but by his own consent. Of consequence, a law made without his consent is, with regard to him, null and void. You cannot say otherwise without destroying the supposition, that none can be governed but by his own consent.

See, now, to what your argument comes. You affirm, all power is derived from the people; and presently excluded one half of the people from having any part or lot in the matter. At another stroke, suppose England to contain eight millions of people, you exclude one or two millions more. At a third, suppose two millions left, you exclude three fourths of these. And the poor pittance that remains, by I know not what figure of speech, you call the people of England!

Hitherto we have endeavoured to view this point in the mere light of reason. And even by this means it manifestly appears that this supposition, which is so high in vogue, which is so generally received, nay, which has been palmed upon us with such confidence, as undeniable and self-evident, is not only false, not only contrary to reason, but contradictory to itself; the very men who are most positive that the people are the source of power, being brought into an inextricable difficulty, by that single question, "Who are the people?" reduced to a necessity of either giving up the point, or owning that by the people they mean scarce a tenth part of them.

But we need not rest the matter entirely on reasoning; let us appeal to matter of fact. And because we cannot have so clear and certain a prospect of what is at too great a distance, whether of time or place, let us only take a view of what has been in our own country for six or seven hundred years. I ask, then, When and where did the people of England (even suppose by that word, *the people,* you mean only a hundred thousand of them) choose their own governors? Did they choose, to go no farther, William the Conqueror? Did they choose King Stephen, or King John? As to those who regularly succeeded their fathers, it is plain the people are out of the question. Did they choose Henry the Fourth, Edward the Fourth, or Henry the Seventh? Who will be so hardy as to affirm it? Did the people of England, or but fifty thousand of them, choose Queen Mary, or Queen Elizabeth? To come nearer to our own times, did they choose King James the First? Perhaps you will say, "But if the people did not give King Charles the supreme power, at least they took it away from him. Surely, you will not deny this." Indeed I will; I deny it utterly. The people of England no more took away his power, than they cut off his head. "Yes, the parliament did, and they are the people." No; the parliament did not. The lower house, the house of commons, is not the parliament, any more than it is the nation. Neither were those who then sat, the house of commons; no, nor one quarter of them. But suppose they had been the whole house of commons, yea, or the whole parliament; by what rule of logic will you prove that seven or eight hundred persons are the people of Eng-

## The Origin of Power.

land? "Why, they are the delegates of the people; they are chosen by them." No; not by one half, not by a quarter, not by a tenth part, of them. So that the people, in the only proper sense of the word, were innocent of the whole affair.

"But you will allow, the people gave the supreme power to King Charles the Second at the Restoration." I will allow no such thing; unless by *the people* you mean General Monk and fifteen thousand soldiers. "However, you will not deny that the people gave the power to King William at the Revolution." Nay, truly, I must deny this too. I cannot possibly allow it. Although I will not say that William the Third obtained the royal power as William the First did; although he did not claim it by right of conquest, which would have been an odious title; yet certain it is, that he did not receive it by any act or deed of the people. Their consent was neither obtained nor asked; they were never consulted in the matter. It was not therefore the people that gave him the power; no, nor even the parliament. It was the convention, and none else. "Who were the convention?" They were a few hundred lords and gentlemen, who, observing the desperate state of public affairs, met together on that important occasion. So that still we have no single instance, in above seven hundred years, of the people of England's conveying the supreme power either to one or more persons.

Indeed I remember in all history, both ancient and modern, but one instance of supreme power conferred by the people; if we mean thereby, though not all the people, yet a great majority of them. This celebrated instance occurred at Naples, in the middle of the last century; where the people, properly speaking, that is, men, women, and children, claimed and exerted their natural right in favor of Thomas Aniello (vulgarly called Masanello), a young fisherman. But will any one say, he was the only governor for these thousand years, who has had a proper right to the supreme power? I believe not; nor, I apprehend, does any one desire that the people should take the same steps in London.

So much both for reason and matter of fact. But one single consideration, if we dwell a little upon it, will bring the question to a short issue. It is allowed, no man can dispose of another's life but by his own consent. I add, No, nor with his consent; for no man has a right to dispose of his own life. The Creator of man has the sole right to take the life which he gave. Now, it is an indisputable truth, *Nihil dat quod non habet,* "none gives what he has not." It plainly follows, that no man can give to another a right which he never had himself; a right which only the Governor of the world has, even the wiser Heathens being judges; but which no man upon the face of the earth either has or can have. No man therefore can give the power of the sword, any such power as implies a right to take away life. Wherever it is, it must descend from God alone, the sole disposer of life and death.

The supposition, then, that the people are the origin of power, is every way indefensible. It is absolutely overturned by the very principle on which it is supposed to stand; namely, that a right of choosing his governors belongs to every partaker of human nature. If this be so, then it belongs to every individual of the human species; consequently, not to freeholders alone, but to all men; not to men only, but to women also; nor only to adult men and women, to those who have lived one-and-twenty years, but to those who have lived eighteen or twenty, as well as those who have lived threescore. But none did ever maintain this, nor probably ever will. Therefore this boasted principle falls to the ground, and the whole superstructure with it. So common sense brings us back to the grand truth, "There is no power but of God."

## THOUGHTS ON THE POWER OF MUSIC.

[*Arminian Magazine*, 1781.  *Works*, vii, 455-7.]

By the power of music, I mean, its power to affect the hearers; to raise various passions in the human mind. Of this we have very surprising accounts in ancient history. We are told, the ancient Greek musicians in particular were able to excite whatever passions they pleased; to inspire love or hate, joy or sorrow, hope or fear, courage, fury, or despair; yea, to raise these one after another, and to vary the passion just according to the variation of the music.

But how is this to be accounted for? No such effects attend the modern music; although it is confessed on all hands, that our instruments excel theirs beyond all degrees of comparison. What was their lyre, their instruments of seven or ten strings, compared to our violin? What were any of their pipes, to our hautboy or German flute? What, all of them put together, all that were in use two or three thousand years ago, to our organ? How is it then, that, with this inconceivable advantage, the modern music has less power than the ancient?

Some have given a very short answer to this, cutting the knot which they could not untie. They have doubted, or affected to doubt, the fact; perhaps have even denied it. But no sensible man will do this, unless he be utterly blinded by prejudice. For it would be denying the faith of all history; seeing no fact is better authenticated. None is delivered down to us by more unquestionable testimony; such as fully satisfies in all other cases. We have, therefore, no more reason to doubt of the power of Timotheus's music, than that of Alexander's arms; and we may deny his taking Persepolis, as well as his burning it through that sudden rage which was excited in him by that musician. And the various effects which were successively wrought in his mind (so beautifully described by Dryden, in his Ode on St. Cecilia's Day) are astonishing instances of the power of a single harp, to transport, as it were, the mind out of itself.

Nay, we read of an instance, even in modern history, of the power of music not inferior to this. A musician being brought to the king of Denmark, and asked, whether he could excite any passion, answered in the affirmative, and was commanded to make the trial upon the king himself. Presently the monarch was all in tears; and, upon the musician's changing his mood, he was quickly roused into such fury, that, snatching a sword from one of his assistants' hands (for they had purposely removed his own), he immediately killed him, and would have killed all in the room, had he not been forcibly withheld.

This alone removes all the incredibility of what is related concerning the ancient music. But why is it that modern music, in general, has no such effect, on the hearers? The grand reason seems to be no other than this,—the whole nature and design of music is altered. The ancient composers studied melody alone; the due arrangement of single notes; and it was by melody alone, that they wrought such wonderful effects. And as this music was directly calculated to move the passions, so they designed it for this very end. But the modern composers study harmony, which, in the present sense of the word, is quite another thing; namely, a contrast of various notes, opposite to, and yet blended with, each other, wherein they,

"Now high, now low, pursue the resonant fugue."

Dr. Gregory says, "this harmony has been known in the world little more than two hundred years." Be that as it may, ever since it was introduced, ever since counterpoint has been invented, as it has altered the grand design of music, so it has well nigh destroyed its effects.

## The Power of Music.

Some indeed have imagined, and attempted to prove, that the ancients were acquainted with this. It seems, there needs but one single argument to demonstrate the contrary. We have many capital pieces of ancient music, that are now in the hands of the curious. Dr. Pepusch, who was well versed in the music of antiquity (perhaps the best of any man in Europe), showed me several large Greek folios, which contained many of their musical compositions. Now is there, or is there not, any counterpoint in these? The learned know there is no such thing. There is not the least trace of it to be found: it is all melody, and no harmony.

And as the nature of music is thus changed, so is likewise the design of it. Our composers do not aim at moving the passions, but at quite another thing; at varying and contrasting the notes a thousand different ways. What has counterpoint to do with the passions? It is applied to a quite different faculty of the mind; not to our joy, or hope, or fear; but merely to the ear, to the imagination, or internal sense. And the pleasure it gives is not upon this principle; not by raising any passion whatever. It no more affects the passions than the judgment: both the one and the other lie quite out of its province.

Need we any other, and can we have any stronger, proof of this, than those modern overtures, voluntaries, or concertos, which consist altogether of artificial sounds, without any words at all? What have any of the passions to do with these? What has judgment, reason, common sense? Just nothing at all. All these are utterly excluded, by delicate, unmeaning sound!

In this respect, the modern music has no connection with common sense, any more than with the passions. In another, it is glaringly, undeniably, contrary to common sense; namely, in allowing, yea, appointing, different words to be sung by different persons at the same time! What can be more shocking to a man of understanding than this? Pray, which of those sentences am I to attend to? I can attend to only one sentence at once; and I hear three or four at one and the same instant! And, to complete the matter, this astonishing jargon has found a place even in the worship of God! It runs through (O pity! O shame!) the greatest part even of our Church music! It is found even in the finest of our anthems, and in the most solemn parts of our public worship! Let any impartial, any unprejudiced person say, whether there can be a more direct mockery of God.*

But to return: Is it strange, that modern music does not answer the end it is designed for? and which it is in no wise calculated for? It is not possible it should. Had Timotheus "pursued the resonant fugue," his music would have been quite harmless. It would have affected Alexander no more than Bucephalus; the finest city then in the world had not been destroyed; but

"*Persepolis stares, Cyrique arx alta maneres.*"
[Persepolis, thou mightst have stood, and the lofty tower of Cyrus.†]

It is true, the modern music has been sometimes observed to have as powerful an effect as the ancient; so that frequently single persons, and sometimes numerous assemblies, have been seen in a flood of tears. But when

---

* "Is not this formality creeping in already by those complex tunes, which it is scarcely possible to sing with devotion? Such is, 'Praise the Lord, ye blessed ones:' such the long quavering hallelujah annexed to the morning song tune, which I defy any man living to sing devoutly. The repeating the same words so often (but especially while another repeats different words, the horrid abuse which runs through the modern church music), as it shocks all common sense, so it necessarily brings in dead formality, and has no more of religion in it than a Lancashire hornpipe. Besides, it is a flat contradiction to our Lord's command, 'Use not vain repetitions.' For what is a vain repetition, if this is not? What end of devotion does it serve? Sing no anthems."—*Minutes of Several Conversations* ("*The Large Minutes*"), 1789. *Works*, v, 225.

[† The line in Virgil, altered by Mr. Wesley as above, is,
"*Trojaque nunc stares, Priamique arx alta maneres.*"
"Old Priam still his empire would enjoy,
And still thy towers had stood, majestic Troy."—PITT.]

was this? Generally, if not always, when a fine solo was sung; when "the sound has been an echo to the sense;" when the music has been extremely simple and inartificial, the composer having attended to melody, not harmony. Then, and then only, the natural power of music to move the passions has appeared. This music was calculated for that end, and effectually answered it.

Upon this ground it is, that so many persons are so much affected by the Scotch or Irish airs. They are composed, not according to art, but nature; they are simple in the highest degree. There is no harmony, according to the present sense of the word, therein; but there is much melody. And this is not only heard, but felt, by all those who retain their native taste; whose taste is not biassed (I might say, corrupted) by attending to counterpoint and complicated music. It is this, it is counterpoint, it is harmony (so called), which destroys the power of music. And if ever this should be banished from our composition, if ever we should return to the simplicity and melody of the ancients, then the effects of our music will be as surprising as any that were wrought by theirs; yea, perhaps they will be as much greater, as modern instruments are more excellent than those of the ancients.

Inverness, June 9, 1779.     JOHN WESLEY.

# LETTERS.

## TO HIS BROTHER SAMUEL.
[*Works*, vi, 597-9.]

LINCOLN COLLEGE, November 17, 1731.

DEAR BROTHER,—Considering the other changes that I remember in myself, I shall not at all wonder if the time comes when we differ as little in our conclusions as we do now in our premises. In most we seem to agree already; especially as to rising, not keeping much company, and sitting by a fire, which I always do, if any one in the room does, whether at home or abroad. But these are the very things about which others will never agree with me. Had I given up these, or but one of them,—rising early, which implies going to bed early (though I never am sleepy now), and keeping so little company, not one man in ten of those that are offended at me, as it is, would ever open their mouth against any of the other particulars. For the sake of these, those are mentioned; the root of the matter lies here. Would I but employ a third of my money, and about half my time, as other folks do, smaller matters would be easily overlooked. But I think *nil tanti est* [Nothing is worth this cost]. As to my hair, I am much more sure that what this enables me to do is according to the Scripture, than I am that the length of it is contrary to it.

I have often thought of a saying of Dr. Hayward's when he examined me for priest's orders: "Do you know what you are about? You are bidding defiance to all mankind. He that would live a Christian priest ought to know that, whether his hand be against every man or no, he must expect every man's hand should be against him." It is not strange that every man's hand who is not a Christian should be against him that endeavours to be so. But is it not hard, that even those that are with us should be against us? that a man's enemies (in some degree) should be those of the same household of faith? Yet so it is. From the time that a man sets himself to his business, very many, even of those who travel the same road, many of those who are before, as well as behind, him, will lay stumbling blocks in his way. One blames him for not going fast enough; another, for having made no greater progress; another, for going too far, which, perhaps, strange as it is, is the more common charge of the two: for this comes from people of all sorts; not only Infidels, not only half Christians, but some of the best of men are very apt to make this reflection: "He lays unnecessary burdens upon himself; he is too precise; he does what God has no where required to be done." True, he has not required it of those that are perfect; and even as to those who are not, all men are not required to use all means; but every man is required to use those which he finds most useful to himself. And who can tell better than himself, whether he finds them so or no? "Who knoweth the things of a man better than the spirit of a man that is in him?"

This being a point of no common concern, I desire to explain myself upon it once for all, and to tell you, freely and clearly, those general positions on which I ground (I think) all those practices, for which (as you would have seen, had you read that paper through) I am generally accused of singularity. First. As to the end of my being, I lay it down for a rule, that I cannot be too happy, or, therefore, too holy; and thence infer, that the more steadily I keep my eye upon the prize of our high calling, the better, and the more of my thoughts, and words, and

THE REV. SAMUEL WESLEY, JR.

The print was published after his death; the legend is,
"late master of the grammar school at Tiverton,
elder brother of the Rev. John Wesley."

## To His Brother Samuel. 345

actions are directly pointed at the attainment of it. Secondly. As to the instituted means of attaining it, I likewise lay it down for a rule, that I am to use them every time I may. Thirdly. As to prudential means, I believe this rule holds of things indifferent in themselves: whatever I know to do me hurt, that to me is not indifferent, but resolutely to be abstained from; whatever I know to do me good, that to me is not indifferent, but resolutely to be embraced.

But it will be said, I am whimsical. True; and what then? If by whimsical be meant simply *singular,* I own it; if *singular without any reason,* I deny it with both my hands, and am ready to give a reason to any that asks me, of every custom wherein I wilfully differ from the world. I grant, in many single actions, I differ unreasonably from others; but not wilfully; no, I shall extremely thank any one who will teach me to help it. But can I totally help it, till I have more breeding, or more prudence? to neither of which I am much disposed naturally; and I greatly fear my acquired stock of either will give me small assistance.

I have but one thing to add, and that is, as to my being formal. If by that be meant, that I am not easy and unaffected enough in my carriage, it is very true; but how shall I help it? I cannot be genteelly behaved by instinct; and if I am to try after it by experience and observation of others, that is not the work of a month, but of years. If by formal be meant, that I am serious, this, too, is very true; but why should I help it? Mirth, I grant, is fit for you; but does it follow that it is fit for me? Are the same tempers, any more than the same words or actions, fit for all circumstances? If you are to "rejoice evermore," because you have put your enemies to flight, am I to do the same while they continually assault me? You are glad, because you are "passed from death to life:" well, but let him be afraid, who knows not whether he is to live or die. Whether this be my condition or no, who can tell better than myself? Him who can, whoever he be, I allow to be a proper judge, whether I do well to be generally as serious as I can.

John Whitelamb wants a gown much, and I am not rich enough to buy him one at present. If you are willing my twenty shillings (that were) should go toward that, I will add ten to them, and let it lie till I have tried my interest with my friends to make up the price of a new one. I am, dear brother,

Yours, and my sister's, affectionate brother.

The rector is much at your service. I fancy I shall, some time or other, have much to say to you about him. All are pretty well at Epworth, my sister Molly says.

## TO THE SAME.

[*Works*, vi, 607-8.]

BRISTOL, May 10, 1739.

DEAR BROTHER,—The having abundance of work upon my hands is only a cause of my not writing sooner. *The* cause was rather my unwillingness to continue an unprofitable dispute.

The Gospel promises to you and me, and our children, and all that are afar off, even as many of those whom the Lord God shall call, as are not disobedient unto the heavenly vision, "the witness of God's Spirit with their spirit, that they are the children of God;" that they are now, at this hour, all accepted in the Beloved; but it witnesses not that they shall be. It is an assurance of present salvation only; therefore, not necessarily perpetual, neither irreversible.

I am one of many witnesses of this matter of fact, that

## To His Brother Samuel.

God does now make good this his promise daily, very frequently during a representation (how made I know not, but not to the outward eye) of Christ either hanging on the cross or standing on the right hand of God. And this I know to be of God, because from that hour the person so affected is a new creature, both as to his inward tempers and outward life. "Old things are passed away; and all things become new."

A very late instance of this I will give you: While we were praying at a society here, on Tuesday the 1st instant, the power of God (so I call it) came so mightily among us, that one, and another, and another, fell down as thunderstruck. In that hour many that were in deep anguish of spirit, were all filled with peace and joy. Ten persons, till then in sin, doubt, and fear, found such a change, that sin had no more dominion over them; and instead of the spirit of fear, they are now filled with that of love, and joy, and a sound mind. A Quaker who stood by was very angry at them, and was biting his lips and knitting his brows, when the Spirit of God came upon him also, so that he fell down as one dead. We prayed over him, and he soon lifted up his head with joy, and joined with us in thanksgiving.

A bystander, one John Haydon, was quite enraged at this, and, being unable to deny something supernatural in it, laboured beyond measure to convince all his acquaintance, that it was a delusion of the devil. I was met in the street the next day by one who informed me that John Haydon was fallen raving mad. It seems he had sat down to dinner, but wanted first to make an end of a sermon he was reading. At the last page he suddenly changed colour, fell off his chair, and began screaming terribly, and beating himself against the ground. I found him on the floor, the room being full of people, whom his wife would have kept away; but he cried out, "No; let them all come; let all the world see the just judgment of God." Two or three were holding him as well as they could. He immediately fixed his eyes on me, and said, "Ay, this is he I said deceived the people; but God hath overtaken me. I said it was a delusion of the devil; but this is no delusion." Then he roared aloud, "O thou devil! Thou cursed devil! Yea, thou legion of devils! Thou canst not stay in me. Christ will cast thee out. I know his work is begun. Tear me to pieces if thou wilt. But thou canst not hurt me." He then beat himself again, and groaned again, with violent sweats, and heaving of the breast. We prayed with him, and God put a new song in his mouth. The words were, which he pronounced with a clear, strong voice, "This is the Lord's doing, and it is marvellous in our eyes. This is the day which the Lord hath made: we will rejoice and be glad in it. Blessed be the Lord God of Israel, from this time forth for evermore." I called again an hour after. We found his body quite worn out, and his voice lost. But his soul was full of joy and love, rejoicing in hope of the glory of God.

I am now in as good health (thanks be to God!) as I ever was since I remember, and I believe shall be so as long as I live; for I do not expect to have a lingering death. The reasons that induce me to think I shall not live long old are such as you would not apprehend to be of any weight. I am under no concern on this head. Let my Master see to it. O may the God of love be with you and my sister more and more!

I am, dear brother, your ever affectionate brother.

## TO HIS BROTHER CHARLES.
[*Works*, vi, 663.]

LONDON, December 26, 1761.

DEAR BROTHER,—Spend as many hours in the congregation as you can: but exercise alone will strengthen your lungs; or electrifying, which I wonder you did not try long ago. Never start at its being a quack medicine. I desire no other; particularly since I was so nearly murdered by being cured of my ague *secundum artem* [scientifically]. You should always (and I hope you do) write standing and sloping.

We are always in danger of enthusiasm: but I think no more now than any time these twenty years. The word of God runs indeed; and loving faith spreads on every side. Do not take my word, or any one's else; but come and see. It is good to be in London now.

It is impossible for me to correct my own books. I sometimes think it strange, that I have not one preacher that will and can. I think every one of them owes me so much service.

Pray tell R. Sheen, I am hugely displeased at his reprinting the Nativity Hymns, and omitting the very best hymn in the collection,—

" All glory to God in the sky," &c.

I beg they may never more be printed without it. Omit one or two and I will thank you. They are *namby-pambical*. I wish you would give us two or three invitatory hymns. We want such exceedingly. My love to Sally. My wife gains ground. Adieu!

## TO THE SAME.

[*Works*, vi, 669-70.]

ATHLONE, June 21, 1767.

DEAR BROTHER,—For some time I have had many thoughts concerning the work of God in these kingdoms. I have been surprised that it has spread so far; and that it has spread no farther. And what hindered? Surely the design of God was, to "bow a nation to his sway:" instead of which, there is still only a Christian here and there; and the rest are yet in the shadow of death: although those who would profit by us have need to make haste, as we are not likely to serve them long.

What, indeed, has hindered? I want to consider this. And must we not first say, *Nos Consules* [We the chiefs]? If we were more holy in heart and life, thoroughly devoted to God, would not all the preachers catch our fire and carry it with them throughout the land? Is not the next hinderance, the littleness of grace (rather than of gifts) in a considerable part of our preachers? They have not the whole mind that was in Christ; they do not steadily walk as he walked. And therefore the hand of the Lord is stayed; though not altogether; though he does work still: but it is not in such a degree as he surely would, were they holy as He that hath sent them is holy.

Is not the third hinderance the littleness of grace in the generality of the people? Therefore, they pray little, and with little fervency, for a general blessing; and therefore their prayer has little power with God. It does not, as once, shut and open heaven. Add to this, that as there is much of the spirit of the world in their hearts, so there is much conformity to the world in their lives. They ought to be both burning and shining lights; but they neither burn nor shine. They are not true to the rules they profess to observe; they are not holy in all manner of conversation. Nay, many of them are salt that has lost its savour; the little savour they once had. Wherewith then shall the rest of the land be seasoned? What wonder that their neighbours are as unholy as ever?

But what can be done to remedy this? I wish you would give an attentive reading to the Minutes of the last conference, and see if it will not be worth our while to enforce them with all our might. We have weight enough, and can enforce them. I know not who can and will when we are gone. Let us now fix things on as firm a foundation as possible, and not depend upon seeing another conference.

Richard Bourke, John Dillon, and one or two more in this kingdom, are truly devoted men; so are a few of the preachers in England. *Si sic omnes* [O that all were so]! What would be able to stand before them?

How go you on in London? How is Mr. Whitefield, and my Lady, and Mr. Madan, and Romaine, and Berridge? Do you converse with those that are most alive, and sparingly and warily with them that are dead while they live?

I hope Sally and your young ones are well. O what a work is it to train up children for heaven!

Peace be with you and yours! Ἔρρωσο [Farewell].

---

## FROM LETTERS TO HIS BROTHER CHARLES.

[1768–1772. *Works*, vi, 671–5.]

I AM at my wit's end with regard to two things,—the Church, and Christian perfection. Unless both you and I stand in the gap *in good earnest,* the Methodists will drop them both. Talking will not avail. We must *do* or be borne away. Will you set shoulder to shoulder? If so, think deeply upon the matter, and tell me what can be done.  *Age, vir esto! nervos intendas tuos* [Come on, act the man! do your utmost]. Peace be with you and yours! Adieu. . . .

But what shall we do? I think it is high time that you and I, at least, should come to a point. Shall we go on in asserting perfection against all the world? Or shall we quietly let it drop? We really must do one or the other; and, I apprehend, the sooner the better. What shall we jointly and explicitly maintain (and recommend to all our preachers), concerning the nature, the time (now, or by and by), and the manner of it? instantaneous, or not?* I am weary of intestine war; of preachers quoting one of us against the other. At length, let us *fix* something for good and all; either the same as formerly, or different from it. Ἔρρωσο [Farewell]. . . .

I find almost all our preachers, in every circuit, have done with Christian perfection. They say, they believe it; but they never preach it; or not once in a quarter. What is to be done? Shall we let it drop, or make a point of it?

O what a thing it is to have *curam animarum* [the care of souls]! You and I are called to this; to save souls from death; to watch over them as those that must give account! If our office implied no more than preaching a few times in a week, I could play with it: so might you. But how small a part of our duty (yours as well as mine) is this? God says to you, as well as me, "Do all thou

---

* "At many times our advances in the race that is set before us are clear and perceptible; at other times they are no more perceptible (at least to ourselves) than the growth of a tree. At any time you may pray,—

'Strength and comfort from thy word,
Imperceptibly supply.'

And when you perceive nothing, it does not follow that the work of God stands still in your soul; especially while your desire is unto him, and while you choose him for your portion."—*Letter to a Young Disciple*, 1773. *Works*, vii, 93-4.

canst, be it more or less, to save the souls for whom my Son has died." Let this voice be ever sounding in our ears; then shall we give up our account with joy. *Eia age, rumpe moras* [Come, come on, make no delay]! I am ashamed of my indolence and inactivity. The good Lord help us both! Adieu! Ἔρρωσθε [Fare ye well]. . . .

I often cry out, *Vitæ me redde priori* [Restore me to my former mode of life]! Let me be again an Oxford Methodist! I am often in doubt whether it would not be best for me to resume all my Oxford rules, great and small. I did then walk closely with God, and redeem the time. But what have I been doing these thirty years?[*] My love to all. Adieu!

## TO MR. RICHARD TOMPSON.[†]

[*Works*, vi, 106.]

JUNE 28, 1755.

SOME days since, I received your favour of the 22d instant, which came exceeding seasonably; for I was just revising my Notes on the fifth chapter of the Romans: one of which I found, upon a closer inspection, seemed to assert such an imputation of Adam's sin to his posterity, as might make way for the "horrible decree." I therefore struck it out immediately; as I would willingly do whatsoever should appear to be any way inconsistent

---

[*] "To this day, I have abundantly more temptation to lukewarmness than to impetuosity; to be a saunterer *inter sylvas Academicas*, [among Academic shades], a philosophical sluggard, than an itinerant preacher. And, in fact, what I now do is so exceeding little, compared with what I am convinced I ought to do, that I am often ashamed before God, and know not how to lift up mine eyes to the height of heaven!"—*Letter to Mr. John Smith*, 1746. *Works*, vi, 633.

[†] This person was a member of the Methodist Society at an early period after its formation. He afterward separated himself from his old friends, and questioned the truth of some of their religious tenets; especially the witness of the Spirit, and Christian perfection. He addressed several letters to Mr. Wesley, under the assumed name of P. V.—EDIT.

with that grand principle, "The Lord is loving to every man; and his mercy is over all his works."

If you have observed any thing in any of the tracts I have published, which you think is not agreeable to Scripture and reason, you will oblige me by pointing it out, and by communicating to me any remarks you have occasionally made. I seek two things in this world,—truth and love. Whoever assists me in this search is a friend indeed, whether personally known, or unknown, to, sir,

Your humble servant.

---

## TO MR. JOHN TREMBATH.
[*Works*, vi, 749-50.]

CORK, August 17, 1760.

MY DEAR BROTHER,—The conversation I had with you yesterday in the afternoon, gave me a good deal of satisfaction. As to some things which I had heard (with regard to your wasting your substance, drinking intemperately, and wronging the poor people at Silberton), I am persuaded they were mistakes; as I suppose it was, that you converse much with careless, unawakened people. And I trust you will be more and more cautious in all these respects, abstaining from the very appearance of evil.

That you had not always attended the preaching when you might have done it, you allowed; but seemed determined to remove that objection; as well as the other, of using such exercises or diversions as give offence to your brethren. I believe you will likewise endeavour to avoid light and trifling conversation, and to talk and behave in all company with that seriousness and usefulness which become a preacher of the Gospel.

## To Mr. John Trembath.

Certainly some years ago you was alive to God. You experienced the life and power of religion. And does not God intend that the trials you meet with should bring you back to this? You cannot stand still; you know this is impossible. You must go forward or backward. Either you must recover that power, and be a Christian altogether, or in a while you will have neither power nor form, inside nor outside.

Extremely opposite both to one and the other, is that aptness to ridicule others, to make them contemptible, by exposing their real or supposed foibles. This I would earnestly advise you to avoid. It hurts yourself; it hurts the hearers; and it greatly hurts those who are so exposed, and tends to make them your irreconcilable enemies. It has also sometimes betrayed you into speaking what was not strictly true. O beware of this above all things! Never amplify, never exaggerate any thing. Be rigorous in adhering to truth. Be exemplary therein. Whatever has been in time past, let all men now know, that John Trembath abhors lying; that he never promises any thing which he does not perform; that his word is equal to his bond. I pray be exact in this. Be a pattern of truth, sincerity, and godly simplicity.

What has exceedingly hurt you in time past, nay, and I fear, to this day, is, want of reading. I scarce ever knew a preacher read so little. And perhaps, by neglecting it, you have lost the taste for it. Hence your talent in preaching does not increase. It is just the same as it was seven years ago. It is lively, but not deep; there is little variety; there is no compass of thought. Reading only can supply this, with meditation and daily prayer. You wrong yourself greatly by omitting this. You can never be a deep preacher without it, any more than a thorough Christian. O begin! Fix some part of every day for private exercises. You may acquire the taste which you have not: what is tedious at first, will afterward be pleasant. Whether you like it or no, read and pray daily. It is for your life; there is no other way; else you will be a trifler all your days, and a pretty, superficial preacher. Do justice to your own soul; give it time and means to grow. Do not starve yourself any longer. Take up your cross and be a Christian altogether. Then will all the children of God rejoice (not grieve) over you; and, in particular,

Yours, &c.

---

## TO LADY MAXWELL.

[*Works*, vii, 15-16.]

NEWCASTLE-UPON-TYNE, June 20, 1764.

WILL it be agreeable to my dear Lady Maxwell, that I trouble her with a letter so soon? and that I write with so little ceremony? that I use no compliment, but all plainness of speech? If it be not, you must tell me so, and I shall know better how to speak for the time to come. Indeed, it would be unpleasing to me to use reserve: The regard I feel for you strongly inclines me to "think aloud," to tell you every thought which rises in my heart. I think God has taken unusual pains, so to speak, to make you a Christian; a Christian indeed, not in name; worshipping God in spirit and in truth; having in you the mind that was in Christ, and walking as Christ also walked. He has given you affliction upon affliction; he has used every possible means to unhinge your soul from things of earth, that it might fix on him alone. How far the design of his love has succeeded, I could not well judge from a short conversation. Your ladyship will therefore give me leave to inquire, Is the heaviness you frequently feel merely owing to weakness of body, and the loss of near relations? I will hope it is not. It might, indeed, at first spring from these outward pressures. But did not the gracious Spirit of God strike in, and take occasion from these to convince you of sin, of unbelief, of the want of Christ? And is not the sense of this one great cause, if not the greatest, of your present distress? If so, the greatest danger is, either that you should stifle that conviction, not suffering yourself to be convinced that you are all sin, the chief of sinners; or, that you should heal the wound slightly, that you should rest before you know Christ is yours, before his Spirit witnesses with your spirit, that you are a child of God. My dear lady, be not afraid to know yourself; yea, to know yourself as you are known. How soon, then, will you know your Advocate with the Father, Jesus Christ the righteous! And why not this day? Why not this hour? If you feel your want, I beseech the God and Father of our Lord Jesus Christ to look upon you now! O give thy servant power to believe! to see and feel how thou hast loved her! Now let her sink down into the arms of thy love; and say unto her soul, "I am thy salvation."

With regard to particular advices, I know not how far your ladyship would have me to proceed. I would not be backward to do any thing in my power; and yet I would not obtrude. But in any respect you may command,

My dear lady,

Your ladyship's affectionate servant.

## TO THE SAME.
[*Works*, vii, 25.]

LONDON, February 8, 1772.

MY DEAR LADY,—I commend you for meddling with points of controversy as little as possible. It is abundantly easier to lose our love in that rough field, than to find truth. This consideration has made me exceedingly thankful to God for giving me a respite from polemical labors. I am glad he has given to others both the power and the will to answer them that trouble me; so that I may not always be forced to hold my weapons in one hand, while I am building with the other.—I rejoice, likewise, not only in the abilities, but in the temper, of Mr. Fletcher. He writes as he lives: I cannot say that I know such another clergyman in England or Ireland. He is all fire; but it is the fire of love. His writings, like his constant conversation, breathe nothing else, to those who read him with an impartial eye. And although Mr. Shirley scruples not to charge him with using subtility and metaphysical distinctions, yet he abundantly clears himself of this charge, in the "Second Check to Antinomianism." Such the last letters are styled, and with great propriety; for such they have really been. They have given a considerable check to those, who were every where making void the law through faith; setting "the righteousness of Christ" in opposition to the law of Christ, and teaching that "without holiness any man may see the Lord."

Notwithstanding both outward and inward trials, I trust you are still on the borders of perfect love. For the Lord is nigh!

> " See the Lord thy Keeper stand
> Omnipotently near!
> Lo! he holds thee by thy hand,
> And banishes thy fear!"

You have no need of fear. Hope unto the end! Are not all things possible to him that believeth? Dare to believe! Seize a blessing now! The Lord increase your faith! In this prayer I know you join with,

My dear lady,

Your ever affectionate servant.

## TO THE SAME.

[*Works*, vii, 27.]

LONDON, August 8, 1788.

MY DEAR LADY,—It is certain, many persons both in Scotland and England would be well pleased to have the same preachers always. But we cannot forsake the plan of acting which we have followed from the beginning. For fifty years God has been pleased to bless the itinerant plan; the last year most of all: it must not be altered, till I am removed; and I hope will remain till our Lord comes to reign upon earth.

I do not know (unless it unfits us for the duties of life) that we can have too great a sensibility of human pain. Methinks I should be afraid of losing any degree of this sensibility. I had a son-in-law (now in Abraham's bosom) who quitted his profession, that of a surgeon, for that very reason; because he said it made him less sensible of human pain. And I have known exceeding few persons who have carried this tenderness of spirit to excess. I recollect but one who was constrained to leave off, in a great measure, visiting the sick, because he could not see any one in pain without fainting away. Mr. Charles Perronet was the first person I was acquainted with who was favored with the same experience as the Marquis de Renty, with regard to the ever-blessed Trinity; Miss Ritchie was the second; Miss Roe (now Mrs. Rogers) the third. I have as yet found but a few instances; so that this is not, as I was at first apt to suppose, the common privilege of all that are "perfect in love."

Pardon me, my dear friend, for my heart is tenderly concerned for you, if I mention one fear I have concerning you, lest on conversing with some, you should be in any degree warped from Christian simplicity. O do not wish to hide that you are a Methodist! Surely it is best to appear just what you are. I believe you will receive this as a proof of the sincerity with which I am,

> My dear lady,
> Your ever affectionate servant.

---

## TO THE REV. MR. VENN.

[*Works*, vii, 303-5.]

BIRMINGHAM, June 22, 1765.

REVEREND AND DEAR SIR,—Having at length a few hours to spare, I sit down to answer your last, which was particularly acceptable to me, because it was wrote with so great openness. I shall write with the same. And herein you and I are just fit to converse together; because we both like to speak blunt and plain, without going a great way round about. I shall likewise take this opportunity of explaining myself on some other heads. I want you to understand me inside and out. Then I say, *Sic sum: Si placeo, utere* [Thus I am: if you like me, use me].

Were I allowed to boast myself a little, I would say, I want no man living, I mean, none but those who are now connected with me, and who bless God for that connection. With these I am able to go through every part of the work to which I am called. Yet I have laboured after union with all whom I believe to be united with Christ. I have sought it again and again; but in vain. They were resolved to stand aloof. And when one and another sincere minister of Christ has been inclined to come nearer to me, others have diligently kept them off, as though thereby they did God service.

To this poor end the doctrine of perfection has been brought in, head and shoulders. And when such concessions were made as would abundantly satisfy any fair

## To the Rev. Mr. Venn.

and candid man, they were no nearer,—rather farther off; for they had no desire to be satisfied. To make this dear breach wider and wider, stories were carefully gleaned up, improved, yea, invented and retailed, both concerning me and "the perfect ones." And when any thing very bad has come to hand, some have rejoiced as though they had found great spoils.

By this means chiefly, the distance between you and me has increased ever since you came to Huddersfield; and perhaps it has not been lessened by that honest, well-meaning man, Mr. Burnet, and by others, who have talked largely of the dogmaticalness, love of power, errors, and irregularities. My dogmaticalness is neither more nor less than a custom of coming to the point at once, and telling my mind flat and plain, without any preface or ceremony. I could indeed premise something of my own imbecility, littleness of judgment, and the like; but, First, I have no time to lose, I must despatch the matter as soon as possible. Secondly, I do not think it frank or ingenuous. I think these prefaces are mere artifice.

The power I have, I never sought.* It was the undesired, unexpected result of the work God was pleased to work by me. I have a thousand times sought to devolve it on others; but as yet I cannot. I therefore suffer it till I can find any to ease me of my burden.

If any one will convince me of my errors, I will heartily thank him. I believe all the Bible, as far as I understand it, and am ready to be convinced. If I am a heretic, I became such by reading the Bible. All my notions I drew from thence; and with little help from men, unless in the single point of justification by faith. But I impose my notions upon none: I will be bold to say, there is no man living farther from it. I make no opinion the term of

---

* "I fear and shun, not desire, authority of any kind."—*Letter to Mr. Joseph Benson*, 1770. *Works*, vii, 69.

union with any man: I think and let think. What I want is, holiness of heart and life. They who have this are my brother, sister, and mother.

"But you hold perfection." True; that is loving God with all our heart, and serving him with all our strength. I teach nothing more, nothing less, than this. And whatever infirmity, defect, ἀνομία, is consistent with this, any man may teach, and I shall not contradict him.

As to irregularity, I hope none of those who cause it do then complain of it. Will they throw a man into the dirt, and beat him because he is dirty? Of all men living, those clergymen ought not to complain, who believe I preach the Gospel as to the substance of it. If they do not ask me to preach in their churches, they are accountable for my preaching in the fields.

I come now directly to your letter, in hopes of establishing a good understanding between us. I agreed to suspend, for a twelvemonth, our stated preaching at Huddersfield, which had been there these many years. If this answered your end, I am glad: my end it did not answer at all. Instead of coming nearer to me, you got farther off. I heard of it from every quarter, though few knew that I did; for I saw no cause to speak against you, because you did against me. I wanted you to do more, not less, good, and therefore durst not do or say any thing to hinder it. And lest I should hinder it, I will make a farther trial, and suspend the preaching at Huddersfield for another year.

To clear the case between us a little farther. I must now adopt your words: "I, no less than you, preach justification by faith only, the absolute necessity of holiness, the increasing mortification of sin, and rejection of all past experiences and attainments. I abhor, as you do, all Antinomian abuse of the doctrine of Christ, and desire to see my people walking even as he walked. Is it then worth while, in order to gratify a few bigoted persons,

## To the Rev. Mr. Venn. 363

or for the sake of the minute differences between us, to encourage all the train of evils which follow contention for opinions, in little matters as much as in great?"

If I was as strenuous with regard to perfection on one side, as you have been on the other, I should deny you to be a sufficient preacher; but this I never did. And yet I assure you, I can advance such reasons for all I teach as would puzzle you and all that condemn me to answer; but I am sick of disputing. Let them beat the air and triumph without an opponent.

"None," you say, "preach in your houses, who do not hold the very same doctrine with you." This is not exactly the case. You are welcome to preach in any of those houses; as I know we agree in the main points; and whereinsoever we differ, you would not preach there contrary to me. "But would it not give you pain to have any other teacher come among those committed to your charge, so as to have your plan disconcerted, your labours depreciated, and the affections of your flock alienated?" It has given me pain when I had reason to fear this was done, both at Leeds, Birstal, and elsewhere. And I was "under a temptation of speaking against you;" but I refrained even among my intimate friends. So far was I from publicly warning my people against one I firmly believed to be much better than myself.

Indeed I trust "the bad blood is now taken away." Let it return no more. Let us begin such a correspondence as has never been yet; and let us avow it before all mankind. Not content with not weakening each other's hands, or speaking against each other, directly or indirectly (which may be effectually done under the notion of exposing this and that error), let us defend each other's characters to the uttermost against either ill or well meaning evil speakers. I am not satisfied with, "Be very civil to the Methodists, but have nothing to do with them." No: I desire to have a league offensive and defensive with every soldier of Christ. We have not only one faith, one hope, one Lord, but are directly engaged in one warfare. We are carrying the war into the devil's own quarters, who therefore summons all his hosts to war. Come then, ye that love him, to the help of the Lord, to the help of the Lord against the mighty! I am now well nigh *miles emeritus senex, sexagenarius* [an old soldier who has served out his time and is entitled to his discharge,— a sexagenarian]; yet I trust to fight a little longer. Come and strengthen the hands, till you supply the place, of your weak, but affectionate brother,

JOHN WESLEY.

---

## TO MR. THOMAS RANKIN.
[*Works*, vii, 7.]

ST. JOHN'S, September 11, 1765.

DEAR TOMMY,—There is a good work in Cornwall. But where the great work goes on well, we should take care to be exact in little things.

I will tell you several of these, just as they occur to my mind. Grace Paddy, at Redruth, met in the select society, though she wore a large glittering necklace, and met no band.

They sing all over Cornwall a tune so full of repetitions and flourishes, that it can scarce be sung with devotion. It is to those words,—

"Praise the Lord, ye blessed ones."

Away with it. Let it be heard no more.

They cannot sing our old common tunes. Teach these every where. Take pains herein.

The societies are not half supplied with books; not even with Jane Cooper's Letters, or the two or three sermons which I printed last year: No, not with the shilling hymn book, or "Primitive Physic."

They almost universally neglect fasting.

The preaching houses are miserable, even the new ones. They have neither light nor air sufficient; and they are far, far too low, and too small. Look at Yarm house.

We have need to use all the common sense God has given us, as well as all the grace. I am, dear Tommy,
    Your affectionate friend and brother.

Recommend the Notes on the Old Testament in good earnest. Every society, as a society, should subscribe. Remind them, every where, that two, four, or six might join together for a copy, and bring the money to their leader weekly.

## TO THE SAME.

[*Works*, vii, 10.]

CLARMAIN, NEAR ARMAGH, June 13, 1775.

DEAR TOMMY,—I am afraid our correspondence for the time to come will be more uncertain than ever; since the sword is drawn: and it is well if they have not on both sides thrown away the scabbard. What will the end of these things be, either in Europe or America? It seems, huge confusion and distress, such as neither we nor our fathers had known! But it is enough, if all issues in glory to God, and peace and good will among men.

I am sorry for poor T. R. I well hoped God had thoroughly healed his backsliding, and so lifted up his head that he would have fallen no more. But the case is not desperate yet: you must in nowise give him up. I have scarcely ever known an habitual drunkard finally reclaimed, before he had relapsed more than once or twice. Your point is, First, save him from the occasions of sin: then incite him, not to cast away hope. Nothing but this, despair of conquering, can totally destroy him.

As long as he keeps up the faintest hope, he will strive against sin.

My brother wrote me word, that he had received a copy of the tract that you have written. Something of the kind may be very seasonable. Never had America such a call to repentance. For unless general reformation prevent general destruction, what a scene will soon be opened! Ruin and desolation must soon overspread the land, and fair houses be turned into ruinous heaps. But what are those strange phenomena which you speak of? Send me an account of just so much as you can depend upon.

Should not you appoint in America (as we do in England and Ireland), one or more general days of fasting and prayer? I am, dear Tommy,

Your affectionate friend and brother.

---

## TO MRS. EMMA MOON, OF YARM.

[*Works*, vi, 762-3.]

LONDON, January 24, 1768.

MY DEAR SISTER,—Formerly, when persons reproached me for doing thus and thus, I have very frequently said, "In truth, I have not done it yet; but by the grace of God, I will." This seems to be the very case with you. You are accused for what you did not, but ought to have done. You ought to have informed me from time to time, not indeed of trifles, or idle reports, but of things which you judged to be a real hinderance to the work of God. And God permitted you to be reminded of this omission by those who intended nothing less.

Opposition from their brethren has been one cause why so many who were set free have not retained their liberty. But perhaps there was another more general cause: they had not proper help. One just saved from sin is like a new-

born child, and needs as careful nursing. But these had it not. How few were as nursing fathers! How few cherished them as a nurse her own children! So that the greater part were weakened, if not destroyed, before their sinews were knit, for want of that prudent and tender care which their state necessarily required. Do all that you can to cherish them that are left; and never forget
Your affectionate brother.

## TO MR. JOHN MASON.
[*Works*, vii, 96.]

PEMBROKE, August 6, 1768.

MY DEAR BROTHER,—I would advise to make a longer trial of Kinsale. I am still in hope that good will be done there. And there has been considerable good done at Bandon; and will be more, if the preachers do not coop themselves up in the house. But no great good will be done at any place without field preaching. I hope you labour to keep the bands regular in every place, which cannot be done without a good deal of care and pains. Take pains, likewise, with the children, and in visiting from house to house; else you will see little fruit of your labour. I believe it will be best to change the preachers more frequently. I am
Your affectionate friend and brother.

## TO THE SAME.
[*Works*, vii, 98.]

NEAR LONDON, January 13 1790.

MY DEAR BROTHER,—As long as I live, the people shall have no share in choosing either stewards or leaders among the Methodists. We have not, and never had, any such custom. We are no republicans, and never intend to be. It would be better for those that are so minded to go quietly away. I have been uniform both in doctrine and discipline for above these fifty years; and it is a little too late for me to turn into a new path now I am grey-headed. Neither good old brother Pascoe (God bless him) expects it from me, nor brother Wood, nor brother Flamank. If you and I should be called hence this year, we may bless God that we have not lived in vain. Come, let us have a few more strokes at Satan's kingdom, and then we shall depart in peace!

I am

Your affectionate friend and brother.

## TO MR. JOSEPH BENSON.
[*Works*, vii, 67.]

SHOREHAM, December 22, 1768.

MY DEAR JOSEPH,—You do not quite take my meaning yet. When I recommend to any one a method or scheme of study, I do not barely consider this or that book separately, but in conjunction with the rest. And what I recommend I know; I know both the style and sentiments of each author; and how he will confirm or illustrate what goes before, and prepare for what comes after. Now, supposing Mr. Stonehouse, Roquet, or any other, to have ever so great learning and judgment, yet he does not enter into my plan. He does not comprehend my views, nor keep his eye fixed on the same point. Therefore, I must insist upon it, the interposing other books between these, till you have read them through, is not good husbandry. It is not making your time and pains go so far as they might go. If you want more books, let me recommend more, who best understand my own

AN EARLY PORTRAIT OF JOSEPH BENSON

scheme.* And do not ramble, however learned the persons may be that advise you so to do. This does indulge curiosity, but does not minister to real improvement, as a stricter method would do. No; you would gain more clearness and strength of judgment by reading those Latin and Greek books (compared with which most of the English are whipped syllabub), than by fourscore modern books. I have seen the proof, as none of your Bristol friends have done, or can do. Therefore, I advise you again, Keep to your plan (though this implies continual self denial), if you would improve your understanding to the highest degree of which it is capable. I am, dear Joseph, Your affectionate brother.

## TO THE SAME.

[*Works*, vii, 80.]

WARRINGTON, May 21, 1781.

DEAR JOSEPH,—As I have not leisure myself, I am exceeding glad that you have entered into the lists with Mr. A——. And I am in hopes you will "reply at large," to all his cavils and objections. If he cites any thing from me, you should answer simply, "I never undertook to defend every sentiment of Mr. W——'s. He does not expect or desire it. He wishes me and every man to think for himself."

If you remember, I do not insist on the term *impression*. I say again, I will thank any one that will find a better; be it *discovery, manifestation, deep sense,* or whatever it may. That *some consciousness* of our being in favour with God is joined with Christian faith, I cannot

---

\* "But beware you be not swallowed up in books: an ounce of love is worth a pound of knowledge."—*Letter to Mr. Joseph Benson*, 1768. *Works*, vii, 67.

"Many persons are in danger of reading too little: you are in danger of reading too much."—*Letter to Mr. Joseph Benson*, 1774. *Works*, vii, 74.

doubt; but it is not the essence of it. A consciousness of pardon cannot be the condition of pardon.

But I am still more glad that you have some thoughts of answering that pernicious book of poor Mr. Madan. Analyze it first with the postscript; then overturn it thoroughly, from the beginning to the end. You may steer between the extremes of too much roughness, and too much smoothness. And see that you are plain enough for women and pretty gentlemen. I allow you a hundred pages. I am, dear Joseph,

Your affectionate friend and brother.

---

## TO MRS. CROSBY.

[*Works*, vii, 29.]

CHESTER, March 18, 1769.

MY DEAR SISTER,—The westerly winds detain me here, I care not how long: good is the will of the Lord. When I am in Ireland, you have only to direct to Dublin, and the letter will find me.

I advise you, as I did Grace Walton formerly, 1. Pray in private or public, as much as you can. 2. Even in public, you may properly enough intermix short exhortations with prayer; but keep as far from what is called preaching as you can: therefore, never take a text; never speak in a continued discourse, without some break, above four or five minutes. Tell the people, "We shall have another prayer meeting at such a time and place." If Hannah Harrison had followed these few directions, she might have been as useful now as ever.

As soon as you have time, write more particularly and circumstantially; and let S. Bosanquet do the same. There is now no hinderance in the way; nothing to hinder your speaking as freely as you please to,

Dear Sally,

Your affectionate brother.

## TO THE SAME.
[*Works*, vii, 30.]

LONDONDERRY, June 13, 1771.

MY DEAR SISTER,—I think the strength of the cause rests there; on your having an extraordinary call. So I am persuaded has every one of our lay preachers; otherwise, I could not countenance his preaching at all. It is plain to me, that the whole work of God termed Methodism is an extraordinary dispensation of his providence. Therefore, I do not wonder if several things occur therein which do not fall under ordinary rules of discipline. St. Paul's ordinary rule was, "I permit not a woman to speak in the congregation." Yet, in extraordinary cases, he made a few exceptions; at Corinth in particular.

I am, my dear sister,
Your affectionate brother.

---

## TO A YOUNG DISCIPLE.
[*Works*, vii, 92.]

WHITBY, June 20, 1772.

IT is of admirable use to bear the weaknesses, nay, and even the faults, of the real children of God. And the temptations to anger which rise herefrom are often more profitable than any other. Yet surely, for the present, they are not joyous but grievous: afterward comes the peaceable fruit. You shall have exactly as much pain and as much disappointment as will be most for your profit, and just sufficient to

> "Keep you dead to all below,
> Only Christ resolved to know."

Never make it matter of reasoning that you have not either a larger or a smaller share of suffering. You shall have exactly what is best both as to kind, degree, and time. O what a blessing is it to be in his hand who "doeth all things well!"

Of all gossiping, religious gossiping is the worst: it adds hypocrisy to uncharitableness, and effectually does the work of the devil in the name of the Lord. The leaders, in every society, may do much toward driving it out from among the Methodists. Let them, in the band or class, observe, 1. "Now we are to talk of no absent person, but simply of God and our own souls." 2. "The rule of our conversation here is to be the rule of all our conversation. Let us observe it (unless in some necessarily exempt cases) at all times and in all places." If this be frequently inculcated, it will have an excellent effect.

Instead of giving a caution once, as to a grown person, you must give it to a child ten times. By this means you may keep a sensible child from an improper familiarity with servants. Cautions should also be given frequently and earnestly to the servants themselves; and they will not always be thrown away, if they have either grace or sense.

## TO THE SAME.
[*Works*, vii, 94.]

AUGUST 20, 1773.

I OFTEN heard my own mother make the same complaint with you. She did not *feel* near so much as my father did; but she *did* ten times more than he did. You must labour to *do* so much the more, and pray that God would supply whatever is wanting. One degree of forgiveness is due to every one, though impenitent; still I love him as I love all men. But the other degree, whereby I should again receive him as a friend, is only due to one who says, "I repent;" that is, convinces me that he does really repent, and is entirely changed.

It is certain God has given you a talent, and I still think it ought to be used. I grant indeed, to be hid and to be still is more agreeable to flesh and blood; but is it more agreeable to Him "who hath left us an example, that we might tread in his steps?"

One cannot be saved from evil tempers, without being devoted to God; neither can a soul be all devoted to God, without being saved from sin: but it is often exceeding hard to judge of others, whether they are saved from all evil tempers, and whether they are all devoted to God, or not; yea, it is hard to judge of ourselves; nay, we cannot do it, without the anointing of the Holy One given for that very purpose. Out of darkness, God will command light to shine. Be plain and open to all; then, whether they are sincere or insincere, you will have a conscience void of offence. You find all things work together for good. They must, while the hairs of your head are all numbered.     Yours affectionately.

---

## TO THE REV. JOHN FLETCHER.
[*Works*, vi, 687-8.]

JANUARY, 1773.

DEAR SIR,—What an amazing work has God wrought in these kingdoms, in less than forty years! And it not only continues, but increases, throughout England, Scotland, and Ireland; nay, it has lately spread into New-York, Pennsylvania, Virginia, Maryland, and Carolina. But the wise men of the world say, "When Mr. Wesley drops, then all this is at an end!" And so it surely will, unless, before God calls him hence, one is found to stand in his place. For οὐκ ἀγαθὸν πολυκοιρανίη. Εἷς κοίρανος ἔστω.* I see more and more, unless there be one προεστώς,†

---
\* It is not good that the supreme power should be lodged in many hands: let there be one chief governor.—EDIT.

† A person who presides over the rest.—EDIT.

the work can never be carried on. The body of the preachers are not united: nor will any part of them submit to the rest; so that either there must be one to preside over all, or the work will indeed come to an end.

But who is sufficient for these things? qualified to preside both over the preachers and people? He must be a man of faith and love, and one that has a single eye to the advancement of the kingdom of God. He must have a clear understanding; a knowledge of men and things, particularly of the Methodist doctrine and discipline; a ready utterance; diligence and activity, with a tolerable share of health. There must be added to these, favour with the people, with the Methodists in general. For unless God turn their eyes and their hearts toward him, he will be quite incapable of the work. He must likewise have some degree of learning; because there are many adversaries, learned as well as unlearned, whose mouths must be stopped. But this cannot be done, unless he be able to meet them on their own ground.

But has God provided one so qualified? Who is he? Thou art the man! God has given you a measure of loving faith; and a single eye to his glory. He has given you some knowledge of men and things; particularly of the old plan of Methodism. You are blessed with some health, activity, and diligence; together with a degree of learning. And to all these, he has lately added, by a way none could have foreseen, favour both with the preachers and the whole people. Come out, in the name of God! Come to the help of the Lord against the mighty! Come while I am alive and capable of labour!

"*Dum superest Lachesi quod torqueat, et pedibus me
Porto meis, nullo dextram subeunte bacillo.*"
[While a remnant of the thread of life is yet unspun, and I am able to walk without the aid of a staff.]

Come while I am able, God assisting, to build you up in faith, to ripen your gifts, and to introduce you to the people. *Nil tanti* [Nothing is of equal moment]. What possible employment can you have which is of so great importance?

But you will naturally say, "I am not equal to the task; I have neither grace nor gifts for such an employment." You say true; it is certain you have not. And who has? But do you not know Him who is able to give them? perhaps not at once, but rather day by day: as each is, so shall your strength be. "But this implies," you may say, "a thousand crosses, such as I feel I am not able to bear." You are not able to bear them now; and they are not now come. Whenever they do come, will he not send them in due number, weight, and measure? And will they not all be for your profit, that you may be a partaker of his holiness?

Without conferring, therefore, with flesh and blood, come and strengthen the hands, comfort the heart, and share the labour, of

        Your affectionate friend and brother.

## TO MR. GEORGE SHADFORD.

[*Works*, vii, 99–100.]

1773.

DEAR GEORGE,—The time is arrived for you to embark for America. You must go down to Bristol, where you will meet with Thomas Rankin, Captain Webb, and his wife.

I let you loose, George, on the great continent of America. Publish your message in the open face of the sun, and do all the good you can.

        I am, dear George,
            Yours affectionately.

## TO MISS BOLTON.

[*Works*, vii, 116–7.]

LONDON, July 18, 1773.

MY DEAR SISTER,—Your late conversation was exceedingly pleasant to me. I had sometimes been almost inclined to think that your affection was lessened; but I now believe it is not. I trust your love is not grown cold. This gave me much satisfaction, though I could not but be concerned at seeing you so encumbered with worldly business. Surely it will not be so always. But God's time is best! Two or three of those little things I have sent you:—

> "With peaceful mind thy race of duty run:
> God nothing does, or suffers to be done,
> But what thou wouldst thyself, if thou couldst see
> Through all events of things as well as he.

> "Let thy repentance be without delay:
> If thou defer it to another day,
> Thou must repent for a day more of sin,
> While a day less remains to do it in.

> "Nor steel nor flint alone produces fire,
> Nor spark arises till they both conspire:
> Nor faith alone, nor works without, is right;
> Salvation rises when they both unite.

> "If gold be offer'd thee, thou dost not say,
> 'To-morrow I will take it, not to-day:'
> Salvation offer'd, why art thou so cool
> To let thyself become to-morrow's fool?

> "Prayer and thanksgiving is the vital breath
> That keeps the spirit of a man from death:
> For prayer attracts into the living soul
> The life that fills the universal whole;
> And giving thanks is breathing forth again
> The praise of Him who is the life of men.

> "Two different painters, artists in their way,
> Have drawn religion in her full display.
> To both she sat: one gazed at her all o'er;
> The other fix'd upon her features more.
> Hervey has figured her with every grace
> That dress could give; but Law has hit her face.

> "The specious sermons of a learned man
> Are little else than flashes in the pan.
> The mere haranguing upon what they call
> Morality, is powder without ball:
> But he who preaches with a Christian grace
> Fires at your vices, and the shot takes place.
>
> "Faith, Hope, and Love, were question'd what they thought
> Of future glory, which Religion taught.
> Now Faith believed it firmly to be true,
> And Hope expected so to find it too:
> Love answer'd, smiling with a conscious glow,
> '*Believe! expect!* I *know* it to be so.'"

Go on in this humble, gentle love; that you may abound therein more and more. Aim at nothing higher than this: and may the God of love still possess you whole, and guide your every thought, and word, and work. Continue to pray for

Your affectionate brother.

---

## TO THE SAME.

[*Works*, vii, 119.]

LONDON, January 9, 1789.

MY DEAR SISTER,—"Sir, you are troubled," said Mr. Law to me, "because you do not understand how God is dealing with you. Perhaps if you did, it would not so well answer his design. He is teaching you to trust him farther than you can see him." He is now teaching you the same lesson. Hitherto you cannot understand his ways. But they are all mercy and truth. And though you do not know now what he does, you shall know hereafter.

I am acquainted with several persons whom I believe to be saved from sin. But there is great variety in the manner wherein God is pleased to lead them. Some of them are called to act much for God; some to rejoice much; some to suffer much. All of these shall receive their crown. But when the Son of Man shall come in his glory, the brightest crown will be given to the sufferers. Look up, thou blessed one! the time is at hand!

I am

Ever yours.

---

## TO SAMUEL SPARROW, ESQ.
[*Works*, vii, 113.]

DECEMBER 28, 1773.

DEAR SIR,— . . . [My brother and I] set out upon two principles: 1. None go to heaven without holiness of heart and life: 2. Whosoever follows after this (whatever his opinions be) is my "brother, and sister, and mother:" and we have not swerved a hair's breadth from either one or the other of these to this day.

Thus it was, that two young men, without a name, without friends, without either power or fortune, "set out from college with principles totally different from those of the common people," to oppose all the world, learned and unlearned; to "combat popular prejudices" of every kind. Our first principle directly attacked all the wickedness, our second, all the bigotry, in the world. Thus they attempted a reformation, not of opinions (feathers, trifles not worth the naming), but of men's tempers and lives; of vice in every kind; of every thing contrary to justice, mercy, or truth. And for this it was, that they carried their lives in their hands,—that both the great vulgar and the small looked upon them as mad dogs, and treated them as such; sometimes saying in terms, "Will nobody knock that mad dog on the head?" . . .

## TO MR. JOHN KING.*

[*Works*, vii, 13.]

NEAR LEEDS, July 28, 1775.

MY DEAR BROTHER,—Always take advice or reproof as a favour: it is the surest mark of love.

I advised you once, and you took it as an affront: nevertheless I will do it once more.

Scream no more, at the peril of your soul. God now warns you by me, whom he has set over you. Speak as earnestly as you can; but do not scream. Speak with all your heart; but with a moderate voice. It was said of our Lord, "He shall not *cry:*" the word properly means, He shall not *scream*. Herein be a follower of me, as I am of Christ. I often speak loud; often vehemently; but I never scream; I never strain myself; I dare not: I know it would be a sin against God and my own soul. Perhaps one reason why that good man, Thomas Walsh, yea, and John Manners too, were in such grievous darkness before they died, was, because they shortened their own lives.

O John, pray for an advisable and teachable temper! By nature you are very far from it: you are stubborn and headstrong. Your last letter was written in a very wrong spirit. If you cannot take advice from others, surely you might take it from

Your affectionate brother.

---

## TO A MEMBER OF THE SOCIETY.

[*Works*, vi, 782-3.]

FEBRUARY 7, 1776.

I HAVE found some of the uneducated poor who have exquisite taste and sentiment; and many, very many,

---

* One of the preachers in America.—EDIT.

of the rich who have scarcely any at all. But I do not speak of this: I want you to converse more, abundantly more, with the poorest of the people, who, if they have not taste, have souls, which you may forward in their way to heaven. And they have (many of them) faith, and the love of God, in a larger measure than any persons I know. Creep in among these, in spite of dirt, and a hundred disgusting circumstances; and thus put off the gentlewoman. Do not confine your conversation to genteel and elegant people.* I should like this as well as you do: but I cannot discover a precedent for it in the life of our Lord, or any of his Apostles. My dear friend, let you and I walk as he walked.

I now understand you with regard to the P——'s; but I fear in this you are too delicate. It is certain their preaching is attended with the power of God to the hearts of many; and why not to yours? Is it not owing to a want of simplicity? "Are you going to hear Mr. Wesley?" said a friend to Mr. Blackwell. "No," he answered, "I am going to hear God: I listen to him, whoever preaches; otherwise I lose all my labour."

"You will only be content to convert worlds? You shall hew wood, or carry brick and mortar; and when you do this in obedience to the order of Providence, it shall be more profitable to your own soul than the other." You may remember Mr. De Renty's other remark: "I then saw that a well-instructed Christian is never hindered by any person or thing. For whatever prevents his doing good works, gives him a fresh opportunity of submitting his will to the will of God; which at that time is more pleasing to God, and more profitable to his soul, than any thing else which he could possibly do."

---

* "In most genteel religious people there is so strange a mixture, that I have seldom much confidence in them. I love the poor; in many of them I find pure, genuine grace, unmixed with paint, folly, and affectation."—*Letter to Miss Furly*, 1757. *Works*, vi, 713.

Never let your expenses exceed your income. To servants I would give full as much as others give for the same service; and not more. It is impossible to lay down any general rules, as to "saving all we can," and "giving all we can." In this, it seems, we must needs be directed, from time to time, by the unction of the Holy One. Evil spirits have undoubtedly abundance of work to do in an evil world; frequently in concurrence with wicked men, and frequently without them.

## TO THE SAME.

[*Works*, vi, 784-5.]

DECEMBER 10, 1777.

You do not at all understand my manner of life. Though I am always in haste, I am never in a hurry; because I never undertake any more work than I can go through with perfect calmness of spirit.* It is true, I travel four or five thousand miles in a year. But I

---

* "In my last journey into the north, all my patience was put to the proof again and again; and all my endeavour to please, yet without success. In my present journey I leap, as broke from chains. I am content with whatever entertainment I meet with, and my companions are always in good humour, "because they are with me." This must be the spirit of all who take journeys with me. If a dinner ill dressed, a hard bed, a poor room, a shower of rain, or a dirty road, will put them out of humour, it lays a burden upon me, greater than all the rest put together. By the grace of God I never fret. I repine at nothing; I am discontented with nothing. And to have persons at my ear, fretting and murmuring at every thing, is like tearing the flesh off my bones. I see God sitting upon his throne, and ruling all things well. Although, therefore, I can bear this also,—to hear his government of the world continually found fault with (for in blaming the things which He alone can alter, we, in effect, blame him); yet it is such a burden to me as I cannot bear without pain; and I bless God when it is removed.

"The doctrine of a particular providence is what exceeding few persons understand; at least, not practically; so as to apply it to every circumstance of life. This I want, to see God acting in every thing, and disposing all, for his own glory and his creature's good."—*Letter to Mr. Ebenezer Blackwell*, 1755. *Works*, vi, 700-1.

generally travel alone in my carriage;* and, consequently, am as retired ten hours in a day, as if I was in a wilderness. On other days, I never spend less than three hours (frequently ten or twelve) in the day alone. So there are few persons in the kingdom who spend so many hours secluded from all company. Yet I find time to visit the sick and the poor; and I must do it, if I believe the Bible, if I believe these are the marks whereby the Shepherd of Israel will know and judge his sheep at the great day; therefore, when there is time and opportunity for it, who can doubt but this is matter of absolute duty? When I was at Oxford, and lived almost like a hermit, I saw not how any busy man could be saved. I scarce thought it possible for a man to retain a Christian spirit, amidst the noise and bustle of the world. God taught me better by my own experience. I had ten times more business in America (that is, at intervals) than ever I had in my life. But it was no hinderance to silence of spirit.

Mr. Boehm was chaplain to Prince George of Denmark; secretary to him and Queen Ann; principal manager of almost all the public charities in the kingdom, and employed in numberless private charities. An intimate friend, knowing this, said to him when they were alone, "Sir, are you not hurt by that amazing hurry of business? I have seen you in your office, surrounded with people, listening to one, dictating to another, and at the same time writing to a third: could you then retain a sense of the presence of God?" He answered, "All that company, and all that business, no more hindered or

---

* "I am not yet quite free from the effects of the fall which I had at Christmas, and perhaps never shall in this world. Sometimes my ankle, sometimes my knee, and frequently my shoulder, complains. But, blessed be God, I have strength sufficient for the work to which I am called. When I cannot walk any farther, I can take a horse, and now and then a chaise; so that hitherto I have not been hindered from visiting any place which I purposed to see before I left London."—*Letter to Mr. Ebenezer Btackwell*, 1766. *Works*, vi, 707.

lessened my communion with God, than if I had been all alone in a church kneeling before the communion table." Was it not the same case with him to whom Gregory Lopez said, "Go and be a hermit in Mexico?" I am concerned for you; I am sorry you should be content with lower degrees of usefulness and holiness than you are called to. But I cannot help it; so I submit; and am still, my dear Miss M——,

Yours in sincere affection.

---

## TO MR. ——.

[*Works*, vii, 228.]

JANUARY, 1780.

MY DEAR BROTHER,—You seem to me not to have well considered the Rules of a Helper, or the rise of Methodism. It pleased God, by me, to awaken, first my brother, and then a few others; who severally desired of me, as a favour, that I would direct them in all things. After my return from Georgia, many were both awakened and converted to God. One, and another, and another of these desired to join with me as sons in the Gospel, to be directed by me. I drew up a few plain rules—(observe, there was no conference in being!), and permitted them to join me on these conditions. Whoever, therefore, violates these conditions, particularly that of being directed by me in the work, does, *ipso facto* [by the act itself], disjoin himself from me. This brother M. has done (but he cannot see that he has done amiss); and he would have it a common cause: that is, he would have all the preachers do the same. He thinks "they have a right so to do." So they have. They have a right to disjoin themselves from me whenever they please. But they cannot, in the nature of the thing, join with me any longer than they are directed by me. And what, if fifty of the present preachers disjoined themselves! What should I lose thereby? Only a great deal of labour and care, which I do not seek; but endure, because no one else either can or will.

You seem likewise to have quite a wrong idea of a conference. For above six years after my return to England, there was no such thing. I then desired some of our preachers to meet me, in order to advise, not control, me. And you may observe, they had no power at all, but what I exercised through them. I chose to exercise the power which God had given me in this manner, both to avoid ostentation, and gently to habituate the people to obey them when I should be taken from their head. But as long as I remain with them, the fundamental rule of Methodism remains inviolate. As long as any preacher joins with me, he is to be directed by me in his work. Do not you see, then, that brother M., whatever his intentions might be, acted as wrong as wrong could be? and that the representing of this as the common cause of the preachers was the way to common destruction? the way to turn all their heads, and to set them in arms? It was a blow at the very root of Methodism. I could not therefore do less than I did: it was the very least that could be done, for fear that evil should spread.

I do not willingly speak of these things at all; but I do it now out of necessity; because I perceive the mind of you, and some others, is a little hurt by not seeing them in a true light. I am

Your affectionate brother.

## TO BISHOP LOWTH.

[*Works*, vii, 230-1.]

AUGUST 10, 1780.

MY LORD,— . . . Will your lordship permit me to speak freely? I dare not do otherwise. I am on the verge of the grave, and know not the hour when I shall drop into it. Suppose there were threescore of those missionaries in the country, could I in conscience recommend these souls to their care? Do they take any care of their own souls? If they do—(I speak it with concern!), I fear they are almost the only missionaries in America that do. My lord, I do not speak rashly: I have been in America; and so have several with whom I have lately conversed. And both I and they know what manner of men the far greater part of these are. They are men who have neither the power of religion, nor the form; men that lay no claim to piety, nor even decency.

Give me leave, my lord, to speak more freely still: perhaps it is the last time I shall trouble your lordship. I know your lordship's abilities and extensive learning: I believe, what is far more, that your lordship fears God. I have heard that your lordship is unfashionably diligent in examining the candidates for holy orders; yea, that your lordship is generally at the pains of examining them yourself. *Examining them!* In what respect? Why, whether they understand a little Latin and Greek, and can answer a few trite questions in the science of divinity! Alas, how little does this avail! Does your lordship examine, whether they serve Christ or Belial? whether they love God or the world? whether they ever had any serious thoughts about heaven or hell? whether they have any real desire to save their own souls, or the souls of others? If not, what have they to do with holy orders? and what will become of the souls committed to their care?

My lord, I do by no means despise learning: I know the value of it too well. But what is this, particularly in a Christian minister, compared to piety? What is it in a man that has no religion? "As a jewel in a swine's snout." . . .

I do not know that Mr. Hoskins had any favour to ask of the society. He asked the favour of your lordship to ordain him, that he might minister to a little flock in America. But your lordship did not see good to ordain him: but your lordship did see good to ordain, and send into America, other persons, who knew something of Greek and Latin; but who knew no more of saving souls, than of catching whales.

In this respect also, I mourn for poor America; for the sheep scattered up and down therein. Part of them have no shepherds at all, particularly in the northern colonies; and the case of the rest is little better, for their own shepherds pity them not. They cannot, for they have no pity on themselves. They take no thought or care about their own souls.

Wishing your lordship every blessing from the great Shepherd and Bishop of souls, I remain, my lord,

Your lordship's dutiful son and servant.

## TO MR. ——.*

[*Works*, vii, 217–18.]

LONDON, November 9, 1782.

DEAR SAMMY,—I abhor the thought of giving to twenty men the power to place or displace the preachers in their congregations. How would he then dare to speak an unpleasing truth? And, if he did, what would become of him? This must never be the case while I live among the Methodists. And Birstal is a leading case, the first of an avowed violation of our plan.† Therefore, the

---

* The direction of this letter is lost; but it appears to have been addressed to Mr. Bradburn, who was then stationed in Bradford, only a few miles from Birstal, where an attempt was made to settle a Methodist chapel upon the plan of independency.—EDIT.

† "Whenever the trustees exert their power of 'placing and displacing preachers,' then,

"1. Itinerant preaching is no more. When the trustees in any place have found and fixed a preacher they like, the rotation of preachers is at

point must be carried for the Methodist preachers now or never; and I alone can carry it, which I will, God being my helper.

You are not a match for the silver tongue, nor brother Hopper. But do not, to please any of your new friends, forsake                      Your true old friend.

## TO THE COMMANDING OFFICER IN LOWESTOFT.

[*Works*, vii, 136.]

LONDON, November 30, 1782.

SIR,—I am informed by some of my friends in Lowestoft, that they have been frequently disturbed at their public worship by some officers quartered in the town. Before I use any other method, I beg of you, sir, who can do it with a word, to prevent our being thus insulted any more. We are men; we are Englishmen: as such we have a natural and a legal right to liberty of conscience. I am, sir,                      Your obedient servant.

---

an end; at least, till they are tired of their favourite preacher, and so turn him out.

"2. While he stays, is not the bridle in his mouth? How dares he speak the full and the whole truth, since, whenever he displeases the trustees, he is liable to lose his bread? How much less will he dare to put a trustee, though ever so ungodly, out of the society?"—*The Case of Birstal House*, 1788. *Works*, vii, 328.

## TO DR. COKE, MR. ASBURY,

### AND OUR BRETHREN IN NORTH AMERICA.*

[*Works*, vii, 311-12.]

BRISTOL, September 10, 1784.

By a very uncommon train of providences many of the provinces of North America are totally disjoined from their mother country, and erected into independent states. The English government has no authority over them either civil or ecclesiastical, any more than over the states of Holland. A civil authority is exercised over them, partly by the congress, partly by the provincial assemblies. But no one either exercises or claims any ecclesiastical authority at all. In this peculiar situation some thousands of the inhabitants of these states desire my advice; and in compliance with their desire, I have drawn up a little sketch.

Lord King's "Account of the Primitive Church" convinced me many years ago, that bishops and presbyters are the same order, and consequently have the same right to ordain. For many years I have been importuned, from time to time, to exercise this right, by ordaining part of our travelling preachers. But I have still refused, not only for peace' sake, but because I was determined as little as possible to violate the established order of the National Church to which I belonged.†

---

* This document is introduced by Mr. Wesley in the following manner: "What is the state of our societies in North America? A. It may best appear by the following letter. If any one is minded to dispute concerning diocesan episcopacy, he may: but I have better work."—EDIT.

† "Some obedience I always paid to the bishops, in obedience to the laws of the land. But I cannot see, that I am under any obligation to obey them farther than those laws require.

"It is in obedience to those laws, that I have never exercised in England the power which I believe God has given me. I firmly believe I am a Scriptural ἐπίσκοπος, as much as any man in England or in Europe. (For the uninterrupted succession I know to be a fable, which no man ever did or can prove.)"—*On the Church: in a Letter to the Rev.* ——, 1785. *Works*, vii, 312.

But the case is widely different between England and North America. Here there are bishops who have a legal jurisdiction: in America there are none, neither any parish ministers. So that for some hundred miles together, there is none either to baptize, or to administer the Lord's Supper. Here, therefore, my scruples are at an end; and I conceive myself at full liberty, as I violate no order, and invade no man's right, by appointing and sending labourers into the harvest.

I have accordingly appointed Dr. Coke and Mr. Francis Asbury to be joint superintendents over our brethren in North America; as also Richard Whatcoat and Thomas Vasey to act as elders among them, by baptizing and administering the Lord's Supper. And I have prepared a liturgy little differing from that of the Church of England (I think, the best constituted national church in the world), which I advise all the travelling preachers to use, on the Lord's day, in all the congregations, reading the Litany only on Wednesdays and Fridays, and praying extempore on all other days. I also advise the elders to administer the Supper of the Lord on every Lord's day.

If any one will point out a more rational and Scriptural way of feeding and guiding those poor sheep in the wilderness, I will gladly embrace it. At present, I cannot see any better method than that I have taken.

It has, indeed, been proposed to desire the English bishops, to ordain part of our preachers for America. But to this I object (1.) I desired the bishop of London to ordain only one; but could not prevail. (2.) If they consented, we know the slowness of their proceedings; but the matter admits of no delay. (3.) If they would ordain them now, they would likewise expect to govern them. And how grievously would this entangle us! (4.) As our American brethren are now totally disentangled both from the state, and from the English hierarchy, we dare not entangle them again, either with the one or the other. They are now at full liberty, simply to follow the Scriptures and the primitive church. And we judge it best that they should stand fast in that liberty, wherewith God has so strangely made them free.

JOHN WESLEY.

## TO THE REV. FREEBORN GARRETTSON,

OF THE METHODIST EPISCOPAL CHURCH, IN AMERICA.

[*Works*, vii, 184.]

DUBLIN, June 16, 1785.

MY DEAR BROTHER,—Dr. Coke gives some account of you in his Journal; so that, although I have not seen you, I am not a stranger to your character. By all means send me, when you have an opportunity, a more particular account of your experience and travels. It is no way improbable that God may find out a way for you to visit England; and it may be the means of your receiving more strength, as well as more light. It is a very desirable thing that the children of God should communicate their experience to each other; and it is generally most profitable when they can do it face to face. Till Providence opens a way for you to see Europe, do all you can for a good Master in America.

I am glad brother Cromwell and you have undertaken that "labour of love" of visiting Nova Scotia; and doubt not but you act in full concert with the little handful who were almost alone till you came. It will be the wisest way to make all those who desire to join together, thoroughly acquainted with the whole Methodist plan: and to accustom them, from the very beginning, to the accurate observance of all our rules. Let none of them rest in being half Christians. Whatever they do, let them do it with their might; and it will be well, as soon as any of them find peace with God, to exhort them to "go on to perfection." The more explicitly and strongly you press all believers to aspire after full sanctification, as attainable now by simple faith, the more the whole work of God will prosper.

I do not expect any great matters from the bishop. I doubt his eye is not single; and if it be not, he will do little good to you, or any one else. It may be a comfort to you that you have no need of him. You want nothing which he can give.

It is a noble proposal of brother Marchington; but I doubt it will not take place. You do not know the state of the English Methodists: they do not roll in money, like many of the American Methodists. It is with the utmost difficulty that we can raise five or six hundred pounds a year to supply our contingent expenses; so that it is entirely impracticable to raise five hundred pounds among them to build houses in America. It is true, they might do much; but it is a sad observation, they that have most money have usually least grace.*

The peace of God be with all your spirits! I am
        Your affectionate friend and brother.

## TO THE SAME.
[*Works*, vii, 186.]

LONDON, January 24, 1789.

MY DEAR BROTHER,—It signifies but little where we are, so we are but fully employed for our good Master. Whether you went, therefore, to the east, it is all one, so you were labouring to promote his work. You are following the order of his providence wherever it appeared, as a holy man strongly expressed it, in a kind of holy

---

* "Most of those in England who have riches love money, even the Methodists; at least those who are called so. The poor are the Christians. I am quite out of conceit with almost all those who have this world's goods."—*Letter to the Rev. Freeborn Garrettson*, 1786. *Works*, vii, 185.

disordered order. But there is one expression that occurs twice or thrice in yours, which gives me some concern: you speak of finding *freedom* to do this or that. This is a word much liable to be abused. If I have plain Scripture, or plain reason, for doing a thing, well. These are my rules, and my only rules. I regard not whether I had freedom or no. This is an unscriptural expression, and a very fallacious rule. I wish to be, in every point, great and small, a Scriptural, rational Christian.

In one instance, formerly, you promised to send me your Journal. Will you break your word, because you do not find freedom to keep it? Is not this enthusiasm? O be not of this way of thinking! You know not whither it may lead you. You are called to

"Square your useful life below
By reason and by grace."

But whatever you do with regard to me you must do quickly, or you will no more in this world.

Your affectionate friend and brother.

---

## TO DR. ADAM CLARKE.
[*Works*, vii, 204.]

BIRMINGHAM, March 26, 1787.

DEAR ADAM,—You have reason to praise God for giving you such favour in the eyes of the poor people of Alderney. And I am in hopes our brother De Queteville will meet with a blessing in watering the seed which is already sown. But I observe in the map, the name of another island, not very far from Alderney. Are there none that understand English in the Isle of Sark? If there are, I cannot tell whether you are not a debtor to those poor souls also.

If confinement hurts you, do not submit to it. Spread yourself abroad through all the four islands. But I

doubt speaking loud hurts you more, if not speaking long
too. Beware of this for conscience' sake. Do not offer
murder for sacrifice; but, before it be too late, take the
advice of, dear Adam,

Your affectionate brother.

---

## TO THE REV. PEARD DICKINSON.

[*Works*, vii, 101.]

LONDONDERRY, June 5, 1787.

DEAR SIR,—The Irish posts are not the quickest in
the world; though I have known one travel full two
miles in an hour. And they are not the most certain.
Letters fail here more frequently than they do in England.

Mr. Heath has need of abundance of faith and
patience. He is in a very unpleasing situation. But this
I am determined on; he shall not want, as long as I
have either money or credit. He is a truly pious and a
very amiable man: his wife and children are cast in the
same mould. I am glad you all showed him, while he
was in London, the respect which he well deserves.

As the work of God increases in so many parts both of
England and Ireland, it would be strange if there were
no increase of it in London; especially while all the
preachers are of one mind, and speak the same thing.
Only do not forget strongly and explicitly to urge the
believers to "go on to perfection." When this is constantly and earnestly done, the word is always clothed
with power.

Truly I claim no thanks for loving and esteeming
Betsy Briggs; for I cannot help it. And I shall be in
danger of quarrelling with you, if you ever love her less
than you do now. Peace be with all your spirits! I am

Your affectionate friend and brother.

## TO THE REV. FRANCIS ASBURY.

[*Works*, vii, 187-8.]

LONDON, September 20, 1788.

THERE is, indeed, a wide difference between the relation wherein you stand to the Americans, and the relation wherein I stand to all the Methodists. You are the elder brother of the American Methodists: I am, under God, the father of the whole family. Therefore, I naturally care for you all in a manner no other person can do. Therefore, I, in a measure, provide for you all; for the supplies which Dr. Coke provides for you, he could not provide were it not for me,—were it not that I not only permit him to collect, but also support him in so doing.

But, in one point, my dear brother, I am a little afraid, both the Doctor and you differ from me. I study to be little; you study to be great. I creep; you strut along. I found a school; you a college! nay, and call it after your own names!* O, beware! Do not seek to be something! Let me be nothing, and "Christ be all in all!"

One instance of this, of your greatness, has given me great concern. How can you, how dare you, suffer yourself to be called bishop? I shudder, I start at the very thought! Men may call me a knave or a fool, a rascal, a scoundrel, and I am content: but they shall never, by my consent, call me *bishop!* For my sake, for God's sake, for Christ's sake, put a full end to this! Let the Presbyterians do what they please, but let the Methodists know their calling better.

Thus, my dear Franky, I have told you all that is in

---

* Cokesbury College. The name was formed from the names of its founders,—Coke and Asbury.—EDIT.

## TO MRS. ADAM CLARKE.

[*Works*, vii, 202-3.]

DUMFRIES, June 1, 1790.

MY DEAR SISTER,—The great question is, What can be done for Adam Clarke? Now, will you save his life? Look round; consider if there be any circuit where he can have much rest, and little work; or shall he and you spend September in my rooms at Kingswood, on condition that he shall preach but twice a week, and ride to the Hot Wells every day? I think he must do this, or die; and I do not want him (neither do you) to run away from us in haste. You need not be told, that this will be attended with some expense: if it be, we can make it easy. I am apt to think this will be the best way. In the mean time, let him do as much as he can, and no more. It is probable I shall stay with you a little longer, as my

---

[* The above letter, it will be perceived from its date, was written in the year after what has been called the leaving of Mr. Wesley's name off the American Minutes (1787),—a measure at which he was much grieved, and for which Mr. Asbury particularly had been blamed, though unjustly. It is known, too, that there were individuals in America unfriendly to Mr. Asbury, who misrepresented him to Mr. Wesley in other respects. . . .

With respect to the title "bishop," the Rev. Henry Moore, the biographer and long the intimate friend and companion of Mr. Wesley, says,—" Mr. Wesley well knew the difference between the *office* and the *title*."—" He gave to those 'Επίσκοποι,' *Episcopoi, bishops*, " whom he ordained, the modest but highly expressive title of *superintendents*, and desired that no other might be used." Mr. Moore adds that Mr. Wesley's objection to the title "bishop," arose from his "hatred of all display;" but he was himself obviously of opinion that in this letter to Mr. Asbury, Mr. Wesley had expressed himself too strongly, and rather inconsistently with his former admissions. " Did he not," says Mr. Moore, " upon this occasion, a little forget what he had written in his address to the societies in America, after their separation from the mother country:

strength does not much decline. I travelled yesterday nearly eighty miles, and preached in the evening without any pain.* The Lord does what pleases him. Peace be with all your spirits!

    I am, my dear sister,
        Yours most affectionately.

---

'They are now at full liberty simply to follow the Scriptures and the primitive Church; and we judge it best that they should stand fast in the liberty wherewith God has so strangely made them free.' But the association in his mind between the assumed *title* and the *display* connected with it in the later ages of the Church, was too strong. He could not, at that moment, separate the plain laborious bishops of the American societies, where there is no legal establishment, from the dignified prelates of the mighty empire of Great Britain. That our brethren who are in that office, are true Scriptural bishops, I have no doubt at all: nor do I wish that the title should be relinquished, as it is grown into use, and is known by every person in the United States, to designate men distinguished only by their simplicity, and abundant labours."—See *Moore's Life of Wesley*, book viii, chap. ii.]

* "From this time [1775] I have, by the grace of God, gone on in the same track, travelling between four and five thousand miles a year, and once in two years going through Great Britain and Ireland; which, by the blessing of God, I am as well able to do now as I was twenty or thirty years ago."—*A Short History of the People Called Methodists*, 1781. *Works*, vii, 396.

"On the 28th of last June I finished my eightieth year. When I was young I had weak eyes, trembling hands, and abundance of infirmities. But, by the blessing of God, I have outlived them all. I have no infirmities now, but what I judge to be inseparable from flesh and blood. This hath God wrought. I am afraid you want the grand medicine which I use—exercise and change of air."—*Letter to the Rev. Walter Sellon*, 1784. *Works*, vii, 248.

"My sight is so far decayed, that I can not well read a small print by candle light; but I can write almost as well as ever I could: and it does me no harm, but rather good, to preach once or twice a day."—*Letter to Mrs. Jane Cock*, 1790. *Works*, vii, 210.

## TO ROBERT C. BRACKENBURY, ESQ.,
OF RAITHBY, LINCOLNSHIRE.
[*Works*, vii, 153-4.]

BRISTOL, September 15, 1790.

DEAR SIR,—Your letter gave me great satisfaction. I wanted to hear where and how you were; and am glad to find you are better in bodily health, and not weary and faint in your mind. My body seems nearly to have done its work, and to be almost worn out. Last month my strength was nearly gone, and I could have sat almost still from morning to night. But, blessed be God, I crept about a little, and made shift to preach once a day. On Monday I ventured a little farther; and after I had preached three times (once in the open air), I found my strength so restored that I could have preached again without inconvenience. I am glad brother D—— has more light with regard to full sanctification. This doctrine is the grand depositum which God has lodged with the people called Methodists; and for the sake of propagating this chiefly he appeared to have raised us up. I congratulate you upon sitting loose to all below; steadfast in the liberty wherewith Christ has made you free. Moderate riding on horseback, chiefly in the south of England, would improve your health. If you choose to accompany me, in any of my little journeys on this side Christmas, whenever you was tired you might go into my carriage. I am not so ready a writer as I was once; but I bless God I can scrawl a little,—enough to assure you that

> I am, dear sir,
> Your affectionate friend and brother.

## TO THE REV. EZEKIEL COOPER,

### OF PHILADELPHIA.

[*Works*, vii, 237.]

NEAR LONDON, February 1, 1791.

MY DEAR BROTHER,—Those that desire to write, or say any thing to me, have no time to lose; for time has shaken me by the hand, and death is not far behind. But I have reason to be thankful for the time that is past: I felt few of the infirmities of old age for fourscore and six years. It was not till a year and a half ago that my strength and my sight failed. And still I am enabled to scrawl a little, and to creep, though I cannot run. Probably I should not be able to do so much, did not many of you assist me by your prayers. I have given a distinct account of the work of God, which has been wrought in Britain and Ireland, for more than half a century. We want some of you to give us a connected relation of what our Lord has been doing in America, from the time that Richard Boardman accepted the invitation, and left his country to serve you. See that you never give place to one thought of separating from your brethren in Europe. Lose no opportunity of declaring to all men, that the Methodists are one people in all the world; and that it is their full determination so to continue,

"Though mountains rise, and oceans roll,
  To sever us in vain."

To the care of our common Lord I commit you; and am

Your affectionate friend and brother.

## TO A FRIEND.*

[*Works*, vii, 237.]

LONDON, February 26, 1791.

DEAR SIR,—Unless the Divine power has raised you up to be as *Athanasius contra mundum* [Athanasius against the world], I see not how you can go through your glorious enterprise, in opposing that execrable villany,† which is the scandal of religion, of England, and of human nature. Unless God has raised you up for this very thing, you will be worn out by the opposition of men and devils. But, "if God be for you, who can be against you?" Are all of them together stronger than God? O "be not weary in well doing!" Go on, in the name of God, and in the power of his might, till even American slavery (the vilest that ever saw the sun) shall vanish away before it.

Reading this morning a tract, wrote by a poor African, I was particularly struck by that circumstance,—that a man who has a black skin, being wronged or outraged by a white man, can have no redress; it being a law, in all our colonies, that the oath of a black against a white goes for nothing. What villany is this!

That He who has guided you from your youth up, may continue to strengthen you in this and all things, is the prayer of, dear sir,

Your affectionate servant.

---

* This letter is supposed to have been addressed to Mr. Wilberforce, and, as its date shows, was written by Mr. Wesley only four days before his death.—EDIT.

† "That execrable sum of all villanies, commonly called the Slave Trade."—*Journal* of February 12, 1772. *Works*, iv, 366. "Slave holding is utterly inconsistent with mercy . . . or justice."—*Thoughts upon Slavery*, *Works*, vi, 287.

# INDEX

Titles are printed in *italics*. The figures refer only to the pages on which the passages in question begin.

*Address to the Clergy, An*, 262.
Admission to societies, see Methodism.
*Advice to the People Called Methodists*, 293.
American Church, Independence of, 389.
*American Colonies, A Calm Address to Our*, 330.
American colonies, Religious conditions in, 386.
American Revolution, 365.
Amusements, 101, 270, 354.
Anthems condemned (*see also* Methodism, music), 340.
Antinomianism (*see also* Calvinism), 202, 203, 362.
*Appeals* (*see also Earnest Appeal, Farther Appeal*), 10.
*Arminian Magazine, The*, 6, 7.
*Arminian Magazine*, Articles from *The*, 74, 92, 122, 205, 254, 259, 287, 337.
*Asbury, Letter to the Rev. Francis*, 388, 394.
Asceticism condemned, 315.

Backsliders, see Penitents.
Bands and Band-meetings (*see also* Classes), 185, 207, 367.
*Bardsley, Letter to Mr. Samuel*, 290.
Benevolence, see Wesley.
*Benson, Letter to Mr. Joseph*, 361, 368, 369.
Benson, Writings of Joseph, 6.
Bible (*see also* Reason, Testament), 8, 12, 122, 128, 132, 200, 213, 245, 247, 264, 274, 278, 287, 292, 329, 354, 361, 392.
Bibliography, see Works.
Bigotry, Precautions against (*see also* Methodism, Opinions, Tolerance), 183.
Birrell, Augustine, on Wesley, 5, 10.
*Birstal House, The Case of*, 387.
*Bishop, Letter to Miss*, 171, 260, 315.
*Bishop of London, Letter to the*, 241.
Bishops, 388, 389, 394, 395.
*Blackwell, Letter to Mr. Ebenezer*, 381, 382.
*Bolton, Letter to Miss*, 376, 377.
Books (*see also* Study), 368.
*Brackenbury, Letter to Robert C., Esq.*, 397.
Business, Christian way of doing, 97.

*C., Letter to Mr.*, 205.
*Calm Address to Our American Colonies, A*, 330.
Calvinsim (*see also* Antinomianism, Predestination), 260.
*Case of Birstal House, The*, 387.
*Catholic Spirit*
  Catholic Spirit, 106.
  Tolerance, 107.
Catholic, see Roman Catholic.
*Chapman, Letter to Mrs.*, 315.
*Character of a Methodist, The*, 291.
Charity (*see also* Love), *Sermon on*, 122.
Cheerfulness and religion (*see also* Happiness), 9, 315.
Children (*see also* Schools), 367, 372.
Christ, Person of, 293, 304.
Christian, Characteristics of a (*see also* Christianity), 312, 325.
*Christianity, A Plain Account of Genuine*, 312.
Christianity, Evidences of, see Evidences.
Christianity, Nature of (*see also* Religion), 9, 219, 319.
*Christian Library, A*, 6, 7.
Christian perfection, see Perfection.
*Christian's Pattern, The* (*see also* à Kempis), 10.
Christian unity, see Schism.
Church, *Farther Thoughts on Separation from the*, 287.
Church, *On the*, 388.
Church, *Sermon of the*, 228.
Church, What constitutes the, 228, 305.
Church Fathers, Importance of knowledge of, 266, 267, 287.
*Church of England, Reasons Against a Separation from the*, 289.
Church of England (*see also* Church, Clergy, Liturgy, Methodism, Ministry), 200, 201, 203, 205, 227, 228, 287, 385, 388.
*Churchey, Letter to Mr. Walter*, 287.
*Circumcision of the Heart, Sermon on the*, 243.
*Clarke, Letter to Dr. Adam*, 392.
*Clarke, Letter to Mrs. Adam*, 395.
Clarke, Writings of Dr. Adam, 6.
Classes and class-meetings (*see also* Bands), 178, 206, 287.
*Clergy, An Address to the* (*see also* Ministry), 262.

400

# Index

*Clergy, Earnest Address to the,* 246.
Clergy and the Methodists (*see also* Church of England), 246, 247.
*Clergyman, A Letter to a,* 249.
*Cock, Letter to Mrs. Jane,* 396.
*Coke, Letter to Dr., Mr. Asbury, etc.,* 388.
Coke, Dr. Thomas, 6, 389, 394.
Cokesbury College, 394.
*Collection of Forms of Prayer, A,* 6.
*Complete English Dictionary, The,* 7, 295.
Conference, Annual, 287, 383, 384.
Conscience, Freedom of, *see* Freedom.
Controversy (*see also* Love), 6, 10, 248, 357, 370.
Conversation, Christian way of, 100.
Conversion, *see* New Birth, Salvation.
Cooke, Miss, *see* Clarke, Mrs. Adam.
*Cooper, Letter to the Rev. Ezekiel,* 398.
Creed, A Protestant, *see* Doctrines.
*Crosby, Letter to Mrs.,* 370, 371.
Curnock, Nehemiah, 10.

*Danger of Riches, Sermon on the,* 74.
*Defense of Aspasio Vindicated, A* (Erskine), 172.
Deism, 325, 326.
*Dickinson, Letter to the Rev. Peard,* 393.
*Dictionary, The Complete English,* 6, 295.
*Disciple, Letter to a Young,* 352, 371, 372.
Discipline, *see* Methodism.
Dissenters, 260, 287, 289, 290.
Divisions, *see Methodism, Short History of,* Schism.
Doctrines of Methodism and Protestantism (*see also* Methodism, Opinions), 304.
*Downes, A Letter to the Rev. Mr.,* 236.
Drunkards, 6, 365.

*Earnest Address to the Clergy, An,* 246.
*Earnest Appeal to Men of Reason and Religion, An,* 209.
Election (*see also* Predestination), 244.
Emory, Bishop John (Wesley's Works), 11.
Enthusiasm, 245, 349, 392.
Epworth, Open air preaching at, 288.
Evidences of Christianity, 323, 326.
Exclusion from societies, *see* Methodism.
*Explanatory Notes upon the New Testament,* 292, 353.

Faith, Nature and office of, 210, 218, 222, 224, 320.
Faith, Salvation by, 124, 173, 225, 294, 306.
Faith and works (*see also* Works), 128, 132, 133, 242, 313, 376.
Fasting, 365, 366.
*Farther Appeal to Men of Reason and Religion, A,* Part i, 294.
*Farther Appeal to Men of Reason and Religion, A,* Part iii, 189, 293.
*Farther Thoughts on Separation from the Church,* 287.

Fathers, *see* Church Fathers.
Feeling and doing, 372.
Field preaching, 206, 225, 230, 287, 288, 362, 367.
*Fletcher, Letter to the Rev. John,* 373.
Fletcher, The Rev. John, 6, 358.
*Free Grace*
  Grace, Free, 30.
  Predestination, 31.
*Friend, Letter to a,* 399.
*Furly, Letter to Miss,* 380.

*G., Letter to the Rev. Mr.,* 8.
*Garrettson, Letter to the Rev. Freeborn,* 390, 391.
*Gospel Ministers, Thoughts Concerning,* 259.
Gospel preaching, 254, 259, 377.
Government, Basis of, 329.
Government and the consent of the governed, 330.
Green, The Rev. Richard (*Bibliography*), 6.

Happiness of the Christian (*see also* Cheerfulness), 317.
Heathen, salvation of, 125.
Hervey, Mr. James, 200, 375.
Higher Life, The, *see* Perfection.
History, *see* Methodism, Methodists.
*History of English Thought in the Eighteenth Century* (Stephen), 8.
Holiness (*see also* Perfection), 173, 294.
Holy Club, *see* Methodism, Beginnings of.
Humility (*see also* Wesley), 88.
Hymns of Charles Wesley, 6, 349.

*Imitation of Christ, see* à Kempis.
Independence, *see* American Church, American colonies, Wesley.
Internal evidence of Christianity, *see* Evidences.
Itinerancy, 359, 386.

Jackson, The Rev. Thomas (Wesley's Works), 11.
Johnson, Dr. Samuel, on Methodist preaching, 9.
*Journal of the Rev. John Wesley* (Edited by Nehemiah Curnock), 10.
Journals, Wesley's, *see* Wesley.
Justification and sanctification, 261.
Justification by faith, *see* Faith.

Kempis, à (*Imitation of Christ*), 6, 10.
*King, Letter to Mr. John,* 379.

*Late Phenomenon, Thoughts upon a,* 175.
*Lavington, A Second Letter to Bishop,* 291, 307.
Law, Mr. William, 376, 377.
Lay preachers, 189, 371.
Leaders, 178, 367.
Leadership, Need for, 373.

## Index

Learning, how esteemed (*see also* Books), 245.
*Letter on Preaching Christ, A*, 254.
*Letter to Mr.* ———, 383.
*Letter to Mr.* ———, 386.
*Letter to the Rev. Francis Asbury*, 388, 394.
*Letter to Mr. Samuel Bardsley*, 290.
*Letter to Mr. Joseph Benson*, 361, 368, 369.
*Letter to Miss Bishop*, 171, 260, 315.
*Letter to the Bishop of London*, 241.
*Letter to Mr. Ebenezer Blackwell*, 381, 382.
*Letter to Miss Bolton*, 376, 377.
*Letter to Robert C. Brackenbury, Esq.*, 397.
*Letter to Mr. C.*, 127.
*Letter to Mrs. Chapman*, 315.
*Letter to Mr. Walter Churchey*, 287.
*Letter to Dr. Adam Clarke*, 392.
*Letter to Mrs. Adam Clarke*, 395.
*Letter to a Clergyman*, 249.
*Letter to Mrs. Jane Cock*, 396.
*Letter to Dr. Coke, Mr. Asbury, etc.*, 388.
*Letter to the Rev. Ezekiel Cooper*, 398.
*Letter to Mrs. Crosby*, 370, 371.
*Letter to the Rev. Peard Dickinson*, 393.
*Letter to a Young Disciple*, 352, 371, 372.
*Letter to the Rev. Mr. Downes*, 236.
*Letter to the Rev. John Fletcher*, 373.
*Letter to a Friend*, 399.
*Letter to Miss Furly*, 380.
*Letter to the Rev. Mr. G.*, 7.
*Letter to the Rev. Freeborn Garrettson*, 390, 391.
*Letter to Mr. John King*, 379.
*Letter, A Second, to Bishop Lavington*, 291, 307.
*Letter to Bishop Lowth*, 384.
*Letter to Mr. John Mason*, 367.
*Letter to Lady Maxwell*, 356, 357, 359.
*Letter to a Member of the Society*, 379, 381.
*Letter to Mr. Merryweather, of Yarm*, 10.
*Letter to the Rev. Dr. Conyers Middleton*, 312.
*Letter to Mrs. Emma Moon*, 366.
*Letter to the Commanding Officer in Lowestoft*, 387.
*Letter to the Rev. Mr. Perronet*, 171.
*Letter to the Rev. Thomas Rankin*, 364, 365.
*Letter to a Roman Catholic*, 303.
*Letter to the Rev. Walter Sellon*, 396.
*Letter to Mr. George Shadford*, 375.
*Letter to Mr. John Smith*, 230, 288, 353.
*Letter to Samuel Sparrow, Esq.*, 378.
*Letter to Mr. Richard Tompson*, 353.
*Letter to Sir Harry Trelawney*, 287.
*Letter to Mr. John Trembath*, 354.
*Letter to the Rev. Mr. Venn*, 360.
*Letter to His Brother, Charles Wesley*, 260, 349, 350, 351.
*Letter to His Brother, Samuel Wesley*, 343, 346.
Letter to Mr. Wilberforce, 399.

Liberal spirit, *see* Tolerance.
Liturgy of Church of England, 287.
Loans to needy, 196.
Love (*see also* Opinions, Wesley), 122, 295, 297, 313, 354, 357, 377.
Love endangered by wealth, 87.
Love, essence of religion (*see also* Religion), 9, 93, 209, 307, 308, 310.
Love needful for the ministry, 269, 284.
Love obtained by faith, 210, 218.
Love-feasts, 185.
*Lowth, Letter to Bishop*, 384.

*Mason, Letter to Mr. John*, 367.
*Maxwell, Letter to Lady*, 356, 357, 359.
Medicine, *see* Sick.
*Member of the Society, Letter to a*, 379, 381.
*Merryweather, Letter to Mr.*, 10.
*Methodism, A Short History of*, 199.
*Methodism Examined and Exposed* (Downes), 236.
*Methodism, History of* (Stevens), 7.
*Methodism, Thoughts upon*, 205.
Methodism, admission to societies, 175.
Methodism and the Church of England (*see also* Church, Clergy), 251, 287.
Methodism and the Church of Rome (*see also* Roman Catholic), 238, 240.
Methodism, beginnings of, 171, 199, 205, 226, 378.
Methodism, defenses of, 6, 171, 199, 209, 236.
Methodism, discipline, 390.
Methodism, doctrines (*see also* Doctrines), 9, 201, 202, 205, 206, 209, 240, 292, 378.
Methodism, essence of (*see also* Opinions, Religion), 9, 11, 207, 208, 246, 289, 291, 292, 294, 295.
Methodism, monarchical organization and spirit, 367, 373, 383, 386.
Methodism, music (*see also* Anthems, Music), 364.
Methodism, progress, 204, 237, 347, 350, 371.
Methodism, results of revival, 232, 239.
Methodism, worship, 9, 206.
*Methodist, The Character of a*, 291.
*Methodist, The Principles of a*, 10.
Methodist, origin of name, 200, 241, 291.
Methodist Episcopal Church established, 389.
*Methodists, Advice to the People Called*, 293.
*Methodists, A Plain Account of the People Called*, 171.
*Methodists, A Short History of the People Called*, 174, 200, 201, 288, 396.
*Middleton, A Letter to the Rev. Dr. Conyers*, 312.
Middleton, The Rev. Dr. Conyers, 194.
*Ministerial Office, Sermon on the*, 287.
Ministers, *see* Gospel.
Ministry, character of English (*see also* Church of England), 273, 279.

Ministry, qualifications for, 263.
Ministry, trials of, 343.
Ministry, unselfishness in, 269, 279.
Ministry, work of, 251, 352.
*Minutes of Several Conversations* ("The Large Minutes"), 6, 244, 340.
*Minutes of Some Late Conversations* ("The Doctrinal Minutes"), 243.
Miracles confined to early centuries, 92.
Money and its use (*see also* Ministry, Riches, Wesley), 103, 197, 300, 381.
Moon, Letter to Mrs. Emma, 366.
Moore, The Rev. Henry (*Life of Wesley*), 395.
*More Excellent Way, Sermon on the*, 92.
Mr. ———, Letter to, 383.
Mr. ———, Letter to, 386.
*Music, Thoughts on the Power of* (*see also* Methodism, music), 337.


*New Testament, Explanatory Notes upon the*, 292, 353.
*Notes on the Old Testament*, 365.
*Notes upon the New Testament, Explanatory*, 292, 353.


Officer, Letter to the Commanding, in Lowestoft, 387.
Old Testament, Notes on the, 365.
Opinions (*see also* Doctrines, Orthodoxy, Schism, Tolerance), 9, 292, 303, 309, 320, 361, 378.
Ordination, Right of, 388, 389.
Orthodoxy (*see also* Opinions), 172.
*Our Lord's Sermon on the Mount, Sermon on*, 244.


Pastoral visiting, 367, 382.
Penitents, meetings for, 187.
*Perfection, A Plain Account of Christian*, 291.
Perfection, Christian, 94, 223, 291, 351, 352, 360, 362, 390, 397.
Perronet, Mr. Charles, 359.
Perronet, Letter to the Rev. Mr., 171.
Persecution for religion (*see also* Suffering), 129, 134, 378.
Pews, Absence of, 206.
*Plain Account of Christian Perfection, A*, 291.
*Plain Account of Genuine Christianity, A*, 312.
*Plain Account of the People Called Methodists, A*, 171.
Pleasure, *see* Cheerfulness.
Poor (*see also* Stewards), 194, 379, 382, 391.
*Power, Thoughts Concerning the Origin of*, 328.
Prayer, 96, 287, 288, 297, 355, 376.
*Prayer, A Collection of Forms of*, 6.
*Preaching Christ, A Letter on*, 254.
Preaching, *see* Field, Gospel, Itinerancy, Lay.

Predestination (*see also* Calvinism, Election), 353.
*Predestination Calmly Considered*, 166.
*Preface to the Sermons*
  Wesley, John, sermons, 13.
  Wesley, John, simplicity, 13.
  Wesley, John, style, 14.
  Wesley, John, teachableness, 16.
  Wesley, John, theology, 16.
  Bible, 14.
*Primitive Physic*, 9, 364.
*Principles of a Methodist, The*, 10.
Private judgment, right of (*see also* Freedom), 214.
Providence, divine, 317, 381, 391.


Rankin, Letter to Mr. Thomas, 364, 365.
Rankin, Thomas, 375.
Reading, *see* Books.
Reason, Value of (*see also* Bible), 214, 216, 220, 245, 365, 392.
*Reasons against a Separation from the Church of England*, 289.
Rebuke, Christian (*see also* Reproving), 262, 272, 379, 394.
Regeneration, *see* New Birth.
Religion, nature of true (*see also* Christianity, Methodism, Salvation), 9, 122, 135, 172, 205, 209, 216, 293, 294, 295, 309.
*Remarks on "A Defense of Aspasio Vindicated,"* 172.
Revivals self-destroying, 208.
*Riches, Sermon on the Danger of*, 74.
Riches, The danger of (*see also* Money), 74, 208, 380, 391.
Rights of man, 331.
Ritualism, *see* Liturgy, Methodism, worship.
*Roman Catholic, A Letter to a*, 303.
Roman Catholic Church (*see also* Methodism and the Church of Rome), 293.


Salary, *see* Ministry.
*Salvation by Faith*
  Salvation by Faith, 17.
  Grace, free, 17, 30.
  Heathen believe in God, 18.
  Devils believe, 18.
  Faith, nature and office, 19, 20.
  Salvation, nature of, 20.
  Perfection, Christian, 22.
Salvation by faith (*see also* Faith), 124, 173, 225, 294.
Salvation, nature of (*see also* Love, Religion), 8, 224, 243, 294.
Sanctification, *see* Justification, Perfection.
Schism (*see also* Opinions), 176, 202, 292, 301, 309.
Schools established, 195.
Science, Knowledge of, important, 265, 276.

# 404    Index

*Scriptural Christianity*
  Scriptural Christianity, 137.
  Christianity, Scriptural, 137.
  Salvation, nature of, 39, 40.
Scriptures, *see* Bible.
Sectarianism, *see* Schism.
Select society, The, 187, 207.
*Sellon, Letter to the Rev. Walter*, 396.
Separation, *see* Church of England, Schism.
*Sermon on Charity*, 122.
*Sermon on the Church*, 228.
*Sermon on the Circumcision of the Heart*, 243.
*Sermon on the Danger of Riches*, 74.
*Sermon on the Ministerial Office*, 287.
*Sermon on the More Excellent Way*, 92.
*Sermon on Our Lord's Sermon on the Mount*, 244.
*Sermon on the Wedding Garment*, 172.
*Sermon on Worldly Folly*, 83.
Sermon on the Mount, 244.
Sermons, *see* Wesley.
*Shadford, Letter to Mr. George*, 375.
*Short History of Methodism, A*, 199.
*Short History of the People Called Methodists, A*, 174, 200, 201, 288, 396.
Sick, care for, 191, 192, 382.
Sinlessness, *see* Perfection.
*Slavery, Thoughts upon*, 399.
Sleep, 96, 343.
*Smith, Letter to Mr. John*, 230, 288, 353.
Societies first organized, 174.
Solitary religion, 315.
*Sparrow, Letter to Samuel, Esq.*, 378.
*Spectator, The* (London), on Wesley, 5.
Stephen, Mr. Leslie (*History of English Thought*), 7.
Stevens, Dr. Abel (*History of Methodism*), 6.
Stewards (*see also* Poor), 190, 367.
Study for Preachers (*see also* Books), 264, 274, 355.
Suffering (*see also* Persecution), 356, 371, 377.
Suffrage, Property qualification, 332.

Teachableness (*see also* Truth, Wesley), 379.
Testament, *see* Bible, New, Old.
*The General Spread of the Gospel*
  Spread of the Gospel, The General, 157.
  Heathenism, 157.
  Missionary work, 157–170.
  Mohammedanism, 157, 158.
  Christianity, degenerate, 158.
  Revivals, 163.
*The New Birth*
  New Birth, The, 46.
*The Way to the Kingdom*
  Way to the Kingdom, The, 61.
  Kingdom, The Way to the, 61.
  Religion, nature of true, 61ff.
  Orthodoxy, 63.
*Thoughts Concerning Gospel Ministers*, 259.

*Thoughts Concerning the Origin of Power*, 328.
*Thoughts on Separation from the Church, Farther*, 287.
*Thoughts on the Power of Music*, 337.
*Thoughts upon a Late Phenomenon*, 175.
*Thoughts upon Methodism*, 205.
*Thoughts upon Slavery*, 399.
Tickets for members, 183.
Tolerance (*see also* Bigotry, Opinions, Wesley), 363.
*Tompson, Letter to Mr. Richard*, 353.
Traditional evidence of Christianity, *see* Evidences.
*Trelawney, Letter to Sir Harry*, 287.
*Trembath, Letter to Mr. John*, 354.
Trinity, Experience of the, 359.
Truth, Love of (*see also* Teachableness), 354.

Unity, Christian, *see* Schism.

*Venn, Letter to the Rev. Mr.*, 360.
Venn, the Rev. Mr., 240, 302.

Walsh, Thomas, 132, 379.
Watch meetings, 103.
*Wedding Garment, Sermon on the*, 172.
Wesley, Charles (*see also* Hymns), 6, 199, 201.
*Wesley, Charles, Letter to*, 260, 349, 350, 351.
*Wesley, The Works of John and Charles* (Green), 6.
Wesley, John, benevolence (*see also* Wesley, money), 330, 395.
Wesley, John, charity (*see also* Love), 8, 307, 309, 363.
Wesley, John, conservatism (preference for monarchical rule, *see also* Methodism), 8, 287, 288, 373.
Wesley, John, defense of his own character, 226.
Wesley, John, dogmatic (*see also* Teachableness), 8, 361.
Wesley, John, early habits, 8, 343, 344, 353.
Wesley, John, hardships and labors, 5, 9, 230.
Wesley, John, health, 396, 397, 398.
Wesley, John, humility, 230, 353, 394.
Wesley, John, independence, 7, 360, 387.
Wesley, John, *Journals*, 6, 10, 238.
Wesley, John, journeys, 6, 381, 382, 396, 397.
Wesley, John, letters (*see also* Letter), 10.
Wesley, John, love of power, 8, 361.
Wesley, John, money (*see also* Money), 197, 229.
Wesley, John, publications, 7.
Wesley, John, sermons, 6, 7, 8, 9, 10.
Wesley, John, simplicity, 7, 8.
Wesley, John, style, 7.
Wesley, John, teachableness (*see also* Teachableness), 8, 180, 361.

Wesley, John, theology, 9.
Wesley, John, writings (*see also Works*), 6.
*Wesley, Samuel, Letter to*, 343, 346.
Whitefield, The Rev. George, 200, 201, 202, 351.
Widows, *see* Poor.
Wilberforce, Letter to Mr., 399.
Witness to the Spirit, 346, 357, 369.

Women and Government, 331.
Women speaking in public, 370, 371.
Works (*see also* Faith), 128, 133, 299, 301, 309, 372.
*Works of John and Charles Wesley, The* (Green), 6.
*Worldly Folly, Sermon on*, 83.

*Young Disciple, Letter to a*, 352, 371, 372.